CONTRASTING CRIMINAL JUSTICE

For Matilde, Rachel, Miriam, Mical and Gavriel: Here and There

Advances in Criminology
Series Editor: David Nelken

Titles in the Series

Engendering Resistance: Agency and Power in Women's Prisons
Mary Bosworth

**Integrating a Victim Perspective within Criminal Justice
International debates**
Edited by Adam Crawford and Jo Goodey

**Gender Criminology
Violence and women in Australia and Japan**
Patricia Easteal, Yoko Hosoi and Leon Wolff

**Contrasting Criminal Justice
Getting from here to there**
Edited by David Nelken

Critique and Radical Discourses on Crime
George Pavlich

**Blood in the Bank
Social and legal aspects of death at work**
Gary Slapper

**Governable Places
Readings on governmentality and crime control**
Edited by Russell Smandych

**Items
Stories of product counterfeiting**
Jon Vagg and Justine Harris

Contrasting Criminal Justice
Getting from here to there

Edited by
DAVID NELKEN
University of Macerata, Italy and Cardiff Law School, University of Wales

LONDON AND NEW YORK

First published 2000 by Dartmouth Publishing Company and Ashgate Publishing

Reissued 2018 by Routledge
2 Park Square, Milton Park, Abingdon, Oxon OX14 4RN
711 Third Avenue, New York, NY 10017, USA

Routledge is an imprint of the Taylor & Francis Group, an informa business

Copyright © David Nelken 2000

All rights reserved. No part of this book may be reprinted or reproduced or utilised in any form or by any electronic, mechanical, or other means, now known or hereafter invented, including photocopying and recording, or in any information storage or retrieval system, without permission in writing from the publishers.

Notice:
Product or corporate names may be trademarks or registered trademarks, and are used only for identification and explanation without intent to infringe.

Publisher's Note
The publisher has gone to great lengths to ensure the quality of this reprint but points out that some imperfections in the original copies may be apparent.

Disclaimer
The publisher has made every effort to trace copyright holders and welcomes correspondence from those they have been unable to contact.

A Library of Congress record exists under LC control number: 00103698

ISBN 13: 978-1-138-72219-4 (hbk)
ISBN 13: 978-1-138-72212-5 (pbk)
ISBN 13: 978-1-315-19377-9 (ebk)

Contents

List of Contributors	ix
Series Preface	xi

PART I: INTRODUCTION

1 Just Comparing   3
David Nelken
Introduction   3
Comparative Law and Comparative Criminal Justice   5
Aims, Issues and Methods   10

2 Virtually There, Researching There, Living There   23
David Nelken
Introduction   23
The Virtues of 'Being There'   24
Virtually There   27
Researching There   35
Living There   41

PART II: VIRTUALLY THERE

3 Protecting the Innocent Through Criminal Justice: A Case Study from Spain, Virtually Compared to Germany and Japan   49
Johannes Feest and Masayuki Murayama
Introduction   49
Virtual Comparison   49
The Catalan Case   50
The Virtual German Case   54
The Virtual Japanese Case   59

Comparisons and Conclusions	63
Does Law Make a Difference?	64
Does Legal Culture Make a Difference?	66
Protecting the Innocent	67

4 Legal Cultures, Political Cultures and Procedural Traditions: Towards a Comparative Interpretation of Covert and Proactive Policing in England and Wales and the Netherlands   77
Chrisje Brants and Stewart Field

Introduction	77
The Research Process: Problems of Comparative Interpretation	78
The Analytical Framework: Legal Culture, Political Culture and Procedural Traditions	80
Introducing Covert and Proactive Policing: Definitions and Dilemmas	84
The Targeting of Covert and Proactive Policing: The Social Construction of Particular Demons	86
Targeting Covert and Proactive Policing	93
Differential Regulatory Response	103
Conclusion	107

5 Comparing Women's Prisons: Epistemological and Methodological Issues   117
Marie-Andrée Bertrand

Introduction	117
A Comparative Study of Women's Prisons	118
Epistemological Issues	122
Methodological Issues	123
The Findings	126
Incarceration Rates as Comparative Indicators	130
Conclusion	132

PART III: RESEARCHING THERE

6 Comparing Legal Cultures: The Comparativist as Participant Observer   139
Jacqueline Hodgson

Introduction	139
Ways to Compare	140
The Comparativist as Participant Observer	145

                                                                    Contents vii

    A Concluding Example   151

7 Prosecutor Culture in Japan and the USA   **157**
David T. Johnson
Introduction   157
Who are the Prosecutors? Some Background Information   160
What Do Japanese Prosecutors Want?   164
The Suspension of Prosecution and the Exercise of Discretion   177
Conclusion   192

8 Contrasts in Victim–Offender Mediation and Appeals to Community in France and England   **205**
Adam Crawford
Introduction   205
Appeals to 'Community' in Mediation   210
Comparative Conceptions of Community   215
Comparative Contexts   218
Conclusion   224

PART IV: LIVING THERE

9 Telling Difference: Of Crime and Criminal Justice in Italy   **233**
David Nelken
Introduction   233
On Not Starting from Here   234
Differences and Absences   240
Drawing the Contrasts   246
Conclusion   259

10 Through *Other* Eyes: On the Limitations and Value of Western Criminology for Teaching and Practice in Trinidad and Tobago   **265**
Maureen Cain
Introduction   265
Age and Crime   266
Policing   270
Policing by Communities in Trinidad and Tobago and St Lucia   275
Conclusion   286

Index   295

List of Contributors

Marie-Andrée Bertrand is Professor Emeritus of Criminology at the University of Montreal, Canada.

Chrisje Brants is Professor of Criminal Law and Criminal Procedure at the University of Utrecht.

Maureen Cain is Reader in the Sociology of Law and Crime, Faculty of Law, University of Birmingham.

Adam Crawford is Senior Lecturer in Law and Deputy Director of the Centre for Criminal Justic Studies, University of Leeds, UK.

Johannes Feest is Professor of Criminal Law at the University of Bremen, Germany.

Stewart Field is Lecturer in Law at the University of Wales at Cardiff.

David T. Johnson is Assistant Professor of Sociology at the University of Hawaii at Manoa, USA.

Jacqueline Hodgson is Lecturer in Law at the University of Warwick, UK.

Masayuki Murayama is Professor of Sociology of Law in the Department of Law, Chiba University, Japan.

David Nelken is Distinguished Professor of Sociology at the University of Macerata, Italy and Distinguished Research Professor of Law at the University of Wales at Cardiff.

Series Preface

This series, building on the success of the *International Library of Criminology, Criminal Justice and Penology* is dedicated to publishing the best of new cutting-edge work in these fields. Volumes published or in preparation include theoretically innovative treatments of the subjects of Foucault and governmentality; mediation; victimology; comparative criminal justice; post-modern policing; and women's prisons.

The contributors to *Contrasting Criminal Justice* tackle a variety of issues raised by research into criminal justice in other cultures. How far does criminal justice reflect general culture? Can collaborative research overcome the problem of translating incommensurable concepts? What are the possibilities for 'virtual comparisons'? How do we 'tell difference'? The authors, who are drawn from a wide variety of countries, offer penetrating and sometimes disturbing reflections on international differences in processes of trial and punishment.

DAVID NELKEN
Series Editor

PART I
INTRODUCTION

1 Just Comparing

David Nelken

Introduction

The contributors to this volume – all of whom work in the field of comparative criminal justice – were asked to provide examples of their research which gave special attention to the methods by which they arrived at their findings. The chapters they have supplied are full of interest, but they need some presentation if this collection is to be more than the sum of its parts. In the first of these introductory chapters I shall therefore try to demonstrate why there is a need for better reflection on the aims, issues and methods of comparative criminal justice and in the next chapter I shall concentrate on the principal questions of epistemology and research method which have shaped the organization of this volume, seeking to show how they influence the interplay between substance and method in each of the chapters.

Even the best of current English-language theorizing about crime control takes much of its sense and point from background assumptions and developments which are most at home in what Europeans term 'Anglo-American culture'. David Garland's important and influential analysis of the way the state is currently seeking to divest at least part of its responsibilities in this sphere (Garland, 1996) has less application in the state-centred societies of Continental Europe where, in some respects, it is only now that the state's responsibility to protect its citizens from street crime is becoming a top priority. Much the same can be said for many of the main arguments in Jock Young's eloquent analysis of what he calls the 'exclusive society' (Young, 1999). Despite the many similarities at the level of practice brought about by the homogenizing and converging influences of the European Union, the debate about solidarity versus exclusion takes rather different forms depending on whether it is the representatives of the state or the members of civil society who are allocated the main role in creating an integrated sense of identity and community. If 'penality' is so much a matter of cultural meaning and not merely of instrumental effectiveness (Garland,

1990) it is obvious that this will vary from culture to culture. Indeed, it is fair to say that many of the important points made by these leading scholars are comparative observations about the similarities and the differences they notice in comparing Britain and the USA.

At the same time there is increasing interest in exploring wider differences in criminal justice, especially, but not only, with respect to other member countries of the European Union. There are now many valuable monographs on different aspects of the criminal process,[1] in addition to articles in both general and specialist journals. There are also the beginnings of distinct schools and approaches, whether positivist (for example, Heiland *et al.*, 1992), interpretivist (for example, Crawford, Chapter 8 in this volume; Nelken, 1994b; Zedner, 1995, 1996), or Foucauldian (Smandych, 1999). But the standard texts in comparative criminal justice still tend to invite 'experts' from different countries to provide 'national reports', rather than get them to address what lies behind their descriptions and interpretations – which is, in any case, a difficult task to undertake without the experience of collaboration or research in different countries. With rare exceptions, even recent collections contain relatively little about the actual process of carrying out cross-cultural research in criminal justice (see, for example, Dorn *et al.*, 1996; Heidensohn and Farrell, 1991; Robert and Van Outrive, 1993; Ruggiero *et al.*, 1995; Ruggiero *et al.*, 1998). At best, this question is addressed by the editors rather than by the contributors themselves (Cole *et al.*, 1987; Fields and Moore, 1996; Findlay and Zvekic, 1993, Heiland *et al.*, 1992). It is this attention to process which is at the heart of this collection.

If we merely juxtapose descriptions of various aspects of the criminal process in different cultures we avoid confronting the central problem of how to assess the validity and reliability of comparative work. We do little to advance the goal of explanation or understanding and provide an unsound basis for policy-making. We beg too many questions if we simply assume that the cultural object 'criminal justice' we know exists elsewhere.[2] How can we be sure we are comparing 'like with like', both in terms of the distinctive elements of the criminal process and of its place in the larger culture? How far does the idea of treating criminal justice as a series of decision stages which can, and should, be studied empirically, reflect Anglo-American assumption and practices?[3] The argument behind this collection is that, whatever answer is given, these questions must at least be faced. For it is only by dealing with such problems of method that we can begin to respond to the sceptical charge that comparative social research is unable to overcome the incommensurability between thoughts and practices belonging to different legal cultures (Legrand, 1995). Certainly, discussions of methodology abstracted from matters of substance can easily become dull, but making substantive claims about other places without considering how we have arrived at them is only too likely to be misleading.

Comparative Law and Comparative Criminal Justice

But perhaps the job is already being done by scholars from other disciplines? Comparative sociology of law may not have found another Max Weber but research into comparative criminal justice certainly dare not ignore what is currently produced not only in sociology and anthropology but also in disciplines such as history, political science or cross-cultural psychology.[4] In addition, however, there seems to be an obvious overlap here with the academic discipline of comparative law. The disciplinary affiliations of the contributors to this volume (both law and sociology) make it appropriate to say something more about this overlap, especially as it is difficult to find much in the way of constructive debate between exponents of sociology of law and comparative law (but see Nelken and Feest, forthcoming).

The research presented in this volume makes it clear that it would be a mistake to treat comparative sociology of law and comparative law as internally unified and competing approaches. It suggests that many of the contrasts usually made between sociology of law and comparative law are overdrawn, or at least apply only to particular representatives of each camp. Some social scientists argue that comparative law does not follow the correct protocols for sociological explanation (Feeley, 1997), but this criticism loses much of its force if one's model of social science is based on hermeneutic interpretation and understanding of difference, rather than the explanation or prediction of variance. At least some writers nominally in one camp may have more in common with those in the other, and may make use of similar methods or concepts.[5] Among sociologists of law, for example, there is open disagreement over whether the focus should be on social behaviour or legal ideology (Cotterrell, 1997; Friedman, 1997); nor is there consensus on whether behaviour explains culture, or whether it is only by first grasping the meaning of culture that one can interpret practice (Blankenburg, 1997; Nelken, 1997b). Some comparative lawyers strongly criticize social scientists for being too quick to relate law to reigning social interests and to existing features of social structure (Watson, 1993). But others – no less influential – recommend a bastardized version of the sociological idea of 'functionalist equivalents', advising students of another legal system to make it their working assumption that the foreign system will have legal rules (somewhere or other) which fulfil the same social function as that served by the rules with which he or she is familiar (Zweigert and Kotz, 1987).

Some sociologists do criticize comparative lawyers for placing too much importance on the complexities of legal texts rather than focusing on the difference rules actually make in practice. In this volume, for example, Feest and Murayama (Chapter 3) suggest that an innocent person runs a similar high risk of miscarriage of justice under very different sets of rules and procedures. But many of the important insights of sociology of law come from trying to work out the relative importance of 'law in books' and 'law in action' as evidence of conflict and change in society.[6] Social scientists can readily acknowledge that, even in practice, law, including criminal law, does not necessarily always correspond to reigning interests and social structure (Nelken, 1987, 1990). Indeed, the only way to explain the political scandals in Italy known as *Tangentopoli* is by emphasizing how and why the criminal law can become distanced from the interests of the powerful – at least in certain cultures and under given circumstances (Nelken, 1996).

However, whilst we should not exaggerate their disagreements, there are many ways in which research carried out by comparative lawyers is sufficiently different from comparative social science for both to have much to gain from each others' approaches. On the one hand, for example, comparative lawyers rely mainly on historical, philosophical and juridical analyses. These scholars are well aware that legal and other rules are not always applied in practice and that legal outcomes do not necessarily turn out as planned. But the sociological significance of such evidence is usually ignored in favour of processing it normatively, as an example of deviance or 'failure', to which the solution is typically a (further) change in the law. Social scientists, on the other hand, are more interested in what *does* happen rather than what *should* happen, looking beyond written rules and documents to the structures and 'infrastructures' (Blankenburg, 1997) which shape the repeated patterns of everyday action. Nevertheless, their approach also carries risks. The importance given to the present rather than to the past or future of law can block an appreciation of law's character as a bearer of tradition which makes the past live in the present. The determination to take practice more seriously than protestations of ideals can sometimes lead to an underestimation of the law's role as a representation of 'counterfactual' values (Van Swaaningen, 1998, 1999), especially in some legal cultures. (The reader must decide how far the chapters included in this volume avoid these opposite errors.)

A second set of considerations – which brings us even closer to the concerns of this volume – relates to the status of the experts or practitioners who are usually the direct or indirect source of claims about other cultures. In all cultures, descriptions of social and legal ideas carry political implications – in some cases, even issuing directly from particular political or social philosophies. When we think of experts in own culture we will normally, without much difficulty, be able to associate them with a given political or policy position. But what knowledge do we have about this factor when we rely on experts from abroad? In much of the comparative law literature there seems to be little recognition or discussion of the extent to which those relied on for descriptions of the aims or results of legal reforms are themselves *part* of the context they are describing, in the sense of favouring one position rather than another. In Italy some academics and practitioners are notoriously pro-judges, others are anti-judges (Nelken, 1996). In France some commentators are strongly against importing ideas from the common law world, whereas others are less antagonistic (Garapon, 1995). In Japan some leading academics are involved in fierce controversy over the need for greater rights-consciousness in their country, and this clearly shapes their arguments about present-day legal culture there (Feldman, 1997). Others are against such developments. The list could go on.

Moreover, cultural variability means that the problem faced here is not always quite the same. In some cultures it is considered appropriate for an academic to identify and be identified as a member of a group. In playing the role of what Gramsci called an 'organic intellectual' your prime duty is understood both by your allies and by your opponents to be the furtherance of a specific group ideal (the relationship between academia and politics in Italy and in Latin America are the examples with which I am most familiar, but there are many others). In consequence, in such societies the issue of social and political affiliation is one of the first questions raised (even if not always openly) in considering the point and validity of academic criticisms of current practices and of corresponding proposals for reform.

In other cultures, however, the approved practice is to do one's best to avoid such identification. In some cases this just makes the process of establishing affiliation more elusive. Alternatively, the extent of political consensus, or of admiration for allegedly neutral criteria based on 'results' or 'efficiency', may be such that academics are indeed less pressed to take sides. Or intellectuals may simply count for less politically! There is no suggestion here that these considerations do not apply to social scientists as well as to legal experts; it is itself a cultural variable whether or not legal academics are more likely to be engaged in persuasive, rather than descriptive, endeavours, or more or less directly involved in shaping the criminal justice system. The point is that, without knowledge about their affiliations and an understanding of the role responsibilities of affiliation in the culture under investigation it can be difficult to decide what credit to give to the arguments of any expert opinion about criminal justice.

Even if we assume that our sources are not 'partial' (or, better still, if we try to make proper allowance for this) there still remains the problem that experts and practitioners are undoubtedly part of their own culture. This is, after all, why we consult them. But this also means that, as insiders, they do not necessarily ask or answer questions pertinent to the outsider researcher (and may not even have the basis for understanding such questions). Thus, in many ways, their descriptions – and also their criticisms – will also belong to their culture. But, without some other means of understanding the culture, we will not be alert to this.

Take, as an example, someone from an 'Anglo-American' background (as Continental Europeans might say) who is reading through an insider's account of the results of the famous New Code of Criminal Procedure introduced in Italy during the late 1980s. This insider viewpoint is likely to be influenced by a widely shared cultural approach in which the role of criminal law is associated *overwhelmingly* with what in Anglo-American parlance is called 'due process' (Nelken, Chapter 9 in this volume). As compared to analyses by writers with a common law background, the evaluation of the outcome of this reform is less likely to turn into an assessment of how it has affected the necessary balance between the potentially incompatible exigencies of 'due process' and 'crime control'. Instead, a series of criticisms will make it seem as if the problem is the continuing lack of 'due process'. Typical insider complaints concern the extent to which the powers of judges and prosecutors under the older inquisitorial system have survived this reform and the attendant need to further increase the rights of the defendant in the interests of finally arriving at a 'just trial process'.

At the level of some pre-trial practices there may still be less protection of the accused than in common law countries (although in other respects these protections may be stronger). But what these insiders rarely criticize is the fact that Italy has grafted an extreme version of the accusatorial process (as seen from an Anglo-American perspective) on to their pre-existing system. It is still assumed that most defendants will have trials, defendants are all still allowed a second trial on the facts, defendants can lie in their own defence, and so on. Little interest is shown in the 'workability' of such a demanding version of the accusatorial process, least of all in relation to the way it works in those countries from which it has been borrowed. Perfecting the ideal is all-important, and a clear line is drawn between questions of principle and what are deemed to be unacceptably pragmatic reasons for compromising ideals.

It is not only the values animating expert criticism which tend to express and reproduce a given legal culture; the same applies to the arguments used to make such assessments. The relative lack of interest amongst legal academics in Italy (and many other civil law countries[7]) in criticisms based on descriptions of the *everyday* functioning of legal institutions is undoubtedly linked to the lack of a tradition of empirical research in studying criminal justice. But there is a further consequence of the lack of an empirical tradition in civil law countries. Within such societies much of the empirical material about crime and its control which academics use actually derives from dossiers prepared by prosecuting magistrates![8]

None of this would be a problem if insiders' opinions and descriptions were treated merely as data to be interpreted. It is when we assume that experts can act as our eyes and ears that serious dangers of potential misunderstanding arise. If we must rely on experts, the best results can usually be obtained by interviewing cosmopolitan 'insiders/outsiders' from the culture under investigation, especially if they also have experience of the investigator's culture. But there is also a greater likelihood that such sophisticated informants will be playing an active role in developments in their own culture and will therefore have interested, as well as interesting, views. And the originating culture will always make some difference (see Nelken, Chapter 9 in this volume).

Much of this discussion may sound like a replay of the inconclusive battle between proponents of systematic legal exposition as opposed to those who espouse socio-legal studies and talk of the need to examine the 'law in context'.[9] Indeed, the claim that law can only be understood in relation to its wider social context should apply more strongly to the attempt to make sense of foreign legal systems since the further one is from familiar reference points the less can be taken for granted with respect to the significance or efficacy of legal rules and practices. Because we cannot assume that our informants have a sociological or anthropological sensibility we will often need to conduct empirical field research for ourselves. Yet many of those who carry out comparative research on police, prosecution or prisons – even if they do travel abroad – devote much less time to familiarizing themselves with the foreign country or setting in which they carry out their research than anthropologists who spend years learning about typically smaller-scale societies.

Can this attitude be justified? Perhaps it depends on the kind of question we are asking? It is one thing, we might argue, for 'Anglo-American' comparative scholars to enquire obsessively whether the continental European instructing judge really does control the action of the police (and therefore offers a solution to their own unresolved problem of police discretion).[10] It is another matter if the comparativist is tempted by broad questions such as 'Could there be a relationship between the mildness or severity of a penal climate and an inquisitorial or an accusatorial system of justice?' (Fennell *et al.*, 1995: xvi). It is certainly interesting that Fennell *et al.* add immediately afterwards 'or is the question absurd?'. As this suggests, those engaged in studying law comparatively can themselves come to recognize the mismatch between their conceptual and technical tools and some of the questions they would like to follow up.[11]

The weakness of traditional approaches becomes all the more evident when comparative enquiries seek to tackle fundamental problems such as: 'How do different societies conceive 'disorder'?' 'How do differences in social, political and legal culture inform perceptions of crime and the role of criminal agencies in responding to it?' or 'What factors underlie the salience of law and order as a political issue?' (Zedner, 1996). Only long and intimate familiarity with a society could even begin to unravel such complex puzzles. But, at the same time, it is likely that such extended research in another culture would also make us rethink the answers we give to apparently more straightforward questions concerning the behaviour and goals of different criminal justice agencies.

Nonetheless, the call for greater sociological sensibility does not, of itself, offer a solution to many of the issues which are intrinsic to all comparative research into legal culture, however it is conducted. What is the best way to make sense of other systems of criminal justice? How closely and definitely can we make connections between legal rules and national cultures? How far can we – and should we – try to stand outside the culture being studied, as well as our own (see Nelken, 1995). First-hand research is likely to be increasingly important in tackling questions of comparative criminal justice, but even at its best it only changes the setting in which the researcher wrestles with such questions.

Aims, Issues and Methods

The topics discussed in this volume range over all the stages of criminal justice including policing, prosecution, defence, trial and imprisonment. The authors describe aspects of criminal justice in a wide variety of settings including England and Wales, France, Germany, Italy, the Netherlands, Spain, Italy, Scandinavia, the USA, Canada, Japan and the West Indies. But the purpose of this collection is to provide examples of how to make progress in sociologically informed research projects into comparative criminal justice, not to give a comprehensive account of legal institutions, rules and procedures in the countries concerned – indeed, in some respects it even presupposes some such level of descriptive knowledge.

The study of contrasts in criminal justice is an integral part of comparative criminology and shares its aims. It may serve to overcome ethnocentrism by helping us come to terms with 'the other' without denying difference or resorting to stereotypes. By showing the interconnections between crime, justice and culture (Nelken, 1994b), it offers a valuable vantage point for examining how crime is constructed by the response of criminal justice agencies. This sort of comparative enquiry also obliges the researcher to be 'reflexive' (Nelken 1994a), in order to avoid, for example, treating the modern Anglo-American 'pragmatic instrumental' approach to law as if it were a universal.

Research into criminal justice abroad can also discover practices which challenge the way in which we do things at home. If the Italian criminal process can more or less de-criminalize cases involving juvenile delinquency (with the important exceptions of those involving immigrants, gypsies or organized crime) why can we not do the same (Nelken, Chapter 9 in this volume)? If prosecutors in Japan succeed in keeping down the number of cases sent to court could we follow their example (Johnson, Chapter 7 in this volume)? It turns out that, far from being the norm, common law countries can be somewhat exceptional, as, for example, in the special proceedings they reserve for white-collar as compared to ordinary criminals (Nelken, 1997d). For some scholars, however, it is a controversial question whether the drawing of policy conclusions should be the aim of comparative research. They argue that it is this concern with 'borrowing' which has prevented comparative work from making its proper contribution to explanatory social science (Feeley, 1997). Hodgson, in Chapter 6 of this volume, also polemicizes against what she calls 'the reformist' approach to 'taking or leaving' single elements of other systems. On the other hand, it can be impossible to separate the normative from the descriptive, especially when we are trying to grasp what the actors themselves are trying to achieve (Nelken, 1997c). Even Hodgson concludes her chapter by suggesting that comparative enquiries can yield sound lessons if they avoid concentrating on single aspects of another system but seek, rather, to rethink their practices as a whole in the light of how things are done elsewhere.

The focus of this volume is not primarily criminal justice policy but rather the prior problem of how to understand and explain difference. Nevertheless, it is certainly possible to extract some practical insights from each of the studies. The project described in Chapter 5 by Marie-Andrée Bertrand – perhaps the most policy-oriented – set out to find a model women's prison. She draws the provocative conclusion that such a prison is not found in the most progressive of cultures, as might be expected. In Chapter 3 Feest and Murayama are concerned with how to make fair comparisons and compare 'like with like', but the problem they examine in pursuing this exercise is the classical policy question of how to improve the effectiveness of legal protections for the innocent. Johnson (Chapter 7) is principally interested in understanding how Japanese prosecutors think, but even he suggests that there may be something to learn from the workings of a group of people so dedicated to avoiding unnecessary recourse to the criminal process.

There is also no necessary connection between an interest in policy questions and the advocacy of foreign practices. In Chapter 4 Brants and Field examine another classical problem of criminal justice policy – the control of police behaviour – both in the Netherlands and in England and

Wales. Yet the question of whether either country could borrow or even learn from the other is not even raised, and the prospect is certainly not encouraged by the evidence of cultural difference which the authors provide. Cain (Chapter 10) is unashamedly committed to policy-useful research but insists that answers must come from home rather than from elsewhere. Other chapters, on the other hand, simply presuppose that borrowing is already taking place, rather than discussing whether or not this would be appropriate. In Chapter 8, Crawford, for example, charts the deeper meaning of the attempt in France to 'borrow' mediation as an 'alternative' to the official system and Nelken, likewise, describes the growing influence of Anglo-American approaches to crime and criminal justice in Italy (see Chapter 9).

It is also worth remembering that, whatever its aims, a given piece of research can, and often will, be used by others for their own purposes. In particular, insiders in a society may find it useful to draw on the prestige of an 'outside observer' who is deemed for that reason to be more objective. There may even be competition to show that the conclusions of such research favour one or the other side in a controversy. Examining how and when this happens can itself provide useful data for further comparative reflection. It may, for example, illustrate cultural variability in the extent to which members of a society are interested in, or willing to accept, outsiders' evaluations or, on the other hand, think that they have little to learn from others!

Leaving aside the specific topics tackled by each of the chapters, what does this collection suggest about the central issues which all comparative researchers into comparative criminal justice have to face? Is the point of the exercise to build and test general hypotheses about crime and crime control (Heiland et al., 1992)?[12] Or is it, rather, to offer hermeneutic interpretations and translations of crime and crime control in culturally specific settings (Nelken, 1994b)? The stakes are high. As I have asked elsewhere:

> Is the goal of comparative work to help further criminology's universalistic pretensions and provide a yardstick to measure how far they have been achieved? Or is it a prophylactic which protects us from such erroneous ambitions by showing us how claims about crime and criminal justice which purport to be universal actually take their sense and limits of applicability from the cultural context in which they are embedded? (Nelken, 1997c: 560)

The form taken by our research will certainly vary depending on whether the criterion of effective comparison is predictive success in measuring the relationship between scientifically operationalized variables or learning how to understand and follow local rules and expectations, more or less as the natives do.

In this volume the most direct discussion of these matters is found in Cain's (Chapter 10) criticism of the way in which some criminological texts (for example, Gottfredson and Hirschi, 1990) wrongly present the alleged relationship between youth and crime as if it were a cultural universal. As she shows, the idea that the peak age of criminality is the late teenage years is highly misleading when applied to the West Indies. Gottfredson and Hirschi are, in fact, unreasonably dismissive of the potential contributions of comparative criminology. But we would do well to distinguish the issue of whether explanation is inherently universalizable from claims that a particular relationship is in fact universal. Is it really a problem if generalizations developed about age and crime do not fit all societies – and, if so, what sort of problem is it? Does Cain's critique actually presuppose the universalizability of criminology by demonstrating that Gottfredson and Hirschi have proposed a falsely universal claim. Or does it seek to show that the search for such claims is inherently implausible? Is the point that Western criminology is wrong or merely that it is wrong for the West Indies? We also need to be clear how far the relationship posited by Gottfredson and Hirschi, and criticized by Cain, is one between age and criminal behaviour or between age and the social reaction to crime. Cain herself suggests (in the light of the West Indies data she presents) that it could also be salutary for the West to ask why it assumes late youth to be the peak age for crime.[13] She points out that, amongst other things, this may reflect the low priority given to white-collar crime, which is certainly not an activity of the young.

Cain's argument also raises a general question about the way in which culture shapes both the making and the reception of theories of crime and criminal justice. Anomie theory was first developed in France and then reworked in the United States with very particular reference to the American dream of egalitarianism and the cultural emphasis on success as measured in money. But it has also been applied with advantage in very different cultural contexts – for example, in Italy to explain the growth of political corruption in the 1980s (Magatti, 1996) and in Japan to account for the relative lack of crime there (Miyazawa, 1997). Is the same theory being employed? I have repeatedly found my Italian students simply incredulous at the idea of describing 'economic success' as a socially mandated value. With the help of a bad translation in the relevant section of Gidden's textbook on sociology which they use for their examinations (a further casualty of intercultural misunderstanding?), they regularly transform Merton's provocative theory back into the banal idea of some individuals trying to achieve success *at the expense of the collectivity.*

An example in this volume of the type of enquiry which involves the testing of hypotheses is offered by Bertrand's questioning of whether 'the place and status of women in women's prisons would constitute a representation of the place and "status" granted to women in each country (Chapter 5). Most of the chapters, however, remain at the level of descriptions of the behaviour of legal actors, of aspects of criminal justice systems, or of relationships between criminal justice and the wider legal culture. At most they *mobilize*, rather than test, specific hypotheses. In part this may be due to the fact that the literature is still poorly furnished with theories explaining how different criminal justice systems fit together, and whether such 'fit' is to be attributed to historical and political affinities (Damaska, 1986) or to structural, functional or other connections. This collection only suggests such links: the findings of Feest and Murayama's 'virtual comparison' could be used to support a functionalist model of interdependence between the different stages of the criminal process; Brants and Field's model of the relationship between legal culture and political culture could also have wider application.

However, as these last examples show, the different directions which can be taken in building theory in comparative criminal justice depend largely on which underlying approach to explanation and understanding is being adopted. Should we be looking for the nearest possible 'functional equivalents' of the stages and goals of the (Anglo-American) criminal process? Are we trying to reach the behaviourist core of criminal justice (the numbers of crimes processed, number of acquittals, the numbers of prisoners) by removing 'the cultural packaging' which prevents us seeing which activities correspond functionally in each system? Must we be careful to translate local terms into scientific Esperanto so as to measure variation in 'decision-making' rather than the elusive concept of 'discretion' across different cultures? Or should we be precisely concerned with the cultural packaging, with the problems of faithfully translating another system's ideas of fairness and justice and of making proper sense of its web and meanings? Is it the essence of the comparative task to penetrate behind the numbers, or even to work out the different meanings of official 'discretion' in cross-cultural terms (Nelken, 1997c)? How else could we proceed when even what is conjured up by the term 'law' itself can be profoundly different in modern European countries belonging to the common law and the civil law worlds (Legrand, 1995)?

All comparative research involves the search for similarities and differences, and the discovery of either one or the other can be of theoretical and practical importance. Setting out to demonstrate that all higher courts have an essential role in governmental social control becomes a provocative argument if the cultures surveyed are as different as Muslim, Chinese, French and British (Shapiro, 1981). Showing essential similarities of outcome between different criminal justice systems even where the cultural differences between systems are less pronounced can still be an important achievement (see the discussion by Feest and Murayama, in Chapter 3, of protections for the accused). In Chapter 5 Bertrand and her collaborators also sought similarities when confirming their pessimistic expectations that there would be little in the way of special provision for women in any of the national prison systems they set out to survey.

The other contributions to this volume, however, are much more fascinated by differences, even if the point of revealing difference, apart from its value in correcting ethnocentrism, is not always made as clear as it might be. Certainly, any postulate that all economically advanced countries *should* be expected to have exactly similar ideas and practices for dealing with crime seems far-fetched. What is of more interest is the attempt to show how one set of differences (for example, in political culture) is linked to other aspects of differences between criminal justice processes (see Brants and Field and Crawford, Chapters 4 and 8 in this volume). It can also be instructive to examine the way in which a researcher becomes conscious of difference, including the process by which he or she recognizes and tries to explain the 'absence' and 'presence' of what is familiar and unfamiliar (see Nelken, Chapter 2 in this volume).

This last concern leads us directly to another important issue in comparative research – the problem of 'starting points'. Difference is important if it contradicts expectations. But where do these differences come from? Of course, one source is the previous scientific literature. Thus in Chapter 7 Johnson explicitly criticizes previous American studies of Japanese prosecutors for assuming that they must broadly share the ideals and goals of American prosecutors. More significantly, however, they also, and perhaps mainly, derive from the researcher's previous socialization. Thus in Chapter 4 Brants and Field describe the painstaking efforts they made to deal with their discovery that they had been socialized into using terms like 'inquisitorial' and 'accusatorial' to mean different things, and to use them for different purposes. In Chapter 9 Nelken discusses how far escaping from one's cultural starting point is possible, desirable or inevitable for a long-stay researcher.

It seems fair to say that few scholars can ultimately justify their particular cultural starting points. Whether or not the expectations they bring with them are especially likely to illuminate the culture which they are investigating is less relevant than the simple fact that they happen to be the ones which have shaped them. But, just for this reason, it is essential to do whatever is possible to understand the shape given to our ideas by such previous socialization. To take only one example, in Chapter 7 Johnson offers us a description of prosecutors' aims and practices in Japan as contrasted to the USA, yet also admits at one point that France and other civil law countries may also exemplify similar differences. Certainly many of his surprised descriptions – such as the concern for truth-finding, the power of prosecutors and judges as elites and even the enormous dossiers which make up complicated cases – also apply just as much to Italy. Thus, a description which purports to be about *Japanese* legal culture turns out to be – in at least some respects – an account of what in Japan differs from the USA rather than what is inherently Japanese.

A final issue, specific to this collection, is the interest shown by most of the authors in the controversial topic of 'legal culture' (Gessner *et al.*, 1996; Nelken, 1995, 1997a; Nelken and Feest, forthcoming). However much they may conceptualize and study it in different ways, this concern for the cultural distinctiveness of criminal justice in different settings undoubtedly also accounts for the preference of most contributors for exploring differences rather than discovering similarities.

At its most straightforward, legal culture refers to the ideas and behaviour of the officials of the legal system (see, for example, Johnson, Chapter 7 in this volume) and of those making demands on law or having demands made on them. More broadly, however, the term serves to name all that is specific about a national system of criminal justice, especially in its relation of correspondence and contrast to the culture in general. Thus, in this volume, we are told about cultural variability in terms of the way in which the boundaries of criminal justice are drawn, as in Brants and Field's discussion of the different meaning of diversion in Holland and in England and Wales (Chapter 4). We are also shown, in Crawford's chapter, the possibility of 'reading' such changes on this margin as clues to important developments in the systems under investigation. There are useful examinations of the relationship between criminal justice, legal culture and political culture in different settings. On the basis of such analyses the current and future trajectories of crime control are shown to be intimately connected to much larger social changes such as the breakdown of 'pillarization' in Holland, or the declining hold of ideologies in Italy.

But working with the concept of legal culture is not unproblematic (Nelken, 1995). Legal culture can either be the description we give to the ideas and actions of legal officials and others or it can be the set of meanings which we use to make sense of these ideas and actions. However, if we say it is both we risk confusion. Another matter concerns the 'unit' to be compared. Can local prosecutors' offices, the common law and the civil law, Italy and England, the West and the Rest be validly compared? Any given legal culture is both an outcome of the past and a projection towards an uncertain future; the local, the other and the global are all increasingly intertwined (as is well demonstrated by Crawford in Chapter 8). Furthermore, some trends, such as growing individualism and rights consciousness, are, arguably, worldwide phenomena (Friedman, 1987, 1994). Consequently, attention must be paid to the opposite dangers, on the one hand, of reifying what is presented as 'English', 'Italian' or any other legal culture, and, on the other hand, of failing to recognize how much one's view of the way the world is going is already influenced by one's own legal culture. The increasing interest in comparison is itself a consequence, and perhaps also partly a cause, of these globalizing developments (Nelken, 1997e). This means that any account we produce of practices in another culture may feed back into changing the object being defined. As if it were not already a sufficiently quixotic project to try to describe another culture – given the enormous range of interpretations in and about any culture[14] – the observer's interpretations themselves join the flux of communications through which cultures reinvent themselves.

The disciplinary resources drawn on by the contributors to this volume include law, sociology, anthropology, history and political science. But this by no means exhausts the range of possibilities. While the attention paid to empirical detail may offer some advance on attempts to develop ideal type of criminal justice systems (see Markovits, 1989), there is still room for more reference to the way in which history shapes current institutions (Mawby, 1990), as well as the part played by ordinary people's conceptions of justice (see, for example, Hamilton and Sanders, 1992). What perhaps most singles out these chapters as sociologically informed contributions is the types of research method they employ. In addition to consulting official and semi-official documents and the secondary literature there are examples of all the usual social research techniques using questionnaires, interviews and observation. Thus the contributors work backwards and forwards not so much between theories and data as between their search for data and the effort to find some way to check its descriptive validity.

The choice to follow any particular approaches to data-gathering is linked to the many considerations which influence the feasibility of a given research project such as the time available and the ability to visit the country concerned and with what sort of commitment. In addition, different research strategies tend to be geared to the aims of given projects. Depending on its purposes, collaboration with experts or a limited period of interviewing abroad may have some advantages to set off against the disadvantages compared with living and working in a country. There are the usual trade-offs, such as being able to cover more cases with questionnaires or interviews as opposed to in-depth observation and so on. The short-termer can pretend a useful naiveté which the long-term researcher must abandon, since that is part of what it means to become an insider/outsider. But, on the other hand, as an insider/outsider, the researcher is likely to learn much more in the course of ordinary life experiences than would be told to even the most naive of researchers.

In practice, none of these methods have necessarily to be pursued in their pure form, nor do they have to be treated as mutually exclusive. Scholars who base their claims on what experts say often do also have direct experience of the country concerned (gained prior to or following contact with the expert[15]); experts are also observers and observers become experts. Those who carry out interviews also observe, the participant observer or expatriate must rely on other sources (including newspaper reports) for the many matters which he or she is unable to experience directly. Often a deliberate strategy using a combination of methods for different purposes could be ideal. There can even be advantages in examining similar issues with different approaches in order to yield the best combination of what David Engel calls, on the one hand, 'cross-sectional engagement' and, on the other hand, 'personal and singular connection between researcher and subject' (Engel, 1999). In this volume, for example, it is interesting that both Johnson, who went to Japan to interview prosecutors, and Feest and Murayama, who collaborated as experts, agree on the importance, in Japan, of the accused being asked to show remorse and the readiness to accept this. Putting the two chapters together also shows how, like most policy choices in criminal justice, the Japanese search for remorse is not unambiguous in its effects. On the one hand it can have the positive result of limiting the number of those being funnelled further into the criminal justice system, but, on the other, it also leads to potentially dangerous consequences in cases where the accused being processed is actually innocent.

Notes

1 For illustrative examples see Downes (1998); Fionda (1995), and Vagg (1994). In relation to the aim of this volume it should be noted that these authors, even while conducting research abroad, chose to rely heavily on local experts (sometimes because of lack of proficiency in local languages). Some of the implications of this choice will emerge later in this chapter and in Chapter 2.
2 The same 'etic' versus 'emic' complications arise if we reformulate our research object in terms of such topics as 'informal justice', 'imposed law' or 'disputes'.
3 See Nelken, chapter 9 in this volume. Van Swanningen (1998, 1999) has recently made this point very well with respect to international criminology.
4 This is not to deny that interdisciplinary work – just because it cuts across academic 'cultures' – can add to the problems of comparative research as well as help solve them.
5 In Chapter 6 of this volume Hodgson relies on the arguments of Legrand (a comparative lawyer) in the course of stressing the need for participant observation of other lega cultures. In Chapter 3 Feest and Maruyama's idea of 'virtual comparison' has much in common with a similar idea found in comparative law (for example, Markensinis 1997).
6 But some of this discussion is rather limited in range, and would be enriched by

Just Comparing   19

consideration of a wider variety of cultures including those where law represents a 'doubly removed ideal' (Lopez-Ayllon, 1995).
7   Faugeron (1993) in his review of research in his country makes the same point about France (see also Hodgson, Chapter 6 in this volume).
8   This is particularly true, for obvious reasons, for information about organized crime. What is little remarked upon by insiders is the fact that these dossiers have been prepared *for the purposes of criminal trials* and therefore by no means seek or provide the sort of empirical information needed for sociological purposes. Even whilst recognizing the considerable effort that goes into compiling such dossiers it is important to appreciate that a prosecutor needs to draw a sharp (for other purposes perhaps oversharp) distinction between the behaviour of those he or she seeks to convict for organized crime and the behaviour of others in the same environment. His or her overall aim is to demonstrate legal responsibility, not examine wider causes.
9   Although the cry is sometimes heard that 'we are all Legal Realists now', this is actually far from true. This can easily be discovered by sitting in on a lecture course in many British law schools – or, still more, following most law courses in continental European countries!
10   A good summary of this debate can be found in Frase (1990).
11   An example of the resources needed in comparing leniency in the USA and Germany can be found in Savelsberg (1994). Interestingly, Melossi (1994) argues that, in Italy, leniency or 'tolerance' has actually become a deliberate strategy of ruling. In this collection some relevant discussions of relative leniency in criminal justice will be found in the chapters by Feest and Murayama, Johnston, Brants and Field and Nelken.
12   The editors of that collection of essays try to apply the theories of 'modernization' and 'civilization' to explain modern trends in crime and punishment.
13   The way the young are treated in Italy could be used to make the same point.
14   The task of describing the 'specificity' or 'peculiarities' of a country's system of criminal justice cannot be treated simply as 'the attribution of a set of behavioural and representational properties to a given population'. It must also involve 'the attempt to encompass an enormous interplay of interpretations of a given social reality' (J. Friedman, 1994: 73).
15   In this collection the collaboration between Brants and Field provides a good illustration of this. Field has also conducted research in the Netherlands, and Brants spent her early years in the UK.

References

Blankenburg, E. (1997), 'Civil Litigation Rates as Indicators for Legal Cultures', in D. Nelken (ed.), *Comparing Legal Cultures*, Aldershot: Dartmouth, 41–68.
Cole, G.F. *et al.* (eds) (1987), *Major Criminal Justice Systems: A Comparative Survey*, Beverly Hills, CA: Sage.
Cotterrell, R. (1997), 'The Concept of Legal Culture', in D. Nelken (ed.), *Comparing Legal Cultures*, Aldershot: Dartmouth, 13–32.
Damaska, M.R. (1986), *The Faces of Justice and State Authority*, New Haven, CT: Yale University Press.
Dorn, N., Jepsen, J. and Savona, N. (eds) (1996), *European Drug Policies and Enforcement*, Basingstoke: Macmillan.

Downes, D. (1988), *Contrasts in Tolerance*, Oxford: Clarendon Press.
Engel, D. (1999), 'Making Connections: Law and Society Researchers and their Subjects', *Law and Society Review*, 33 (1), 3–16.
Faugeron, C. (1993), 'Du Penal à la Discipline: L'Ordre et Le Controle Penal en France. Bilan de la Recherche en France depuis 1980', in P. Robert and L. Van Outrive (eds), *Crime et Justice en Europe*, Paris: L'Harmattan, 115–67.
Feeley, M. (1997), 'Comparative Law for Criminologists: Comparing for What Purpose?', in D. Nelken (ed.), *Comparing Legal Cultures*, Aldershot: Dartmouth, 93–104.
Feldman, E. (1997), 'Patient's Rights, Citizen's Movements and Japanese Legal Culture, in D. Nelken (ed.), *Comparing Legal Cultures*, Aldershot: Dartmouth, 215–36.
Fennell, R., Swart, B., Jorg, N. and Harding, A. (1995), 'Introduction', in C. Harding, P. Fennell, N. Jorg, and B. Swart (eds), *Criminal Justice in Europe: A Comparative Study*, Oxford: Clarendon Press, xv–xix.
Fields, C.B. and Moore, R.H. (eds) (1996), *Comparative Criminal Justice*, Prospect Heights, Ill: Waveland Press.
Findlay, M. and Zvekic, U. (eds) (1993), *Alternative Policing Styles*, Deventer: Kluwer.
Fionda, J. (1995), *Public Prosecutors and Discretion: A Comparative Study*, Oxford: Clarendon Press.
Frase, R.S. (1990), 'Comparative Criminal Justice as a Guide to American Law Reform', *California Law Review*, 79, 539.
Friedman, J. (1994), *Cultural Identity and Global Process*, London: Sage.
Friedman, L. (1987), *Total Justice*, Boston, MA: Beacon Press.
Friedman, L. (1994), 'Is there a Modern Legal Culture?', *Ratio Juris*, 7, 117–31.
Friedman, L. (1997), 'The Concept of Legal Culture: A Reply,' in D. Nelken (ed.), *Comparing Legal Cultures*, Aldershot: Dartmouth, 33–40.
Garapon, A. (1995), 'The Shock of Globalisation and French Legal Culture', in D. Nelken (ed.), special issue on 'Legal Culture, Diversity and Globalisation', *Social and Legal Studies*, 4 (4), 492–506.
Garland, D. (1990), *Punishment and Modern Society*, Oxford: Oxford University Press.
Garland, D. (1996), 'The Limits of the Sovereign State: Strategies of Crime Control in Contemporary Society', *British Journal of Criminology*, 36 (4), 445–71.
Gessner, V., Hoeland, A. and Varga, C. (eds) (1996), *European Legal Cultures*, Aldershot: Dartmouth.
Gottfredson, M. and Hirschi, T. (1990), *A General Theory of Crime*, Stanford, CA: Stanford University Press.
Hamilton, V.L., and Sanders, J. (1992), *Everyday Justice: Responsibility and the Individual in Japan and the United States*, New Haven, CT: Yale University Press.
Heidensohn, F. and Farrell, M. (1991), *Crime in Europe*, London: Routledge.
Heiland, H.G., Shelley, L.I. and Katoh, H. (eds) (1992), *Crime and Control in Comparative Perspectives*, Berlin: De Gruyter.

Legrand, P. (1995), 'Legal Traditions in Western Europe: The Limits of Commonality', in R. Jagtenberg et al. (eds), *Transfrontier Mobility of Law*, Deventer: Kluwer, 63–84.
Lopez-Ayllon, F., (1995), 'Notes on Mexican Legal Culture', in D. Nelken (ed.), *Comparing Legal Cultures*, Aldershot: Dartmouth, 478–92.
Magatti, M. (1996), *Corruzione Politica e Società Italiana*, Bologna: Il Mulino.
Markensinis, B. (1997), *Foreign Law and Comparative Methodology*, Oxford: Hart Publishing.
Markovits, I. (1989), 'Playing the Opposites Game: On Mirjan Damaska's *The Faces of Justice and State Authority*', *Michigan Law Review*, **13**, 13–41.
Mawby, R. (1990), *Comparative Policing Issues*, London: Unwin Hyman.
Melossi, D. (1994), 'The "Economy" of Illegalities: Normal Crimes, Elites and Social Control in Comparative Analysis', in D. Nelken (ed.), *The Futures of Criminology*, London: Sage, 202–19.
Miyazawa, S. (1997), 'The Enigma of Japan as a Testing Ground for Cross-cultural Studies', in D. Nelken (ed.), *Comparing Legal Cultures*, Aldershot: Dartmouth, 195–214.
Nelken, D. (1987), 'Criminal Law and Criminal Justice: Some Notes on their Irrelation', in Ian Dennis (ed.), *Criminal Law and Justice*, London: Sweet and Maxwell, 139–77.
Nelken, D. (1990), 'Alternative Logics in Criminal Justice', in Roy Light (ed.), *Public and Private Provisions in Criminal Justice*, Proceedings of the British Criminology Conference, Bristol Centre for Criminal Justice, Bristol, 1–19.
Nelken, D. (1994a), 'Reflexive Criminology?', in D. Nelken (ed.), *The Futures of Criminology*, London: Sage, 7–42.
Nelken, D. (1994b), 'The Future of Comparative Criminology', in D. Nelken (ed.), *The Futures of Criminology*, London: Sage, 220–43.
Nelken, D. (1995), 'Disclosing/Invoking Legal Culture', in D. Nelken (ed.), *Legal Culture, Diversity and Globalisation*, special issue of *Social and Legal Studies*, London: Sage, **4** (4), 435–53.
Nelken, D. (1996), Judicial Politics and Corruption in Italy', in M. Levi and D. Nelken (eds), *The Corruption of Politics and the Politics of Corruption*, Oxford: Blackwell, 95–113.
Nelken, D. (ed.) (1997a), *Comparing Legal Cultures*, Aldershot: Dartmouth.
Nelken, D. (1997b), 'Puzzling out Legal Culture: A Comment on Blankenburg', in D. Nelken (ed.), *Comparing Legal Cultures*, Aldershot: Dartmouth, 58–88.
Nelken, D. (1997c), 'Studying Criminal Justice Comparatively', in M. Maguire, R. Morgan and R. Reiner (eds), *The Oxford Handbook of Criminology*, (2nd edn), Oxford: Oxford University Press, 559–76.
Nelken, D. (1997d), 'White-Collar Crime', in M. Maguire, R. Morgan and R. Reiner (eds), *The Oxford Handbook of Criminology*, (2nd edn), Oxford: Oxford University Press, 891–924.
Nelken, D. (1997e), 'The Globalization of Criminal Justice: Prospects and Problems', in M. Freeman (ed.), *Law and Opinion at the Turn of the Century*, Oxford: Oxford University Press, 251–79.

Nelken, D. and Feest, J. (eds) (forthcoming), *Adapting Legal Cultures*.
Robert, P. and Van Outrive, L. (eds) (1993), *Crime et Justice en Europe*, Paris: L'Harmattan.
Ruggiero, V., Ryan, H. and Sim, J. (eds) (1995), *Western European Penal Systems*, London: Sage.
Ruggiero, V., South, N. and Taylor, I. (eds), (1998), *The New European Criminology: Crime and Social Order in Europe*, London: Routledge.
Savelsberg, J. (1994), 'Knowledge, Domination, and Criminal Punishment', *American Journal of Sociology*, 99, 911–43.
Shapiro, M. (1981), *Courts*, Chicago: Chicago University Press.
Smandych, R. (ed.) (1999), *Governable Places: Readings on Governmentality and Crime Control*, Aldershot: Dartmouth.
Vagg, J. (1994), *Prison Systems*, Oxford: Clarendon Press.
Van Swaaningen, R. (1998), *Critical Criminology in Europe*, London: Sage.
Van Swaaningen, R. (1999), 'Reclaiming Critical Criminology: Social Justice and the European Tradition', *Theoretical Criminology*, 3 (1), 5–29.
Watson, A. (1993), *Legal Transplants*, 2nd edn., Athens: University of Georgia Press.
Young, J. (1999), *The Exclusive Society*, London: Sage.
Zedner, L. (1995), 'In Pursuit of the Vernacular: Comparing Law and Order Discourse in Britain and Germany', in D. Nelken (ed.) special issue on 'Legal Culture, Diversity and Globalisation', *Social and Legal Studies*, 4 (4), 517–34.
Zedner, L. (1996), 'German Criminal Justice Culture', paper presented at the *Onati Workshop on Changing Legal Cultures*, 1, 13–14 July.
Zweigert, K. and Kotz, H. (1987), *An Introduction to Comparative Law*, Oxford: Oxford University Press.

2 Virtually There, Researching There, Living There

David Nelken

Introduction

This volume could have been organized round the substantive topics discussed in the individual chapters, such as the stage of criminal justice being considered or the relationship between crime control and legal culture. But I have chosen instead to present the chapters in terms of the way in which they have dealt with the central epistemological and methodological problem of comparative research – how we can ever know another culture. The contributors to this volume tackle this problem either by relying mainly on foreign experts, by going abroad to interview legal officials or by drawing on their own experience of living and working in the country concerned – by being 'virtually there', 'researching there' or 'living there'. Thus this volume begins with chapters built round the findings of collaborative investigation, the following chapters are based on relatively limited period of interviewing abroad, and the collection ends with two chapters written by expatriates.

In the remainder of this chapter I shall first say something more about the relationship between the choice of research methods and the organization of the volume. I shall then go on to summarize the arguments of the individual chapters giving special attention to the difference of substance which tend to be associated with the use of such different research stategies. Throughout my exposition, however, I shall also seek to show the extent of variety *within* each of these approaches, as well as between them.

The Virtues of 'Being There'

The way in which the chapters are arranged, as if along a continuum from least to greatest engagement with another culture, might seem to suggest that the ideal form of research is that based on living and working in another country. And, in fact, moving from a reliance on foreign experts to extended ethnography does offer increased opportunities for coming to understand another culture. This can be easily shown if we return to our running example concerning the New Code of Criminal Procedure in Italy introduced in 1989. In typical discussions of this reform in English, based largely on what Italian experts have written in the criminal procedure literature, attention is given to the Code's failure to shift the balance of power between prosecution and defence. Criticism is levelled at the modifications introduced almost immediately by the legislature in 1992 which was concerned about the effects of the Code on the fight against organized crime. (Since 1997 this issue has become the subject of further struggle between the Constitutional Court and parliament.) It is noted too that the adoption of the new Code has also done little to resolve endemic problems of the system, such as delay, and may even have exacerbated them.

However, from a sociological point of view, talking about success and failure in terms of the 'gap' between the aims and achievement of a legal reform, though the very stuff of legal and political polemic, is problematic enough even in one's own home society (Nelken, 1981). Transferred to a foreign context, the enquiry becomes even more difficult. The difficulty lies in determining retrospectively what counts as the aim, or aims, of a legal reform. Once enacted there is likely to be wide and continuing disagreement over what the aims really were and hence over whether its aims have been sufficiently fulfilled. First-hand interviewing offers some opportunity to examine these complexities, and it will usually reveal that much depends on which expert one consults and that judges, prosecutors and defence lawyers, as groups of interested parties, may all have very different ideas – as well as disagreements among themselves.

Arguing about the success or failure of the Code is therefore, as we should have expected, not only or principally a matter of assessing its practical outcomes, especially in cultures like Italy where empirical research into criminal justice is so little practised. Rather, such debate forms part of a continuing battle for ideals and interests between agencies and actors inside and outside the criminal justice system. Living and working in Italy provides ample opportunities for examining the links between the debate over the good and bad effects of the new Code and the way in which this is linked to other changing aspects of law and politics in the country, such as the battles over organized crime and political corruption. What experts or practitioners say, and the process of talking about change itself, become data to be explained and interpreted in seeking to understand a given system of criminal justice. To judge by their proposals for change, for many of those involved in these debates, the alleged failures of the new Code represent its successes! Long-term involvement in a culture also offers one of the most reliable routes to grasping the intellectual and political affiliations of those participating in such debates. Once it is possible to see where the different experts or practitioners relied on as authorities are 'coming from', attention can turn to asking how and why they reach their conclusions as to whether the reform is working or not, what changes they would like to see and what they would like to see in its place.

This said, it is important to remember that observant participation (which is, in any case, not always practical) is not necessarily the best method to use for all purposes. In practice, all three of the approaches to research illustrated in this volume may have to face similar problems in knowing who to trust and then conveying credibility. Even the insider/outsider, or 'observing participant', cannot possibly experience everything at first hand. So, to this extent, his or her research is also in some sense virtual. However his or her findings are (re)presented, they are also largely the result of interviews and consultation of experts and practitioners and they are often obtained in ways which are less systematic and representative than those followed by the other approaches. The insider/outsider's main advantage stems from the fact that consulting experts and interviewing practitioners can be more fruitful when you already have enough cultural background to identify the right questions to ask. But, as the chapters in this volume suggest, there may be more than one way of acquiring such background. Rather than advocating 'observant participation' as an ideal method of research we should be more interested in clarifying some of its special strengths (and weaknesses). Of all methods, this way of researching does provide the most time and opportunity to experience a wide range of formal and informal contacts and experiences. But living and working in another country can also mean that the researcher does not have the same freedom to move around as a visitor does, and becoming more of an insider can also be counterproductive in other ways (Horowitz, 1986).

If the amount of time spent in a culture correlated with success in understanding it the native would always be the best anthropologist. And it matters how that time is used. We should also not assume any necessary relationship between time spent in a culture and a tendency either to appreciate or to criticize its institutions. American comparative lawyers in the 1970s needed only a short time in Europe to satisfy themselves that the vaunted judicial oversight of the police was a 'myth'. Marshall Clinard's short visit to Switzerland led him to a positive assessment of the country's way with crime (Clinard, 1978), but Balvig's even shorter visit (1987) led him to different conclusions. Downes (1988) needed only a short period to be impressed with prison policy in the Netherlands. His Dutch critics were more cynical. On the basis of relatively short research visits, Crawford (Chapter 8 in this volume) criticizes King, who lived for some years in France, for failing to see the downside of the French approach to crime prevention (King, 1989). What seems to be most relevant to these disagreements is the way in which the study of foreign cultures is often really more about the home country. In this respect, we can reasonably expect those who spend more time in a country to usually become less interested in examining it for the lessons it supposedly has to teach those back home (except when writing for an audience in their country of origin).

Actually living in a country offers the possibility of being able to experience in everyday life whether you have a grasp of the way in which the culture works. Yet this sort of 'recipe knowledge' – just because it is close to that possessed by insiders – will not necessarily be easy to reformulate in the language of social science. In fact, one danger which those actually living in another culture are supposedly exposed to is that of 'going native'. An academic expatriate does not really risk this in most cases. Being 'resocialized' into a new culture is rarely as compelling as first socialization, especially when previous links are maintained. What can and does happen is that the observer finds him or herself increasingly concerned with the practical concerns of the country in which he or she is living rather than that from which he or she has moved. He or she is likely to be asked, or tempted, to take part in the debates and conflicts of the new society and can even be drawn in to these debates by parties to such conflicts against his or her will. As an Anglo-American criminologist transplanted to Italy during the *Tangentopoli* investigations it mattered to insiders whether I was 'for' or 'against' the judges. Now that the problem of street crime is increasingly hitting the headlines it again becomes crucial to consider my position. How should I disentangle the elements that could be influencing the trend towards a more populist approach to crime? Should this be understood (and opposed) as further evidence of the spread of American hegemonic ideas? Should it be welcomed as a sign of a more democratic, bottom-up, approach to the problem of crime and the fear of crime? Or should it simply be registered as proof of worldwide growth in individualist, consumer-based approach to politics and law (Friedman, 1987, 1994) which, in Italy, is accompanying the inevitable decline of (solidaristic) ideologies?

As the relationship between the host society and the researcher changes and his or her starting point changes, new – often more apt – questions can be formulated. In this positive sense the researcher does begin to 'go native'. The 'observing participant' can also be led to examine how and why his or her own point of view has changed over time, *possibly to question whether he or she ever really understood his or her own culture of origin*. As he or she looks back 'with other eyes' (Cain, Chapter 10 in this volume) he or she may come to realize that previously he or she saw it only as an insider, and therefore as an ethnocentric native (Eve, 1993, 1996). The problem then becomes how to lose one type of ethnocentrism without taking on another.

A final advantage of actually living in a country for comparative work derives from being better placed to convey convincingly the experience of what Geertz calls 'being there' (Geertz, 1988). Whether this is seen as some sort of reaction to the otherwise paralysing postmodern 'crisis of representation' or, more straightforwardly, as a way of dealing with the suspicion that one has not really got to grips with the culture being re-presented, there is no doubt that the descriptions that most influence an audience often take the form of vignettes drawn from life. Thus the more opportunities to do this the more convincing the story which can be told. In this volume, for example, we hear about the attempt to appeal to the better side of a recidivist rapist in Japan, share the problems of a small businessman in Trinidad trying to solve his security problems, and hear the complaints of an Italian drug dealer in Copenhagen. But, in addition, we also share the experience of outsider/insiders (Cain and Nelken) as they negotiate their place within the culture they have adopted, or which is adopting them. The story *of* the research comes to join the stories *in* the research.[1]

In reading the following summaries of the chapters in this collection it is therefore worth bearing in mind the various methodological problems which the authors are facing. What do experts and legal officials know about their cultures? Who count as experts and why? How do *they* know? What are the similarities and difference between experts and practitioners? If experts and practitioners are in agreement is this because the experts obtain their information from practitioners? Or because practitioners are doubling as experts? How does a visitor learn about a new culture? Should he or she try to think like a native insider? Or can he or she do 'better' than the natives? The differences between the cultures being examined are found not only in the substance of their rules, procedures and institutions but also in which methods it is appropriate to use to understand them.

Virtually There

Chapters 3 to 5 in this collection are all expressly concerned with the potential for international collaboration in comparative research. Rather than seeking to study a foreign culture at first hand, their aim is to describe successfully other systems of criminal justice by means of intercultural cooperation. In this way the researcher is 'virtually there', by being both there and not there.[2] He or she is there in the person of the expert being relied on (but for that same reason is not really there in first person).

Chapter 3 by Johannes Feest and Masayuki Murayama describes the result of an ingenious thought experiment. Starting from a careful description of the actual case of an American student arrested and tried in Spain on a false charge of participating in an illegal squatting demonstration, the authors ask themselves what would have been the likely outcome given the same sequence of events in the countries whose criminal justice they know best – namely, Germany and Japan.

To answer this question the authors take us through all the relevant stages of investigation and trial, paying careful attention to often subtle differences in the criminal process in all three jurisdictions. They point out that this sort of case may be more or less likely to enter the criminal justice system, depending on the likelihood of squatters' demonstrations and the strategies used by the police in handling them. They note the differences in when the accused is told of his/her rights, when they can call a lawyer, how easy it is to get a lawyer, how long the police can keep the accused in custody while they carry out their investigations, whether the accused has the right to silence and what this means in practice. They describe how quickly an accused goes before a judge, what are the advantages and the risks for the defendant of seeking expedited proceedings or the benefit of discretionary measures in return for full or partial confession, the possibilities open to the defence at the trial stage, whether character witnesses can and will be heard, the extent to which there can be an appeal, the importance attached to the bringing or not of certain evidence, and whether the imposition of a fine in addition to, or in substitution for, a prison sentence is possible.

All three jurisdictions belong to the family of civil law. But in Spain and Germany the 'legality principle' applies, which basically requires prosecution whenever there is evidence of crime. The Japanese system, on the other hand, provides more leeway to suspend charges and prosecution. It is partly for this reason that one of the principle differences between the Japanese system and others emerges. The Japanese criminal process offers less protections to the defendant, the Japanese suspect can be kept longest in prison (23 days), and the defence lawyer has the most limited role of all the countries surveyed. But, it is suggested, given the ample discretion of the prosecutor, cases involving a miscarriage of justice are probably less likely to be sent to trial in the first place (the statistics suggest two-thirds of similar cases are not charged). Japanese prosecutors are likely to give considerable weight to the kind of person telling the story, his or her alibi claim and, in general, they are reluctant to take cases forward which risk ending up in non-conviction (compare Chapter 7 by Johnson in this volume). Importantly, however, if the case does go to court there is a high chance it could end in a conviction. The accused is less likely to receive a prison sentence because of the relatively long period of permitted pre-detention he or she will have experienced (even longer if he or she pleads not guilty), which may be considered a sufficient punishment. However, the fact that the (innocent) accused so strongly denies the charges could rebound against him or her because it shows a crucial lack of remorse – as confirmed in Johnson's chapter.

Feest and Murayama describe their enquiry as 'virtual' mainly because the case which arose in Spain has not actually occurred, as far as they know, in these other jurisdictions. I am stressing that their comparison is virtual in the sense that the authors base their findings on interrogating each other rather than on getting to know foreign systems at first hand (even though Johannes Feest was working in Spain at the time of the case his comments on it rely exclusively on the opinions of local experts). Yet the methodology adopted by the authors can be more useful than the many investigations based only on interviewing practitioners and experts about what ought to be the case, since they attend not only to what the rules say (and what legal actors say *should* occur) but also to what is likely to happen as a result of the various strategies open to the parties to the criminal process. They also use statistical evidence to show the choices usually made. Conducting this sort of experiment by interviewing and observing practioners would have been rather unrealistic. If we imagine a project set up to visit different countries in order to seek practitioners' opinions on the likelihood of similar miscarriages of justice involving a known case of factual (and not only procedural) innocence it is difficult to imagine those interviewed replying coolly that, in all likelihood, the hapless defendant would face a prison sentence of one year or more. And setting out to observe such miscarriages of justice is even more implausible.

In the spirit of the Legal Realists, Feest and Murayama suggest that it is not only the law but also practice in the 'shadow of the law' which is important. The law is a condition and resource but the way in which it is used strategically is all-important. Although the authors' intention seems mainly to be that of successful description as a means of prediction, they do not exaggerate the certainty of their predictions. Thus they warn that certain kinds of different consideration could lead to decisions either way – for example, the fact that the accused in this case was a foreigner could make an acquittal either more or less likely. And, in fact, the practitioners may have had the last laugh here because the Spanish Court of Appeal did acquit the student, against the expectations of all the experts.

Feest and Murayama also try to link the differences they describe to wider aspects of legal political and general culture. They suggest that Japan sticks to the 'opportunity principle', notwithstanding its civil law trial institutions, so as to allow prosecution and defence the chance to establish the truth of guilt together, rather than in conflict. They explain the low prospects for acquittal in Germany – notwithstanding its culture of rights – as a consequence of the 'smooth bureaucratic meshing' of judges and prosecutors which leaves little room for the defence role. They argue that the actual trial outcome in Spain may depend on the fact that it is still consolidating its transition to democracy. However, concern for prediction may not always be the best route to take if we are interested in interpreting the meaning of differences in legal culture and can even testify to a behaviourist preference for demonstrating that outcomes can be predicted without taking too seriously the ostensible reasoning by which they are reached. What is sacrificed here is any sustained interrogation of what prosecutors and others in each jurisdiction think they are doing and why (the task Johnson sets himself in Chapter 7 on Japan and the USA). The starting and final point of their enquiry is their assumption that all criminal justice systems have to handle the 'built-in conflict' of how to maximize convictions of the guilty while simultaneously maximizing the acquittal of the innocent. Feest and Murayama are interested in working out what happened to their real defendant and what would happen to their hypothetical innocent defendants. They are less preoccupied with how different systems or agencies may inflect their functional goals in culturally specific ways.

Despite the apparent interest in the strategic use of rules, the methodology used in this study is therefore not one that is really designed to lead to 'understanding' legal culture from the inside. The various similarities that the authors discover – in the ways that maximum charges are used strategically by the police, in the tendency for maximum deadlines to become the norm, in the extent to which defence lawyers come to be incorporated in the system, in the pattern of sentencing well below the maximum – may not even be known by the legal actors themselves and seem, above all, to correspond to a functionalist 'system logic'. Indeed, one strong conclusion (not expressly argued for by the authors) which could be drawn from their comparison has to do with the 'functional' interconnection between the extent of protections at each stage of the criminal process. They demonstrate that each jurisdiction has some really crucial pre-trial and post-trial filters, as well as others which are more formalistic and typically presuppose that the required critical attention has been, or will be, given at another stage. It is then difficult to avoid concluding that there are 'functional equivalents' in each system for legitimizing even unsound cases of police arrests and that the systems 'self-correct' to reach rather similar outcomes. This chapter thus provides confirmation, in a comparative civil law context, for McBarnet's provocative claim, in her study of Scottish trials, that 'due process is *for* crime control' (McBarnet, 1981) and offers disturbing insight into the ease by which the innocent can be convicted.

Valuable as this study is, we should be careful not to take from it more than the authors themselves would claim. The charges under discussion in their 'virtual' cases regarded public order offences, and involved a situation (admittedly not infrequent) where the courts must make a choice between the word of the police and that of the defendant. We do not know how far the findings of this virtual comparison could, or should, be applied to other types of crime – or even this sort of crime at other levels of seriousness.

Questions which are marginal for Feest and Murayama turn out to be at the heart of the collaboration between Chrisje Brants and Stewart Field described in Chapter 4. Their study is about the link between criminal justice and culture and their method requires painstaking attempts to learn to appreciate what is distinctive about the articulation, in a foreign context, of apparently familiar ideas. The task is that of interpreting the past more than predicting the future, except insofar as it is conditioned by the past.

Brants and Field set out to explain how two different jurisdictions have reacted to the rise of covert and proactive policing. They argue that similar causes, such as the increasing use of electronic technology changes in police organization and international cooperation between police forces converging trends in crime are promoting similar developments in many modern criminal justice systems. But, they claim, national and cultural differences in structures and attitudes shape the adoption and adaptation of such policing methods. They therefore explore the contrasting legal cultures, political cultures and procedural traditions in the Netherlands and in England and Wales which create differences in the way the targets for such police actions are constructed, the extent and terms in which their use is found problematic and the regulatory response which is then followed.

In their chapter Feest and Murayama tell us relatively little about how they managed to reach common understandings of the questions they wished to answer. No doubt they followed some of the same protocols as Brants and Field; but much of the plausibility of their exercise depends on their conception of criminal justice primarily as a series of functionally similar organizational decisions, and it is this perspective which allowed them to leave tricky problems of translation and meaning to one side. But issues of cultural understanding and misunderstanding are exactly the matters that Brants and Field wish to tackle. They draw attention to the continued difficulties of reaching shared meanings between experts in different legal cultures, even after long extended collaboration. Such collaboration, they say, requires a high degree of mutual trust and involves 'negotiating' mutually acceptable descriptions of legal practice in each of their home countries. Both authors are constantly concerned about the dangers in not comparing like with like.

The lesson that they seek to drive home is that the correct interpretation of even the smallest detail of criminal justice organization requires sensitivity to 'broader institutional and ideological contexts'. They explain, for example, that, in England and Wales, the idea of 'diversion' refers to a choice to take cases *out* of the system, as part of a pragmatic effort to avoid the negative, self fulfilling side-effects caused when people are drawn into the criminal justice process. In the Netherlands, on the other hand, diversion is part of a continuum of responses which are considered *intrinsic* to the criminal justice system; it is seen mainly as a matter of rerouting offenders from the punishment option to more positive methods of conflict resolution. Again, in England and Wales, diversion is seen as a somewhat 'guilty secret' which compromises the ideals of adversarialness in the interests of making the criminal process more expeditious. Diversion in the Netherlands, on the other hand, is understood as an aspect of the wider 'politics of accommodation' which encourages an ample use of prosecution and other official discretion. Once such differences are pinned down, the authors are able to show how both these contrasting ways of approaching the boundaries of criminal justice can have both good and bad consequences. The broad Dutch approach, for example, too easily allows the gathering of police intelligence without it having to be justified as necessary or directly connected to imminent prosecutions. In much the same way, the concern over proactive and covert forms of police activity in each country also relates to the way in which cultural conceptions of the proper boundaries of criminal justice are being fought over within each of the cultures concerned. In the Netherlands it is seen as part of the growing challenge to the political culture of trusting the elites; in England it is viewed in terms of the difficulties in holding the police accountable.

Brants and Field's socio-historical account of the relationship between these forms of policing and the environing legal and political contexts in the cultures under investigation is important, carefully documented and rather too detailed for easy summary. We learn how proactive police methods in England and Wales were first used to deal with 'problems' such as drugs and football hooliganism but were then legitimized by the 1990s slogan to target 'the criminal not the crime', so as to be applied to burglary, car crime and eventually to the struggle against organized crime. These high-profile techniques prove useful to the police because they give the impression that they are 'doing something' and providing 'value for money'. They both help defuse public expectations regarding the difficulties of apprehending other sorts of opportunistic crime and also help ease police anxieties over the limits to their investigative capacities introduced by the PACE rules. In the Netherlands, on the other hand, the 'management of crime' has always been seen as an essential role of the police. Organized crime is a longstanding

'Dutch demon' and intelligence-gathering and the spread of disinformation is routine. Those who are suspected of being key criminals are targeted and harassed with all sorts of other administrative regulations as part of the process of defining and managing 'risk populations'. But when it became clear that the exercise of police power was no longer being kept under hierarchical control, this helped cause (and indexed) the breakdown of the political culture of 'pillarization' which depended on a high level of trust in elites who corporatively arranged the pacification of the lower classes.

Many of Brants and Field's methodological strategies can be applied beyond their case study. Of particular value is their examination of the relationship between legal culture and political culture and the way in which changes in one affect the other. They set out a fruitful model for examining procedural traditions in criminal law as the site of intersections amongst four aspects of culture: traditions, institutions, intellectual formations and 'lived structures of feeling'. Important as it is to capture contrasts in conceptions and context between cultures, the authors are also aware of the dangers of reifying differences between national systems of criminal justice. They draw attention to the interaction between the local and the global and how influences from the USA and the European Union are affecting both the Netherlands and England and Wales. The adoption of new policing techniques and the controversies which surround their adoption is a good illustration of an area of cultural flux in criminal justice which is not restricted to any particular jurisdiction.

The final example of collaborative research in this collection is represented by Marie-Andrée Bertrand's chapter which describes a collective international project, carried out between 1993 and 1997, examining the conditions in 18 closed prisons and six closed prisons for women located in the USA, Canada and in six European countries. The project, based at the Montreal Centre of Criminology, sought to discover exceptional institutions which focused on women's needs and could thus serve as a model 'to put pressure on Canadian correctional authorities' to improve conditions for women inmates.

Although members of the research team did spend very short periods in the institutions they were studying, these were mainly inspection visits; moreover, different members of the team each visited different sites and then pooled their findings. The project also relied heavily on input from local experts for advice about the local situation. Interestingly, however, the researchers rejected the general objections made by some of these experts to the validity of seeking to compare prisons between common law and civil law countries and countries with high and low detention rates.

In keeping with the brief given to the contributors to this volume, Bertrand focuses principally on the methodological problems encountered in carrying out the project. She explains that the intention was to combine a Schultzian epistemology with a materialist feminist standpoint in examining the structural conditions to be expected and actually observed in women's prisons. Rejecting oversimplified distinctions between positivist and qualitative methodologies she demonstrates the neglect of women in the study of national incarceration rates and the extent to which such rates can disguise important differences amongst prison conditions. Bertrand describes how the project required intense exchanges between the researchers and legal officials at the local and national level and with local experts. Where possible, researchers also spoke with women in the prisons they studied, but this was often hampered by language problems as well as being subject to the selection of prisoner guides by the prison administration.

The project's aim was to describe examples of prisons distinguished for accessibility and modern, high-quality, gender-specific mental health, education and physical services, and work opportunities. What the researchers found, as they rather feared they would, was a generally depressing level of limited and out-of-date work options, poor health facilities, and severe restrictions on family contacts, as well as discrimination against women prisoners (for example, in the denial, in some prisons, of equal opportunities to follow post-secondary education). Despite women representing a relatively low risk there was disproportionate effort to control them and a tendency to 'infantilize' them as compared to men. However, there were also considerable differences between prisons; against expectations, prisons in common law jurisdictions generally had better health facilities and family access provisions. Durham even had a self-governing unit for women.

The researchers hypothesized a direct link between criminal justice and wider culture predicting that 'the place and status of women in women's prisons would constitute a representation of the place and "status" granted to women in each country'. They expected, for example, that the degree of equality in prison would match the level of sexual equality in the wider culture. Here, however, the findings of the project turned out to be surprising. The model women's prison turned out to be the state prison in the US state of Minnesota (a state with prison rates in line with those in Europe rather than the US average) rather than any of those in Scandinavia where some of the most discriminatory regimes were to be found, despite the country's deserved reputation for sexual progressiveness in the wider culture. However, no explanation of this paradox is advanced here. The findings of Bertrand's project illustrate some of the well known tensions which have to be mediated between practical goals and the search for understanding and explanation. Its main goal was to find a model prison, theorizing the relationship between prisons and the wider legal and general culture took second place.[3]

Researching There

The next three chapters in this volume describe studies in which researchers carried out extended periods of empirical research in foreign sites. The first of these chapters, by Jacqueline Hodgson, which is entitled 'Comparing Legal Cultures: the Comparativist as Participant Observer', offers some methodological reflections drawn from her research into the roles of defence and prosecution in the UK and France. Her discussion concerns the problems of understanding what she calls 'the different expectations of those occupying roles in the two systems'. Her overview, short as it is, highlights many of the advantages of seeking sociological understanding of other systems of criminal justice at first hand.

Hodgson criticizes the type of research carried out by comparative law scholars for being in too much of a hurry to learn practical lessons and too uninterested in questions of (sociological) explanation and understanding. Those motivated by reformist goals, according to her, tend to produce formalistic accounts of foreign legal systems which pay insufficient attention to the way in which rules are used and to the meaning of legal ideas in their social context. The remedy for this is 'participant observation' of the system in question. Like it or not, the comparativist must recognize that he or she is engaged in a form of legal anthropology. It is insufficient to rely merely on interviewing legal actors because of the danger that this will produce 'presentational data' – the selective account of practice which it is possible and appropriate for social actors to present in the moment of interview. Interviews accompanied by ethnographic observation are an improvement. This gives the researcher a time of adjustment 'to become familiar' with the new setting and to obtain data outside of formal interview situations. Crucially, it also provides the opportunity for 'open ended' enquiry which can lead to the discovery of new questions whose existence could not be guessed at by relying only on what is written in relevant textbooks, whether French or British. Some things are never written down because they belong to 'craft rules of thumb', some matters are secrets which should not be written down, some matters cannot be reduced to writing because theory and practice do not coincide and so on. Such an approach, she argues, is the only reliable method for finally resolving the vexed question – so central to the main debate in comparative criminal justice as conducted by comparative lawyers – regarding the degree of supervision actually exercised by prosecutors over police enquiries in civil law countries and at what stage of the proceedings.

Hodgson also describes some of the challenges which researchers face in their 'on-site' search for similarities and differences, including the difficulty of knowing what to compare with what, the temptation, on the one hand, to assume 'functional equivalents' between the stages of criminal justice and to assign it universal goals, and, on the other hand, the need for patient dialectical interchange between cultures which fully recognizes the problems of translation, history, and cultural bias, as the researcher moves between his or her home culture and that under investigation. She notes the need to 'unlearn' textbook categories such as 'civil law' or 'inquisitorial systems' (which are, in any case, undergoing rapid change) and to learn to adopt the insiders' views of how their systems differ from such 'ideal types'. She suggests that ethnographic research provides the best opportunity to grasp foreign ideas about the significance of prosecutor and judicial independence and why it matters. But she also underlines the need to alternate between empathy with insiders to discover what they are doing (or think they are doing) and the outsider's point of view.

Of course, a brief visit by a foreign academic can hardly be termed 'participant' observation. Although personal investigation coupled with questioning represents participation in a research project, it hardly counts as *participation in what is being observed*. Hodgson notes the advantages of naiveté for this type of research. But naiveté is precisely what a genuine participant does not have, or cannot afford to display. She rightly comments that empirical investigation carried out by academics into the operations of the criminal process is relatively unfamiliar, or even unknown, in France. But, again, if this role is so unusual for insiders it is hardly consistent with the idea of participant observation. It is for these reasons that I have placed academics who move to another country and do actually participate in its academic and political life in another category.

More importantly, we also should avoid exaggerating the insights made possible by this approach to comparative work as compared to its rivals. How far is legal anthropology feasible in modern complex societies? Is it suitable for all purposes? Can legal culture be understood by immersion in practical contexts or does it require historical and other sorts of illumination? Even the line between explanatory and reformist enquiries cannot be drawn too sharply (Nelken, 1997a). Despite her polemic against reformers, Hodgson ends her chapter on a normative note by returning to her starting point regarding the different methods for supervising police decision-making in civil law and common law jurisdictions. Her objection is to the search for snap solutions. Rather than draw 'all or nothing' conclusions, it is better to use other ideas and practices as something to 'think with', with the aim of re-examining your own system in the light of other.

Chapters 7 and 8 also describe prolonged visits to research sites, although neither, any more than Hodgson's project, could properly be described as true examples of participant observation. Fascinating as each study is in its own right, a reading of these contributions, in relation to Hodgson's discussion of the aims of first-hand research, also reveals the different directions in which such an approach can be taken. David Johnson, in Chapter 7, also sets out to understand differences in 'role expectations' but does this by means of systematic large-scale interviewing of Japanese prosecutors rather than through ethnographic research. Although he also did carry out some observation of trainees and makes good use of biographies of famous prosecutors which serve as inspirational materials, for him, legal culture is essentially a matter of how prosecutors and other legal actors think and act. Johnson's main aim is to demonstrate the false assumptions and errors in the scholarly literature about Japanese (and American) prosecutors. Rather than moving backwards and forwards between his own culture and that under observation Johnson tries to produce the same stimulus for all his interviewees in order to standardize his findings. Rather than becoming part of the research process himself, he follows the positivist protocols of trying to keep the researcher out of the picture. On the other hand, Crawford's method, in Chapter 8, is smaller in scale yet also more ambitious. Like Hodgson, he regards interviewing and immersion in another context as essential, but much of what interests him cannot 'be seen' on the spot. This leads him to seek the wider picture through a larger interpretation of legal culture in an attempt to grasp that which shapes (as well as is shaped by) the ideas and practices of legal actors – a process that he describes as the 'unravelling of cognitive structures'.

Johnson's survey of 235 Japanese prosecutors collected information about a range of background variables: age, gender, educational background (prosecutors have to pass a very demanding examination), reasons for choosing a career in the legal system and the job of prosecutor in particular (the desire to do justice, the appeal of investigation, the fit between job and personality and the influence of significant others) and so on. His main interest, however, was to understand why prosecutors in Japan so often go out of their way not to charge suspects. He warns against assumptions in the scholarly literature which perpetuate the idea that prosecutors must have universal aims such as the desire to maximize convictions. Such assumptions, he argues, are based on alleged prosecution practices in the USA which are even not true there. But he also questions the opposite assumption which claims that Japanese prosecutors set out to rehabilitate or reintegrate offenders in the community.

Of the possible objectives of prosecution which the respondents were asked to consider, 13 were taken seriously. The leading goals were discovering the truth and making the correct decision whether to charge with an offence. Anglo-American themes such as 'disposing efficiently of as many cases as possible' were low down on the list, and 'prosecuting and convicting as many cases as possible' was espoused by a mere 8 per cent. But there was also only limited confirmation of the characterization of the Japanese system, put forward by some scholars, as one dedicated to 'reintegrative stigmatization'. The objective of 'invoking public condemnation of the crime' was given high priority by less than a third of the sample. Many of those interviewed did not even understand the question: 'Why would we want that?', they asked. Japanese prosecutors had little interest in repairing relationships between offenders and victims, but they were diligent in searching for signs of remorse in the offender. Indeed, this professional goal plays a far more important role in the system than the token remorse of guilty pleas which triggers sentence reduction after plea bargains in the USA and the UK. Johnson concludes that it is the less adversary nature of the criminal process in Japan, together with other critical aspects of criminal justice there, such as light caseloads, political quiescence, and the absence of juries, which enable prosecutors to work for objectives other than the punitive ends of retribution and general deterrence.

Johnson relies mainly on the replies of his survey respondents in order to understand what guides them in making difficult decisions about whether to charge. However, he fills out their answers by referring to other influences which shape the prosecutors' culture – especially two important biographical stories which all prosecutors know. The first of these describes the risk of being taken in by offenders' wiles but produces the unexpected lesson that prosecutors mature by being deceived, and that what is truly unforgivable is an erroneous conviction not a mistaken acquittal. At the same time a second text emphasizes the importance of 'not letting the wicked sleep' and proclaims the special necessity of taking firm action against political corruption. On the other hand, in the USA, although there are also many pressures to drop cases, prosecutors do worry a great deal about the political backlash from mistaken acquittals. The principal reason for this is the high level of public concern about crime. In Japan crime is far less of a 'public problem' than in the USA (which may thus be both cause and consequence of prosecutors' behaviour). Johnson argues persuasively that Japanese prosecutors' prudence in charging is ultimately explicable in terms of a combination of cultural differences and a lack of structural pressure on them to produce a high level of convictions.

Johnson's focus is on what Lawrence Friedman defines as 'internal legal culture' (see, *inter alia*, Nelken, 1997b). Thus he describes prosecutors' legal culture as the 'ideas values, expectations and attitudes they have about criminal law, behaviour and justice'. But he also has important points to make about the relationship between this and wider aspects of Japanese culture. He attributes particular significance to the Japanese belief that human nature is perfectible, in contrast to the Christian doctrine of original sin. As a vivid example Johnson offers an account of a recidivist rapist who, court personnel insisted, could nonetheless be reformed if he only would take to the writing of poetic *Haiku*. There are also intriguing insights into the relationship between culture and crime control. Johnson quotes the view that defendants in the USA contribute to their own stigmatization by rejecting the authority of the courts thus excluding the possibility of benefiting from the demonstration of remorse in place of punishment. But, as he himself shows, the internal legal culture of the American courts leaves precious little room for offering and believing in remorse.

Both the strengths and limits of his chosen methodology emerge with great clarity from Johnson's chapter. On the one hand, many important descriptive findings could only be obtained with such a large sample, including the percentage of cases where prosecution was suspended (30–40 per cent) and the discovery that women prosecutors are predominately assigned to less sensitive trial duties. (Trial with its high rate of conviction is seen as mainly ceremonial in relation to the earlier discretionary decisions of the prosecutor.) Even his arguments about which objectives count as most important for Japanese prosecutors carry more weight because they are based on such a large sample.

Conversely, large-scale survey and interview methods are subject to well known criticisms, which are probably even more pertinent in carrying out research in an unfamiliar context. Are answers given in the interview setting a reliable guide to everyday behaviour? Is the context of saying that of doing? How far can we take what prosecutors say they do as a reliable guide to what they actually do? It is significant that the questions Johnson wanted to ask about whether prosecutors *actually* achieved their objectives were ruled off-limits, although the reason he was given – the fear that evidence of lenience might be used by the defence and might therefore become self-fulfilling – was in line with his overall argument about prosecutors' caution in bringing prosecutions. Johnson rightly argues that, whatever other information we rely on, we can hardly dispense with asking subjects what they are trying to achieve and what they think they are achieving. But is it even plausible to argue that prosecutors actually act with 13 goals in mind? And what about the possibility of cultural variation even in the degree to which subjects believe that their interview replies should mirror their actual behaviour? All this thus demonstrates that a single research method is capable of providing us with only part of the picture.

Crawford's chapter, like Hodgson's, is based on research in France. His interest lies in explaining the development of victim–offender mediation and reparation in that country as compared to England and Wales, and to account for the appeal of such criminal justice initiatives. At first sight, the developments in each jurisdiction seem quite similar, and they appear to be initiatives that are particularly easy to transfer and borrow – so much so that they are often used as examples of the 'convergence' of criminal justice systems. Crawford, however, sets out to demonstrate that not all is as it seems. Taking as his guiding idea the 'cultural embeddedness' of strategies of crime control he seeks to illustrate how 'strategies are shaped by, and reflect, their meaning, appeal and place within different judicial and wider social structures'.

Instead of examining how mediation and reparation schemes are implemented in practice in each country – for example, by studying the 'gap' between the aims and effects of particular schemes – Crawford chooses to stand back from the practical effects of this innovation in order to examine how criminal justice is connected to legal culture. He argues that, in these terms, mediation can be seen both as a critique of the existing criminal justice system (and its sedimented cultural and political presuppositions), as well as a call for more responsiveness to the 'community'. His chapter, which concentrates on the second of these themes (although the two are, of course, linked by the identification of the official system with the state), offers a sophisticated reading of the contrasting meanings of mediation in two different settings.

In the French context the move to introduce mediation can be seen as part of a project of 'bringing law to the people' both by making the criminal justice response more immediate and by subtly transforming its referent. However, it is not about involving the 'community' in the actual delivery of criminal justice, for this potential conception of the 'community' has a meaning and appeal which is strongly tied to the Anglo-American type of political and social order. Historically, the French state is the representation of the larger community and the fundamental task of social institutions is to lead those who are not yet part of the *polis* into becoming *bona fide* French citizens. Thus, such integration is seen not as a result of coercion but as the guarantor of mutuality. Conveniently, such an ambitious and endless project risks opening up a dissonance between the imaginary and the real. Relatively independent systems of regional and local government also counterbalance the role of the 'strong state'.

England and Wales has a less ambitious concept of the state and has also witnessed the steady weakening of local government powers. This means that the 'community' has a much greater opportunity for a political role. Here, community is the celebration of difference and diversity, and its celebration of voluntary action nourishes a barely concealed anti-statism. Introduced into the French context, however, the Anglo-American idea and practice of mediation becomes a further expression of the clash between local and global legal cultures and demonstrates how the legitimacy of the 'strong state' is being eroded from above and below.

Living There

The final two chapters in this volume illustrate the sort of comparative research which is the product of more long-term engagement with another culture. They are written by authors who can be seen as part of a new breed of expatriate academics, moving between countries by choice rather than as a result of forced emigration, and hence less inclined to erase the past even as they engage with their new cultures. Maureen Cain spent a total of eight years in the West Indies and still returns; so far I have been in Italy for ten years. Such scholars who live in, and may even intend to stay in, the country under investigation may be described as 'observing participants'[4] who attain the status of insider/outsiders. There may not always be much difference between first-hand ethnographic research projects carried out by visitors to another country and that carried out by academics actually living and working there – and, in fact, the duration of *specific* research projects may not even be longer. What is important is the extent – and benefits – of wider participation in the general life of the country, which can, as for these authors, include an active consulting/critical role in relation to the criminal justice system itself. Those such as Hodgson, who only visit other countries, are unlikely to be called 'family' and 'sister' by strangers in the road, as happened to Maureen Cain. Crawford, it is true, says that he has been asked to give the occasional seminar in France, yet, unlike Nelken, he does not teach there full-time. But even expatriates are not all alike, nor their situations equal. Maureen Cain was called upon to play a different role in the West Indies as compared to that open to David Nelken in Italy. There are also differences in what each author has chosen to discuss. Cain's reflections concentrate mainly on some of the issues raised by 'action research', whereas Nelken is more concerned with the relationship between describing another culture and the starting point of such a description.

Nelken's chapter, 'Telling Difference: Of Crime and Criminal Justice in Italy', begins with a central puzzle of comparative enquiry. What can we do about the degree to which our account of another society is shaped by, and responsive to, our previous cultural expectations? Does this mean that comparative descriptions tell us more about the observer's society of origin than about that being observed? In dealing with this problem he first discusses how far it is possible or even desirable to try to escape the influence of our own starting points and then goes on to discuss differences in crime, criminal justice and discourses about crime between Italy and England and Wales. Certainly, Nelken argues, his previous socialization in what Italians call Anglo-American culture explains much of what he finds most striking about Italy and it is important to appreciate this fully. Nevertheless, he claims, there is, in any case, no view from nowhere. His account of Italian criminal justice should therefore not be treated merely as an idiosyncratic view of Italy as seen by an Englishman, but as one part of a larger picture. Moreover, Anglo-American ideas and practices are in various ways currently becoming more influential in Italy, partly because of wider changes within the society itself. Nelken's role as an observing participant gives him a special vantage point for observing changes in criminal justice in Italy as a field of contest and interaction between the local and the global.

All comparison is about the search for commonalties and differences. But for an observer, especially a long-term observing participant, the study of similarity and difference comes to be pursued largely in terms of reflection on absence and presence. Using the examples of the state and the community, Nelken highlights some of the complexities in understanding the full significance of that which is absent, noting that each of these may be all-important as an ideal *precisely because it is absent*.[5] He also asks what makes a presence or absence 'significant' both in the society under observation and in that of origin. In his conclusion he raises the problem of how far a set of observations of difference can plausibly be used to construct an explanation of what makes a culture distinctive.

The main part of Nelken's chapter offers a description of some of the main features of criminal justice in Italy. He discusses difficulties in the interpretation of crime rates and victim survey data, describes the cultural specificity of current changes there in the organization of the criminal process and points to important emerging trends in discourses about crime and criminal justice. Nelken suggests that there are numerous 'telling' differences between criminal justice in Italy and the UK, some of which reflect aspects of social structure and culture specific to Italy, whilst others can be attributed to wider contrasts between common law and civil law countries. Illustrative examples in the realm of crime and its control have to do with crimes such as juvenile delinquency, political corruption, organized crime and with what is described in Italy as 'micro-criminality'. As far as the broader aims of the criminal process are concerned, the importance publicly attributed on all sides to so-called *garantismo* (due process protections) in Italy seems disproportionately higher than political support for 'crime control'. Populist exploitation of the politics of 'law and order' is, as yet, much less evident than in England or in other common law countries – but it may be about to arrive in a big way.

Chapter 10 by Maureen Cain completes this collection of comparative studies of criminal justice. As would be expected of an 'observing participant', Cain draws directly on her own experience of teaching and action rather than limiting herself to retailing what professionals or experts have to tell us about criminal justice in the countries under observation. In her university work (in which she was expected to reveal the truths of Western criminology) she increasingly felt uneasy about

... teaching about youth cultures in a society which is not rigidly age stratified; of teaching community policing and democratic accountability while lacking a language to describe a post-colonial service lacking a sense of direction, having lost its *raison d'être*, of talking ethnic minorities where historically – and, arguably, today as well – it is the culture and identity of the black former *majority* which is under threat. The examples are as numerous as the topics in a year-long course.

In the first part of her chapter Cain therefore tackles what she sees as the arrogance and theoretical imperialism of much Western criminology. She uses the example of the alleged relationship between age rates and crime to illustrate the lack of sensitivity of criminology to cultural variability. The claim that the peak age of crime lies in the 15 to 25 age group, after which offenders grow out of such behaviour, is clearly misleading in the context of the West Indies where 70 per cent of offenders are over 25 and there are often 'cradle to grave' alternative lifestyles. In the absence of either unemployment or social security benefit there is considerable routine stealing to meet 'grown-up' needs, and petty larceny is typically carried out with an eye to resale. One important sector of crime, drug dealing and related activities, depends organizationally on the continued participation of mature people. Other central types of crime such as state complicity in street crime, the dependence of legitimate lifestyles on the liquidity provided by illegitimate ones, and familial violence equally presuppose the relative maturity of offenders. Cain notes that her students seemed to give more credence to what was in their textbooks rather than what was true of their reality, but policy-makers, too, had given little thought to the implications of having to deal with a relatively mature offending population.

In the second part of her chapter Cain focuses on the special challenges of rethinking the role of post-colonial police forces in the West Indies. The colonial force, she says, was established to serve the needs of the metropolis and the planter class, to ensure a steady supply of disciplined labour and to face down challenges to their culture and trade. Now, after independence, the islands increasingly struggle with the effects of tourism and drug trafficking, both of which increase street crime and stranger violence, and 'bring in money at a lifestyle price'. The new resource-starved police forces tend to combine passivity with sporadic raids against drugs dealing and other crimes. For each newly identified problem a specialized police unit is created, and each island has a slightly different way of organizing policing in accordance with sometimes considerable historical and political differences. One of the few really positive developments had to do with the role of municipal police forces. As a leading Western criminologist, actually living and working in the islands, Cain found herself taking an important part in the debate over the future of policing and, in particular, the appropriateness of 'community policing'. She argued for more central coordination, more professionalism and better resources, before moving to encourage debate over what the community wants from the police. Other scholars claimed that, at least in some of the islands, ensuring better responsiveness to the community must come before increasing professionalism. (As with my experience in Italy I suspect that Cain may sometimes, quite logically, find herself arguing one line 'at home' and another abroad.)

Cain recommends looking for 'best practice' on the ground rather than resorting to foreign models. She examines the potential for self-policing in residential neighbourhoods and the range of self-help strategies adopted by small businesses, and many of her findings are optimistic. 'Neighbourhood watch' schemes in Trinidad do much to improve community spirit and even control crime, despite the fact that crime comes low on the list of their priorities. People facing the risk of crime invent ingenious strategies for sharing the costs of protecting their businesses. Hotel owners show imagination in working out fruitful collaboration between themselves and beach vendors.

Cain concludes strongly that 'each society is responsible for the crime patterns which it creates through its modes of social organization'. For her:

> As the nations of the West Indies are responsible for a society which creates angry adult males without means or life chances, so also, in the same way, is the UK responsible for the pressures and opportunities it creates for its criminal male children and youths.

We could add that what the comparative study of criminal justice demonstrates is that such links between crime patterns and social structure are also, in many ways, a product of the dialectic between rule-breaking and the way it is handled. But is Cain right that it is a given 'national society' which is responsible for its crime patterns? She herself indicates the all-important features of the wider context represented by political inheritance and economic interdependence. Crime patterns in the West Indies, as in other places, are increasingly affected by globalization (see Nelken, 1997c and Findlay, 1999 with special reference to 'developing economies'). Ideas about 'criminal justice', especially currently influential Anglo-American models,[6] are borrowed with little attention being paid to their cultural origins or social preconditions, and (sometimes) change the contexts in which they are introduced. Even the 'best practices' which she says should be the starting point of indigenous reform, such as Neighbourhood Watch committees, are often more than not foreign imports, even if then reworked for local needs. Whether or not the researcher seeks to make it so or tries to resist it, the effects of globalization means that 'here' and 'there' are increasingly interrelated.

Notes

1 Although the chapter by Feest and Murayama is categorized here as an example of collaboration between experts their 'virtual experiment' is rooted in the 'real' story of an American student trying to extract himself from the accusation of having been involved in a squatters' demonstration in Spain. The story carries more conviction because it is reported by Johannes Feest who was living and working in Spain as Director of the Oñati Institute of Sociology of Law.
2 This use of the term is to be distinguished from the sense it has acquired as a result of the communications revolution, which could also have interesting implications for comparative research. The user of the Internet also encounters members of other cultures without actually having to 'go there', but the meeting involves contact without the mediation of experts and takes place in a 'virtual space' with its own emerging rules and culture.
3 More might also have been said about the possibilities of resistance in different prisons and how this is affected by different legal cultures (see Bosworth, 1999).
4 There is, of course, more than one route to becoming an 'observing participant'. Young (1991) uses the term to describe his research in the Northern English police force once he returned there after taking an anthropology degree.
5 Brants and Field also note how something becomes an issue for debate when you do not have it (or think you do not have it).
6 Van Swaaningen (1999) points out that such processes of borrowing are cyclical. If criminology is now being exported to Europe from English-speaking countries, the two main schools of criminology were originally imported to English-speaking countries from Europe (and from Italy in particular).

References

Balvig, F. (1987), *The Snow White Image: The Hidden Reality of Crime in Switzerland*, Scandinavian Studies in Criminology, Oslo: Norwegian University Press.
Bosworth, M. (1999), *Engendering Resistance*, Aldershot: Dartmouth.
Clinard, M.B. (1978), *Cities With Little Crime*, Cambridge: Cambridge University Press.
Downes, D. (1988), *Contrasts in Tolerance*, Oxford: Clarendon Press.
Eve, M. (1993), 'Paradigmi Nazionali: Percezioni del "Particularismo", in Italia e in Inghilterra', *Rassegna Italiana di Sociologia*, xxxiv, 3.
Eve, M. (1996), 'Comparing Italy: The Case of Corruption', in D. Forgacs and R. Lumley (eds), *Italian Cultural Studies*, Oxford: Oxford University Press, 34–51.
Findlay, M. (1999), *The Globalization of Crime*, Cambridge: Cambridge University Press.
Franke, H. (1990), 'Dutch Tolerance: Facts and Fallacies', *British Journal of Criminology*, 30 (1), 81–93.
Friedman, L. (1987), *Total Justice*, Boston, MA: Beacon Press.
Friedman, L. (1994), 'Is there a Modern Legal Culture?', *Ratio Juris*, 7, 117–31.
Geertz, C. (1988), *Works and Lives*, Cambridge: Polity Press.

Horowitz, R. (1986), 'Remaining an Outsider: Membership as a Threat to Research Rapport', *Urban Life*, **14** (4), 409–30.
King, M. (1989), 'Social Crime Prevention à la Thatcher', in D. Nelken (ed.), *Criminal Justice on the Margin*, special issue of *Howard Journal of Criminal Justice*, 291–312.
McBarnet, D.J. (1981), *Conviction: Law, the State and the Construction of Justice*, London: Macmillan.
Nelken, D. (1981), 'The "Gap Problem" in the Sociology of Law: A Theoretical Review', in *Windsor Yearbook of Access to Justice, 1981*, Ontario: Windsor, 35–62.
Nelken, D. (1997a), 'Understanding Criminal Justice Comparatively,' in M. Maguire, R. Morgan and R. Reiner (eds), *The Oxford Handbook of Criminology*, (2nd edn) Oxford: Oxford University Press, 559–76.
Nelken, D. (ed.) (1997b), *Comparing Legal Cultures*, Aldershot: Dartmouth.
Nelken, D. (1997c), 'The Globalization of Criminal Justice: Prospects and Problems', in M. Freeman (ed.), *Law and Opinion at the Turn of the Century*, Oxford: Oxford University Press, 251–79.
Van Swaaningen, R. (1999), 'Reclaiming Critical Criminology: Social Justice and the European Tradition', *Theoretical Criminology*, **3** (1), 5–29.
Young, M. (1991), *An Inside Job*, Oxford: Oxford University Press.

PART II
VIRTUALLY THERE

PART II
VIRTUALLY THERE

3 Protecting the Innocent Through Criminal Justice: A Case Study from Spain, Virtually Compared to Germany and Japan

Johannes Feest and Masayuki Murayama

Introduction

The Code of Criminal Procedure of the now defunct German Democratic Republic stated as its goal 'to secure that every culpable person and no innocent one is brought to penal account'. Most criminal justice systems avoid stating openly such a clearly impossible double goal. Nonetheless one can try to distinguish criminal justice systems in terms of how they handle this built-in conflict. The starting point of the following 'virtual comparison' is the case of a person whom we believe to be innocent even though he was convicted and sentenced to two years' imprisonment in Catalunia, Spain. Starting from this specific, real case we will try to compare what would most likely have happened in Germany and in Japan. Our primary goal is to test the viability of 'virtual comparison', but we also hope to gain some new insights into the three criminal justice cultures involved.[1]

Virtual Comparison

There are several standard ways to compare criminal justice cultures (Miyazawa, 1992; Nelken, 1997). Legal comparativists will usually start from the law in the books, whereas sociologists will start from statistical data or from ethnographic description about what purports to be the law in action. Both Miyazawa and Nelken suggest that these approaches are not mutually exclusive and should be used to supplement each other.

We suggest that one could also start from a specific, more or less well documented case and its handling by a particular criminal justice system. This case could then be evaluated by experts of other penal systems as to its probable fate in those other systems, taking into account both law and legal culture (in the broadest sense). Starting from a specific, real case has the advantage that it provides us with rich details and forces us to decide whether those details can be imagined in the context more familiar to us.

Such an approach has obvious limitations that derive primarily from the fact that we are looking at only one case; in order to produce more generalizable results, it would have to be supplemented by other similar studies. Another major limitation concerns the trustworthiness of the authors' transposition of the case into their respective legal cultures; in order to test the reliability of their accounts one would have to check it with other people familiar with criminal justice reality there.

The following two attempts at such a 'virtual comparison' take as a starting point a case that originated in 1996 in Barcelona, Catalunia, and will therefore be referred to as the 'Catalan case'.[2] First, we present the actual Catalan case and then the same case as it might have developed in Germany and Japan. Following this, we try to identify differences and speculate about possible reasons for them.

The Catalan Case

Arrest

On the evening of 28 October 1996 the protagonist of our story, a young American scholar, was arrested as he emerged from a subway station near his home. It turned out that, earlier in the day, the police had removed squatters from an abandoned cinema in which they had lived for a number of months. This eviction had provoked a demonstration by sympathizers, culminating in what the police saw as an 'assault' on the local police station. The riot police had already broken up the demonstration and were pursuing smaller groups into side streets and also into the subway station. The protagonist, who speaks Spanish very well, tried to argue with a police officer who was barring him from crossing the street, but found himself pushed to the ground, clubbed by two police officers and arrested at 22.30.

At the police station, at 23.30, he was informed that he was accused of the offence of *desorden público* (public disorder).[3] This accusation was based on the word of one police officer (who was only referred to as '*No. 66.412 Cuerpo Nacional de la Policía*') who had identified him as the person he had seen half an hour before the arrest (that is at 22.00) 'throw stones at the police and who had later addressed verbal abuse against the police'.

The arrested young man was informed of his right to remain silent, to designate a lawyer to be present during his testimony (otherwise an *ex officio* lawyer would be assigned) and to designate a person to be informed about his detention. A form signed by the defendant shows that he asked for his room-mate to be informed and agreed to be assisted by the *ex officio* defence lawyer. He was then stripsearched and put into a dark cell.

Fifteen to sixteen hours after the arrest, on 29 October, he was allowed to meet an *ex officio* lawyer. The first thing this lawyer said was that he trusted that the protagonist would see a judge and be out of jail within hours. Based on this assumption, the lawyer decided against filing a petition of *habeas corpus*. The protagonist told the police that he preferred to give his testimony in front of a judge. As a result, he was asked only technical questions regarding his address, age, nationality, employment status, monthly salary and so on. Twenty minutes or half an hour later, the protagonist was back in his cell.

On 30 October, he was presented before a *juez de instrucción* (investigating magistrate) and, in the presence of his lawyer, informed of the charges, which now turned out to be *desorden público* (public disorder) and *manifestación ilícita* (illegal demonstration).[4] He was also informed that the police had supposedly found in the pockets of his parka two iron ball bearings, but denied all allegations. During the evening of 30 October he was released on his own recognizance, 48½ hours after his arrest. By this time, at least one local university professor had informally intervened in his favour. On the same day, the *juez de instrucción* decided to make this a *procedimiento abreviado* (abbreviated, speedy proceedings) and to transfer the matter to the *ministerio fiscal* (prosecutor).

Prosecution

A few days later[5] the prosecution (*fiscal*) accused the defendant, together with other young people arrested at the same time, of joining a demonstration, the participants of which shouted 'slogans of increasingly violent character' and threw objects of all sorts, mainly stones, against the main door of the police station, causing damage to cars and facilities. He was specifically accused of participating in the demonstration 'in a particularly vandalistic fashion' by throwing 'objects at the police force assembled there'. The prosecution asked for the trial of all the arrested people together to start immediately.

Trial

Originally, the joint trial was to take place on 15 November 1996,[6] but it had to be postponed for technical reasons until 18 December. A single judge conducted the trial. The defendant was represented by his *ex-officio* lawyer. The judge refused to hear all character witnesses suggested by the defence (for example the local university professor). Although he did hear the testimony of a photo journalist, the judge refused to admit as evidence the videotape of the arrest he had filmed. At the end, the only evidence against the defendant was the testimony of the arresting policeman, who claimed to have recognized the accused throwing stones at the police and later finding the iron ball bearings in the pockets of his parka. At the time indicated by the arresting officer the accused was, however, still teaching at a language school at a different part of the city, according to evidence offered to the court. The defendant also denied ever having had iron ball bearings in his possession, nor were these produced as evidence at the trial.

On 23 December 1996, the judge convicted the accused of an offence of *desórdenes públicos* (public disorders) as well as an offence of *manifestación ilícita* (illegal demonstration). In the written reasons from the same date, the judge argues that the accused was, if only by a single police officer, identified unambiguously on the basis of his clothes, 'after having received a push, which the accused directed at him without the intention of attacking the police force, but with the intention to disturb the public peace'. The judge added: 'Therefore the allegations to the contrary made by the accused with respect to the time do not prove at all the impossibility that he could have taken part (*la imposibilidad de que tuviera participación*).' At an earlier point in the decision, the judge asserted that the totality of the incriminated acts had happened over a sufficiently long timespan to 'make unnecessary the mathematical determination of the exact hour as the only temporal proof of the event (*eludir la determinación matemática de una hora concreta y determinada como único asentamiénto temporal del suceso*)'.

The accused, who had no previous criminal record, was sentenced to a total of two years in prison (one for each offence) and an eight-month fine at a rate of 1000 pesetas per day – that is, a total of 240 000 pesetas or US$1600. Spanish law gives the judge discretion to suspend prison sentences of up to two years, but this is done only after the conviction has come into force of law – that is, after the appeal has been denied. In practice, to suspend such sentences is the rule.

Appeal

The protagonist defence lawyer received the written decision of the trial court on 15 January and lodged an appeal on 27 January. In this appeal a number of reasons are listed as proof that the protagonist could not have been committing an offence at the specified time at the place of the action:

- He had been teaching until 22.00.
- His subway ticket was marked 22.11.
- By the time of his arrival at his home subway station, the demonstration had already been broken up.
- He was not part of the squatter movement.

Meanwhile, the protagonist had been awarded a scholarship for a postgraduate programme in the USA. He was able to leave Spain without any problems.

Fourteen months later, on 20 May 1998, the *Audiencia de Barcelona* (Appeal Court) reversed the lower court's verdict and acquitted the protagonist. The Appeal Court found that, legally, no *manifestación ilícita* (illegal demonstration) was possible after the police had broken up the demonstration, and all the defendants were therefore acquitted of this offence. As to the offence of *desórdenes públicos* (public disorders) the court found no sufficient evidence that the accused had participated actively in the disturbances. The decision came as a surprise to knowledgeable local observers, who had predicted that the appeal would not be successful. The reason given for this prediction was that an acquittal would imply possible offences on the part of the testifying police officer.

The Protagonist as a Foreigner

Did it make a difference that the protagonist was a foreigner? Throughout the proceedings, we wondered whether it made a difference that the protagonist was a foreigner in Spain. Even though his birth in Oxford (England) was explicitly noted by the police, the prosecution and the court, and the fact that he was called '*un ocupa americano*' (an American squatter) in the newspapers, there are no indications that he was treated any differently from the other accused people. Moreover, the fact that he was not the only one acquitted on appeal seems to confirm this. Doubts remain, however. After his release from police custody, he talked to representatives of the American consulate who were supportive but felt it unwise to intervene in an ongoing judicial proceeding. Whether they intervened informally at a later stage is unknown.

The Virtual German Case

Events of the Catalan type have in fact happened in Germany. With many houses standing empty in the inner cities, squatting is a common occurrence. Since this behaviour is punishable as *Hausfriedensbruch* (illegal entry), it has traditionally been understood that the police have to intervene and remove the perpetrators. Since the early 1980s, the police have, however, increasingly refused to be used as instruments of force by slum landlords and real estate speculators. A new style of police work has developed, which consists in negotiating with squatters as well as landlords about possibilities of a peaceful solution, always, of course, in the shadow of the law – that is, the forcible removal of squatters by the police. As a result squatters are now rarely forcibly removed and squatting is now seldom seen as a problem. Political demonstrations and clashes with the police occur, however, with a certain regularity in other contexts such as nuclear energy, ecology and demonstrations by right-wing groups.

German demonstration legislation has a recent history of both liberalizations and restrengthening.[7] Today, the mere participation in an unannounced or even forbidden demonstration is no longer a punishable offence.[8] If the police found the protagonist in possession of objects that are objectively 'suitable and meant'[9] to injure persons or damage objects, they could charge him with a violation of the public assembly law.[10] Since, in this case, the police would see the protagonist as an active participant in a situation of collective violence, they could charge him with *Landfriedensbruch* (breach of the peace).[11] Carrying 'any weapon in order to use it in the act' would make it an aggravated case[12] and since the iron ball bearings could theoretically qualify as such weapons, the police would be likely to use this to strengthen their case for an arrest. In addition, in a physical clash between a demonstrator and a police officer, the offence of 'resisting officers in the pursuit of their duty with violence or threats of violence'[13] will be routinely used.

Arrest/Pre-trial Detention

In the virtual German case the arrest would have happened in much the same way, if the officer thought he recognized the person as someone whom he had seen throwing stones at the police earlier – even more so if incriminating evidence was found in his pockets. The police would be likely to charge the highest possible offences, in order to make the arrest stick (and possibly lay the ground for pre-trial detention).

The protagonist would have a right to make a telephone call, which, in practice, would only take place if he knew someone to call at such a late hour. He would not immediately be informed about the charges and his rights, since the German law (§ 163a, StPO) reserves this right for the first formal hearing, which may be postponed for hours, while officers can still have informal chats with the detained person.

In police custody, it is unlikely that the protagonist would have been provided with an *ex-officio* lawyer. This is obligatory only in connection with a felony or where the pre-trial detention period exceeds three months (§ 140, para. 1, StPO). If he can produce a lawyer of his own, this lawyer has no right to be present during any interrogation by either the police or the prosecution.[14] A hearing before an investigating judge, where the lawyer's presence was guaranteed (should the protagonist have one), was abolished in Germany in the 1960s.

By law, the police would have had to release the protagonist at the end of the day following the day of the arrest and there are no known violations of this norm in practice. This means that the protagonist would have been released before midnight of 29 October (that is, about 22 hours earlier than in Catalunia).

The police could have asked the prosecutor for a judicial remand decision putting the protagonist into pre-trial detention. In a case like this (alleged violence against the police, foreign defendant, denying the charges) such a course of action is not completely out of the question, but it is also not very likely, given the fact that this was a first-time offender who had a regular income, regular accommodation and even some support among local university people. The fact that he denied the charges would not work against him, since the police had had an opportunity to check his alibi and there was not much chance of him tampering with the evidence. Also, because a detention hearing would be a possibility, the protagonist's lawyer (if he had one) would have a right to be present and to assist his client.

Prosecution

The police would send a case file to the prosecutor. Even though the German prosecution has a mandate to also collect exonerating evidence and may conduct their own supplementary investigation,[15] this is rarely done. The legality principle requires them, as a rule, to bring the case to court. The ever more important exceptions to this rule – allowing the prosecution to fine the offender and dismiss the case – would not work here, since they depend on the consent of the defendant.

Most probably, the German prosecutors would not collect any additional information, but would bring the case to court on the basis of information contained in the police file. The charges against the protagonist could not involve 'unlawful demonstration', since this does not exist in Germany as a criminal offence. At best this could amount to an administrative violation, carrying a fine.[16] The indictment would most likely be based on *Landfriedensbruch* (breach of the peace). For this it would have to be proved that the accused personally engaged in acts of aggression against persons or objects 'perpetrated in a crowd with unified strength and in a manner endangering public security'.[17] Charges would most likely also include resisting a police officer. Any of the other possibilities (the aggravated forms of the offences) seem unlikely, since they require more evidence, especially with respect to the subjective side (*mens rea*) of the offence.

The prosecutor might want to have a case like this handled in expedited proceedings. In the past this would have been unlikely (only 4 per cent of all cases were handled in this way), but the legislator has recently tried to upgrade this type of proceedings. In our case, the use of expedited proceedings seems unlikely, since they are designed for cases in which the facts are simple or the evidence clear. Also, the highest punishment foreseen in this kind of trial is one year's imprisonment, and the prosecution is likely to press for more serious charges, at least for some of the defendants.[18]

The defence attorney is, in principle, entitled to review the prosecutor's case file.[19] He would find there the arresting officer with his full name and title (and not as a mere number). He would also be able to find out, before the trial, whether the prosecution had done its job, which is to investigate both 'incriminating but also exonerating circumstances'[20] (for example, whether the defendant's alibi had been checked). This would enable the defence to prepare for the trial, and ask alibi, as well as character, witnesses to attend.

Trial

Since the protagonist is at large, the case would be unlikely to come for trial within a month or two. More probably, it would take six months or more. In Germany, the case would go to a single professional judge (art. 24, GVG), possibly assisted by two lay assessors (art. 25, GVG). First, the professional judge alone would decide whether 'the results of the preparatory proceedings indicate that the accused is sufficiently suspected of a criminal act'.[21] Since this decision is made on the basis of the prosecutor's file, it would probably be affirmative in this case.

The protagonist would not necessarily have the assistance of an ex-*officio* defence counsel. This is not one of the cases for which German law explicitly foresees *Pflichtverteidigung* (mandatory defence, § 140, para. 1, StPO). But it is likely that the protagonist's lawyer would have appeared and made a case for the 'necessity' of learned defence on the grounds of the difficulty of the factual and legal issues (§ 140, para. 2, StPO) and that the court would have agreed, if only to avoid an easy appeal.

In a regular trial, all the evidence for the offence would have to be produced orally in court (principles of immediacy and orality). The judge would be in charge of deciding which witnesses need to be heard;[22] but German law makes it rather difficult for the judge to refuse to hear a witness whom the defence lawyer has brought in person to the trial. All of this would, of course, be different in expedited proceedings, where the judge would be able to make short shrift. But, as we have seen, expedited proceedings would be quite unlikely.

The court in Germany is supposed to decide 'according to its own conviction based upon the evidence of the trial'.[23] Given the fact that the protagonist is not a 'typical' squatter, that there was no second police witness and that the police did not produce the ball bearings allegedly found on the protagonist, there is more than an outside chance that the a German court might have acquitted him.[24] But, as a rule, police witnesses are seen as more reliable than defendants. If the court believed the police officers, it would convict for both breach of the peace and resisting an officer. Nevertheless, an unconditional prison sentence of two years would be more than surprising.

Legally, as we have seen, a sentence of up to three years' imprisonment would be possible for the offence of *Landfriedensbruch* (§ 125, StGB), the equivalent of *desordenes públicos* (breach of the peace).[25] However, there are a number of reasons why this sentencing frame would be used only in its lower reaches:

- Empirical research shows that judicial sentences tend to be somewhat below those asked by the prosecutors.[26]
- Judicial statistics show that sentences in Germany usually remain within the lower third of the sentencing frame; in the present case, the sentence would certainly not be longer than one year.[27]
- Remaining doubts as to the facts will often lead to an informal 'discount' with respect to the punishment.
- A first offender will rarely receive a prison sentence, if there are (as in the case of § 125, StGB) no mandatory minimum sentences.
- The same is true for a person with a good social prognosis.
- Even if the court decides to impose a prison sentence, such a sentence would immediately be suspended (first offender, good prognosis);[28] since there was no pre-trial detention, this outcome is even more likely.
- As already mentioned, a two-year prison sentence is explicitly ruled out in expedited proceedings (*beschleunigtes Verfahren*).

The most probable outcome of the German case would therefore be a sentence of up to one year of imprisonment (probably less); such a sentence would immediately be suspened, since the court would hardly be able to find a basis for saying that this student would be likely to reoffend. There can be no fine besides the prison sentence, since German law allows this only 'if the perpetrator gained a profit or acted to gain a profit by the act'.[29]

Appeal

Under German law both the protagonist and the prosecutor have a right to appeal the conviction as well as the sentence. The protagonist or his lawyer would surely have appealed the conviction on the merits (*Berufung*). In this case it is not even necessary (but possible) to give reasons. The appeal is decided by the *Landgericht* which, in all bigger cities, will be nearby – maybe even in the same building. There the case would get a complete new hearing, with witnesses and all, before a panel consisting of a professional judge and two lay assessors. The psychology of the situation would be very similar to the first trial, except that the higher court tends to feel some loyalty towards the lower court and, therefore the likelihood of a reversal is small. But the case could be further appealed on points of law to the *Oberlandesgericht* at which only the legal aspects of the case would be reviewed. If, in trial court, the defence had unsuccessfully asked for the ball bearings to be produced, this could certainly be a very good ground for a reversal of the lower court's decision. If the conviction is reversed, the case would be sent back to a different *Landgericht* for a new trial. This is likely to lead to an acquittal; but there is always the possibility that the lower court would convict again on a different charge (for example, resisting an officer).

Outcome

In Germany the most likely scenario would have been as follows: arrest by police on charges carrying high punishment; 25.5 hours of police detention; no pre-trial detention; no expedited proceedings; reduced charges in the prosecution's indictment; trial by a single judge of the lower criminal court; conviction and short prison sentence; sentence suspended with a probation period of three to five years; unsuccessful first appeal (on the merits); successful appeal on points of law.

Would it have made a difference that the protagonist was not a German citizen? On the one hand, it is unlikely that the German police would have treated him differently from the other arrested persons. At any rate, they would not have treated him worse, since he does not fit the present image of the unwanted foreigner (a person who looks different, does not speak the language of the land, is probably an asylum seeker and so on). On the other hand, even this 'privileged' foreigner may have had to fight expulsion from

Germany, since the new (1991) German Alien Law foresees the expulsion of non-citizens, who 'have participated in violent acts in the pursuit of political goals'.[30]

The Virtual Japanese Case

Events of the Catalan type – the eviction of squatters followed by a massive demonstration of sympathizers – are practically inconceivable in Japan. An eviction of illegal occupants could happen but it would be a scattered individual phenomenon, which would not take on such social or political significance.

It is, however, conceivable that demonstrators with some social or political cause would clash with the police and that participants of the demonstration could be arrested for one or more offences against Road Traffic Law[31] and the Penal Code.[32] If the police believed that the protagonist threw stones or something hard, he would be considered to have violated the Road Traffic Law. It is also possible that the behaviour could be perceived as an obstruction to the execution of the police's public duties, although it is debatable whether the behaviour would really be in violation of the Penal Code if the physical or verbal aggression was not directly directed at police officers. The demonstration would be unlikely to be considered as a collectively violent public disturbance unless the demonstration was massive as well as violent. Therefore, in what follows, it is assumed that, in Japan, there would be two possible charges against the protagonist – if any.

Arrest/Pre-trial Detention

In Japan it would not be surprising for the protagonist to be advised about his rights only an hour or so after he was arrested, at the police gaol.[33] He would have the right to remain silent but may not refuse to be interrogated by the police.[34] If he knew something about free legal advice for suspects, he might be able to call a lawyer,[35] but this lawyer would meet him only once free of charge and would not be present during police interrogations. The interrogations would not be tape-recorded but would be written down in a way the police considered to be appropriate. The protagonist would not have the right to designate a person to be informed about his arrest. Before being put in his cell, he would be stripsearched. He would then be detained for 72 hours in the police gaol,[36] especially since he denied the charges.[37] He would have no legal means to challenge the legality of the arrest during this period.

Before the arrest period of 72 hours had expired, the prosecutor would most probably apply to the court for pre-trial detention.[38] In this case there would be a detention hearing. Criteria for detention are reasonable suspicion of an offence and at least one of the following circumstances:

- no place to stay
- a possibility of tampering with evidence
- a possibility of escape.[39]

Our protagonist has a place to stay, but since he denies the charges, the judge would probably decide to detain him for ten days. At the prosecution's request the judge may (and, in many cases, will) renew the detention for ten days.[40] It is most likely that the protagonist of our case would be detained for a total of 23 days.[41] The prosecutor must either indict or release the suspect before the detention period expires.

At the detention hearing our protagonist would have his first serious opportunity to get information about the free legal advice scheme. If he has not asked for a duty lawyer to meet him during the police arrest, he could ask for a meeting with a duty lawyer now.[42] At the end of this meeting he would have to decide whether or not to retain this lawyer. If the accused is indigent, he could apply for pre-trial legal aid but, in practice, the duty lawyer would make this decision while considering the substance of the case, as well as the suspect's financial circumstances.[43] Since our protagonist is still a student without a stable income and also because he denies the charges, which makes the case more difficult because of the possibility of wrongful conviction, he would be likely to get legal aid.

The suspect's rights are not very extensive in Japan. Even if the suspect retains counsel, the lawyer does not have the right to attend the detention hearing. Furthermore, the lawyer in Japan does not have access to the investigation documents, even after the investigation is completed. The prosecutor can restrict the communication between the suspect and his lawyer by specifying the date, time and duration of their meeting. In our case this might happen because the protagonist denies the charges.[44]

Prosecution

Prosecution in Japan operates on the opportunity principle and exercises a wide range of discretion.[45] In our case, the defence lawyer will try to take advantage of that by making the prosecutor either dismiss the case or opt for the summary procedure. Summary procedure is more desirable for the defence than regular trial, since the judge can impose only a fine. But summary procedure requires the consent of the accused and this is unlikely in our case because he wants an acquittal and not a fine. But if the defence lawyer could obtain some exonerating evidence, such as an alibi, it is unlikely that the prosecutor would indict him for trial. This would also be the most likely scenario if the accused has been willing to talk to the police and/or the prosecutor about his side of the story. Furthermore, he is a student and has no criminal record, nor is he a socially marginal person. In such a case, the prosecutors might conclude that the pre-trial detention has been enough to 'punish' him, even if they still suspect that the accused might have performed the alleged behaviour. Moreover, the Japanese prosecutor does not like to risk non-conviction, so exonerating evidence could be decisive.

With a good defence lawyer, it is therefore most likely that the case would result in the suspension of prosecution. There is, however, the possibility that the police would feel that they cannot tolerate the alleged behaviour, either because the authority of the police is at stake or because the political implication of the case is significant. In this event the police might insist that the accused be punished heavily. In our case, the fact that the accused has denied the charge could result in such an attitude on the part of the police. Then the accused would be indicted, unless the prosecutor considered the evidence to be too weak to prosecute.[46]

There is no legal requirement for the time limit of indictment, except that, for obstruction cases, the statute of limitations runs out in three years. However, in our virtual case, the prosecutor would decide whether or not to indict before the detention period expired.[47]

Trial

When the court receives the indictment, it would send it to the accused without delay. At the same time, the court would ask whether the defendant had already retained a lawyer for his defence and, if he had not, whether he wanted to have one. Upon his request, the court would appoint a defence lawyer if he had not already retained one.[48]

Naturally the accused would like to get out of gaol as soon as possible. However, bail can be granted by the court only after indictment. The defence lawyer, particularly when retained, would apply for bail but might be reluctant to do so for the following reasons:

- The amount of bail might be too high for the defendant to pay.[49]
- Since the defendant denies the charge, the court would probably refuse bail.[50]
- The defence might be able to increase the possibility of lighter sentence – and, hopefully, the suspension of his sentence – by his detention throughout the trial period.

Our protagonist's lawyer would probably not apply for bail for the first two reasons. Since the post-indictment detention lasts for two months, our protagonist might be detained throughout the trial. If the trial takes more than one or two sessions,[51] he might be released upon the expiration of the two months during the trial.[52]

The case would be tried by a single judge.[53] The first date of trial would be set about one month after the court received the indictment.[54] If both parties agreed, the case could be tried in a simplified way, which mainly means that the hearsay rule is bypassed. However, since our protagonist denies the charge, the simplified trial procedure would not be taken. During the trial the judge would decide which witnesses should be heard. Since the defendant denies the charges, it is improbable that the judge would refuse to hear witnesses for the defence. The judge would also be free to evaluate the evidence. Because our protagonist denied the charge throughout the pre-trial and trial stages, and also because the prosecution failed to submit the ball bearings in trial, the judge might find him not guilty.[55] However, as far as we can speculate, based on the statistics, the chances for our protagonist are rather bleak, since once the accused has been prosecuted it is extremely difficult to obtain an acquittal.[56] Even when the charge is disputed, the trial result would be similar.[57] If the case comes to trial at all, conviction would be the likely outcome.

Once convicted, the judge will sentence the protagonist to imprisonment. The obstruction of the execution of public duties carries a penalty of up to three years' imprisonment. In our case the outcome would probably be a prison sentence of approximately one year.[58] But it is also highly probable that this sentence would be suspended, because:

1   most sentences for this offence are suspended;[59]
2   our protagonist has no prior record and his offence is not the most serious of its kind; and
3   the defendant is not socially marginal.

If the court found the defendant guilty of throwing metal ball bearings as well as obstructing police duties, the defendant would be sentenced not only to suspended imprisonment but also to a fine of up to 50 000 yen (US$ 357), possibly around 30 000 yen (US$ 212). Although legally possible, the fine would not be suspended.[60]

Appeal

Our protagonist would appeal against the conviction to the Court of Appeal. The appeal must be made within two weeks after the conviction. The Court of Appeal consists of three professional judges. The court would review the original judgment in accordance with the arguments submitted by the defence. If the defence argued that the conviction was based on wrong fact-finding, the court might open a new trial and examine certain facts. Because the police failed to produce the ball bearings during the trial, the Court of Appeal might possibly reverse the conviction. However, statistics indicate that this is unlikely. Nor would the reversal of the conviction be probable if the defence argued that the conviction was based on illegal procedure.[61]

Our protagonist could further appeal by taking his case to the Supreme Court, arguing that there was an unconstitutional or other grave illegal procedure in the conviction procedure. However, the possibility of reversal would be more remote than for the first appeal.

If the defence finds new evidence against the conviction after it was finalized, the prisoner could ask the first instance court to open a new trial, but it is rare for a new trial to be granted.[62]

Result

The most likely outcome of the Japanese virtual case would be as follows: arrest by the police on charges carrying punishment of up to three years' imprisonment; 72 hours of arrest by the police and the prosecutor; 23 days of pre-trial detention; the suspension of prosecution.

The less likely, but possible, outcome is: indicted for the obstruction of public duties and a violation of the Road Traffic Law; trial by a single judge at the first instance; conviction and sentences of about one year's imprisonment and a fine of approximately 30 000 yen; imprisonment suspended with a probation period of about three years; unsuccessful appeal and claim for a new trial.

Would it make a difference if the protagonist was not a Japanese citizen? As our protagonist comes from the USA, it is unlikely that the police would treat him worse than the other arrestees. If anything, he might be treated better than the Japanese. For instance, the police might release him if he was cooperative and did not challenge the police outright, even if he denied the charge. The probability that the prosecutor would not prosecute might also be higher.[63]

Comparisons and Conclusions

In our virtual comparison, we find not only many similarities but also the following interesting differences in outcome:

64 *Contrasting Criminal Justice*

- The time spent in police arrest is shorter in Germany than in Japan and Spain.
- Pre-trial detention (remand) is ordered only in Japan, and not in Germany and Spain.
- The total period spent in gaol is much longer in Japan (23 days/552 hours) than in Spain (48.5 hours) or in Germany (25 hours).
- The prosecutor often interrogates a suspect as an essential part of pre-trial investigation in Japan, but this is much more rare in Spain and Germany.
- The case would be brought to trial in Germany and Spain, but probably not in Japan.
- The sentence of the trial court would higher in Spain than in Germany and Japan (if it were brought to trial in Japan).
- While it is highly probable that there would ultimately be no formal punishment in any of the three countries, the length of the criminal proceedings is much longer in Germany and Spain than in Japan.

All three countries studied are usually seen as members of the civil law family.[64] With respect to criminal law, this means that they are regarded as adherents to the inquisitorial model – in other words, the emphasis is on the 'objective' pursuit of truth, not on 'procedural truth' brought about through conflict between the parties. But while Spain has kept closest to the original model of the investigating magistrate (*juez de instrucción*), Germany has abolished this figure completely and assigned the pre-trial investigation to the prosecutor (*Staatsanwalt*). In Japan, although the American adversarial structure has had more influence on the formal aspects of the trial procedure, the ideal for the prosecution is, like in Spain and Germany, the 'objective' pursuit of 'truth'.

In what follows we will analyse whether the differences we found in handling our case can be attributed to differences in law or in legal culture. Finally, we will return to the question of what all this means in terms of the differential protection of innocent defendants.

Does Law Make a Difference?

Clearly, differences in law play an important role in the explanation of the different lengths of arrest, since there are different upper limits in the three countries. We should note, however, that the police culture in all three countries seems to call for making maximum use of these respective legal limits. The fact that the protagonist would be kept in gaol for a further 20 days in Japan cannot be attributed to major differences in terms of criteria for detention. The only major legal difference is that a ceiling of that sort exists only in Japan and not in Germany or Spain. Such an upper limit seems to encourage the decision in favour of pre-trial detention.[65]

The difference in pre-trial detention is also related to the difference in interrogation practice of the prosecutor. Japanese law allows the police and prosecutor to interrogate a detained suspect without the presence of a defence lawyer, and such an interrogation becomes a crucial element of investigation when a suspect initially denies the charge. In Germany and Spain the law also allows the prosecutor to interrogate a suspect, but this is still the exception rather than the rule. The difference to Japan could be due to the fact that, in Germany, the defence lawyer has the right to be present at prosecutorial interrogations and, in Spain, even at police interrogations.[66] Spain is the only one of the three countries where the law allows a defence lawyer to attend police interrogations. However, no major difference seems to follow from that. The difference in interrogation practice seems to be related with differences in the scope and manner of prosecutorial discretion.

That the case would be brought to trial in Germany and Spain appears to be a logical consequence of the principle of compulsory prosecution (the 'legality principle'). Even though there are now many legal exceptions to this principle, they do not apply to the case at hand. While there are still possibilities not to indict cases of this sort in Germany or Spain, the opportunity principle makes non-prosecution much easier in Japan.

Despite differences in trial procedure, the three countries share the strong tendency for the judiciary to convict. However, this must be seen in the whole context of the criminal procedure, not as the characteristic of trial procedure alone.[67]

Sentencing differences have little to do with the law. Whereas punishment provided by the law is more severe in Germany and Japan than in Spain, actual punishment imposed is lighter in the former than in the latter. Apparently, sentencing practice is formed by extra-legal factors.

Law makes a difference with respect to the length of criminal proceedings. While there are no formal legal limits to the length of proceedings in Germany,[68] the Japanese 23-day rule for detention cases appears to have the effect that prosecutors decide, during this period, on what cases to concentrate. The same is true, in our case, with respect to the abbreviated trial procedures in Spain; it is, however, interesting to note that the shortness of the trial proceedings is set off by the length of the appeal process. Obviously, law makes a difference here, but only in interaction with other factors to which we return in the next section.

Does Legal Culture Make a Difference?

It is well known that legal principles and norms do not function in a social vacuum. How legal principles and norms are translated into practice depends on the institutional structure and the internal legal culture of the respective criminal justice system. We will briefly outline what we know about the legal cultural features in the three countries that seem to be relevant for explaining the outcome(s) of our case. For Germany and Japan, we will mainly make explicit some of the background assumptions we have implicitly made during our attempt to 'describe' how the original case would have developed in our respective countries.

German legal culture is characterized by a largely unbroken tradition of professional autonomy centred around the image of independent judges (Blankenburg, 1996: 249ff). In the sphere of criminal justice, prosecutors have tried to share this role since they were given quasi-judicial functions for handling routine cases out of court. While prosecutors are the main actors in the pre-trial phase, they take a back seat during the trial. Judges and prosecutors have identical training, have their offices in the same court buildings, meet frequently and largely share a common outlook on offences and offenders, as well as on adequate sanctions. In some parts of Germany, civil servants in criminal justice alternate between serving as prosecutors and as judges. All of this makes the handling of criminal cases a rather smooth and bureaucratic affair. It takes an unusually able defence lawyer to make a difference in this tightly knit system. Lawyers, including those who work mainly as defence lawyers, traditionally do not belong to the court subculture. It is only since the 1970s and 1980s that a specialized criminal defence bar has developed in Germany. This is why we think that once our protagonist had been charged by the prosecution, his conviction would be a forgone conclusion.

While Spain shares some of that tradition with Germany, the developments since the end of the Franco regime have made for important differences. There has been a considerable rejuvenation and feminization of the judicial career. However, there is a widespread feeling that the new judges arrive insufficiently prepared for their task. The pressure to fill vacancies is such as to make attempts to organize training courses for the prospective judges largely in vain. It can happen that a graduate from law school finds himself within a few months acting as judge in the courtroom (Toharia, 1996). Yet criminal justice personnel with longer practical experience also find themselves at a loss because of recent large-scale changes of the relevant codes and because of the introduction of the jury into the Spanish system. Some of the mechanisms through which especially the new generation of legal practitioners is coping with this difficult situation have recently been identified (Casanovas, 1997). Among them are cooperative behaviour rather than corporative exclusiveness (this applies to judges, prosecutors, lawyers, clerks and so on) and collective reasoning through informal conversations with many other professional actors. This goes a long way to explain why legal rules seem to play only a secondary role in trying the Catalan case.

The Japanese prosecutors are not mere gatekeepers at the entrance of the criminal trial. They, more than the judges, practically decide the fate of the accused. In this sense, the opportunity principle of prosecution is, in its practical interpretation, stretched to such an extent that it allows the prosecutor almost unlimited legal power to dispose of cases.[69] This prosecutorial practice was developed in the pre-war period, at a time when both judges and prosecutors belonged to the Ministry of Justice and when judges did not see themselves as in any way adversaries of the prosecutors. But there was also no strong opposition from the defence side, probably because the prosecutor's wide discretion to suspend was not against the interests of the accused. Under these conditions, the post-war introduction of American criminal procedure has had only a small effect on Japanese practice. For most Japanese defence lawyers, the idea that the accused should be able to stand for trial to prove their innocence is very foreign indeed. That is why we think that our case would not have come to trial in Japan. However, once prosecuted, the conviction of our protagonist is almost a forgone conclusion as in Germany. Although the judiciary became independent of the Ministry of Justice after the Second World War, judges are organized very much like the hierarchy of civil servants under the Supreme Court, and their relationship with the prosecutors is closer than with the private attorneys, sharing with the prosecutors the ethos of civil law criminal procedure, 'the objective pursuit of truth'. The combination of the inquisitorial pre-trial structure and the more adversarial trial structure tends to burden the defence and make it difficult for defence lawyers to prepare for trial. The fact that the prosecutors on the one hand choose only well prepared cases for trial and drop many cases on the other also tends to intensify the prospect of conviction (see, further, Hirano, 1989: 129).

Protecting the Innocent

All criminal justice systems are facing the dilemma that they attempt simultaneously to protect potential innocence and to punish potential guilt. Criminal justice cultures seem to differ in the ways in which they tackle this dilemma. This hypothesis can obviously not be checked by means of our virtual comparative case study; it will need to be checked against other cases and other criminal justice systems. The present study can, however, serve to produce some preliminary ideas on this subject.

From our case study we derive the notion that, in Japan, the potentially innocent are mainly protected by the prosecutor not going to trial with doubtful cases. In Germany (and presumably Spain), many more potentially innocent people are charged and are protected mainly through trial and appeal mechanisms. The flip side of this is that, in Japan, the potentially guilty get a prophylactic 'punishment' by means of a minimum pre-trial detention period.[70] Even though the Japanese system seems to avoid punishing the innocent by highly selective prosecution, serious miscarriages of justice could still occur. There have been well known cases where death row prisoners were released after new trials. All of these cases were confession cases, in which the confessions were later denied by the accused themselves. These cases indicate that the present pre-trial procedure which allow the police to extract confessions from the accused who are more or less under their total control could lead to the miscarriage of justice, particularly when defence lawyers do not work actively (see also Foote, 1991: 415). This problem also could be seen as a consequence of the strong commitment of the prosecutors to conviction, once they opt for trial.

The protection of the innocent in Germany (and presumably in Spain) is handled through a bureaucratic mechanism, in which the police investigation is checked by prosecutors and then by a hierarchy of courts. In a contested case, this is likely to work in favour of an atypical defendant, like our protagonist. But if in doubt, prosecutors will eventually send the case to court, to be on the safe side. At the same time, the built-in distance between the police and the criminal justice agencies (prosecution and courts) seems to be greater than in Japan and Spain. This works in favour of a defendant, who is able to retain a good defence lawyer who will eventually be able to clear up mistakes in fact as well as law.[71] The downside of this criminal justice culture is the long period of uncertainty ('punishment by proceedings') suffered by the innocent defendant.

Notes

1 For the purpose of this chapter we are using a broad definition of the term 'legal culture', encompassing not only the attitudes, values and opinions towards the law held by either the law staff or the general population (Friedman), but also the normative, institutional and behavioural features to be found in the respective criminal justice systems. For such a broader conception see Blankenburg (1997) and Gessner (1997).

2 A more detailed documentation of the case was presented at the SLSA Conference in Cardiff and discussed by a panel of international experts (Alldridge, Sanders, Felstiner, Sebba, Kurczewski, Murayama and Feest). The accused, who holds a BA from the University of California, Santa Barbara and an International Master's degree in the Sociology of Law from the IISL, Oñati, also participated in this discussion.

3 Art. 557 of the Spanish *Codigo Penal* (Penal Code) makes punishable by imprisonment

of a minimum of six months and a maximum of three years those, who 'acting in groups, and with the goal to commit an offence against the public peace disturb public order, causing injuries to persons, producing damage to property, obstructing public street or the access to same in a manner that is dangerous for those who circulate through them...'.
4   Art. 513 of the *Codigo Penal* does not envisage punishment for merely participating in illegal demonstrations. Those participants, however, who carry weapon or similar dangerous instruments during the demonstration, can be punished by one to two years' imprisonment. Participants who, in this context, commit violent acts against the authorities are punishable with the penalty that accompanies the respective offence, whereby the upper half of the sentencing frame is to be used (Art. 514.3, *Codigo Penal*).
5   The exact date is unknown but, in Spain, legally, the normal deadline for abbreviated proceedings is five days.
6   Also in the Spanish context, this is very fast. Even in cases of abbreviated procedures, 'the speed at which the case was dealt in court is not the general rule in Spain' as one Spanish criminologist told us.
7   In 1970 a major reform attempted to make the criminal law more compatible with the constitutional right of public assembly. Since then, there have been several changes (1985, 1989) trying to strengthen the criminal law against 'unpeaceful demonstrations'.
8   According to the *Versammlungsgesetz* (law on public assemblies) only the organizers of an unannounced or forbidden demonstration may be punished with up to one year in prison (§ 26, *Versammlungsgesetz*).
9   '*geeignet und bestimmt*' (§ 27, *Versammlungsgesetz*).
10 Punishable with up to one year in prison or a fine.
11 § 125, StGB (Penal Code): 'Whoever, as perpetrator or accessory, takes part in acts of violence against human beings or objects...perpetrated in a crowd with unified strength and in a manner endangering public security...will be punished by imprisonment not exceeding 3 years or by a fine.'
12 § 125a, StGB: punishable by six months up to ten years' imprisonment.
13 § 113, StGB: punishable by imprisonment not exceeding two years or a fine; in aggravated cases – that is, involving 'weapons' – the imprisonment may be from six months to five years.
14 This practice was questioned by the Council of Europe Committee for the Prevention of Torture, after they visited German prisons and police stations in 1991. The committee suggested that the defendant should have a right to a lawyer from the very beginning of police custody and that such a lawyer should have the right to present during police interrogations (*Report to the Government of the Federal Republic of Germany on the Visit to Germany Carried out by the European Committee for the Prevention of Torture etc.*, Strasbourg 1993, para. 30). The German government flatly denied the necessity to change German law or practice (*Response of the Government etc.*, Strasbourg 1993, pp. 7f).
15 § 163a, para. 3, StPO (Code of Criminal Procedure).
16 § 29, lit. 2 *Versammlungsgesetz* makes it an administrative violation not to leave the scene of a public assembly that has been declared dissolved by the authority. This can be fined with up to 1000 German marks.
17 § 125, StGB.
18 § 417, StPO. The provision has been redrafted in 1994 in the context of efforts to fight organized crime.

19 § 147, StPO. The prosecutor can deny access under certain conditions, as long as the investigation has not been formally closed.
20 § 170, StPO.
21 § 203, StPO. This filter is not very effective. In the overwhelming majority of all cases, the trial judge will go along with the prosecutor's case. Only about one percent of the cases prosecuted are not bound over for trial (Kühne, 1999: 259).
22 § 245, para. 1, StPO.
23 § 261, StPO: *freie Beweiswürdigung* (free evaluation of evidence).
24 In 1996 only 50 per cent of all suspects charged with *Landfriedensbruch* were convicted by the courts (Statistisches Bundesamt, *Rechtspflege, Strafverfolgung*, Wiesbaden, 1997, pp. 42–3.
25 If the court convicts also for resisting an officer, this would be dealt with as a 'merger of acts' (§ 52, StGB), resulting in the imposition of only one sentence. This sentence would be determined on the basis of the sentencing frame of the law which provides for the severest sentence. In our case, this would be *Landfriedendsbruch*.
26 Schünemann (1988: 265–80).
27 In 1996 of all sentences passed on offences against the state and public order only about 4 per cent surpassed one year of imprisonment, more than 50 per cent of which were suspended (Statistisches Bundesamt, *Rechtspflege, Strafverfolgung*, Wiesbaden, 1997, pp. 48–9).
28 § 56, para. 1, StGB.
29 § 41, StGB.
30 § 46, para. 1, *Ausländergesetz*.
31 The Road Traffic Law (§76.4.4) prohibits anyone to throw a stone, a piece of metal, and so on, which could hurt a person or a car on the street. The penalty is a fine of up to 50 000 yen.
32 Obstruction of public officials in the exercise of their duties (§ 95.1, Penal Code): punishable by up to three years' imprisonment. Public disturbance by collective violence (§ 106, Penal Code): active participants can be punished by six months' to seven years' imprisonment, passive participants by a fine of up to 100 000 yen. Since the latter provision is considered a rather draconian measure, it is hardly invoked.
33 In theory, an arrest is made when a police officer detains a suspect at the scene. However, in practice, the official decision to arrest is made at the police station. At this point, a police officer would inform the suspect of the charge. This could take place more or less than one hour after the suspect is arrested at the scene.
34 It has been disputed among academics whether the arrested accused can refuse to be interrogated. However, the practice does not allow the arrested accused to refuse interrogation.
35 In 1992 all the Japanese Bar associations set up a duty lawyer scheme, in which they provide free legal advice for arrested or detained suspects for the first meeting. Some, but not all, of the prefecture police cooperate in telling the suspect about this opportunity.
36 When the police arrest a suspect, they must, within 48 hours, either release or send him, with the investigation documents, to the prosecutor who must then either release, indict or ask the court for his detention within 24 hours. This means that the prosecution can, in effect, detain the suspect for 72 hours in total.
37 If he admits to the charge, he can be released before or (rarely) after being put into the police gaol. Of suspects charged with obstruction in 1996, 28 per cent were not put into the police gaol and 4 per cent were released from the gaol before being sent to the prosecutor.

Protecting the Innocent Through Criminal Justice 71

38 Among the suspects sent to the prosecutor on a charge of obstruction in 1996, 88 per cent were detained by the court at the prosecutor's request. Less than 8 per cent were released by the prosecutors. The obstruction cases in these statistics include several different offences in that category, but the general picture should not be very different. In general, once the suspect is arrested and sent to the prosecutor he or she is very likely to be further detained by the court.
39 Possible functions of the pre-trial detention are (1) to prevent escape, (2) to prevent the tampering of evidence, (3) to prevent further offences, (4) to 'punish' and (5) to interrogate. When a suspect denies the charge, it is important for the police and the prosecutor to interrogate a suspect during pre-trial detention. There have been heated debates on whether such practice could put pressure upon the accused to make a false confession.
40 In general, almost all detention applications are granted. In 1996 the rate was 99 per cent. In more than half of the obstruction cases, the duration of detention was requested by the prosecutor and granted by the court with no exceptions.
41 When the charge is public disturbance by collective violence, the pre-trial detention is renewable one more time, but within five days. In this case, the number of detention days from arrest can be up to 28 days.
42 The duty lawyer scheme is financed by each bar association, but not by the state.
43 The legal aid association decides whether the legal aid for pre-trial defence is granted to a particular applicant. However, since the budget for legal aid is very limited, the lawyer who meets the suspect as duty lawyer virtually determines whether or not the suspect should apply for the legal aid. The legal aid for suspects is not financed by the state, but by donations from the bar associations and the accused. It is an established practice that the accused often tries to get a lenient decision from the prosecutor or the judge by paying civil compensation to the victim or making donation to the legal aid association when the offence involves no victim. The latter is called redemption money. Since the state subsidy for legal aid can be used only for civil cases, the legal aid association uses the redemption money for criminal legal aid.
44 A major advantage for prosecution in Japan in comparison with Spain and Germany is the detention practice that a suspect is detained at a police cell attached to a police station, thus putting a suspect under their control. Such a practice clearly exacerbates the plight of the detained accused. Otherwise, we have reservations about to what extent the Japanese police have procedural advantages in comparison with their Spanish and German counterparts. With respect to the 'the enabling legal environment' for the police in comparison with the North American situation see Miyazawa (1992: 16–25).
45 In 1996 the prosecutors did not indict 44 per cent of all the Penal Code offenders, excluding traffic negligence (when the latter is included, the non-prosecution rate is 79 per cent) and 26 per cent of all the Non-Penal Code offenders, excluding violations of the Road Traffic Law. More specifically, 67 per cent of obstruction suspects were not prosecuted and 95 per cent of them were suspended in that year.
46 When the police refer a case to the prosecutor, they can express their opinion about the prosecutor's disposition of the case. Although the data is old (late 1960s), a statistical analysis of prosecutors' documents shows that police opinion was the most significant variable in deciding whether or not prosecution was suspended in theft and assault and battery cases (Mitsui, 1974: 1693).
47 Sometimes there are cases in which a suspect is released without further disposition by the prosecutor upon the expiration of detention. In practice, such an incident indicates that the case is very difficult – sometimes impossible – for the prosecutor to indict.

When a suspect is not detained, he or she could be indicted a year after the alleged offence.

48 Whether the defendant is indigent or not, the law requires the court to appoint counsel in offences which carry a penalty of more than three years' imprisonment. In our virtual case, the court would not be legally required to appoint defence counsel for the defendant. In offences whose maximum penalty is three years' imprisonment or less, the court must appoint defence counsel only for the indigent. But in practice every defendant can get defence counsel appointed by the court, if he or she wants to. Therefore, 97 per cent of the defendants at first instance were defended by lawyers in 1996. On conviction, the court may order a non-indigent defendant to pay all or part of the trial cost, including the cost of defence counsel.

49 In obstruction cases, 45 out of 49 defendants, who were granted bail, were ordered to submit the amount between 1 000 000 yen (US$ 7143) and 3 000 000 yen (US$ 21 429) in 1996.

50 The court can deny bail when there is a reasonable cause to suspect that the defendant will tamper with evidence. When the defendant denies the charge, the court tends to suspect the possibility of tampering with evidence.

51 A trial session takes place once or twice a month.

52 The renewal of detention is possible, but the renewed detention lasts for only a month. Further application for renewal must be made every month. In obstruction cases 77 per cent of the detained defendants were released during trial either by bail (22 per cent) or on the expiration of detention (55 per cent) in 1996.

53 There is no jury and there are no lay assessors in Japan.

54 During the period between the indictment and the first trial, the court must appoint defence counsel, if necessary, and the parties must make preparations for trial, such as exchanging documents for evidence and asking possible witnesses to attend the trial. Therefore, if a case is complex, a first trial could be opened much later.

55 The judge may be less willing to convict a defendant who has no prior record and who denies the charge throughout the pre-trial and trial stages, particularly when there is no independent evidence which supports the trustworthiness of the police story. In our case, the police failed to produce the ball bearings during the trial.

56 In 1996 the guilty rate was 98.7 per cent in all the criminal trial cases in the district courts. The not guilty rate was 0.06 per cent, while the rate of dismissal for technical reasons was 0.2 per cent. In the obstruction cases tried at first instance, all the defendants were convicted in 1996.

57 In 1996, 15 per cent of the defendants in obstruction cases denied a part or all of the alleged facts, but all were found guilty of a part or all of the charge.

58 In 96 per cent of the obstruction cases convicted in 1996, the penalty was between six months' and less than two years' imprisonment. It is an established practice that the prosecutor recommends less than the maximum sentence and that the court further discounts the sentence to be imposed upon a defendant.

59 In 1996 75 per cent of the prison sentences in the obstruction cases were suspended.

60 Fines of up to 500 000 yen can be suspended under certain conditions, but are rarely suspended in practice. In Road Traffic Law cases, only one out of 266 defendants was given a suspended fine sentence at first instance in 1996.

61 If there is a grave inconsistency in the original judgment, the Court of Appeal would reverse the conviction. In such a case, it is more or less established practice that the Court would declare the defendant not guilty rather than send the case back to the first instance court, though the latter is normal according to the law. Otherwise, it is likely that the original conviction would be sustained. The main function of appeal in Japan is

to reduce an original sentence, but not to challenge fact-finding by the first instance court. In 1996 the original judgments were reversed in 18 per cent of the Court of Appeal cases. However, the reversal for wrong fact-finding occurred in only 1 per cent of all the Court of Appeal cases, while reversal on grounds of illegal procedure occurred in less than 1 per cent.

62 For ten years, from 1981 to 1990, only 1 per cent of the prisoners and 98 per cent of prosecutors succeeded in their claims to open a new trial. Prosecutors' cases were mostly wrong identification cases (Matsuo, 1997: 269 and Tables 10.3 and 10.4 at 269 and 275).

63 There seem to be many complex factors which might affect the outcome of the case. Nationality, ethnicity or race is just one factor, but it could also interact with other factors like social class, status, political power and so on. Generally, the police do not want to make political trouble with another country.

64 It is, clearly, the most regrettable limitation of our study that we did not manage to include a scholar from the common law world.

65 For a similar mechanism cf. the German six-month deadline, after which detention cases come automatically under the jurisdiction of the high court (*Oberlandesgericht*). This deadline was introduced as a means to cut down the average detention time. It is, however, well known that it has had the effect that once you are placed on remand in Germany, the likelihood that you stay there for (at least) close to six months is substantial (more than 40 per cent of all cases).

66 In Japan the interrogation of a suspect by the prosecutor is significant not only for deciding whether a suspect is to be put on trial or not, but also for producing evidence which could be introduced in trial as an exception to the hearsay rule. Therefore, it is possible that differences in evidentiary rules have effects on the pre-trial practice.

67 McBarnet (1981) argues that common law is also designed to ensure a high conviction rate despite the rhetoric of justice and due process. According to her, the law pertaining to the criminal procedure from arrest to trial is made to favour crime control rather than due process. However, we suspect that jury trial in common law countries would have a different outcome from trial by a professional judge in civil law countries.

68 This is one of the reasons why Germany is frequently criticized by the European Court of Human Rights.

69 The opportunity principle is an aspect of the pre-war criminal justice system which widely adopted ideas of the German new school (*moderne Schule*). Ideas of the German new school could grow in Japan more than in Germany, probably because there was less cultural constraint, such as legal rights (cf. Kawashima, 1968). However 'almost unlimited legal power' does not mean that there is no institutional control over the exercise of discretion. This control is, however, more internal than external.

70 These characteristics of the Japanese criminal justice administration were discussed by previous studies in various ways. See Foote (1992: 317); Murayama (1992: 221).

71 But this will not work for the many defendants, who cannot pay well qualified and motivated defence lawyers. Therefore, a substantial number of unwarranted convictions will end up in force of law and can only be reopened under very restrictive conditions. See the still unsurpassed research organized by Peters (1970) on miscarriages of justice in Germany.

References

Blankenburg, Erhard (1996), 'Changes in Political Regimes and Continuity of the Rule of Law in Germany', in Herbert Jacob et al., *Courts, Law and Politics in Comparative Perspective*, Newhaven/London: Yale University Press.
Blankenburg, Erhard (1997), 'Civil Litigation Rates as Indicators for Legal Cultures', in D. Nelken (ed.), *Comparing Legal Cultures*, Aldershot: Dartmouth, 41–68.
Casanovas, Pompeu (1997), 'Notes on Legal Young Professionals' Culture in Spain. An Interpretative Hypothesis of some Statistical and Field Data', paper presented at the Workshop on 'Judges: Selection and Evaluation', IISL, Oñati.
Foote, Daniel H. (1991), 'Confessions and the Right of Silence in Japan', *The Journal of International and Comparative Law*, 21.
Foote, Daniel H. (1992), 'Benevolent Paternalism of Japanese Criminal Justice', *California Law Review*, 80.
Friedman, Lawrence (1969), 'Legal Culture and Social Development', *Law and Society Review*, 29–44.
Gessner, Volkmar (1997), 'Teaching Legal Culture', in J. Feest and E. Blankenburg (eds), *Changing Legal Cultures*, Oñati: International Institute for the Sociology of Law, 83–90.
Hirano, Ryuichi (1989), 'Diagnoses of the Current Code of Criminal Procedure', *Law in Japan*, 22.
Kawashima, Takeyoshi (1968), *Nihonjin no Ho Ishiki* (The Legal Consciousness of the Japanese) Tokyo: Iwanami Shopen.
Kühne, H.H. (1999), *Strafprozesslehre*, (5th edn), Heidelberg: C.F. Müller.
Matsuo, Koya (1997) *Keiji Sosho Ho (The Law of Criminal Procedure) (Volume 2)*, Tokyo: Kobundo.
McBarnett, Doreen J. (1981), *Conviction: Law, the State and the Construction of Justice*, London: Macmillan.
Mitsui, Makoto (1974), 'Kensatsukan no Kiso Yuyo Sairyo' (The Prosecutor's Discretion to Suspend Prosecution), *Hogakn Kyokai Zasshi*, 91.
Miyazawa, Setsuo (1992), *Policing in Japan: A Study on Making Crime*, Albany, NY: State University of New York Press.
Miyazawa, Setsuo (1997), 'The Enigma of Japan as a Testing Ground for Cross-cultural Criminological Studies', in D. Nelkin (ed.), *Comparing Legal Cultures*, Aldershot: Dartmouth, 195–214.
Murayama, Masayuki (1992), 'Postwar Trends in the Administration of Japanese Criminal Justice: Lenient but Intolerant on Something Else?', *Journal of the Japanese–Netherlands Institute*, 4.
Nelken, David (1997), 'Understanding Criminal Justice Comparatively', in M. Maguire, R. Morgan and R. Reiner (eds), *The Oxford Handbook of Criminology*, (2nd edn), Oxford: Oxford University Press, 559–76.
Peters, Karl (1970), *Fehlerquellen im Strafprozess. Eine Untersuchung der Wiederaufnahmeverfahren in der Bundesrepublik*, Karlsruhe: C.F. Müller.
Schünemann, Bernd (1988), 'Daten und Hypothesen zum Rollenspiel zwischen

Richter und Staatsanwalt bei der Strafzumessung', in G. Kaiser *et al.* (eds), *Kriminologische Forschung in den 80er Jahren. Projektberichte aus der Bundesrepublik Deutschland*, Freiburg: Max Planck Institute.

Toharia, José Juan (1996), 'La administración de justicia en España', in O. Alzaga *et al.* (eds), *Entre dos siglos. Reflexiones sobre la democracia española*, Madrid: Alianza Editorial.

4 Legal Cultures, Political Cultures and Procedural Traditions: Towards a Comparative Interpretation of Covert and Proactive Policing in England and Wales and the Netherlands

Chrisje Brants and Stewart Field

Introduction

The larger part of this chapter reports a particular study of the way in which two jurisdictions – the Netherlands and England and Wales – have reacted to certain new developments in police investigative techniques, namely, the rise of covert and proactive policing.[1] This is a phenomenon noticeable in most Western European countries because many of the pressures behind it are supranational, such as developments in (electronic) technology, the growth of international police cooperation associated with Europeanization and globalization and thus converging social trends in crime. Yet covert and proactive policing techniques, despite certain similarities, do not represent culturally neutral technologies because different institutional and cultural contexts give them distinct social meanings and connotations in particular countries. Contrasting legal cultures, political cultures and procedural traditions all create differences in the way in which the targets for covert and proactive policing methods have been socially constructed, the extent to which, and the terms in which, their use has been regarded as problematic, and the regulatory responses which have followed. However, before turning to the specifics of this analysis, we have chosen, given the methodological and conceptual themes of this volume, to start by explaining how the research came about and to say something about the interpretative concepts on which it is based.

The Research Process: Problems of Comparative Interpretation

This study represents a comparative and collaborative (re)interpretation of trends suggested by the empirical work of indigenous researchers (*Inzake Opsporing*, 1996; Maguire and John, 1995; Dunninghan and Norris, 1996; Dorn *et al.*, 1992; Greer, 1995; Greer and South, 1998).[2] We have developed a detailed technical definition of covert and proactive policing which is intended to address that enduring problem of cross(legal)cultural work – 'Are we comparing like with like?'. But in going beyond technical definition to interpret the contrasting social meaning of covert and proactive policing, differences in legal cultures have become central to our analysis and these, in turn, are necessarily related to broader aspects of culture and tradition. Lucia Zedner has highlighted the problem in this kind of interpretative exercise: 'it is rarely possible to attain equivalent familiarity with two cultures. We are necessarily the child of the one and, at best, the distant cousin of the other' (Zedner, 1995: 519).

We have attempted to solve this problem by academic cross(legal) cultural collaboration. This chapter emerges from a long-term research link between the Willem Pompe Institute for Criminal Law and Criminal Justice, the University of Utrecht, and the Cardiff Law School, University of Wales. One author is genuinely bilingual with equal facility in both Dutch and English but her formal legal studies were pursued entirely in the Netherlands. The other speaks and reads no Dutch and his entire education in law has been in English law. There is thus no difficulty of language (in that all collaboration has been through English, a mother tongue of both researchers) except – and this is, of course, an important qualification – where language defines legal concepts. However, each of the co-authors is very largely dependent on the other for a detailed contextualized account of how that other's legal system works. Over a period of time (and through a number of publications) (Jörg *et al.*, 1995; Brants and Field, 1995a, 1995b, 1997), out of this interdependence has come a mode of genuinely joint writing in which the authors have sought to 'negotiate' mutually acceptable descriptions of legal practice in the two countries.

Yet because the precise words used to describe particular elements of a legal system reflect broad aspects of institution and ideology, one discovers routinely, in the process of negotiation, the cultural contingency of meanings of particular legal concepts and notions. Forms of words that are natural and uncontroversial to someone brought up in a common law, adversarial tradition may be startling and contentious to someone from a Continental inquisitorial tradition and vice versa. Even describing a Continental system as inquisitorial – a reflex natural to a lawyer educated in England – is liable to meet strong reaction, given the stress in the Netherlands – and France as well – on the extent to which historic inquisitorial tradition has been qualified in modern times. In these countries, the native tendency is to talk of the system as 'mixed' (Delmas-Marty, 1991) or of a system that is 'moderately' inquisitorial (Brants and Field, 1997: 406) or of the 'inquisitorial tradition'. Similarly, Continental lawyers describe their own trial stage as based on the fundamental principles of 'orality' and 'adversariality' (to contrast it with the preceding pre-trial stage) and yet the terms jar with English observers exactly because of the relative absence – that is, relative to English practice – of both from the Continental trial. And what of those two other organizing principles, 'immediacy' and *le principe contradictoire*, so well known on the Continent but for which there is no linguistic equivalent in English? This is not because English criminal process is not marked by 'immediacy' or *le contradictoire* but because the fundamental accusatorial basis of the English system entrenches so much 'immediacy' and *le contradictoire* that the 'principles' are almost taken for granted (Spencer, 1998).

Another example more specific to Dutch–British comparison may merit slightly more detailed examination. It concerns 'diversion' from criminal process. The authors have written together on the topic only to discover that English and Dutch jurists[3] attribute completely different meanings to the concept. In England and Wales diversion has been regarded, certainly until recently, as primarily the taking of a case out of the criminal justice system. The justifications for this have been a rather uneasy mix of, on the one hand, managerial concern to process cases more quickly and cheaply by eliminating those judged low priority and, on the other, a view that state intervention was positively harmful in labelling and stigmatizing young people. Yet, in contrast, the Dutch see diversion as an intrinsic part of the criminal justice system – as one of a continuum of pragmatic alternatives for resolving social conflicts and issues. This originated from the significant influence of the 1970s Dutch abolitionist movement, and especially Louk Hulsman, in stressing the meaningful resolution of conflict through reparation and mediation – through mechanisms that 'divert' from retributive punishment, but not necessarily positive institutional response. Thus differing notions of diversion exist not because of the lack of common institutional pressures – for example, to process cases cheaply – but because the cultural attitudes through which these pressures have been filtered differ. Even more fundamentally one could argue that, in this, Dutch legal culture reflects broader aspects of Dutch political culture in which the resolution of conflicts through negotiation finds a semi-institutional expression in a 'politics of accommodation' central to Dutch social stability and political legitimation.[4] Although this is changing – and we shall return to both the politics of accommodation and some of the reasons for, and consequences of, such changes later – one of its strongest legacies has been in the field of criminal justice where it has produced a tendency to rely on more consensual and less overtly punitive methods of social control rather than on strictly upholding the criminal law. The rules of criminal law and criminal procedure therefore leave very wide margins of discretion for the criminal justice authorities to refrain from the use of traditional criminal sanctions and to rely on methods of diversion that, in England and Wales, would not be regarded as criminal justice. For the English and Welsh, plea bargaining and diversion remain only half-acknowledged, rather guilty secrets in which the ideals of adversarial contest have to make way for the pragmatism of resource constraints – and perhaps the crime control pressures to maximize rapid convictions (McBarnet, 1981: ch. 4).

We hope we have said enough to indicate that, even with two native speakers writing in English, we are continually negotiating different concepts through language. Inevitably this is a process that evolves over time, requires a significant amount of trust between co-authors and a recognition that even describing the smallest detail of legal systems requires sensitivity to broader institutional and ideological contexts.

The Analytical Framework: Legal Culture, Political Culture and Procedural Traditions

Our research does indeed start from a fairly concrete point of departure: particular (defence) rights, particular (policing) techniques and their interaction with particular procedural traditions. Nevertheless it seeks to embed its explanations in more general ways of seeing, accepting the task for comparative lawyers set out recently by Cotterrell – that is, to examine legal concepts, doctrine and procedures in the context of the social, political and economic matrix within which they exist (Cotterrell, 1997: 13–14). In recent years scholars in comparative law have been using the concept of 'legal cultures' as a means of thus contextualizing the analysis of comparative legal practices) (Nelken, 1997; Gessner *et al.*, 1996).

The use of 'culture' as a general analytical category for bringing together active social components into more generalizing explanations of social phenomena is not new. In retrospect, Raymond Williams' defence from the 1950s and 1960s onwards of a broad concept of culture – against more restricted notions in which 'culture' is confined to a limited body of artistic works – represents a crucial moment in the UK.[5] He graphically defined culture as a process by which 'patterns learned and created in the mind' are communicated and made active in relationships, conventions and institutions' (Williams, 1961: 89). Two key ideas are expressed here. First, culture is more than either social behaviours or attitudes viewed in isolation: it is the active social process by which these are brought into interrelationship that is important. Second, and consequentially, for Williams, culture could be expressed as much through the creation and sustaining of social *institutions* as more personal projects such as artistic or intellectual works.[6] The same emphases can be found in David Garland's influential analysis of the cultural forms and meanings of punishment (Garland, 1990, especially chs 9–12). Drawing on the classical founding sociologists (and Foucault) rather than directly from Williams, he argues that:

... the frameworks of meaning which we call culture...must be viewed as inextricably bound up with material forms of action, ways of life, and situational conditions. The intricate, interwoven webs of significance which make up the fabric of a culture develop in a kind of dialectical relationship with social patterns of action.... (Garland, 1990: 90)

This leads him also to conclude that institutions such as punishment must themselves be seen as cultural artefact, 'embodying and expressing society's cultural forms' (Garland, 1990: 193). Political, economic or organizational forms are aspects of culture in its broadest sense because they are 'frameworks of meaning within which social action takes place'.[7] This is in contradistinction to Lawrence Friedman's recent usage which limits (legal) culture to the realm of personal ideologies about law: 'ideas, values, expectations and attitudes, beliefs towards law and legal institutions which some public or some part of the public holds', making legal culture a 'measurable phenomenon' like public opinion (Friedman, 1997: 34, criticized by Cotterrell, 1997). Similarly the stress on meaning puts Williams and Garland a long way from those who have tried to see culture simply in terms of behaviours (Blankenburg, 1997; see also Nelken, 1997 in critique).[8]

The importance of this for the development of a concept of legal culture is easy to see. The centrality of institutional structures to legal cultures is clearer than it might be to, say, artistic or leisure culture. Characteristically, a legal culture is most evident in the ideas that inform the creation, maintenance and revision of the particular institutional forms that order the society in which it exists. Certainly, one could imagine a legal culture that existed in individual intellectual and/or imaginative work without institutional expression, but even then it would inevitably be offering a vision – perhaps an alternative vision – of institutional practices. Thus what we draw from Garland and Williams' analysis is the sense that only by bringing out the active relationships between legal (and other) frames of interpretation and narrower institutional and doctrinal components of legal systems can either be fully understood. Indeed, one would want to qualify Williams' formulation set out above in that it presents the interrelationships as unidirectional: what is needed is a sense of the reflexive or interactive connections between relationships, conventions and institutions on the one hand and 'patterns learned and created in the mind' on the other. The form of the institutions expresses the ideas and, often, the ideas are reaffirmed and validated by institutional practice over time (see our discussion below of procedural traditions and Garland, 1990: 193 ff. for a sense of these reciprocal influences in the context of punishment).

The concept of legal culture has not escaped criticism, the most significant being that is unhelpfully vague and tends to encourage totalization (Cotterrell, 1997: 17). The danger is that one may impose general unity on what may be extremely diverse elements of ideas, practices, values and traditions and, instead of making connections, make wholes. This suggests that there is an argument for distinguishing different elements in a legal cultural process. In relation to culture in general, Raymond Williams distinguished four such elements: traditions, institutions and (intellectual) formations, to which he added the more informal lived experience of culture that he termed a 'structure of feeling' (Williams, 1977: 115). By making the distinctions, the necessary connections *between* elements can then be remade and emphasized. In trying to achieve this bringing together of four elements of (legal) culture we will make extensive use of a concept at the intersection between them – that of procedural traditions in criminal process. This may be most directly seen as an institutional element, but it clearly interacts with underlying cultural and political formations: for example, the existence, role and relative independence and power of prosecutors and investigating judges clearly relates to contrasting intellectual formations which construct the state as a powerful and benevolent guarantor of the public interest or as something more sinister (Jörg et al., 1995).[9] And particular procedural (that is, institutional) forms derive normative force from their association with the past, and these sustain and perpetuate broader ways of seeing the law. Such traditions speak not only to developed philosophical discourses (Williams' intellectual formations) but to many barely articulated, taken for granted, deeply ingrained attitudes about law, the state and its relations with the individual – as well as the selected versions of history on which they depend (Williams' structure of feeling). This then has an influence beyond the existing procedural forms of the particular moment in that it shapes the way in which new problems are defined and constituted. The way in which judges, legislators and legal practitioners react to new developments in technologies or social forces and process them legally is filtered, often unthinkingly, through a sense of tradition: the new is incorporated into the patterns of the old, while often transforming them in more or less subtle ways.

This normative effect of tradition on ways of seeing in law is well captured by Merryman:

> A legal tradition, as the term implies, is not a set of rules about contracts, corporations and crimes, although such rules will almost always be in some sense a reflection of that tradition. Rather it is a set of deeply rooted, historically conditioned attitudes about the nature of law, about the role of law in society, about the proper organization and operation of a legal system, and about the way law is or should be made, applied, studied, perfected and taught. The legal tradition relates the legal system to the culture of which it is a partial expression. It puts the legal system into cultural perspective. (Merryman, 1985: 2)[10]

The interrelationships and associations above – with their stress on normative attitudes to the way the (legal) world should operate – suggest close interactions between legal culture and broader political culture (the sphere of state decision-making). But this raises a key definitional problem for the analysis that follows: how are we to differentiate a *legal* culture from a political *culture*? In some authoritarian dictatorships opposition is partly organized around images of due process and human rights held and expounded by radical lawyers and political groups which represent visions of alternative institutional possibilities. Are these lawyers or groups constructing an oppositional political culture or an oppositional legal culture? In part this will depend on the tradition of the particular culture – whether it is a jurisdiction with a tradition of appeal to legality – and in part on how the vision is expressed in the particular instance. If it is expressed through lawyers opposing the state through the courts then it is perhaps easier to see it as an alternative legal culture, whereas if it is done through political meetings, demonstrations or pamphletering then it may be more easily viewed as an alternative political culture. But the same groups and individuals may express themselves in a variety of forms and in ways that cut across these separations: what if a political demonstration is about specifically legal reform, such as the incorporation of human rights conventions into domestic law?

We are not arguing here that political and legal cultures are synonymous: many aspects of political culture relate to no established institutional forms and do not aspire to do so – for example, (unlawful) multiple voting in

Northern Ireland may be said to be part of the political culture but is hardly an aspect of legal culture. But once political argument evokes general notions of appropriate institutional forms for the ordering of social practice – a central definitional domain for law – the distinction may be as much about particular modes of expression as subject matter, and also about the degree to which the institutional forms are 'established'. Some political practices, if repeated enough, attain such normative force as to become constitutional (legal) conventions (the self-limitation of monarchical power in several countries being an obvious example). Particular arguments about discretion in particular contexts may shade into arguments about discretion (as opposed to rules) generally. Political and legal culture become intermeshed and subject to reciprocal influence.[11] Legal culture may not only underpin political culture but may be informed by it. In other words, there may be a balanced and self-sustaining relationship between the two that implies that, as a society evolves politically and socially, so too will its legal culture evolve. It may well be, however, that such mutually informed evolution is not necessarily an even process but one that takes place in fits and starts, especially in times of fundamental social change or political upheaval or uncertainty. Given the inherent conservatism of law, legal culture may come to lag behind political culture or even to run counter to it. It is no coincidence that during great revolutionary events the law and legal institutions are prime targets of (forced) change.

We make these general remarks in order to clarify the general concepts that inform the analysis. In what follows[12] we introduce covert and proactive policing by setting out its definition and the dilemmas it poses for criminal process. We then examine the contrasting ways in which the targeting of these investigative methods has been socially constructed differently in the two jurisdictions, reflecting important differences in political culture and making its use and form subtly different in the two countries. Then, we seek to explain how the political and legal culture of each country has interacted with its procedural traditions to shape the way in which the *problems* posed by such policing have been defined. Finally, we consider the way the regulatory resources available to deal with these problems are themselves conditioned by the very same aspects of legal and political culture and procedural tradition. Where appropriate we draw on Williams' distinctions.

Introducing Covert and Proactive Policing: Definitions and Dilemmas

Definitions

What the terms covert and proactive policing seek to capture is a trend whereby, rather than starting inquiries into specific offences after they have been committed, police forces increasingly target particular 'known' offenders who are expected to commit future crimes (hence, the term 'proactive' policing). Alternatively, they may also dispense altogether with the concept of known offender and target 'risk groups' thought likely to become involved in (future) criminal activity. Information-gathering techniques – such as the use of (participating) informers, undercover police operations and (electronic) surveillance – are then used which have secrecy as their common denominator (hence 'covert' policing).[13] Covert techniques may potentially be used both reactively as well as proactively – that is, after, as well as before, the relevant offence is committed. More frequently, the demands of secrecy mean that such methods will be used proactively or perhaps at the very beginning of the reactive phase – that is, after the offence but before arrest,[14] since after arrest, suspects are more inclined to be on their guard.

The purpose of proactive intelligence-gathering may or may not be to gather evidence for the future prosecution of a criminal offence. Hoogenboom has suggested that intelligence-gathering without subsequent prosecution is a defining characteristic of proactive policing (Hoogenboom, 1995: 570). But as we will see, whether or not prosecution follows intelligence-gathering depends on how criminal policy is constructed: in the Netherlands, some proactively gathered intelligence is used for prosecution and a great deal is not, while in the UK proactive methods are still predominantly regarded, certainly by the regular police, as a preliminary to criminal prosecutions. The idea of purpose other than criminal prosecution should not then be regarded as a defining – because necessary – feature of proactive policing, but rather as a related development that brings the potential of such policing into sharper focus and considerably compounds problems of control.

Dilemmas

The issues here can be simply stated in outline. Jurisdictions from both the adversarial and inquisitorial traditions of criminal procedure seek to ensure that the evidence produced at trial will enable legal truth to be found by procedural means considered fair by prevailing social standards (see Jörg *et al.*, 1995; Brants and Field, 1995a). Within the adversarial tradition the search for the truth and procedural fairness are said to be assured by the autonomous pre-trial responsibility of the parties – under presumed conditions of rough equality of arms – to seek out and present evidence which supports their own contentions. For the inquisitorial tradition it is the monitoring and supervising of the police investigation by prosecuting and examining magistrates which ensures that both inculpatory and exculpatory evidence is placed before the court.

The problem posed by covert and/or proactive policing is that its timing and secrecy have profound implications for these traditional mechanisms for checking and rendering the police investigation accountable at trial. The timing of proactive investigation is important because it exacerbates a problem traditional to defence participation in reactive investigations – namely, that the defence arrives too late on the scene. Rights of access to legal advice accrue at best on arrest and, in many European countries within the inquisitorial tradition, only after 24 or 48 hours (Van De Wyngaert, 1993). If most of the investigation has by then been completed, the defence's capacity to participate – to object to surveillance or the targeting of the suspect – is inevitably limited. The best that one can then do is to assert a right to information about the investigation. From this, effective rights to assert one's case and challenge adverse decisions may flow. The problem then is that the covert nature of the policing may mean not just that defence access to information about the policing methods is postponed, but also that the police will usually argue that covert operations demand that the defence should *never* be given the identity, for example, of those who have informed or the location of surveillance posts or told how undercover operations were conducted. This makes full defence participation in the pre-trial and trial process problematic. In turn, this has profound implications for the equality of arms that is the basis of adversarial claims to find the truth and to fairness of procedure.

Less obviously, such forms of policing threaten judicial monitoring and supervising systems within the inquisitorial tradition: overloaded prosecutors and examining magistrates find it difficult to look below the surface of apparently straightforward dossiers without the promptings of defence intervention. Without knowledge of the police investigation the defence find it difficult to play this key role.[15] This may be less important if judges or prosecutors know what is going on but there is evidence that, sometimes, the police do not think they need to know (and the judges and prosecutors themselves sometimes do not seem to want to know). In the end the danger is that much that might be relevant to issues of guilt, culpability and sentence are buried in unread files or (worse) never committed to paper.

The Targeting of Covert and Proactive Policing: The Social Construction of Particular Demons

There is much that is supranational in these developments (not least the 'persuasive' influence of the US Drugs Enforcement Agency and, more recently, developments in police cooperation under the third pillar of the European Union). However, it is clear that receptiveness to these technologies, their targets and the way in which they interact with the procedural forms of the criminal process vary in the UK when compared with the Netherlands.

The Rise of Proactive and Covert Policing in the UK

In the UK, traditional attitudes towards covert policing have to be understood in the light of political and ideological controversies surrounding the introduction, as late as the mid-nineteenth century, of an organized professional state police in the face of extensive resistance. The critique offered by a variety of diverse social groups of an organized state police was couched exactly in terms of opposition to 'the continental spy system' of policing:

> ... [i]n France it was popularly held – and with some justification – that there were spies and informers everywhere; once admit a police force into England, and the long-cherished liberties of Englishmen will be swept away in a regime of terror and oppression. (Critchley, 1978: 35)

It was not that spying did not take place[16] but that its existence was widely denied and rejected: 'it was the fond belief of the English people that the employment of spies was unBritish...' (Thompson, 1968: 532 ff).[17] Thompson demonstrates clearly the weight of this cultural inheritance – that rejection and denial of intrusive and inquisitorial foreign methods was part of the 'birthright' and self-identity of the 'free-born Englishman' in the late eighteenth and early nineteenth centuries. Thus the early police forces had to be presented as a uniformed presence to make them politically acceptable. That this traditional view derived from highly selective interpretations of both past and present is demonstrated by the long tradition of precisely such undercover methods in the context of Ireland. Those who were not 'freeborn Englishmen' could not expect the same protections. But cultural and political sensibilities about policing in traditional crime contexts seems to have led to more limitations on its use than either on the Continent or in the USA (Fijnaut and Marx, 1995: 8–9; Marx, 1995: 325). Certainly some surveillance work, and even some undercover work, went on in British policing after the development of organized police forces, but the detective branch remained small and low key and was expected to avoid a number of practices necessary to covert policing (Armstrong and Hobbs, 1995: 178).

It was only in the mid-1980s that it became clear that these long established traditions of cultural hostility to the police penetration of the private sphere had been substantially qualified. Until around 1985 proactive investigation had been the guiding principle behind certain specialist squads (particularly drugs squads and regional crime squads) where the predominant targets were drugs and, to a lesser extent, armed robbery. It had not achieved much broader use in 'regular policing'.[18] Only in 1985 was football hooliganism added as a further major target (Armstrong and Hobbs, 1995). Noticeably the National Football Intelligence Unit, charged with national and international coordination of intelligence dates only from 1990 despite longstanding problems. Armstrong and Hobbs (1995) have suggested that the expansion to the policing of football hooliganism in the mid-1980s was not happenstance. It was a relatively non-contentious target which, by enabling the media to present undercover police as unambiguous heroes in the war against crime, may have played a part in legitimizing similar practices in other areas (implying that the use of such methods would need some special justification).

It was only in the early 1990s that street crime and (to a lesser extent) the potential threat of organized crime became more clearly targeted. The officially endorsed argument was that small numbers of offenders committed a high proportion of offences and that selective targeting made proactive methods both viable and necessary.[19] After the Audit Commission (1993) urged the police to 'target the criminal not the crime', proactive methods became widely used as an evidence-gathering preliminary to strategies of high-profile, mass, coordinated dawn arrests and criminal prosecutions for burglary and car crime.[20] Alongside this there has been the development of official police and Government concern over organised crime. This was late emerging – at least by Dutch standards – and remains relatively low key (see below). It was not until the beginning of 1995 that a House of Commons Select Committee on Home Affairs decided to examine organized crime as a serious problem, in the context of regular policing and crime control.[21] The comparatively tardy emergence of concern is reflected in the relatively slow moves to develop a specialized police service to deal with organized crime. The National Crime Intelligence Service (NCIS), coordinating separate police units dealing with such matters as football hooliganism, drugs and international crime, was not set up until 1993 and suffered from a lack of resources, an uneasy relationship with local forces and regional crime squads and squabbles about whether it should have an operational arm.[22] Only in 1997 did the Police Act put NCIS on a statutory footing and introduce, for the first time, a National Crime Squad with a remit 'to prevent and detect serious crime of relevance to more than one police area in England and Wales'.[23] This seems likely to reinforce the tendency towards the new methods, as does the redeployment of the security services as external threats have become less potent and the defence of budgets favours retargeting domestic 'threats'.

How are we to interpret these trends in state procedures in terms of the intellectual formations and 'structures of feeling' of contemporary political culture? Throughout the 1980s government rhetoric on crime had been central to its self-identity as a force for the reassertion of social disciplines lost in the allegedly lax 1960s. The appeal and success of this 'authoritarian populism' in the context of relative economic decline has been well-documented (Hall, 1980; Downes and Morgan, 1997). From 1992 the law and order temperature was especially high, with renewed government emphasis on 'getting tough on crime'. With the Conservative government trailing badly in the polls, Michael Howard – with political ambitions of his own and an openly populist style – became Home Secretary in 1993 – the year of the furore caused by the murder of 2 year-old Jamie Bulger by two pre-teenage boys. Tony Blair had become Shadow Home Secretary in 1992 and Leader of the Opposition in 1994 and, with him, arrived 'New Labour' with its absolute conviction that a tough crime stance was vital to winning the next election. Sensitivities about civil liberties and state accountability were politically less potent than sometimes overdramatized crime threats.[24]

Nevertheless, the government had had to confront the inherent tension between its 'strong state' rhetoric and its radical right-wing aspirations to reduce public spending. During the 1990s a cooler relationship between the Conservative government and senior police officers developed as attempts to reform police management cultures and strategies led to demands that the individual forces demonstrate efficiency by achieving performance-related targets (Leishman *et al.*, 1996, especially chs 1, 3, 13, 14). For the police, the shift to covert and proactive policing could be seen as a way of providing evidence of 'value for money' for state spending on policing by addressing a high-profile concern with new high-profile methods (already endorsed by the Audit Commission). The fact that covert and proactive policing could be packaged as new and technological was no doubt helpful; that one could take journalists along on raids timed and coordinated to maximize publicity made it all the more so. The new methods also provided a response to police anxiety about the requirements of the 1984 Police and Criminal Evidence Act and its Codes of Practice, which made it more difficult to exert prolonged psychological pressure on suspects to confess in the police station (a traditional way of securing convictions for street crime quickly and easily). These interlinked developments, seeming to reconcile the drama necessary for political presentations with new managerial concerns (Lacey, 1994), formed the background to the key policy shift towards the proactive targeting of prolific street offenders. Not surprisingly, scepticism within government about the potential of covert and proactive policing was little in evidence.

The development of such techniques may also be seen as part of a profound shift in criminological assumptions charted in an important article by David Garland. He outlines a series of modern state adaptations – some of them contradictory – to the apparent incapacity of government agencies to control crime in insecure postmodern cities (Garland, 1996: esp. 458). Amongst these is 'denial' – a sometimes hysterical political response that simply reaffirms, in the face of the evidence, that state punishment, if harsher and more certain, can deal with the problem. Another response in clear tension with this operates at the administrative level: it seeks to lower citizens' expectations of the state's capacity to control crime by redefining success and failure. The rise of covert and proactive policing fits neatly into these contradictory responses. On a political level it provides some answer to the presentational need of modern governments (particularly those with a strong law and order rhetoric) to show that 'something is being done' – a way to respond to media panics about youth crime or sensational events or something to deny their message of the state's incapacity to deliver security. On the other hand proactive and covert policing can also be seen as part of an attempt to *redefine* success and failure. Garland suggests that the British police are now seeking to claim success in detecting *serious* crime or *serious* criminals while reducing public expectations that they can control routine, opportunist crime. Covert or proactive policing provides a technique specifically adapted to the targeting of particular crime problems and the concentration of resources on them. It is a technique that requires a rather particular demon.

The Rise of Proactive and Covert Policing in the Netherlands

In contrast, use of the 'new' methods in the Netherlands has had a rather different social focus. Here, the above-mentioned 'politics of accommodation' combines with a restrained media tradition – the product of the absence of a tabloid press comparable to that of the UK – to produce lower levels of public anxiety about street crime. This has led to a greater emphasis on living with ordinary street crime (Downes, 1988). In terms of Garland's argument on the criminology of adapting to high crime levels, the policy of the Netherlands has been much more based on administrative *management* of (street) crime rather than overt and dramatized repression and grandiose political claims about its efficacy (Garland, 1996). Although this can be seen as evidence of foreign stereotypes of Dutch 'pragmatic tolerance' this should not be confused with a lack of concern for social discipline (for a similar point in relation to Dutch policy toward prostitution, see Brants (1999)). It is more that the style of social discipline suits Dutch ways of doing things, which are based on coordinated management of problems by criminal justice and other elites (see Brants and Field, 1995b; and compare Germany, generally Blankenburg, 1997, Zedner, 1995 on law and order, and Busch and Funk, 1995 on covert and proactive policing).

Legal Cultures, Political Cultures and Procedural Traditions 91

Extensive Dutch use of covert and proactive policing has the longer history in ordinary crime contexts (Busch and Funk, 1995). In the 1970s it became clear that the use of undercover agents, informers and surveillance teams had become an integral part of Dutch police work – especially, but not exclusively, in relation to drugs offences. This was recognized in the setting up of a separate national Criminal Intelligence Department (CID) at the end of the decade. From the late 1980s onwards it was organized crime that became the 'particular demon' of official Dutch debate rather than the individual opportunist street crime that is seen as so alarming in the UK. The fear in the Netherlands was of new forms of sophisticated networks or organizations reaching across crime definitions, involved in traditional 'mafia' type work (drugs, gambling, prostitution enforced by violence) but also environmental crime (the highly lucrative trade in illegal waste-dumping) and white-collar crime (fraud, corruption, money-laundering). In 1991 a survey of all the regional CIDs produced a police estimate of 599 criminal groups connected to serious or organized crime, with 10 per cent being assessed as 'highly organized' (Klerks, 1995: 135–6). Although later criminological work cast serious doubt on such police assessments, they reinforced the importance of organized crime as the key criminal policy priority and led to significant changes in the way in which covert and proactive policing was used. In the 1970s, the strategy was to use surveillance and informers to facilitate arrests and conviction, initially of any individuals involved in the drug trade and later targeting organizers. However, with the 1990s focus on criminal networks and organizations, state intelligence-gathering became used more as a basis for disruption of networks in which criminal prosecution often played a marginal role. The spreading of disinformation through the media, the use of intelligence to chart networks (with a view to further surveillance and possibly breaking them up in future), the pinpointing of key figures both in and outside of the organization (for example, lawyers involved in money-laundering) all became regular tactics. The latest development has been that organizations, under surveillance because they were suspected of involvement in organized crime, might find themselves targeted by inspectors dealing with tax, social security, immigration, working conditions, building regulations and gaming licences. Although some leading figures have been prosecuted for the offences in relation to which the initial or related suspicion arose, intelligence-gathering has become a goal in itself, while 'administrative harassment' is now seen as a strategy that may well be more successful than the lengthy, costly and not always successful business of criminal law.

Such developments in the Netherlands demonstrate the potential for proactive policing to go beyond the criminal justice system and the targeting of (future) criminality and become part of a process of defining and managing 'risk populations' (Riehle, 1985). Such methods provide a means for the surveillance of groups (usually those on the margins of the society and its economy) considered as threats to social order in a larger and vaguer sense than as criminals (perhaps because of their nationality, race, family or social contacts, previous conduct or political beliefs). Much can therefore be done to justify flexible systems of surveillance and regulation by the construction of vague categories such as 'organized' crime. Four Dutch criminologists, eventually commissioned to look into police definitions of organized crime, found that the figures given for crime organizations (for example, those cited above) were little more than a hoax. Yet the figures produced legitimated the extensive surveillance of a particular sector of the population.[25]

These successive transformations in the social construction of the crime problem relate to changes in social and political culture in the Netherlands. Much has been written about the 'pillarization'[26] of Dutch society and its pervasive effect on all important social, political and legal components of Dutch culture. The salient feature of pillarization was bargaining and compromise between the elites at the top of the four main 'pillars' of Dutch society (Catholics, Calvinists, secular conservatives and social democrats), for which reason it is also known as 'the politics of accommodation'. The 'price' that society paid for the relative peacefulness of this arrangement, was that, of necessity, it entailed secrecy at the top and pacification of the 'lower levels' of society. The politics of accommodation were therefore also the politics of acquiescience and paternalism, with a consequent relative immunity of the elite from criticism and, compared to most other countries, an inordinate measure of faith in government and the state. In turn, this allowed the public prosecution service to make use of wide discretion to promote diversionary policies and also supported the self-censorship within the mass media which enabled such patterns to remain unchallenged and thus regarded as self-evident. However, a loosening of the tight bonds of pillarization and, with it, the structure that provided for informal social control has led to growing social unrest about crime in general and an increasing tendency for the public and political parties to call for more and stricter use of formal means of social control. Yet it is perhaps indicative that the 'administration' response to organized crime outlined above has taken the rather 'traditional' form of 'managing' rather than fighting crime, although it has been presented in the media and sold to the politicians as an indispensable part of the 'war on organized crime'.

We have contrasted Dutch patterns of low visibility surveillance and disruption of so-called 'criminal' organizations with British media-directed, overtly repressive use of criminal sanctions against street criminals. In each country, by socially constructing a particular crime problem, on which scarce resources could be focused, policing solutions could be seen to have a new credibility. However, the challenge for policing was established by very different domestic social constructions of crime and social order which reflect very different dominant political cultures. How, then, was each country to manage possible tensions between the new policing forms and domestic legal culture, not least their procedural traditions in criminal process? In what ways has proactive and covert policing proved problematic?

Targeting Covert and Proactive Policing

Contexts: The Relationship between Political and Legal Cultures

In this sub-section we explore contrasts in the relationship between legal and political culture in the two countries. We then use these general reflections to try to understand the way in which proactive and covert policing had a different social, political and legal significance in the two countries.

England and Wales E.P. Thompson and others have charted historically the cultural notion of the 'rule of law' as part of the Englishman's birthright. Historians have commented that this ideology of law – a very particular legal culture – was central to political legitimacy in eighteenth-century Britain (Hay, 1975; Thompson, 1975; Brewer and Styles, 1980; Hall and McLennan, 1981). Thompson has traced the line of this 'culture of constitutionalism' back to the anti-monarchist struggles and the jurists of the sixteenth and seventeenth centuries and argues that it was still a key cultural element well into the nineteenth century (Thompson, 1975: 269; Thompson, 1968). The appeal of its rhetoric was, as we have seen, still strong enough to pose significant constraints on the policing strategies of the 1830s and 1840s. This constitutional birthright had characteristics that were culturally specific: it was viewed less as a system of positive abstract rights (such as right to privacy) and more as a set of concrete freedoms, won in historic political conflicts, from particular forms of state intrusions.[27]

> The common Englishman was not so much democratic, in any positive sense, as anti-absolutist. He felt himself to be an individualist, with few affirmative rights, but protected by the laws [nb. plural] against the intrusion of arbitrary power. (Thompson, 1968: 87)

In addition to this, much was made of individual citizen participation in criminal justice and the capacity to assert one's own rights *directly* in state processes. Brewer and Styles (1980) describe the cultural significance in legitimating the rule of law in the eighteenth century, of hue and cry, private prosecution, jury service and a citizen judiciary (although the concept of citizen entailed was admittedly limited). This was all part of the 'assertion of the popular right to secure the fair and equitable enactment of justice'. The effect of this legal culture, rooted in *particular* restraints on power and individual rights of participation, has been a view that it is the direct actions of the 'people' that secure and preserve liberty. Accompanying this has been a scepticism about guarantees of freedom dependent on the state and a residual concept of liberty (a citizen may do anything not specifically proscribed by the law). Yet the rejection of entrenched abstractions of constitutional rights has meant that this legal culture is more dependent on the contemporary political culture for its maintenance than elsewhere.

This has important consequences for the 1990s – a period in which covert and proactive methods seem to have become broadly accepted, with very little immediate critique, into the accumulating range of police investigative techniques. Stuart Hall argued that one of the characteristics of the 'authoritarian populism' of the 1980s was that government and senior sections of the police sought to use the modern mass media of communication to shape public opinion by constructing a 'definition of the crisis' – in short, to construct a political culture favourable to its interests (Hall, 1980: 3–4). The early 1990s witnessed a vivid replay of this scenario with something like cross-party support – again for reasons of (Labour) political strategy. The tabloid demonization of football hooligans, joy riders, burglars and car thieves became an important factor in limiting questions asked about the new means used to deal with them. In the process, one of the weaknesses of the language of the 'free-born' Englishman was again exploited: that those who are defined as outside this category cannot be expected to enjoy its protections. Questions of appropriate legal form are side-stepped by a naive instrumentalism, in which the only question – and one to which 'too easy' answers are characteristically found[28] – is 'What will work?'. An ancient legal tradition can sometimes stand in opposition to a contemporary political culture (see Thompson, 1980).

The Netherlands Dutch criminal law and criminal procedure, like most continental European systems, are rooted in the eighteenth-century traditions of Enlightenment and Revolution. These reflect a concept of political society in which the state is regarded more positively than in Anglo-Saxon political culture – as something fundamental to the rational realization of the 'common good'. However, because of the immense powers needed to carry out such essential tasks, the state is regarded with some suspicion: by their very nature, these powers represent a continuous threat to the liberty of the individual. Yet precisely because that liberty is not merely an individual interest but part of the common good, only the state can secure and uphold it. The solution to these apparent paradoxes is to demand that state power be exercised through particular forms: great weight is attached to the primacy of written rules of law, entrenched constitutional rights of the individual and the division of power within the state (which implies judicial scrutiny of executive action). Although the practical constitutional arrangements that this theory implies are no longer strictly applied in the Netherlands, it nevertheless still influences both intellectual formations – elaborated constitutional accounts – and common sense concepts about criminal justice (or structures of feeling, in Williams' terms).

The difficulty is that a tension developed between these aspects of legal or constitutional culture and very specific aspects of Dutch social–political culture rooted in the system of 'pillarization' described above. The criminal justice system, as such, was not part of any pillar, but was, nevertheless, most definitely part of the establishment, and therefore of the politics of accommodation, allowing its functionaries their fair share of immunity and trust. This applied especially to the judiciary and the prosecution service and goes some way to explaining the far-reaching discretionary powers they have. Compromise and consensus – essential to the politics of accommodation – require flexible solutions to social problems (such as crime) that are less divisive and conflictual than criminal justice. Once it is acknowledged that criminal justice cannot solve social problems and should be used as a last resort, a flexible and pragmatic attitude to rules and regulations is necessarily implied. Herein lies the basis of fundamental tension between a legal–constitutional culture – which stresses the primacy of the written law and the necessity of monitoring and control rooted in legal values – and the social–political culture. Until recently, the ability to achieve balance between these two aspects of Dutch culture – legal and political – allowed Dutch criminal justice to gain a reputation for tolerance and pragmatism *and* respect for individual rights.

During the final quarter of the twentieth century, however, developments in the Netherlands have gradually made inconsistencies and incompatibilities in these interrelated assumptions increasingly visible. The relatively stable relationship between legal and political culture has been fundamentally altered. Pillarization has been undermined by secularization, the rise of the welfare state and social democracy, the undermining of automatic elite authority, and individualization and fragmentation of social relations (all of which were, in the Netherlands, the lasting legacy of the 1960s). This has changed perceptions of the delicate balance in criminal process and the relationships between its participants, undermining the commitment to legal principles and, in the final event, casting doubt on the legitimacy of crime control. The politics of accommodation, however, had left such an indelible mark that the legal culture did not begin to show signs of strain until the 1980s. It was only then that the competing tensions under which the criminal justice system operated came to be regarded as no longer sustainable (although there remains a deep and more lasting 'structure of feeling' derived from the tradition). These contradictions gave rise to what became a criminal justice crisis that, in the Netherlands, centred around the issue of proactive policing.

Legal Cultures and the Accountability of Policing

In this section we want to explore certain specific elements of these legal cultures which relate to police accountability. The general assumptions set out above mean that a great deal of (legal) cultural capital is invested in particular procedural elements which are considered fundamental to the legitimacy of the criminal process (and thus the state). We will stress the significance of three constitutional aspects of Dutch criminal process: Continental notions of the *Rechtstaat*, the centrality of the European Convention on Human Rights, and the judicial supervision of the police (predominantly by the public prosecutor). In contrast, within the adversarial culture of England and Wales, it is defence autonomy and rights to participate fully in challenging the prosecution case at public trial that are accorded the highest symbolic value. These differences are, of course, themselves reflections of the different attitudes discussed above towards the state and different histories: a concept of rights guaranteed by (a particular form of) the state as opposed to a space of liberty chiselled out around its margins.

We have argued that, in England and Wales, there exists a residual concept of liberty as something expressed in, and defined by, *particular* restraints on state intrusion. A paradoxical consequence of this is that, when it is applied to the state, it means that the police may do anything that is not specifically illegal. New policing methods can exist outside the legal framework of criminal procedure. For the Dutch this idea of police powers, defined in an unstructured series of negative prohibitions, seems like power in legal limbo. The *Rechtstaat* concept of continental Europe demands that infringements of citizens' rights and freedoms require a specific and positive basis in the written law (usually the Code of Criminal Procedure): this is viewed as part of the fundamental legitimating principle of legality. For the Dutch, therefore, proactive and covert investigations posed a specific constitutional challenge in that, until very recently, with the exception of telephone tapping, the only written legal authority for covert techniques was the vague provision which defines the general functions of the police.[29] For many jurists this was an insufficiently precise legal basis to found infringements of fundamental freedoms such as the European Convention's right to privacy. Indeed, the courts' acceptance of a variety of such practices on that basis could be seen as evacuating the legality principle of its 'bite'.

This need for specific legal authority for intrusive policing acts is reinforced by the direct applicability, and central cultural importance, of the European Convention in 'completing' domestic law in the Netherlands. Swart and Young have argued that 'the Convention is at the heart of every debate in the Netherlands on the quality of criminal justice' (Swart and Young, 1995: 60–61) and that the ECHR is now to Dutch case law what the national constitution is to countries like Germany or the USA. ECHR definitions of the right to a fair trial and the right to privacy, and the legal conditions under which the latter may be infringed, become fundamental questions for the national legal order. For the British, until the enactment of the Human Rights Act 1998, the ECHR was an external (if increasingly important) political influence on the legislative and jurisprudential development of law, rather than something that dominated legal culture. Thus, for example, the fact that police bugging practices in *R* v. *Khan* might be in breach of Article 6 or 8 of the Convention could not be regarded as a decisive factor in deciding whether to exclude the evidence produced.[30]

Another key contrast between Dutch and British legal cultures is the attitude towards police autonomy in investigation. Perhaps the most remarkable feature of the structure of investigation in England and Wales, viewed from the Continent, is the degree of openly accepted, and indeed vaunted, police autonomy to investigate without external review. One could argue that this is just part of adversarial logic: the tradition entrenches the autonomy of parties to seek out and present their own evidence. But more than that, in England and Wales police autonomy is often presented as a due process guarantee – 'the police are answerable to the law and to the law alone'[31] in that the separation of government and policing is seen as part of the relationship between separation of powers and the rule of law. This was reinforced in the early twentieth century by the judiciary's reinvention of the doctrine of constabulary independence just as local control of the police threatened to become democratic control (Lustgarten, 1986). Added to this has been the increasingly sophisticated police use of the media since the 1970s to reinforce the rhetoric of police professionalism and thus their unique qualifications to make the allegedly technical choices involved in policing policy and strategy.[32] If the police are only accountable to law, in the absence of pre-trial prosecuting and investigating magistrates, pre-trial autonomy is not just accepted but lauded, since any controls should be exercised through public trial.

There may be broad police autonomy in the Netherlands but, in terms of legal culture, it is defined as problematic because it is strongly felt that investigations should be judicially supervised. It is the prosecuting magistrate that is the central figure in supervision (Jörg *et al.*, 1995, Fionda, 1995: 96): in the early stages of a case it is his or her role to direct the police investigation, both by providing guidelines on appropriate action in general and by ordering or approving investigative acts in specific instances. Attitudes towards the public prosecutor are shaped by the fact that the system is a product of longterm historical development, marked by few publicized scandals and a confidence and trust undiminished by combined roles – magistrate, bureaucrat, criminal justice policy-maker (Brants and Field, 1995b). The accountability of Dutch criminal justice, and its structures of authority correspond closely to Damaska's ideal type of hierarchical/pyramidal organization (Jörg et al., 1995). The cultural assumption that underpins this form of state accountability is the notion that the state is the benevolent and powerful guarantor of the public interest and can be trusted to 'police' itself provided that it is appropriately organized (Brants and Field, 1995a; Field et al., 1995).

In contrast, much more of the cultural investment of the adversarial tradition is in full rights of defence participation in challenging the whole of the prosecution case at public trial. Although much of the procedural detail now associated with adversarial trials – the rule against hearsay, the (relatively) passive judge, the questioning primarily through partisan counsel – only emerged with the arrival of the defence lawyer from the second half of the eighteenth century, the idea of criminal trial as 'altercation' between accused and accusing witnesses dates back at least to Elizabethan times (Langbein, 1978, 1983: 123–34, 1997). And, although rights of confrontation might be qualified in some important categories of case, for hundreds of years English commentators asserted the superiority of their legal culture over that of the Continent exactly because these rights could be asserted on the basis of longstanding tradition (Friedman, 1998: 703–4). Viewed in the light of the emphasis on citizen participation in English–Welsh legal culture, the strong rhetorical force attached to rights to cross-examination and to confront one's accuser in person are easily comprehensible. If the state is not to be trusted, then it is for each 'free-born' Englishman to defend his own interests. Further, and perhaps more pragmatically, once police investigations developed higher degrees of institutional autonomy and more substantial resources during the twentieth century, the metaphor of 'balance' in England and Wales has often been used (with its half-articulated appeal to the adversarial version of equality of arms) to demand and protect (relatively) strong defence rights to participate even in the early stages of that process.

The Social Construction of Proactive and Covert Policing Methods as a Problem

In this section we set out the extent to which covert and proactive has been publicly defined as problematic in terms of the elements of legal ideology and institution outlined above.

The Netherlands By the beginning of the 1990s telephone tapping (sometimes without authorization), bugging, the use of long-distance microphones and homing devices were all in widespread use in police investigations. Added to this was the practice of so-called 'looking-in operations' which was a euphemism for burglaries by the police who would enter houses, sheds and companies of suspects – without, of course, reporting it in a written form (*proces-verbaal*) – in order to establish whether it was worth making an official search (*NRC Handelsblad*, 25 March 1994). Most of these lacked an explicit legal basis but were regarded by the courts as being sufficiently justified in law by the Code of Criminal Procedure's general definition of the functions of the police.

The police then developed the so-called 'Delta' method whereby criminal informers were allowed to import large amounts of drugs into the country and sell them to establish their credibility with targeted organizations. Soon significant amounts of drugs were being 'lost', informers allowed to keep the receipts of crime and new investigative operations financed by drug-related transactions (*Het Parool*, 30 March 1994). Surveillance operations sometimes lasted for many months. There was a reasonable suspicion that some targets had committed serious offences; others were suspected of planning to commit an offence; in some cases, suspicion did not arise until after surveillance and in others the target seemed to have been chosen because of his or her presumed connections, however tenuous, with 'organized crime'. Only occasionally was the purpose of such intelligence-gathering the prosecution of the target.

This kind of covert and proactive policing – particularly when not geared to prosecution – led to the widespread undermining of the prosecutor's pivotal role. While in theory public prosecutors are required to monitor pretrial investigation, their ability to do so depends on information provided by the police. However, since the police were not inclined to pass on information on the secret use of illegal proactive methods, public prosecutors were not informed of police operations unless their cooperation – or through them, that of an investigating magistrate – was required for legally obtaining evidence. And as the purpose of proactive policing evolved towards intelligence-gathering without immediate links to specific cases, the necessity for informing the prosecutor diminished accordingly. Indeed, the increasingly secret nature of such operations prompted a policy of 'need to know' even within specialized police departments and, as for outsiders, who needs to know if there is to be no prosecution?

Eventually in 1993 the Chief Commissioner of Police, the Chief Public Prosecutor and the Mayor of Amsterdam, having discovered something of what was going on, announced the disbanding of Interregional (Police) Team North Holland/Utrecht (IRT). The scandal was also partly prompted by a case in which information about the investigation had been deliberately withheld from the defence, prosecution and court. The public perception was that the police had somehow been allowed to get 'out of control'. The Ministers of Justice and Home Affairs were forced to resign, but even this failed to satisfy parliament and an official parliamentary inquiry (*Commissie Van Traa*) was instigated.[33] The commission found evidence of widescale use of methods of investigation that were, in the words of a later government report, 'unacceptable in terms of Rechtstaat and legality' (Ministry of Justice, 1996: 3). The commission noted a fundamental breakdown in traditional forms of hierarchical control of the police by the public prosecution service. The very foundations of the system – faith in its ability to 'police itself' through supervisory mechanisms – had been severely shaken. It remains to be seen whether public confidence in the integrity of the criminal justice system as a whole – traditionally a fundamental characteristic of Dutch society – has been lastingly undermined.

England and Wales In England and Wales, stress on police autonomy, the residual concept of liberty and the fact that Article 8 of the ECHR had not been hitherto directly applicable, meant that the use of covert and proactive techniques without particular legal authority posed few problems in terms of English/Welsh legal culture (although it might be subject to political critique from civil liberties organizations). The police could, like any citizen, do anything that was not specifically forbidden: electronic and physical surveillance, undercover operations/infiltration by police officers and the use of informers required no prior authority from outside the police service regardless of their intensity or duration. Some but not all covert techniques required the authority of the chief constable of the relevant force.[34] Hierarchical monitoring took place within the police hierarchy: there was/is no requirement that the Crown Prosecution Service be consulted beforehand. Furthermore, the CPS is not a judicial organization: its constitutional function is not defined as being the control of the police or its investigation.

The procedural tradition thus left (and leaves) much to regulation at trial. At trial, evidence is, according to the adversarial theory, tested vigorously by full defence participation and the right to challenge the prosecution case through cross-examination. Thus the strong doctrine of hearsay in England – expression of the cultural significance of these traditions – has prevented the widespread use of testimony by undercover officers or participating informers because anonymity is not as readily guaranteed as in the Netherlands (Spencer, 1998; Cape and Spronken, 1998). Where the investigation is both covert *and* proactive in the sense that the relevant offence[35] has not yet occurred, usually the main evidence which the prosecution seeks to advance is accumulated at the time of that offence because the police will be waiting for the defendant (staking out the bank or other scene of crime). Usually this results in such probative evidence that the police do not want to use information gained in the proactive phase (such as the testimony of informers or undercover agents). But, if the detail of the covert and proactive policing never becomes subject to debate at public trial, the capacity of criminal process to hold the police to account is accordingly weakened. Whether there will be public scrutiny at trial depends on whether the defence know the detail of the investigation. Here, appeals to the procedural tradition of adversarial confrontation looked set at one point in the 1990s to place strong constraints on covert and proactive policing. A development in case law in relation to the disclosure of evidence to the defence in the 1990s, prompted by revelations of miscarriages of justice, led to a reassertion through judicial reinterpretation of the participation rights of the defence. The Court Appeal in *Ward*[36] decided that the 'common law right to a fair trial' and rules of natural justice required that almost all records of investigation, including the use of proactive and covert methods, be made available to the defence so that its reliability and fairness could be challenged in open court.[37] As the Court of Appeal explained in an earlier miscarriage of justice case, the great advantage of the adversarial system was the ability of the defence to test the prosecution case in open court through oral cross-examination of prosecution witnesses. Because this could be undermined by inequality of investigative resources, extensive duties of disclosure were vital to ameliorate this imbalance of arms.[38] Left like that, one might have said that judicial intervention in the name of the English common law had done that for which Dutch legal culture had used the *Rechtstaat* and the ECHR – reasserting the due process safeguards of the traditional legal culture.

This was to have a profound, but shortlived, impact on the regulation of covert and proactive policing. Almost immediately the British police began a vigorous media campaign complaining that defence lawyers were beginning to force the state to drop cases by demanding disclosure of the role of informants and their identity or confidential information on surveillance techniques (Rose, 1995; Gibb, 1994). By this time, the political climate could not have been less like a British version of the 'politics of accommodation'. A Home Office consultation paper supported these views without any systematic empirical evidence on the extent of the problem (Home Office, 1995: para. 14). The Home Secretary quickly defined that problem in terms of acquittals based on the defence exploitation of technicalities and introduced the plans that were radically to curtail prosecution disclosure in the Criminal Procedure and Investigations Act 1996. Thus, it has been made quite clear that any stability in the procedural traditions of English legal culture that might exist, is – given the British doctrine of parliamentary sovereignty – always subject to the greater volatility of political debate and the British political culture.

As for that political culture, much has been played out through the mass media. Gradually, stories on covert policing methods have begun to emerge, focusing on the use of informers, their incitement of offences, the price paid in money and immunities for their services, as well as the corruption of some informer–police relationships and the effects of hidden rivalries between investigators.[39] But, as yet, we have not witnessed public revelations that innocent persons have been wrongly convicted, something that public debate in Britain now seems to require to shift it from crime control values, partly because covert and proactive investigations tend to be directed at those already suspect – at 'known faces'. A much publicized example was the Colin Stagg affair: a female undercover police officer in a murder case befriended the principal suspect and sent him a series of letters including episodes of sexual fantasy as she tried to persuade him to confess (Harding, 1997; Ames, 1994; Doherty, 1994). The trial judge ruled inadmissible certain alleged comments made to the undercover officer, said to demonstrate knowledge of details of the killing not released to the press, and condemned the undercover operation as 'deception of the grossest kind'. Yet some sections of the tabloid press – notably the *Mail on Sunday* – apparently encouraged by nods and winks from police contacts (Harding, 1997), ran the story in terms of a guilty man acquitted on a technicality and released 'evidence' not heard at trial that allegedly implicated the suspect. Thus, while the operation drew a great deal of condemnation from legal groups, for others – and these tended to be those more influential at the Home Office from 1993 – the episode demonstrated again excessive legal control over the effective pursuit of the truth. Not surprisingly, in a climate in which both major parties were seeking to outdo each other in sometimes simpleminded crime control rhetoric, no parliamentary or judicial inquiry followed and the general terms of covert policing were not put in question. Much media coverage has consisted of uncritical reporting of the successes of such proactive operations in cutting crime on the basis of police-produced statistics that are extremely dubious (Field, 1998).

Only in 1997, in rather precise political circumstances, did the issues raised by police covert methods begin to trouble British politicians. It had became apparent that the police were now engaging in a widespread practice of entering premises covertly to plant electronic surveillance devices. This had no lawful basis in that such entry involved at least a civil trespass and, very possibly, criminal damage. The lack of specific legal authority made a condemnation by the European Court of Human Rights inevitable. The then Conservative government tried to legalize the practice without introducing any mechanism for prior judicial authorization and thus do the minimum necessary to bring domestic law in line with the ECHR.[40] Initially this strategy seemed likely to succeed: only the small Liberal Democrat group in the House of Commons was arguing for prior approval by a circuit judge. But there followed a belated revival of what E.P. Thompson once described as the 'very ancient cultural tradition in Britain of bloody-mindedness towards the intrusion of authority' (Thompson, 1980: 178). An unlikely alliance developed of liberal forces with right-wing newspapers such as the *Daily Mail, Daily Telegraph, The Times*, and the *Economist*, along with senior Conservative Peers, Law Lords, the Lord Chief Justice and lawyers' organizations (*Guardian*, 1997; Wadham and Colvin, 1997; Travis, 1997). From one perspective what was striking was the tardiness with which the issue was taken up by the official opposition: a critique of crime control measures based on the constitutional need to control intrusive state powers seems to have been perceived as politically dangerous (Young, 1997). On the other hand, the rhetorical points of reference in the campaign are telling, especially those of the right-wing newspapers: the *Daily Telegraph*, quoting *Entick* v. *Carrington* found the bill contrary to the 'genius of the common law'; its correspondents found it contrary to 'ancient common law freedoms that have set British citizenship apart' and evoked the traditional sanctity of the Englishman's home. It is, of course, easy to mock the chauvinism involved, the ritual invocation of the Spanish Inquisition, the role accorded to the 'Mother of Parliaments' in protecting traditional liberties, the classically bourgeois juxtaposition of 'liberty and property'.[41] Yet this sometimes unreasoned rhetorical force calls us back to Williams' concept of a 'structure of feeling' – something less intellectually assured but more forcefully felt than an 'intellectual formation'. There is also something here that recalls Thompson's 'free-born Englishman', that suggests that there remains an inherited force to the legal culture which, even if based on highly selective interpretations of the past and convenient omissions, may nevertheless sometimes confront the immediacies of politics and policy.

Differential Regulatory Response

The Netherlands

The regulatory response to proactive and covert policing illustrates the idea that procedural traditions can influence not just the way the issues are constructed but also the institutional resources available to respond. The Dutch, rather than enhancing defence rights during the proactive phase, have chosen, first, to reassert judicial control of police investigations (especially to reassert the authority of the prosecutor) and second, to provide the specific legal authority for the use of investigative powers that the *Rechtstaat* and the ECHR are said to demand. A bill published in 1997 by the Ministry of Justice[42] places responsibility for deciding whether specific proactive methods should be used firmly in the hands of the public prosecutor. The bill entered into force on 1 February, 2000 and allows proactive investigation (that is, without the stringent requirements of reasonable suspicion of individuals) for organized crime only (although it shies away from any useful definition of the phenomenon). All methods involving 'serious' violations of privacy are now said to demand more specific legal authority to satisfy the 'legality' requirements of the ECHR with their stress on clear criteria. Systematic surveillance of suspects, the covert entry and limited search of non-residential premises, the use of informers (whether or not they are participating) and undercover infiltration by the police or citizens will all require prior authorization from the public prosecutor. Telephone taps and bugging will require authorization from the investigating magistrate.[43]

As for the fundamental question of access to information, the government bill requires that an index be placed in the dossier of all special investigation methods. The bill's explanatory memorandum explains that this obligation is to enable the prosecutor to control and supervise investigative acts in the proactive phase and the trial judge to check the reliability and legality of the information.[44] The bill also sets out innovative new powers to allow the *rechter-commissaris* (examining magistrate) to investigate the reliability and legality of police investigations which have not led directly to evidence presented in court but which, for example, may have generated initial suspicions. If, say, a question arises about the running of an informer who is not going to testify, the examining magistrate, on his or her own initiative, or at the request of defence, prosecutor or trial judge, may interview the police officers running the informer and, in exceptional cases, the informer.

It is by these means – essentially reaffirming the traditionally active truthfinding role of the investigating magistrate and the trial judge and the supervisory role of the public prosecutor – that the bill seeks to reconcile the secrecy needs of proactive methods with suspects' rights under the ECHR. In terms of defence rights, the system does little more than meet the absolute minimum requirement of the European Court under Article 6(3)d – namely, that the defence must be able to 'challenge the evidence at some point in the procedure'.[45] This does not mean confrontation publicly or at trial, and defence rights to know and discuss information or confront a witness remain often qualified or contingent upon a reasoned request by the defence (see Field and Jörg, 1998). This still leaves the defendants in the position of having to demonstrate the relevance of material to their case before they have had access to it. Thus Dutch legal culture traditions have made rather more of the danger of breaches in the structure of legal authority that the *Rechtstaat* demands and the minimum standards of the ECHR than the importance of the fullest defence participation in the dialogue over guilt: traditions of trust in the state (and thus in magistrates) continue to shape response. The unanswered question is whether the broader transformations in Dutch social and political culture – individualization and fragmentation of social relations, the decline of pillarization and loss of trust in elites – will not require much more fundamental change in legal culture. It may not be long before the debate is less about particular discretions and powers of police, prosecutors and judges and more about how magistrates and police discretion generally must be more and more closely structured and individuals given more active roles in processes that affect them, signalling a further juridification of social relations.

England and Wales

In England and Wales the debates have led to two significant legislative developments: the Criminal Procedure and Investigations Act 1996 and the Police Act 1997. The first responds to police demands for greater secrecy in covert and proactive policing by restricting defence rights to know the detail of the police investigation and thus to enter into dialogue over the authenticity of its results. Such a move, which inevitably limits any due process guarantees that are based on defence participation and public trial, might be thought to require, in the name of balance, a more developed system of pretrial judicial supervision or monitoring. But both Acts, in different ways, point to the institutional difficulty of constructing such systems in a jurisdiction where the traditional judicial role has been limited to that of procedural referee at trial. Traditions have shaped and do shape institutions, and this affects both the way in which solutions can be conceived and their practicability.

The Police Act 1997 introduces, for the first time, a limited requirement of prior judicial authority for 'intrusive surveillance'. Permission will now be required from 'surveillance commissioners' – who will be serving or former high court judges – for bugging operations involving entry into, or interference with, premises without the consent of the occupier.[46] From the standpoint of institutional tradition the interesting issue is the nature of the judicial authority.[47] Countries like the Netherlands can more easily adopt systems of prior judicial authority because they already have professional magistrates with direct continuing daily responsibility for monitoring police investigations. In England and Wales prior authorization will remain an isolated decision rather than one step in a structured judicial monitoring process. The Judicial Commissioners – who will number only five or six and who may well still be holding high judicial office – are likely to be

London-based and therefore less accessible outside the capital, and probably unfamiliar with local conditions and particular officers (Ewing and Gearty, 1997). Hence the call of the Liberal Democrats during the debates for Circuit judges (of whom there are over 550) to be given the responsibility (Lester, 1997). But even if this had been accepted, supervising police investigations would have been a marginal part of those judges' professional responsibilities. The traditional model of the judicial role means that to provide the training and institutional resources for serious judicial scrutiny of intrusive surveillance would have required some serious institutional innovation. But to do this, the issue has to be seen not as a specific political problem relating to particular police powers, but as a general question of appropriate institutional forms for accountability in an adversarial jurisdiction which presumes equality of arms yet embraces a police force that is increasingly sophisticated, organized and coordinated in the use of the new (electronic and biological) technologies. There is, as yet, no sign of the redrawing of a general legal culture about police accountability from the specifics of particular political controversy.

The Criminal Procedure and Investigations Act 1996 deals with the key information issue raised by the new investigative methods: it purports to achieve balance in weighing the needs of the police to keep sensitive material secret and the defence right to know the detail of the investigation. The defence will have a right to material that might undermine the prosecution case[48] and to a schedule of non-sensitive material. A schedule of 'sensitive' material drawn up by the police – which will include details of informers, surveillance and undercover operations – will not be revealed.[49] If it wants further disclosure, the defence must set out its case in general terms so that the prosecution can decide whether it holds further relevant material.[50] A judge will become involved if (a) the defence wish to challenge the prosecution claim that it holds no (further) relevant material or (b) the prosecution wish to avoid disclosing material that it considers relevant but 'sensitive'. Judges will then decide in preliminary proceedings whether the information is relevant or sufficiently central to a plausible line of defence to require disclosure.

Remarkably, in terms of adversarial tradition, the effect of this is that aspects of the truth will be judicially determined (albeit provisionally) pre-trial and very often with only limited defence participation in the decision.[51] If the issue is relevance, the judicial role is triggered by a defence claim but as they have not seen the schedule of 'sensitive material', they will be working in the dark and relying on the judge to find out what is relevant. If the question is one of the public interest in disclosure – where there is relevant material that is considered sensitive – the hearings will probably start *ex parte* without even a defence presence.[52] It is not clear how judges will determine these disputes, but protecting legitimate defence interests will require a significant step away from the passive pre-trial of the adversarial tradition. The government hardly seemed to acknowledge this, being apparently more concerned to restrict the inconvenience of defence participation rights than to imagine how guarantees of reliability and fairness in investigation could be maintained. Had it done so it might have had to confront the institutional difficulties: simply going through prosecution materials in the 1990s has been said to put significant strains on the workload of Crown Court judges (Glynn, 1993: 847) and, under the new regime, if judges are not simply to take prosecution case-papers on face value they might well have to hear witnesses such as police officers in chambers. Where are these judges to come from? The very absence of a pre-trial role has enabled England and Wales to maintain a very small prestigious cadre of full-time judges hardly adapted to the kind of supervision that proactive policing will require if defence participation is limited. Again, institutional forms and traditions are interwoven.

Conclusion

We hope this particular study illustrates some ways in which procedural tradition and broader legal and political culture can illuminate comparative questions in criminal justice. Procedural tradition must be seen not just as an institutional form but also as a cultural filter that shapes the way in which different countries define and respond to new policing technologies. But procedural tradition must itself be seen in a broader context. First, it is embedded within a broader legal and constitutional culture (*Rechtstaat* versus rule of law and a domestically incorporated ECHR versus a strong tradition of parliamentary sovereignty). Second, the intellectual formations and structures of feeling that constitute different political cultures socially construct the problem of crime in contrasting ways and (re)define the terrain on which criminal process must act. Thus the forms of policing we discuss may have a very different impact within different jurisdictions of 'similar' procedural traditions.[53] Third, legal institutional forms may be affected by tensions between political and legal cultures as jurisdictions strive to manage change. In the Netherlands, the approach to state accountability expressed in its legal culture is having to confront – or perhaps, will have to confront – changes in the political culture of trust. In England and Wales, the demonization of its targets through the mass media has obscured the importance of the challenge of covert and proactive policing to its traditions of state accountability. The fundamental questions – the vulnerability of an adversarial process built around equality of arms to an increasingly technologically sophisticated police force – have hardly been posed in terms of a rethinking of legal cultures.[54] Left as isolated political controversy, it is hard to think through the institutional changes that would be needed to confront the new situation. A full explanation of these diverse responses over a range of jurisdictions is as important a task for scholars of comparative legal cultures as it is for scholars of covert and proactive policing. This chapter is intended as a first tentative attempt at bilateral comparison.

Notes

1 Our thanks to Peter Alldridge for very helpful comments on an earlier draft. The usual disclaimers apply.
2 It may well be that one key progression in research on covert and proactive policing in the future will be towards gathering empirical data on a direct comparative basis. This will not be easy: leaving aside the problems of qualitative cross(legal)cultural research (Nelken, 1997), covert and proactive policing is, almost by definition, a practice surrounded by secrecy and therefore poses special difficulties of access for 'outsiders'. Yet the importance of assessing the normative implications of proactive investigation – both its potential risks to democratic policing and standards of fairness in criminal process – make some kind of comparative interpretation of experience in Europe imperative.
3 To use a peculiarly Continental phrase.
4 For an analysis in English see Andeweg and Irwin (1993), especially ch. 2.
5 In the 1950s and early 1960 Williams was consciously working against the dominant tradition of Arnold, Eliot and Leavis. Thus part of his aim was a broadening, an opening out of the whole notion of culture to embrace 'a total human order' or a 'whole way of life'. See his *Culture and Society* (1958) for his retracing of the broader uses to the nineteenth century and also his *Long Revolution* (1961) and *Politics and Letters* (1979: 154–5).
6 Hence his stress that working-class culture should not be seen as expressed merely through a few proletarian novels but also through the creation of democratic institutions in the trade unions, the cooperative movement or within political parties.
7 For a sustained attempt to see the history of English state formation as cultural form see Corrigan and Sayer (1985).
8 When Williams comments that 'historically, culture was cultivation of something – it was an activity...' it is clear that he is arguing this as one of a web of overlaying linguistic uses that are seen as representing aspects of the overall concept (Williams, 1979: 154).
9 Contrast the differential effect of utilitarianism and philosophic radicalism in the UK and on the Continent in Halevy (1928).
10 For further discussion of the concept of legal tradition see Krygier (1986).
11 For a defence of the connections between general culture and legal culture see Nelken (1997: 82–8) in critique of Blankenburg (1997).
12 This part draws on Brants and Field (1995a) and Field and Pelser (1998).
13 This would embrace: a) observation and surveillance either directly (by tailing or the use of observation posts) or through electronic means (including bugging and interception of communications); b) police infiltration of criminal gangs/networks by use of

Legal Cultures, Political Cultures and Procedural Traditions 109

informers and undercover police officers; c) other kinds of undercover work, such as controlled delivery of illegal goods and services and front store operations.

14 Some definitions extend 'proactive investigation' to include acts performed after the offence but before a reasonable suspicion has arisen. We, for the sake of clarity, take the point of offence to be the key definitional moment.

15 For a stress on the importance of defence prompting in Dutch pre-trial criminal process, see Field et al., (1995).

16 Paid informers were the prime investigative and enforcement technique in the UK just prior to the development of an organized police force. Cf. Greer (1995: 13–15) and also Thompson (1968: 532 ff.).

17 On fear of French republican influence see Armstrong and Hobbs (1995: 177–8).

18 Again, MI5 and Special Branch were (still) using such methods in Northern Ireland.

19 According to the Home Office 7 per cent of males convicted of six or more offences account for 65 per cent of recorded offences (Home Office, 1991).

20 The most high-profile operations have been Operations Bumblebee, Gemini and Eagle-Eye. Operation Bumblebee (originally) in London used some limited undercover operations in setting up fake 'fencing' stores, but mainly involved informers and surveillance to target known burglars (*Guardian*, 17 June 1994). Operation Gemini in Gloucestershire, has directed similar methods at both burglary and car-related crime (*Guardian*, 30 July 1995). For an assessment of these and one other such initiative see Stockdale and Gresham (1995). Operation Eagle Eye has used enhanced intelligence, closed circuit television, other surveillance techniques and information from the public in an operation against street robbery.

21 Even then the Committee concluded that the problem was not as acute as in the rest of Europe – although they saw several potential sources of expansion, especially through connections with East/Central Europe (House of Commons Select Committee on Home Affairs, 1995).

22 *Guardian*, 26 March 1995, 6.

23 Police Act 1997, Parts 1 and 2.

24 For a detailed and sober assessment of the key period after the arrival of Michael Howard at the Home Office in 1993, see Windlesham (1996, especially Part II).

25 For example, the involvement of Turkish immigrants in drug trafficking in the Netherlands is well known. Dutch police files, examined by the criminologists for the parliamentary Van Traa Commission, suggested that around 7000 Turks in the country had connections with the trade. However, close examination revealed that most of these alleged connections lacked substance and many had been included because they were Turks who frequented certain cafes or other 'suspect' places, had contact with other suspects, or were part of their family. Only a quarter of the files showed clear indications of involvement in drug trafficking.

26 'Pillarization' is a direct translation from the Dutch *verzuiling* that is sometimes used in English, but 'the politics of accommodation' is the more common term. See Lijphart (1975), De Haan (1990: 66–70) and Downes (1988: 74ff).

27 Rights especially to freedom from arbitrary arrest and entrance and search of the home, along with more qualified freedoms to liberty, thought, speech and conscience.

28 See Field (1998) for a critique of some assessments of the crime control results of covert and proactive policing.

29 Articles 141 and 142 of the Code of Criminal Procedure and the former Article 26, now Article 2, Police Act 1993.

30 R v. *Khan* [1996] 3 All ER 289.

31 R v. *MPC, ex parte* Blackburn [1968] 2 QB 118 at 136 (*per* Lord Denning).

32 Sir Robert Mark's period as Metropolitan Police Commissioner gave new impetus to the process in the 1970s.
33 *Inzake Opsporing*, 1996. The commission of inquiry (Commission Van Traa) held public and televised sessions, commissioned a vast amount of research, heard hundreds of witnesses and experts, and published its findings in a report that ran to 11 volumes.
34 For example, the use of technical bugging devices (see Bevan and Lidstone, 1991: 210–14 for a summary of the rules) and participating informers (see Greer and South, 1998). Condemnation at Strasbourg had meant that telephone tapping required the authority of the Home Secretary (Interception of Telecommunications Act 1985). Bugging other than via a public telephone system requires the consent of the Home Secretary if it is carried out by MI5 in pursuit of its new mandate under the Security Service Act 1996 to investigate 'serious crime' but before the 1997 Police Act (see below) the only prior authority for any kind of electronic surveillance required in police investigation was that of the chief constable.
35 That is, the principal offence for which the police are trying to catch the target, as opposed to some more trivial preliminary or precursor offence.
36 *R v. Ward* (1993) 96 Cr App R 1 at 25 and 57.
37 Only if a judge on application by the prosecution ruled that the public interest in concealing sensitive material outweighed defence rights to information could material be withheld.
38 *R v. McIlkenny* [1992] 2 All ER 417 at 425–6.
39 The flavour can be gleaned from the newspaper headings: see Rose (1997), Davies (1997a, 1997b), Connett (1997).
40 Police Bill, announced July 1996: see Campbell (1996), 'Howard sets statutory code for police bugs', *Guardian*, 3 July 1996.
41 See leading articles 'Will Bugging be Warranted?', 'A Liberty-taking Bill' and 'Liberty and Property', *Daily Telegraph*, 3, 14 and 22 January 1997; Letter to the Editor: 'Holes in Howard's Police Bill', *Daily Telegraph*, 16 January 1997; leading article: 'Bugging Should be by Judicial Warrant', *Daily Mail*, 14 January 1997.
42 II K, 1996–1997, 25403 nrs. A, B, 1–3.
43 In some of these cases permission must come from the Procurators-General advised by a Central Review Committee. For details see Field and Jörg (1998).
44 This confirms the ending of the special practice that had developed and which lead to the IRT scandal, of certain proactive investigations (those involving the importation and sale of cannabis under controlled circumstances) being conducted but concealed from Prosecutor and *Rechter-Commissaris* (examining magistrate).
45 See *Kostovski v. The Netherlands*, ECHR 20.11.1989, Series A no. 106.
46 The relevant premises are dwellings, hotel bedrooms or offices or where the device is likely to pick up matters subject to legal privilege (client/lawyer discussions) or material held in confidence and acquired or created in a professional context (which specifically includes journalism). There is also special protection in respect of lawyers, doctors, journalists and others who hold confidential records: (Police Act 1997, s. 99).
47 There are other anxieties for civil libertarians about the detail of the Act that we do not have time to deal with.
48 S. 3(1) It is apparently not enough to require disclosure that material 'may be relevant to' the defence case.
49 Home Office (1997), para. 6.12.
50 S. 5(4).
51 Provisionally because the trial judge might decide during the course of the trial that the

information had to be revealed after all. Note that preparatory hearings are defined as part of the trial, so technically decisions there are not part of the pre-trial process.
52 JUSTICE in its recent consultation paper on disclosure suggested that such *ex parte* applications have become very frequent, being used in relation to almost all informer cases (JUSTICE, 1995).
53 For some suggestive, rather than extensively documented, ideas on the way national differences may be ascribed in part to different traditions of citizen–state relations see also Marx (1995) and Nadelman (1995).
54 For a start which received very little media attention, see JUSTICE (1998).

References

Ames, J. (1994), 'Nickel Case Acquittal: Good News for Justice', *Law Society Gazette*, **91** (34), 4.
Andeweg R.B. and Irwin, G.A. (1993), *Dutch Government and Politics*, London: Macmillan.
Armstrong, G. and Hobbs, D. (1995), 'The Policing of Soccer Hooliganism', in C. Fijnaut and G. Marx (eds), *Undercover: Police Surveillance in Comparative Perspective*, The Hague: Kluwer Law International.
Audit Commission (1993), *Tackling Crime Effectively*, London: Audit Commission.
Bevan V. and Lidstone, K. (1991), *The Investigation of Crime*, London: Butterworths.
Blankenburg, E. (1997), 'Civil Litigation Rates as Indicators for Legal Cultures' in D. Nelken (ed.) (1997), *Comparing Legal Cultures*, Aldershot: Dartmouth.
Brants, C. and Field, S. (1995a), *Participation Rights and Proactive Policing: Convergence and Drift in European Criminal Process*, Deventer: Kluwer.
Brants, C. and Field, S. (1995b), 'Discretion and Accountability in Prosecution: A Comparative Perspective on Keeping Crime out of Court', in P. Fennell, C. Harding, N. Jörg and B. Swart (eds) (1995), *Criminal Justice in Europe*, Oxford: Clarendon Press.
Brants, C. and Field, S. (1997), 'Les méthodes d'enquête proactives et le contrôle des risques', *Déviance et Société*, **21** (4), 401.
Brants, C. (1999), 'Prostitution and Regulated Tolerance in the Netherlands', *Journal of Law and Society*, **25** (4), 621.
Brewer, J. and Styles, J. (1980), 'Popular Attitudes to Law in the 18th Century', in J. Brewer and J. Styles (eds), *An Ungovernable People*, London: Hutchinson.
Busch, H. and Funk, A. (1995), 'Undercover Tactics as an Element of Preventive Crime Fighting in the Federal Republic of Germany', in C. Fijnaut and G. Marx (eds), *Undercover: Police Surveillance in Comparative Perspective*, The Hague: Kluwer Law International.
Campbell, D. (1996), 'Howard Sets Statistical Code for Police Bugs', *Guardian*, 3 July.
Cape, E. and Spronken, T. (1998), 'Proactive Policing: Limiting the Role of the Defence Lawyer', in S. Field and C. Pelser (eds), *Invading the Private? State*

Accountability and New Police Investigative Methods in Europe, Aldershot: Dartmouth.
Connett, D. (1997), 'Tactics under Fire as Police use more Informants', *Observer*, 30 March.
Corrigan, P. and Sayer, D. (1985), *The Great Arch: English State Formation as Cultural Revolution*, Oxford: Blackwell.
Cotterrell, R. (1997), 'The Concept of Legal Culture', in D. Nelken (ed.), *Comparing Legal Cultures*, Aldershot: Dartmouth.
Critchley, T.A. (1978), *A History of the Police in England and Wales*, London: Constable.
Davies, N. (1997a), 'Police Yardie Scandal', *Guardian*, 3 February.
Davies, N. (1997b), 'Second Front: How the Yardies Duped the Yard', *Guardian*, 3 February.
De Haan, W. (1990), *The Politics of Redress. Crime, Punishment and Penal Abolition*, London: Unwin Hyman.
Delmas-Marty, M. (Chair) (1991), *La Mise en Etat des Affaires Pénales*, Paris: La Documentation Française.
Doherty, M. (1994), 'Watching the Detectives', *New Law Journal*, **144** (66–70), 1525–6.
Dorn, N., Murji, K. and South, N. (1992), *Traffickers: Drug Markets and Law Enforcement*, London: Routledge.
Downes, D. (1988), *Contrasts in Tolerance. Post-war Penal Policy in the Netherlands and England and Wales*, Oxford: Clarendon Press.
Downes, D. and Morgan, R. (1997), 'Dumping the Hostages to Fortune? The Politics of Law and Order in Post-War Britain' in M. Maguire, R. Morgan and R. Reiner, *The Oxford Handbook of Criminology*, Oxford: Clarendon Press.
Dunninghan, C. and Norris, C. (1996), 'The Nark's Game', *New Law Journal*, 22 March.
Ewing, K. and Gearty, G. (1997), 'Check Mission Control', *Guardian*, 12 February.
Field, S. (1998), 'Invading the Private? Towards Conclusions', in S. Field and C. Pelser (eds), *Invading the Private? State Accountability and New Police Investigative Methods in Europe*, Aldershot: Dartmouth.
Field, S. and Jörg, N. (1998), 'Judicial Regulation of Covert and Proactive Policing in the Netherlands and England and Wales', in S. Field and C. Pelser (eds), *Invading the Private? State Accountability and New Police Investigative Methods in Europe*, Aldershot: Dartmouth.
Field, S., Alldridge, P. and Jörg, N. (1995), 'Prosecutors, Examining Judges and Control of Police Investigations', in P. Fennell, C. Harding, N. Jörg and B. Swart (eds), *Criminal Justice in Europe*, Oxford: Clarendon Press.
Field, S. and Pelser, C. (1998), *Invading the Private? State Accountability and New Police Investigative Methods in Europe*, Aldershot: Dartmouth.
Fijnaut, C. and Marx, G. (eds) (1995), *Undercover: Police Surveillance in Comparative Perspective*, The Hague: Kluwer Law International.
Fionda, I. (1995), *Public Prosecutors and Discretion: A Comparative Study*, Oxford: Clarendon Press.

Friedman, L.M. (1997), 'The Concept of Legal Culture: A Reply', in D. Nelken (ed.), *Comparing Legal Cultures*, Aldershot: Dartmouth.
Friedman, R.D. (1998), 'Thoughts from Across the Water on Hearsay and Confrontation', *Criminal Law Review*, 697.
Garland, D. (1990), *Punishment and Modern Society*, Oxford: Oxford University Press.
Garland, D. (1996), 'The Limits of the Sovereign State', *British Journal of Criminology*, **36** (4), 445.
Gessner, V., Hoeland, A. and Varga, C. (eds) (1996), *European Legal Cultures*, Aldershot: Dartmouth.
Gibb, F. (1994), 'DPP Blames Law on Disclosure for Guilty going Free', *The Times*, 29 November.
Glynn, J. (1993), 'The Royal Commission on Criminal Justice: (4) Disclosure', *Criminal Law Review*, 841.
Greer, S. (1995), *Supergrasses, A Study in Anti-Terrorist Law Enforcement in Northern Ireland*, Oxford: Clarendon Press.
Greer, S. and South, N. (1998), 'The Criminal Informant: Police Management, Supervision and Control', in S. Field and C. Pelser (eds), *Invading the Private? State Accountability and New Police Investigative Methods in Europe*, Aldershot: Dartmouth.
Guardian (1997), 'Editorial', 17 and 21 January.
Halevy, F. (1928), *The Growth of Philosophic Radicalism*, London: Faber and Faber.
Hall, S. (1980), *Drifting into a Law and Order Society*, London: Cobden Trust.
Hall, S. and McLennan, G. (1981), 'Custom and Law: Law and Crime as Historical Processes', in Open University Course Team D335, *Law and Disorder: Histories of Crime and Justice*, Milton Keynes: Open University Press.
Harding, L. (1997), 'Stagg at Bay', *Guardian*, 15 January.
Hay, D. (1975), 'Property, Authority and the Criminal Law', in D. Hay, P. Linebaugh and E.P. Thompson, *Albion's Fatal Tree*, London: Allen Lane.
Home Office (1991), *Digest of Information on Criminal Justice System*, London: HMSO.
Home Office (1995), *Disclosure: A Consultation Document*, Cm 2864, London: HMSO.
Hoogenboom, B. (1995), 'Over de betrekkelijkheid van het debat over opsporingsmethoden. Proactivering in relatie tot bijzondere opsporingsdiensten en particuliere recherche', *Delikt en Delinkwent*, **25** (6), 570.
House of Commons Select Committee on Home Affairs (1995), House of Commons papers session 1994–5, *Third Report: Organised Crime*, Vol. 1, London: HMSO.
Inzake Opsporing: Enquêtecommissie opsporingsmethoden, Bijl, Hand. TK 1995–96, 24072.
Jörg, N., Field, S. and Brants, C. (1995), 'Are Inquisitorial and Adversarial Systems Converging?', in P. Fennell, C. Harding, N. Jörg and B. Swart (eds), *Criminal Justice in Europe*, Oxford: Clarendon Press.

JUSTICE (1995), *Disclosure: A Consultation Paper, the JUSTICE Response*, London: JUSTICE.
JUSTICE (1998), *Under Surveillance: Covert Policing and Human Rights Standards*, London: JUSTICE.
Klerks, P. (1995), 'Covert Policing in the Netherlands', in C. Fijnaut and G. Marx (eds), *Undercover: Police Surveillance in Comparative Perspective*, The Hague: Kluwer International.
Krygier, M. (1986), 'Law as Tradition', *Law and Philosophy*, 5, 237.
Lacey, N. (1994), 'Government as Manager, Citizen as Consumer: The Case of the Criminal Justice Act 1991', *Michigan Law Review*, 57 (4), 534.
Langbein, J. (1978), 'The Criminal Trial before the Lawyers', *University of Chicago Law Review*, 45 (2), 263.
Langbein, J. (1983), 'Shaping the Eighteenth-Century Criminal Trial: A View from the Ryder Sources', *University of Chicago Law Review*, 50 (1), 1.
Langbein, J. (1997), 'The Privilege and Common Law Criminal Procedure: The Sixteenth to the Eighteenth Centuries', in R.H. Helmholz et al., *The Privilege against Self-Incrimination: Its Origins and Development*, Chicago: University of Chicago Press.
Leishman, F., Loveday, B. and Savage, S. (1996), *Core Issues in Policing*, London: Longman.
Lijphart, A. (1975), *The Politics of Accommodation*, (2nd rev. edn), Berkeley and Los Angeles, CA: University of California Press.
Lester, A. (1997), 'A Question of Balance', *Observer*, 19 January.
Lustgarten, L. (1986), *The Governance of the Police*, London: Sweet and Maxwell.
Maguire, M. and John, T. (1995), *Intelligence, Surveillance and Informants: Integrated Approaches*, Police Research Group Crime Detection and Prevention Series, Paper 64, London: Home Office.
Marx, G. (1995), 'Undercover in Comparative Perspective: Some Implications for Knowledge and Social Research', in C. Fijnaut and G. Marx (eds), *Undercover: Police Surveillance in Comparative Perspective*, The Hague: Kluwer Law International.
McBarnet, D.J. (1981), *Conviction: Law, the State and the Construction of Justice*, London: Macmillan.
Merryman, J.H. (1985), *The Civil Law Tradition*, (2nd edn), Stanford, CA: Stanford University Press.
Ministry of Justice (1996), *In juiste verhouding, Beleidsvoornemens m.b.t., Rechtshandshaving en veiligheid*, Den Haag: SDU .
Nadelman, E. (1995), 'The DEA in Europe', in C. Fijnaut and G. Marx (eds), *Undercover: Police Surveillance in Comparative Perspective*, The Hague: Kluwer Law International.
Nelken, D. (1997), 'Puzzling out Legal Culture: A Comment on Blankenburg', in D. Nelken (ed.), *Comparing Legal Cultures*, Aldershot: Dartmouth.
Riehle, E. (1985), 'Verdacht, Gefahr und Risiko: der V-mann: ein weiterer Sehrritt auf dem Wege zu einer anderen Polizei', *Kriminologisches Journal*, 44.
Rose, D. (1995), 'On the Dangerous Road to a Police State', *Observer*, 21 May.
Rose, D. (1997), 'Drugs Catch Sunk by Crime Squad', *Observer*, 26 January.

Spencer, J. (1998), 'Proactive Policing and the Principles of Immediacy and Orality', in S. Field and C. Pelser (eds), *Invading the Private? State Accountability and New Police Investigative Methods in Europe*, Aldershot: Dartmouth.
Stockdale, J. and Gresham, P. (1995), *Combating Burglary: An Evaluation of Three Strategies*, Crime Detection and Prevention Series Paper 59, London: Home Office Police Research Group.
Swart, B. and Young, J. (1995), 'The European Convention on Human Rights and Criminal Justice in the Netherlands and the United Kingdom', in P. Fennell, C. Harding, N. Jörg and B. Swart (eds), *Criminal Justice in Europe*, Oxford: Clarendon Press.
Thompson, E.P. (1968), *The Making of the English Working Class*, London: Penguin.
Thompson, E.P. (1975), *Whigs and Hunters*, London: Allen Lane.
Thompson, E.P. (1980), *Writing by Candlelight*, London: Merlin.
Travis, A. (1997), 'Straw U-Turn on "spybill"', *Guardian*, 27 January.
Van De Wyngaert, C. (1993), *Criminal Procedure Systems in the European Community*, London: Butterworths.
Wadham, J. and Colvin, M. (1997), 'Good as Far as it Goes', *Guardian*, 17 January.
Williams, R. (1958), *Culture and Society*, London: Chatto and Windus.
Williams, R. (1961), *The Long Revolution*, London: Penguin.
Williams, R. (1979), *Politics and Letters*, London: NLB.
Windlesham, L. (1996), *Responses to Crime: Legislating with the Tide*, Oxford: Clarendon Press.
Young, H. (1997), 'Wake up and Defend our Basic Freedoms', *Guardian*, 4 March.
Zedner, L. (1995), 'In Pursuit of the Vernacular: Comparing Law and Order Discourse in Britain and Germany', *Social and Legal Studies*, **4** (4), 517.

5 Comparing Women's Prisons: Epistemological and Methodological Issues

Marie-Andrée Bertrand

Introduction

Depending on their epistemological and methodological persuasion, social scientists entertain different views on the feasibility and uses of comparisons. At one extreme of an imagined spectrum, the positivists–quantitativists seem to have no qualms about comparing because, to them, social facts are real things posited out there, to be studied by distanced neutral observers with methods as close as possible to those of the natural scientists; they love secondary and tertiary data such as censuses and surveys and, when they occasionally collect original data, it is 'to add depth' to the information already gathered. Their research results can be set out in one table of packed mathematical symbols that makes for a beautiful comparative *exposé*. At the other end of the spectrum, social scientists, closer to the subjectivist–qualitativist stance, often feel handicapped when asked to make a comparison. For one thing, they know that what they see[1] is a representation – a social construction of the observer's socialization, culture, gender, age, social position, ethnic appurtenance and so on. To avoid gathering information that is the result of multiple reconstructions, they study 'the scenario' directly, themselves, using the least invasive and the most natural techniques. At the analytical stage, they will let the material speak for itself, and the differences and similarities 'appear'. The process is lengthy, and the results not reducible to a single statistical table.

The above picture is of course a Manichean one. It is also slightly obsolete. Nowadays, hard positivism is not very fashionable among objectivists. The 'in' thing is post-positivism in which naïve realism is being replaced with critical realism. Methodologically, the post-positivists pride themselves on *triangulation* and make increasing use of qualitative 'techniques'. Changes are taking place in the subjectivists' camp as well: 'structural' constructivism is 'in', and qualitative methodologists are busy defending the *scientificness* of their methods (Poupart, 1997) while standpointists claim *strong objectivity* (Harding, 1991).

What precedes is meant as an introduction to the case in point – a comparative study of women's prisons in which a *verstehen* approach and qualitative methods were used.

A Comparative Study of Women's Prisons

The international comparative research on women's prisons (Bertrand et al., 1998) went on from 1993 until late 1997. It was conducted by a team of professors and students[2] attached to the School of Criminology and the International Centre for Comparative Criminology at the University of Montreal, and supported by the Social Science and Humanities Council of Canada, with occasional grants from the Correctional Service of Canada and the International Centre for Comparative Criminology.

The team went out to observe 16 closed prisons for women and eight 'open' ones in eight different countries: England and Scotland, Germany, Denmark, Norway, Finland, Canada and the United States (see Table 5.1). Epistemologically, the team was inspired by Schutz's life-world theory (*Lebenswelt*) and concept of subjective understanding (*verstehen*)[3] (Schutz, 1962, 1964, 1966, 1982; Schutz and Luckmann, 1973), and by Berger and Luckmann's social constructivism (1967). In making their critical examination of their subject – women's prisons – the researchers had chosen to take the materialist feminist perspective (Delphy, 1970, 1975; Guillaumin, 1978; Juteau and Laurin, 1988) and to use MacKinnon's radical feminist critique of the state (1989). Their minimalist, or even abolitionist, position on prisons and captivity owed much to Christie (1981, 1993), Cohen and Taylor (1972), Foucault (1975), Goffman (1968), Hulsman with Bernat de Celis (1982), and Mathiesen (1974 and 1990).

Methodologically, the team relied mostly on qualitative techniques, non-participant observation, plus open and semi-structured interviews (Lofland, 1971; Schatzman and Strauss, 1973; Strauss, 1987) of the prison staff, local actors and national experts. The researchers also made use of secondary and tertiary sources of quantitative data such as national and international incarceration rates and statistics of the prisons' populations. They also delved into analytic documents like the prisons' history and inmates' handbooks (prison guides).

Comparing Women's Prisons 119

Table 5.1 List of Sites Studied

Country	Closed prisons	Open prisons
Canada	Montreal (Maison Tanguay) Kingston (Prison for Women) Minimum security facility – MacNeil House Orsainville (Centre de détention de Québec) women's section Burnaby (Correctional Centre for Women) Open living unit	Montreal (Maison Thérèse Casgrain, Society Elizabeth Fry) Kingston (Joyce Detweiller House, Elizabeth Fry Society) Quebec (Centre Expansion – Femmes)
United States	Framingham (Massachusetts Correctional Institution) Pittsburgh (County Jail) Waynesburg (State Correctional Institution for Women) Shakopee (Minnesota Correctional Facility) Independent living centre	Boston (Neil J. Houston House, Social Justice for Women) Pittsburgh (The Program Centre, The Program for Female Offenders)
England	Durham (Her Majesty's Prison) Holloway (Her Majesty's Prison)	
Scotland	Corton Vale (Her Majesty's Prison)	
Germany	(East) Butzow (West) Vechta	Bremen
Denmark	Ringe	Horserod
Finland	Hameenlinna	
Norway	Bredtveit	Ostensjoveien
N=8	N=16	N=8

The Intellectual Agenda

At the knowledge ('scientific') level, the research group wanted to see if the well documented theses on the obsolescent and discriminatory character of penal institutions for women were still valid in the 1990s. Their general hypothesis was that women's prisons constitute a very telling *social representation* of the place and status 'granted' to women in each country, to be interpreted in its proper context – that of the country's criminal justice system. Furthermore, having observed the Canadian and US penal systems and men's prisons for some years, the research directors hypothesized that the programmes and regimes in women's prisons would leave more to be desired than those in men's prisons in the same country.

The working hypotheses were as follows:

1 In the 1990s, in advanced countries, prisons for women will still be seriously lacking in up-to-date education, training and work programmes. On each of those fronts, nothing 'inside' will resemble even remotely what the average woman can access in her country and social milieu. Also, work and training programmes in prisons for women will be more outdated than is the case in men's prisons. But the more 'humane' the national criminal justice system and the more advanced sex equality in the country, the less will be the observable distance between the internal and external conditions, and between men's and women's prisons.

2 While more decent than they were 20 years ago, physical and mental health services will still be very deficient. Inmates will have no direct access to doctors, psychiatrists and psychologists, nor to one of their choice. Referrals will be made by the staff on a discretionary basis. There will be nothing specific to meet women's particular health needs.

3 Despite the existence of human rights charters in each of the countries under study, family contacts and sexual relations with spouses or long-time partners will be scarce and allowed on a discretionary basis. Statutory provisions for vacations in the family each year, as in Germany, may reduce the effect of incarceration on family dissociation.

4 In all the countries the physical constraints on inmates' movements inside the prison and in the adjacent spaces, and the organizational and psychological control of their use of time will be disproportionate to the known risks that 90 per cent of the women inmates represent inside and to the community at large; the great majority of female inmates could safely be transferred to open prisons or community centres. The routine in the women's prisons and the way in which prison staff exercise their power over inmates will prove to be unnecessarily burdensome and infantilizing, compared to the regimes in men's prisons.

Comparing Women's Prisons 121

There are documented exceptions to these obsolescent and irrational approaches and there are also known examples of prisons geared to women's needs (see below). However, it remains to be seen how useful to women these actually are.

The Political Agenda and the Choice of Sites

The research was undertaken at a time of upheaval in prisons for women in Canada. The one and only federal penitentiary for long-term women convicts was being closed and the plans were to replace it by four less centralized facilities more in line with women's needs. Since it was a good time to put pressure on the Canadian correctional authorities by collecting and disseminating information on plausible alternatives to traditional prisons for women, the team entertained a political agenda as well as an intellectual one. The overall study aimed to highlight documented and contrasting evidence of different models, original formulas, experiences in decarceration and minimum imprisonment and progressive up-to-date work and training programmes geared to women's needs. However, the above-mentioned 'intellectual' or scientific agenda required that detailed observations also be gathered on all major detention centre(s) for women, especially in Canada, however archaic those might be.

The selection of the non-traditional sites, programmes and formulas was made after a careful review of the literature and in consultation with feminist criminologists and national experts. In many instances it was primarily the documented exceptionality of institutions that determined the choice. Such was the case with Shakopee, in Minnesota, USA, known for the quality of its work and education programme and its focused attention on women's needs; Ringe, in Denmark, for its complete mix of genders; the BC correctional institution for women at Burnaby in Canada, for its extra-modernity and the newness of some of its programmes; and, more generally, the German prisons for women known for their mother–child units and the Frankfurt prison for women. On the issue of decarceration and minimum imprisonment, the team looked to the Scandinavian 'model' and these countries' low incarceration rates. While Finnish and Norwegian prisons for women were not particularly original or *avant-garde*, it was the countries' overall penal reputation that attracted the researchers, as well as the co-correctional character of the central prison for women at Hameenlinna in Finland, and the new open prison for women near Oslo in Norway.

The observation grid was designed to collect data on four issues related to the hypotheses:

1 the current training and work programme in terms of its accessibility and modernity;
2 the quality and gender-specificity of the mental and physical health services;
3 the institutional arrangements meant to help maintain or restore the relations between inmates and those close to them, especially their partners and children;
4 the prison's disciplinary regime, the constraints on physical freedom to come and go, to relate to the outside, and the levels of security compared to the inmates' relative 'dangerousness' and to the arrangements in men's prisons.

Epistemological Issues

The research concerned women's prisons studied from a feminist materialist perspective as structural entities of the state apparatus, rather than women prisoners themselves. While such an objective was theoretically compatible with a subjectivist–qualitativist approach à la Schutz and à la Strauss, things proved more difficult in practice. The researchers realized that they could not plan to interview directly Danish, Norwegian, Finnish and German prisoners due to lack of proficiency in some of the languages, and that the use of intermediaries would not yield interesting and meaningful information. But the language barrier was not the only one. For instance, even in English- and French-speaking countries or states, it was far from guaranteed that the prison authorities would have allowed the researchers to formally interview a sample of inmates. More importantly, if the interviews were to lead to significant information, the time spent inside, limited as it was by financial contingencies, was too short (three weeks maximum) to allow for the establishment of a trusting relationship. Clearly, attempts had to be made to compensate for the lack of formal systematic input from the inmates.

To overcome these problems the researchers devised some strategies. They decided to sit in inmates' meetings as often as possible, engage systematically in conversations with small groups of prisoners at mealtimes and to interact with individual prisoners while they were taking part in their training and work programmes. At the preplanning stage the team learned, through its local informants, that a significant proportion of the inmates in European prisons – up to 30 per cent – were foreigners, speaking Spanish, French, Italian and some English with whom they would be able to converse.[4] Finally, they hoped that, in some cases,[5] inmates would be asked by the administration to act as their guides, as happens in Canadian and US prisons, and even though the team knew full well that it was not 'any'

Comparing Women's Prisons 123

inmate who would be asked or allowed to chaperone them, they planned to take maximum advantage of such opportunities and make good use of these hours of contact.

Methodological Issues

In studies lasting over four years, not only does the scenario change, but the observers also evolve and mature. This means the *measure* – the *constant* which must be relied on – becomes evanescent. With regard to the scenario itself, important modifications took place in two of the closed prisons after the study visit,[6] and this made the team very conscious of the time-limited character of the observations collected. For their part, the researchers became more familiar with the field and the method. As the study progressed, their observations became more complete and the interviews more cleverly done and, as a result, information gathered during the later site visits was much richer than that collected earlier: on the whole, the data collected in the later stages of the study were of a different quality. Furthermore, there were variations in the number of observers on the site. In principle, the field study was to be conducted by teams of at least three observers in as many locations as was financially possible and acceptable to the hosts. But, in fact, nine closed prisons – those of England (2), Scotland (1), Germany (3), Norway (2) and Finland (1) – were studied by one researcher alone. These field visits, however, took place in the middle or last part of the study and were carried out by the two study directors – both experienced researchers who were familiar with women's prisons. At the other extreme, in the first year of the study, three closed prisons were researched by the entire team. Third, the time spent 'inside' varied. While 'large' closed prisons could take on the observers for many days or weeks, that was not possible in small community centres housing 10–15 residents, and these were studied for shorter periods, usually by two observers. Yet another variation in the method of approach derived from the fact that, in Germany and Norway, national experts[7] accompanied the researcher inside. As those experts are well known to the staff their presence must have influenced the latters' reactions to the researcher and to the study.

To 'normalize' the quality of the data and render the information comparable from site to site, the team resorted to the following strategies:

1 Individual notes were shared and analysed in full team meetings.
2 Three team members became responsible for writing 'agreed upon group reports' on the sites that had been studied by more than one team member.

3   Preliminary reports on the Norwegian, Danish, German, and Finnish prisons were sent for review to local actors and national experts,[8] who had acted as informants. (The researcher who had carried out the observation in Northern European countries went back to discuss her reports with her consultants, fill up the blanks, correct the factual errors and nuance her interpretations, then sent back final reports to the same correspondents who wrote their comments.)
4   Reports on the UK prisons were read by one English expert[9] who had himself studied Durham prison (though not the women's section) and who made very useful comments on English and Scottish prisons and other sites.

In sum, intense and methodical teamwork was used to compensate for the lack of uniformity in the number of observers and quality of their observations. Substantial oral and written feedback was requested and obtained from local actors and experts on those reports written in situations where the team was on less familiar ground and where the sites had been studied by one researcher alone.

Comparability of the Sites: Questions and Comments

Prisons for women are few. In fact, in the majority of the countries or states where the research team was to conduct its observations and that had been chosen for the originality of one or two programmes, there was only one closed prison for women: this was the case in Scotland, Norway, Denmark, Finland, and the US state of Minnesota. In other countries, where there was a relative choice (England, Canada and other US states), the team studied more than one institution in their search for diversity.

Penologists who read the first research reports raised some interesting questions about the comparability of prison sites. For instance, they asked whether it was legitimate to compare penal institutions deriving their rules from two different legal systems, the Romano-Germanic one in Europe, and the common law one in the UK, USA and Canada, since the former often makes greater use of presentence detention than the latter. Again, with regard to differences emanating from the socio-juridical systems, they asked whether account should be taken of the fact that they engender different sentencing guidelines and legislative clauses and the presence or absence of a parole system, all of which impacts on the length of the sentences served, which in turn has a serious effect on the imprisonment rates. The first question can be answered quickly; the institutions studied in the research were *prisons receiving sentenced prisoners only*. Some occasionally or regularly held a few women awaiting trial (generally for humanitarian or 'proximity') reasons, but such pre-trial inmates were not counted in the population studied, nor did the team observe their detention conditions. The second question is more complex and I have no complete answer to it because the research did not make a detailed comparative examination of the national sentencing policies. The question, however, seems to postulate disparities that are not found in practice between the two systems: for instance, not all common law countries or states have a parole system (for example, the state of Minnesota does not have one) and conditional early release, subject to supervision, is practised in some European countries but is nevertheless subject to supervision, as is the case in some German *Länder* and in Norway, even though it is not called 'parole'.

A third question was 'Is it not unwise to compare prisons located in countries with such widely distant incarceration rates, like, for instance, the Scandinavian ones (60–70) as against the United States (500+)?' There are several answers to this: First, in this study detention rates were taken as intervening variables hypothetically affecting the conditions to which prisoners in general, and women in particular, would be subjected. In terms of a low rate of imprisonment, for instance, the assumptions were that it might mean smaller prisons, manageable groups of inmates which make for a less difficult life inside; it might also be taken as an indicator of a criminal policy aiming in general at decency, moderation and humanness. However, the latter assumption proved mistaken, at least regarding women's prisons, as shown later. Second, and more importantly, the research team was not studying all or any US prisons but that of the state of Minnesota[10] where the detention rate is comparable to that of Finland and Norway and slightly lower than that of England and Scotland (see Table 5.2). Third, the chosen countries were comparable and relatively similar on one key aspect of the study – that is, their social policies that affect women's lives. All are democratic First World countries with a concern for their citizens' quality of life; all of them also have a reputation for pursuing sex equality in education, at work, and in social and political life – a concern that hypothetically could, or should, impact on correctional policies and practices.

In fact, it is in the USA, a country denounced by criminologists for its correctional policies, that the team found a women's prison and two post-penal resources that leave less to be desired and are best geared to women's needs. Faced with that result which struck them as paradoxical, and trying to make sense of it, two penologists formulated the following comment and suggestion: 'in very large countries like the US, one is bound to find among the hundreds of carceral and post-carceral institutions for women some "less worse" than others'. My answer to that is that, while that statistical rule makes much sense in advanced First World countries (I doubt whether there are 'nice' prisons for women in India and Russia, whatever the number

Table 5.2 Detention Rate and Percentage of Women Among Prisoners

	Detention rates (per 100,000)	Women prisoners (%)
Norway	60.0	4.6
Finland	61.8	3.5
Denmark	71.0	4.8
Germany	81.0	4.3
England and Wales	89.0	3.7
Canada	114.3	6.5
Scotland	115.0	3.0
United States	529.0	5.7
Minnesota	78.0	5.5
Massachusetts	143.0	6.7
Pennsylvania	192.0	4.7

* The figures quoted are those of 1993 for Europe and Canada and 1991 in the USA.

Sources:
Europe: Council of Europe (1994–95); *United States*: Bureau of Justice Statistics (1992, 1993a, 1993b); *Canada*: Centre canadien de la statistique juridique (1993).

of carceral institutions) it is not applicable here. The American prison in question – the one located at Shakope – is the only correctional institution for women in the state of Minnesota, and its mandate is nearly identical to that of the central prisons for women in Finland, Denmark, Norway and Scotland. True, there are federal prisons in the USA in addition to the state ones, but the former receive less than one-tenth of the total convicted offenders; indeed, not one woman from Minnesota was incarcerated in any federal institution at the time of the study. Hence, all women sentenced to prison in the state had to be incarcerated at Shakopee.

The Findings

The first hypothesis on the obsolescence and paucity of work and training programmes proved true in the great majority of the cases (13 out of the 16 closed prisons). The only complete exception was to be found at Shakopee in Minnesota where not only are the programmes up-to-date but they are also numerous, diverse and women-oriented. There existed other exceptions to the rule of obsolescence – at Burnaby Vechta, Holloway and Durham –

but these exceptions affected only parts of the institutions' general routine and were opened to small groups of inmates on a discretionary basis. The general rule was the following: at the time of the study, 80–90 per cent of all women inmates in 15 of the 16 closed prisons (the exception here being Shakopee), in Europe and in North America, worked and/or were trained in laundries, knitting and sewing workshops, the prison kitchen, or on small industrial contracts manufacturing pencils, plastic toys and dishes. Everywhere newcomers were allocated house cleaning duties. Access to post-secondary education was positively denied to all women imprisoned in Scandinavia, Germany, Canada and Scotland, while men prisoners in those countries get some access to university courses. The only prisons for women among those studied where inmates had access to post-secondary education through correspondence courses were Holloway and Durham in England, and Shakopee in the USA. A litigation case involving a Canadian woman inmate who had been denied equal access to post-secondary education was won in the Federal Court of Justice in 1992 and the woman had to be transferred to a BC men's prison to attend classes at Simon Fraser University together with her male fellow inmates.[11]

The second hypothesis had to do with the mental and physical health services, in terms of their relative lack of quality and accessibility. The assumption of poor accessibility proved correct: nowhere did the inmates have direct access to a physician or to one of their choice when there was more than one attached to the institution. However, the relative absence of quality was disproved in common law countries where modernity of the equipment, the variety of services and the staff competence ran contrary to the hypothesis. Among the health professionals were many women who showed great concern for the particular needs of women inmates. There was nothing of this sort in Scandinavia and Germany, where there is almost no health service inside, except perhaps a small, not very inviting, infirmary where an inmate can be kept under a nurse's surveillance for a couple of hours. 'Serious cases' (decided by whom?) are sent to the nearby hospital. In-house psychological services are non-existent in Continental European prisons, but are abundant in common law countries. In Northern Europe, severely mentally disturbed inmates are sent to a central facility. Only recently have self-help groups such as AA and NA been admitted into European prisons for women.

The third hypothesis on the lack of prison facilities for family visiting inside was partly disproved. In common law countries there existed nearly everywhere, except at Shakopee, family trailers in the prison grounds, or special rooms in the prison itself, where the inmate could spend up to 72 hours with her spouse or long-time male partner, and with her young children, at regular intervals (every six weeks) after the first months or years of imprisonment. However, as hypothesized, access to the family trailer or special visitation room was a privilege that could be taken away for a number of reasons, and the limited availability of the facility created serious constraints. In Germany, as expected and according to the country's prison law, prisoners are allowed to spend two to three weeks in their family per year; however, that proved unhelpful to the majority of women inmates who, after a short period inside, no longer had a waiting spouse, had no home to go to, and, in fact, no more family. The central location and 'uniqueness' of women's prisons (the fact that there is only one per country or state) contribute decisively to family dislocation and to the growing estrangement of women inmates from their loved ones and social milieu. The prisons' location and 'uniqueness' have been judged discriminatory when compared to the decentralized and diverse men's prisons, and this seems particularly unfair because familial and other affective relations are usually of greater importance to women than men in our societies. That inequality in treatment has been recognized in courts in more than one country and partially corrected by sending sentenced women to men's regional or local facilities (in Finland, Norway, Canada). Finally, the material organization of women's prisons – the fact that in general all inmates at all phases of their detention time are in the same building – prevents any serious attempt at classification and progressive release, another factor conducive to family and social dislocation and increased rigidity in the security controls.

As hypothesized, there is no place for lesbian relations in women's prisons but a certain tolerance of 'decent' manifestations of affection between women lovers is observable. However, nowhere were lesbian inmates allowed to receive their loved one in the trailer or family room, although the house of a woman friend and lover is considered an acceptable residence on release.

In Germany, as expected, every prison for women must have a mother-and-child unit to house children up to school age, although in some of the *Länder* only very young children are accepted in residence. Finland, England and Scotland also have mother-and-child facilities for very young children. However, the presence of children in the prison has become the subject of heated debates everywhere, and the practice seems to be undergoing transformation. For instance, in Germany – notably at Vechta – a mother of a young child will quickly be sent with her child to the open prison. In Finland only very young children (up to 18 months) and those born during their mothers' detention are now accepted inside. Shakopee which used to have young children inside has ended that practice. The research team's interest and faith in mother-and-child units was seriously shaken by the effects of its application in the German prisons of Vechta and Butzow where it was obvious that it had created two classes of prisoners – the mothers with

Comparing Women's Prisons 129

their children, and the mothers without. The mothers' units had become first-class luxury residences, and the mothers with children had become privileged inmates with regard to freedom of movement, quality of accommodation, and the rights to stay away from all chores. Why should mothers of seven-year-old children be treated differently?

Our fourth hypothesis on the strict and infantilizing constraints imposed on women's spatial mobility and use of time in closed prisons proved true everywhere except at Durham where, inside the unit, the small group of women self-govern themselves and organize their programmes. Self-governance is also the rule at Ringe, in Denmark. At the opposite extreme, the team observed complete movement and time electronic surveillance, inside and outside the prison, at the new institution of Burnaby in Canada, and rigid 'old style key and guards' control at the 'medieval' prison of Vechta in Germany. On the issue of time control, it was at Shakopee that the constraint was strictest, but the rationale is that women really have much to do in their work time which is seldom the case in women's prisons. On the other hand, at Shakopee the inmates enjoy more freedom of movement than elsewhere. For one thing, the prison ground is unfenced even though inmates must commute between their residence to the core building to study or work and eat. At night, the rooms are not locked (as is also the case at Durham), and the inmates can go downstairs to the common room to read, watch TV, talk with the duty officer or with other inmates who happen to be awake, or eat something as one does at home when one is unable to sleep and hungry. Elsewhere, inmates are locked in at night, kept in fortresses with perimetric security controls out of all proportion to their 'dangerousness' and the risks that they may escape. Escapes are rare. The verdict of the staff at all prisons studied was unanimous: '90 per cent of sentenced women inmates should be sent to minimum security institutions or open prisons'.

As expected, there were exceptions to obsolescence, paucity of programmes and excessive security. For example, the team observed complete mixing of the sexes at the closed institution of Ringe and the open prison of Horserod in Denmark, but contrary to the hopes that such an unusual formula may create, its application at Ringe does not have positive effects on women. The prison receives 16 women of all ages (18 to 64) who live day and night with 80 young boys (of 16 to 24), in units of 20 people (16 boys, 4 women). According to the women and many of the staff members, this arrangement makes the women's lives difficult and, as Ringe is the only closed prison to which sentenced women may be sent, there is no choice. The system originated from the suggestion of the founder of the Ringe prison for young men that women should be 'integrated' into the youths' prison, to 'render life inside more normal for young boys sentenced to closed imprisonment'. The open prison of Horserod is also a mixed one, although, in that case, living with persons of the other sex is not forced upon anyone. Inmates can choose to live in a 'women's only pavillion', a men's one, a mixed one or a 'family' one with children. There are also four work and training programmes that are reported as having positive effects on the women involved: one in Germany, the cook and chef cook training programme at Vechta, a mixed training programme which is very successful both inside and on the labour market; and three in Canada and England – the flower shops and the horticultural programmes at Burnaby and Holloway, which are well attended and the dog training programme at Burnaby.

As already shown in Table 5.2, there are differences in the detention rate in North America as compared to European countries: the former incarcerate considerably more people than the latter. There are also discrepancies in the percentages of women among incarcerated people between countries. National detention rates do not speak of women's detention rate (the number of women inmates per 100 000 women in the population) nor of women's detention conditions, and must be considered for what they are – one of the indicators of a country's (male) criminal policy.

Incarceration Rates as Comparative Indicators

Incarceration rates are widely used by criminologists. They are considered by some as key indicators of the general humanness or inhumanness of a country's penal policy. The *good* countries, penologically speaking, have the *low rate*. However, the comparative study on women's prisons shows that this indicator is very misleading, for the following reasons:

1 Leaving aside the 'woman question' the number of prisoners sometimes grossly misrepresents the number of offenders sentenced to imprisonment. That is precisely what Nils Christie shows with regard to his own country: while there were only 2500 prisoners in Norway in 1991, a further 4500 had been sentenced to imprisonment and were waiting for a prison place (Christie, 1993: 35).
2 Nationally aggregated rates are deceptive if taken to represent anything 'real' in decentralized countries where, by constitutional decision, the administration of justice is a matter of state or provincial competence, as in the USA and Canada and, to some extent, in Germany. Some years ago, in the USA, the states' rates of imprisonment ran from 66 in North Dakota to 1187 in the District of Columbia (ibid.: 84). The national average, in such a case, is not an enlightening indicator.
3 Ethnically neutral rates say nothing of the 'detention probability' of any group, be it the majority or one of the minorities. The US Bureau of

Prisons has adopted the habit of publishing detention rates by ethnic groups, which are very telling indicators.

4   All researchers in penology and criminology are well aware of the gender ratio and know that women, who constitute 51 per cent of the population, account for 10–15 per cent of all arrestees and 5 per cent of the sentenced prisoners in developed countries. Nevertheless, criminologists continue to use *gender-blind incarceration ratios*. In fact, men's 'real' detention rate is twice the 'gender-blind' one.

Would gender-specific detention ratios tell a more enlightening story? I have attempted in Table 5.3 to demonstrate that such might be the case, comparing national rates to 'men only' rates, then to the women-specific ones and, finally, to the percentage of women among the incarcerated population. We see, for instance, that while Denmark's national gender-blind rate was 71 in 1993, its 'men only' one was 144. Denmark was in the second-best position among the six countries on those two counts. However, in terms of the women-specific rate, Denmark lies in fourth place. Canada, which comes sixth with its gender-blind national rate of 115, keeps its place with its gender-specific men's rate of 242, but comes last with its women-specific rate of 14.2, behind the USA. We also see that, while it is true that there are a small proportion of women imprisoned in Denmark and Ger-

Table 5.3   National versus Gender-Specific Incarceration Rates in Six Countries, 1993

	National rates	Men's rate[1]	Women's rate[2]	Women's % among inmates
Norway	60	118	5.5	4.6
Denmark	71	144	7.0	4.8
Germany	81	163	6.9	4.3
England and Wales	89	179	6.5	3.7
Canada	115	242	14.2	6.5
United States	504	862	9.0	5.7

[1]   Number of male prisoners per 100 000 men. All ages.
[2]   Number of women prisoners per 100 000 women. All ages.

Sources:
European countries: Council of Europe (1994–95). The figures are for 1993; *Canada*: Centre canadien de la statistique (1993). The figures quoted are for 1993; *United States*: Bureau of Justice Statistics (1993, 1993a, 1993b). The figures quoted are for 1991.

many compared to Canada and the USA, there are more proportionately in those two countries than in England and Wales which have lowest percentage of women among all incarcerated people (3.7 per cent).

In Scandinavia, based on the detention ratio, the research team had expected to find minimum imprisonment of women and attempts at decarceration. It found neither if by minimum imprisonment one understands not only 'as few inmates as possible' or 'the fewest' (we have seen that if that is true for men, it is not for women since England and Wales, with a high detention rate, have in fact a smaller proportion of imprisoned women) but also 'prison conditions as little constrained as possible', 'for periods as short as possible'. What the researchers saw in Norway, Denmark and Finland, were very constraining conditions, no programmes to speak of, and material (building) conditions that deny the possibility of classification. Despite these countries' reputation for their policies of sex equality, the access women have to education, their complete choice of employment and their remarkable place in the political arena, the research showed that: women prisoners' salaries in Norway are inferior to those of men; female inmates in the co-correctional prison of Hameenlinna in Finland are prevented from working in jobs that pay better and lead to qualifications; and in Norway and Finland, as in Germany, women were granted access to open prisons between 10–15 years later than men prisoners – not a strong indication of short periods of detention in closed prisons. Finally, as previously mentioned, all women inmates in Scandinavia are prevented from following the post-secondary courses accessible to men prisoners.

In short, national gender-blind incarceration rates obfuscate the proportion of men imprisoned in relation to their gender group and misrepresent, in the international comparisons, women's national detention rates. In the case of women, low detention rates have been shown to co-exist with the most detestable and boring prison conditions, and sex discrimination coincides with model penal policies.

Conclusion

The chosen perspective in this study on women's prisons allowed the researchers to understand the prisons' conditions from within (*verstehen*) and in context (in the life-world) and permitted comparison and contrast. The 'qualitative look' (the non-participant observation of the individual prisons and the dialogues with their habitants and local experts) have shed considerable light on the material conditions of the prisons and their consequences on life inside. Yet it is from the feminist standpoint that it has become possible to 'see', and hence theorize the differential effects of gender-

Comparing Women's Prisons 133

neutral correctional policies – such as family vacations which, finally, compounds women's solitude, or the disfunction between the sex equality professed in the social and political sphere and the inequalities practised in the correctional field or, finally, the representation of, and the rewards offered to, the 'good' mother through the material organization of the mother-and-child units. In all these respects structural and materialist analyses have proved very useful.

However, the qualitative analysts needed an interlocutor with whom to debate. They had to engage in dialectical conversation with other visions, such as that of the quantitativist and its cherished aggregated figures on national crime and detention rates. In fact, for the critical penologist, national, centralized, gender-blind and ethnically neutral data sit there in need of deconstruction.

Notes

1   To *see*, or in French *regarder*, come from the Greek *teoria*.
2   Two of the research team members, Louise L. Biron and myself, were then professors at the School of Criminology and affiliated researchers of the International Centre of Comparative Criminology. Three were graduate students: Concetta di Pisa, Andrée B. Fagnan, and Julia McLean. Concetta di Pisa's and Julia McLean's master's and doctoral dissertations, on alternatives to imprisonment and women's prisons, were based on the data they themselves collected during the study.
3   Schutz's theory of interpretive understanding is to be distinguished from the one held by Max Weber and his critics, explained in Schutz (1954: 257–73).
4   On-site, the researchers saw that foreign inmates, quite isolated in the prison, took pleasure and pride in exchanging with visitors in languages little known to the staff and other inmates.
5   In fact, that was the case in four closed prisons and one open.
6   In both cases, the change had to do with the level of security which went from relatively low to medium high or high.
7   Respectively Johannes Feest, Professor of Criminal Law at Bremen University and member of Prison Reform International and Evy Frantzsen, research assistant at the Oslo Institute of Criminology. Liv Finstad, Professor at the Institute, was of great help in programming the study visit.
8   In Norway, Liv Finstad, Evy Frantzsen and Cecile Hoigard, researchers and professors attached to the Institute of Criminology at the University of Oslo had read the primary report on the closed prison of Bredtveit and on the open prison of Ostensjovien when the author met them in the summer of 1994. Later on, Evy Frantzsen also read the final report and commented on it. Nils Christie and Stanley Cohen read the reports on the Danish, German, Finnish and Norwegian prisons for women on the occasion of their visit to the School of Criminology in Montreal, in 1994 and made very pertinent comments. In Denmark, Annika Snare, Professor of Criminal Law and Criminology at the University of Copenhagen received the preliminary report on the closed prison of Ringe and the open prison of Horserod and made careful critiques, correcting errors of facts and interpretation. The Danish prison at Ringe had been studied by two researchers

for a full week; the open prison of Horserod was visited for one day by one researcher alone.

In Finland, Pirkko Villikka, head of the education programme and vice-director of the Hameenlinna Prison, and Tarja Poso, Professor of Social Policy at the University of Tampere, and author of articles and books on the social control of women and women's place in the political and social life in the country, both read the preliminary report. Tarja Poso sent comments on the final one.

Johannes Feest helped the author plan her visits to the two West German prisons for women and, as mentioned earlier, accompanied her inside. He discussed with her the preliminary reports on the three German prisons studied, and then received and commented on the final reports. Mrs Helga Einsele, founder of the German mother-and-child units in women's prisons was consulted before the visits to the German prisons, and was also given access to the report of the interview she had given to the author on the history and present state of these facilities. She disagreed with one point of the report, the 'use of the child's presence inside to bring the mother inmate to conform', that the author had understood to mean a form of *chantage*. The author agreed to make the necessary change in nuance in her later publications. Uta Kruger, Professor of Criminology at the police department of Hamburg, read and made comments on the reports on the three German prisons. No German senior criminologist, however, seemed familiar with the East German prison of Butzow and hence no one helpfully critiqued the author's report on that site.

9   Professor Stanley Cohen.
10 In fact, the team paid short visits to two other state prisons in the USA – those of Massachussets and Pennsylvania – so that they could contextualize the neighbouring correctional community centres of Boston and Pittsburgh which were integral parts of the study programme.
11 *Horii* v. *Canada*, 1991, 1FC142 (C.A.).

References

Berger, Peter and Luckmann, Thomas (1967), *The Social Construction of Reality*, Garden City, NY.: Doubleday Inc.
Bertrand, Marie-Andrée with Biron, Louise L., Di Pisa, Concetta, Fagnan, Andrée B. and McLean, Julia (1998), *Prisons pour femmes*, Montreal: Les Éditions du Méridien.
Bureau of Justice Statistics (1992), *Jail Inmates*, Washington, D.C.: U.S. Department of Justice, Office of Justice Programs.
Bureau of Justice Statistics (1993a), *Sourcebook on Criminal Justice Statistics 1992 and 1993*, Washington, D.C.: U.S. Department of Justice, Office of Justice Programs.
Bureau of Justice Statistics (1993b), *Prisoners 1993*, Washington, D.C.: U.S. Department of Justice, Office of Justice Programs.
Centre Canadien de la Statistique Juridique (1993), *Services correctionnels pour adultes au Canada, 1993*, Ottawa, Ontario: Statistique Canada.
Christie, Nils (1981), *Limits to Pain*, Oxford: Martin Robinson.
Christie, Nils (1993), *Crime Control as Industry*, London: Routledge.

Cohen, Stanley and Taylor, Laurie (1972), *Psychological Survival. The Experience of Long-Term Imprisonment*, New York: Pantheon Books.
Council of Europe (1994–95), *Bulletin d'information pénologique*, (18, 19, 20), December.
Delphy, Christine (1970), 'L'ennemi principal', *Partisans*, **54–55**, 157–72.
Delphy, Christine (1975), 'Pour un féminisme matérialiste', *L'Arc*, **61**, 61–68.
Foucault, Michel (1975), *Surveiller et punir: naissance de la prison*. Paris: Éditions Gallimard.
Goffman, Erving (1968), *Asiles, étude sur la condition sociale des malades mentaux*, Paris: Minuit.
Guillaumin, Colette (1978), 'Pratique de pouvoir et idée de nature (1) l'appropriation des femmes', *Questions féministes*, **2**, 5–50.
Harding, Sandra (1991), *Whose Science? Whose Knowledge? Thinking from Women's Lives*, Ithaca, NY: Cornell University Press.
Hulsman, Louk (1987), *The Criminal Justice System as a Social Problem: An Abolitionist Perspective*. Part One, Rotterdam: Erasmus University Press.
Hulsman, Louk with Bernat de Celis, Jacqueline (1982), *Peines Perdues: Le Système Pénal en Question*, Paris: Éditions le Centurion.
Juteau, Danielle and Laurin, Nicole (1988), 'L'évolution des formes d'appropriation des femmes', *Revue canadienne de sociologie et d'anthropologie*, **25** (2), 188–207.
Lofland, John (1971), *Analysing Social Settings. A Guide to Qualitative Observations and Analysis*, Belmont, CA: Wadsworth.
MacKinnon, Catherine, A. (1989), *Towards a Feminist Theory of the State*, Cambridge, MA: Harvard University Press.
Mathiesen, Thomas (1974), *The Politics of Abolition*, New York: Halsted.
Mathiesen, Thomas (1990), *Prisons on Trial*, London: Routledge.
Poupart, Jean (1993), 'Discours et débats autour de la scientificité des entretiens de recherche', *Sociologie et sociétés*, **25** (2), 93–110.
Schatzman, Leonard and Strauss, Anselm L. (1973), *Field Research: Strategies for Natural Sociology*, Englewood Cliffs, NJ: Prentice Hall.
Schutz, Alfred (1954), 'Concepts in Theory Formation', *The Journal of Philosophy*, **51** (9), 257–73.
Schutz, Alfred (1962, 1964, 1966), *Collected Papers*, The Hague: Martinus Nijhoff.
Schutz, Alfred (1982), *Life Forms and Meaning Structure*, London: Routledge.
Schutz, Alfred and Luckmann, Thomas (1973), *The Structure of the Lifeworld*. Evanston, Ill: Northwestern University Press.
Strauss, Anselm (1987), *Qualitative Analysis for Social Scientists*, Cambridge and New York, Cambridge University Press.

PART III
RESEARCHING THERE

6 Comparing Legal Cultures: The Comparativist as Participant Observer

Jacqueline Hodgson

Introduction

The contributions to this collection testify to the variety of comparative criminal justice research being conducted and to the new perspectives which it can offer. However, comparative work is not simply a method, a new twist on old problems: to view it as such is 'to deny, in sum, any substantive content to comparative work about law and to ensure that it ultimately loses its status as a discrete, autonomous intellectual domain' (Legrand, 1995: 264). Comparing criminal processes raises questions not only about the nature of criminal justice, but also about the nature of comparative work itself – where, why and how we do it. The aim of this chapter is to reflect upon the process of comparative work itself and, in particular, the role of qualitative empirical research and the wider lessons it presents to the comparativist.

Comparative legal studies embraces a diverse range of scholarship, from detailed positivist descriptions of foreign legal systems, to the use and development of legal and social theory as a tool for comparison and analysis. In many ways, the study of other legal systems is no different from any other research enterprise: the results are constrained by the methods. The answers we produce are largely determined by the questions we ask and so we should choose our research tools with care. What I would like to argue here is that the comparativist (whether or not conducting empirical work) is engaging in a form of legal anthropology and is a participant observer (see also Legrand, 1995: 266; 1996: 238; Zedner, 1995: 18). She is attempting to permeate another culture, at the very least to understand its institutional structures, laws and procedures, but hopefully also its languages, customs, ideologies, legal cultures and practices. The interpretation of her findings, and indeed the search itself, are influenced by her own legal cultural perspective and the ways in which she gathers and reports information. Knowledge of the issues and the problems inherent in such a task will result in greater awareness of the impact of self on the production of knowledge, going some way to avoiding the presentation of cultural bias as objective fact.

Ways to Compare

My own research is concerned with the working practices of those involved in the investigation and prosecution of crime in France. The choice of France does not represent a belief in its stereotypicality as an inquisitorial[1] process but, rather, one example[2] in this broad category of systems. One of the first tasks in a new endeavour such as this is to study earlier accounts – expositions and comparisons of the French criminal justice process and wider comparative work. When this is done, it soon becomes clear that there are few established frameworks or systematic approaches to the study of foreign legal systems in general, or, more specifically, to the study of criminal processes. Instead, we find a range of studies paying more or less attention to theory, method and coverage. Some, such as Damaska (1975), present descriptive 'models' as an aid to analysis, providing an overview and exposition of institutional structures and procedures. He characterizes the 'adversarial' and 'inquisitorial' systems by their wider structures of authority – coordinate and hierarchical respectively. This sets the beginning of a theoretical framework, but is necessarily general and masks important differences between individual systems. However, most accounts lack any overt theoretical framework. There are descriptions of the institutional structures and legal procedures in different countries; descriptions of how the same function is addressed, such as prosecutorial discretion, the exclusion of evidence, or the provision of expert witnesses; there are policy reform-driven studies seeking foreign cures to domestic ills (this is especially so of many American studies in the glut of comparative work in the 1970s and early 1980s); and there are a handful of attempts to empirically test hypotheses such as judicial investigative supervision. However, in the absence of reflection upon how and why these studies are conducted, there are significant gaps in the account which they provide. In addition, many studies stop at descriptions of foreign legal systems and how they differ to or resemble the author's own jurisdiction. There is no reflection on what new meanings are given to domestic structures, no mirroring (Rogowski, 1996b) and no dialectic analysis (Puchalska-Tych and Salter, 1996).

Formalist Non-contextual Accounts

Many studies are formal descriptions of institutions, rules and processes, providing a static backdrop – an official picture – but telling us nothing of the daily workings of, and practices within, the legal system. Taken as an account of the formal rhetoric of the system[3] such descriptions can be useful, but they are deficient in their provision of an idealized version with no interpretative context.[4] Describing the law relating to the provision of custodial legal advice contained in the Police and Criminal Evidence Act 1984, for example, may reflect one strand of official rhetoric, but it would be misleading in its suggestion that universal legal advice is afforded to all suspects, since data revealing request and refusal rates for legal advice, level of lawyer attendance and quality of legal advice, reveal that the aspiration is far from being realized (see, for example, McConville and Hodgson, 1993).[5] Similarly, accounts of the role of the *juge d'instruction* in supervising a criminal investigation must also include information relating to the frequency with which the *juge* is used and the nature of her role in day-to-day practice. Close examination of the *Code de Procédure Pénale* reveals that it is actually the prosecutor (*procureur*) who plays a central part in the supervision of investigations and, in all but the most serious of cases, may retain that control. What then becomes of interest is how that role is played in practice, how it is viewed by the *procureur* and what constitutes 'supervision'. A number of different and contradictory explanations may be uncovered. It is this level of understanding that is missing in the existing literature. Formalist accounts are reductionist and decontextualized. For them, '[t]he debate within legal theory as to the "nature of law" is assumed to have been concluded in favour of positivism' (Puchalska-Tych and Salter, 1996: 160). A contextual approach to the comparative study of law and legal processes is vital to our understanding of legal culture: rules, procedures and judicial decisions are insufficient. Just as with the study of domestic law and legal problems, this approach creates only an illusion of understanding.[6] In addition, a formalist approach takes no account of the social, economic and political influences on the formation and development of legal structures and processes, or policy – be it the French Revolution or the high numbers of prisoners awaiting trial. This further reduces its usefulness to the comparative lawyer not only in evaluating features of the legal system in their native context, but also making difficult any judgment as to the possible value of foreign concepts and their likely successful adaptation elsewhere.

The Lack of Comparable Empirical Data

A second general problem is that of what precisely to compare. How do we select relevant material? There is a wealth of critical empirical research in the criminal justice area, relating both to the UK and the USA. However, a search for comparable data on the French criminal process reveals a relative empirical vacuum. Some, such as Goldstein and Marcus (1977) and Leigh and Zedner (1992), have conducted a limited amount of empirical work, consisting primarily of (an unspecified number of) interviews and some court observation. This produces useful insights into the views of key legal personnel concerning the operation of the criminal justice process, but caution must be exercised. Consciously or unconsciously, interview subjects may offer up presentational data[7] which does not reflect daily routines and experiences: this needs to be tested against more sustained periods of observation.[8] French literature, although sometimes critical, (Merle and Vitu, 1979) does not reflect an empirical tradition, and debate tends to be conducted within a doctrinal and theoretical context.[9] The lack of critical empirical studies in the field of comparative criminal justice can, and does, lead to the drawing of false comparisons. For example, it has become popular to contrast the (negative) lack of external police supervision in England and Wales with the (positive) use of the *juge d'instruction*. It is argued that miscarriage of justice would be less likely were somebody independent of the police responsible for impartially investigating the case, including uncovering exculpatory evidence (Devlin, 1979; Berlins and Dyer, 1986; Mansfield and Wardle 1993; Rose, 1996). This may be so, but the UK police versus the French *juge d'instruction* is an uneven, unbalanced comparison, as it contrasts our critical empirical knowledge of the police construction of the prosecution case in England and Wales with a formal account of a minority procedure in France, that of *instruction*. Apart from the fact that a *juge* is involved in less than 10 per cent of all cases, this comparison makes no enquiry into the efficacy of such a procedure. It weighs official rhetoric (from a discourse existing outside so-called 'inquisitorial' systems, which are themselves critical of the *juge d'instruction*) against an account based on critical empirical research.

This is often the case with policy-driven research in which the would-be reformer is captive to her own false model of the foreign jurisdiction. The Anglo-American obsession with the role of the *juge d'instruction*, rather than the *procureur*, in supervising criminal investigations is a classic example. The French, similarly misty-eyed, look with admiration at the English system of jury trial and the writ of *habeas corpus* as if they represented typical modes of case disposition. Goldstein and Marcus (1977) and Langbein and Weinreb (1978) debated keenly which was the correct 'model' of inquisitorial systems for comparison. Others, undeterred by the lack of comparable data, have launched into widescale comparison and conclusion. For example, Frase (1990) is critical of the US police for *de facto* exercising wider powers than are lawfully allowed them, so leaving the suspect unprotected, but then goes on to eulogize the French police hierarchy and its 'prosecution' supervision, offering no evidence of how effective these controls are in practice. Mendelson (1983) concludes that the French system provides a better way of obtaining confessions whilst at the same time protecting the rights of individuals, but his account is distorted by comparison of the majority practice of plea bargaining in the USA, with the minority procedure of *instruction* in the French system. In addition, he takes no account of the heavy reliance placed on the police through *commission rogatoires*, where the *juge* delegates portions of the investigation to the *police judiciaire*.

Functionalism and Ethnocentrism

Ethnocentric research design and interpretation of data are the constant enemies of the comparativist and also lead to false comparisons. In an attempt to select relevant data, the comparativist may focus only on those areas considered to be of direct functional equivalence (Rose, 1991). This definition and form of functionalism may be a helpful way of looking at phenomena in a very broad sense[10] – criminal investigation, sentencing, human rights – but it may produce false units of analysis if it defines areas of interest from a domestic and therefore culturally biased perspective. Legrand (1995) talks of 'restaging' another legal culture within the parameters of one's own. This can skew the whole picture by omitting what is important or overdrawing perceived equivalence. For example, it is not enough to compare the sentencing of the English criminal judge with that of the French without also taking account of the fact that the French prosecutor, unlike her English counterpart, makes a sentence recommendation to the court. Even a comparison of the prosecutor in England and Wales with the *procureur* in France requires qualification (and here we encounter the almost constant problem of translation[11] where no equivalent word exists). They both prosecute cases in court, but while the former is trained as a lawyer, the latter is trained (in common with the *juge d'instruction* and the *juge* trying the case) as a *magistrat*. This, together with her wider role and responsibilities, makes the *procureur* a different creature from our own Crown Prosecutor. To represent her as the same would be a false ordering – a kind of reproduction in the researcher's own legal cultural image. Similarly, one cannot examine the role of the defence lawyer in assisting suspects held in police custody in England and Wales and in France without considering the wider safeguards in place and the expectations which arise when supervision of the detention period is placed in the hands of someone outside the police. One may even wonder whether Goldstein and Marcus's (1977) illuminating and critical account is a little hasty in equating the functional benefits of plea bargaining with those of *correctionalisation* in France.[12] This is the reduction of the offence to a less serious charge, avoiding the need for a lengthy jury trial before the *cour d'assises*. Whilst this brings clear benefits to the courts in terms of case turnover and the defendant is prosecuted for a lesser offence (although forfeiting the right to jury trial) and remains free to deny the charges, there is no evidence that this is the result of routine bargaining between the prosecution and defence with any pressure placed upon the latter. Rather, it appears to be a unilateral decision.

Theory: Why, How and What to Compare

A final difficulty with much comparative work is the lack of theoretical grounding. Procedures, institutions and statistics are plucked out and compared with little or no thought as to how they fit into the wider criminal justice process.[13] Comparison is made as an 'add-on' to the domestic critique. By treating it as a method, rather than a perspective, it becomes 'constrained, mechanical and apolitical...no more than a handmaiden to contract, property or constitutional law' (Legrand, 1995: 264). Used as a perspective we can learn much more. By reflecting upon the institutional structures and experiences of other legal cultures we can begin to reassess our understanding of our own legal culture and values.[14] These observed differences provide a constant foil – an 'other' against which to view a system. The comparativist must think about why, how and what she is comparing in order to avoid inexplicit theorizing and a false objectivity in the presentation of data. This means making explicit the models which she is comparing, rather than assuming them to be shared by the reader.

The way in which comparison is approached is important in this process of reflection. The observation of another legal culture, the problems of immersion, of comprehension, of not being accepted or understood by either your own or another community, of 'going native', of understanding context and of conveying information and nuances from another culture in a way which will be understood by one's own culture are not problems exclusive to comparative studies, whether in law or other fields. Any ethnographic study encounters these phenomena – the need to penetrate without becoming or assimilating another culture; the need to see as one's research subjects see, without becoming one of them; to penetrate the internal whilst maintaining a foothold in the external. Even issues such as language and

Comparing Legal Cultures 145

historical context, so important to comparative work, are also crucial to the ethnographer. In my own participant observation study of criminal defence lawyers in England and Wales, it was important to understand the training, values and legal culture of solicitors and their staff, but also how they came to occupy the professional position they now hold. Knowledge of the past informs our understanding of the present. Ethnographic work may not always face the problem of translating from one language, such as French, to another, but in studying other communities it often becomes apparent that they have their own language – a discourse laden with the values of its subjects or borrowed from official rhetoric and used in self-serving ways. An important element in understanding that community will be to uncover the meanings behind what its members say. It is in these kinds of ways that I believe issues surrounding ethnography and participant observation have something to contribute to the process of comparison. Hooked on descriptions of institutions, official rules and legal personnel, or historical differences, comparativists seem to forget that they are presenting data subjectively acquired and so the normal caveats apply – how and why the data was gathered and how it is presented must be made explicit. Data is not objective fact (if, indeed, this exists) but an interpretation (not simply in the linguistic sense). To deny the methodological process and context is to return to a normative and positivist account of law and the production of knowledge.

The Comparativist as Participant Observer

My own research project seeks to understand the role of pre-trial actors in the investigation and prosecution of criminal cases in France. This is a broadly stated objective as I am conscious of the dangers of casting the research net too narrowly in relatively uncharted waters. It is not only the daily routine and experiences of these personnel that I am trying to discover, but also the (possibly contradictory) expectations which they might have concerning their role and that of other legal actors performing different functions. In what are these beliefs and expectations grounded and how, if at all, do they relate to official rhetorics that exist within French criminal justice? The nature of my enquiry has led me to conduct fieldwork in five sites, including Paris, spending time with *juges d'instruction, procureurs* and police. This qualitative work is complemented by interviews towards the end of the observation period at each site and questionnaires administered across other regions of the country. It is unsurprising, therefore, that I should concentrate my mind on issues of participant observation, given my preferred methodology. However, its relevance extends beyond the narrow confines of my own project, striking at the heart of what I believe to be the role of the comparativist – to permeate and interpret another culture. By prolonged observation and interaction in the field, the aim of the participant observer is to 'use the culture of the setting (the socially acquired and shared knowledge available to the participants or members of the setting) to account for the observed patterns of human activity' (Van Maanen, 1983: 38).[15] In my own research, my preferred term is direct observation: (McConville and Hodgson, 1993: 6; McConville et al., 1994: 13) although placed among the community under study, and thus inevitably participating in what is observed, the researcher does not participate as her research subjects do. However, participant observation, as referred to within sociological literature, includes a continuum of activity from the covert and fully participant observer to the overt researcher whose observations may be limited in ways agreed by research subjects. Participant observation is considered to be the main tool in ethnographic studies – here, in understanding a legal system within the context of its culture. I would like to consider some participant observation issues and their relevance to comparative studies in more detail.

Open-endedness

A clear benefit of ethnographic work is the ability of the researcher to immerse herself in the field in order to try to identify important and relevant issues, without the total constraint of precoded categories. That is not to say that research should be wholly unstructured (it can be systematically replicated in a number of sites or settings), but rather, that space is needed to cross-check initial hypotheses and to generate new ones in the field. Once the researcher has a framework within which to work, further data can then be gathered in a more focused way. So, too, can the comparativist benefit from an open-endedness to her project, avoiding predetermined (and possibly ethnocentric) categories and attempting to learn from the jurisdiction more directly. My own preconceptions about the French criminal justice process arose from a discourse based on Anglo-American concerns and interests in forms (or perhaps one iconic form, the *juge d'instruction*) of judicial supervision. This remains of interest, but in a much wider context which includes the day-to-day pressures of those responsible for supervising criminal investigations and the police detention of suspects, as well as the competing rhetorics within the French criminal process concerning judicial independence. This latter point especially is not evident in the Anglo-American literature, nor to any great extent in French texts. It has emerged only through spending time with *procureurs, juges d'instruction, juges des enfants* and, to a lesser extent, trial judges, and setting their views and comments in the context of, for example, French revolutionary ideology and current political reform.¹⁶ Whilst at one level there is concern over the wide powers of the *juge d'instruction* in particular – and modification of her role is never far from the reform agenda – many *magistrats* would jealously guard the independent nature of her position as an investigator, in contrast to that of the *procureur* who is under, and may receive written instructions from, the minister of justice. This independent status is seen as crucial in cases involving political figures and those in the world of business, and criticisms of the wide powers, together with the youth and inexperience of some *juges d'instruction*, is dismissed by some *magistrats* as a politically motivated red herring. This is one small example, but uncovering these contradictory discourses¹⁷ has begun to reshape my thinking of French judicial roles, past and present.¹⁸ It also illustrates the need to remain responsive to the data gathered in formulating new models for understanding.

Some have criticized participant observation as subjective and therefore unscientific, and we have seen the preference of many comparativists for precoding. Yet, such rigid categorization from the outset, formulated in the researcher's own terms and language, produces responses also within these confines, and she learns little beyond that of which she already has some knowledge. Using participant observation, the researcher is able to study social relationships and complex interdependencies, unrestricted by the need to identify all categories of data before entering the field. This is vital for the comparativist too – to go beyond (often externally) pre-set categories and explore a legal culture in its own setting. In this way one can get closer to the subject of study.

Immersion and Going Native

The researcher studying any new community requires time to adapt to her new environment, to identify key players and to locate and evaluate information sources, before data of sufficient quality can be gathered. She can then begin to understand the context in which legal institutions and actors operate and to allow the legal culture to speak in its own voice rather than a projection of her own. This may lead to a new perspective on the meaning of words and concepts and the processes understood to be behind them. The comparativist also requires substantial periods of study in order to soak up and begin to interpret another legal culture. Brief forays will make it difficult to go beyond the superficial. By immersing herself into the broader legal culture, the researcher can move beyond static descriptions and begin to understand the legal process in a variety of contexts. For example, in most instances, supervision of the police by the *procureur* consists of the police telephoning the *procureur* during the first few hours after a suspect's arrest and at the end of the detention period. I had expected a more proactive model of supervision, but *procureurs* rarely aspired to anything beyond this. This gave new meaning to my understanding of the concept of 'supervision' in this context. Finding your way around the literature in another jurisdiction can be difficult and time-consuming – especially when academic traditions and subject boundaries differ widely.[19] It was some time before I moved beyond French official accounts and texts and dry critiques, and finally located commentaries based in a broader and more critical context.

Another factor which especially affects the comparativist is language. Understanding a new context and conveying it in the research subject's own terms, rather than those of the observer, is especially difficult when not only the culture, but also the language is different.[20] Many words, such as *juge d'instruction*, have no obvious translation, and others can be misleading in appearing to convey some functional equivalence, such as *procureur*. The latter is responsible for the prosecution of cases, but as we saw above, has a wider role than, and different training from, the English Crown Prosecutor. To imagine the English prosecutor supervising the police investigation does not reflect the position in France. Interestingly, Tomlinson (1983) describes the *procureur* as a career civil servant under the minister of justice and Cooper (1991) as a member of the Crown Prosecution Service trained as a magistrate. To an audience in England and Wales, words such as magistrate and judge refer to lay and professional trial judges and so to translate *magistrat* or *juge* (both of which describe the French *procureur*) in this way is unhelpful.

The initial role adopted by, or assigned to, the researcher will influence the type and amount of information to which she will be allowed access. For the participant observer, this is frequently about providing a plausible explanation of her research objectives, both to facilitate relationships and to locate relevant sources of information. It may be that the researcher is unsure of her precise objectives and to avoid foreclosing issues may ask her research subjects to suggest areas meriting attention and investigation. When comparing legal cultures too, the way in which the comparativist defines her role both to herself and to others may, to some extent, determine the nature of the data sought and provided. A reform agenda will yield quite different information from a general enquiry. In addition, those under study may also have their own views as to the researcher's role. In the early stages of my fieldwork in France I was often asked which system I thought to be better – the English or the French. It became clear that most French legal actors I encountered assumed that I was engaged in a reform exercise. This was reinforced by their own concerns with the French legal process and an interest in things adversarial. When studying another legal culture, the naïveté of the foreigner is unthreatening and may ease her path initially and provide

Comparing Legal Cultures 149

ready access to documentation, but this is a card which must not be overplayed if the research enterprise is to be taken seriously.

After some time in the field the participant observer becomes at ease with her new environment and may even begin to feel a part of it, though regular debriefing is important in order to retain a critical perspective. Nevertheless, somehow she remains an outsider, and there is a tension in retaining the complementary but necessarily separate roles which may place a strain on the fieldworker.

The ethnographer who becomes immersed in other people's realities is never quite the same afterward. The total immersion creates a kind of disorientation – culture shock – arising from the need to identify with and at the same time remain distant from the process being studied. (Sanday, 1983: 20)

I have experienced this in a number of research projects, including the current French study. One can feel as though straddling two roles or identities – never fully accepted by the culture under study, as one's role there is only temporary and one is never 'one of them', yet defensive about that culture when returning 'home'.

Although a proper period of immersion and adaptation is necessary, the participant observer must beware of 'going native'. This is when she loses her sense of critical perspective and begins to see and evaluate things as (she perceives that) her research subjects do. In my own doctoral research of criminal defence lawyers, the firm I was studying was involved in some of the, now infamous, West Midlands Serious Crime Squad cases. Because of the appalling nature and scale of systematic police corruption they revealed, I found myself identifying more and more with the lawyers opposing this, failing to see some of the other, negative, aspects of their work. This became apparent only when I pulled out of the field for debriefing.[21] The comparativist must also beware of overidentification with her research subjects. A new and different legal culture looks most appealing when it seems not to suffer from the flaws that we know only to well in our own system. Goldstein and Marcus criticize Langbein and Weinreb's idealism in relation to inquisitorial models. It is vital to continually re-evaluate what one finds in a foreign legal culture and not to lose one's critical perspective.

Analysis and Reflection

All observation is subjective. In evaluating the validity of research findings, one looks to the range of data, the methods employed in its generation and the evidence produced to support the theory or conclusion advanced. Asking the minister of justice about the ways in which police detention of suspects are regulated will provide one perspective, not a definitive account. A very different response may be produced when the same question is put to suspects themselves, to defence lawyers, police or to the *procureurs* responsible for supervising the police. Overlaying this with direct observation of the process may reveal additional factors which, when placed in the context of comment and explanation from police, *procureurs* and so on (rather than the researcher's interpretation alone), begins to build up a more complete picture. Clearly, it is not enough to rely on the subjective view of either the researcher or those researched. Data needs to be cross-checked against alternative sources. The perceived objectivity of the comparativist is also problematic, as is the subjectivity of any researcher,[22] if not properly recognized. The researcher is never invisible, neither to the subjects of her study, nor in the process of writing up.[23] The reporting of information in the context of contrasting legal systems or categorizations does not make it objective (Frankenberg, 1985: 411; also Legrand, 1995: 266). The comparativist must be sensitive to the limitations of her data, especially if only limited resources are relied on. In addition is the specific factor of legal cultural bias: 'As a foreigner, one's first knowledge of another legal system is always mediated in the sense that one necessarily views others within the meanings constructed in one's own language and legal language' (Legrand, 1995: 266). Legal language exists in the context of a legal culture. This is not overcome, or somehow neutralized by the act of comparing and contrasting legal systems. The comparativist must beware of constructing models and precoding information from the bias of her own legal culture. For example, even the notion of a civil law tradition has been criticized by some as an invention of common lawyers – an 'other' to give meaning to the concept of common law (Rogowski, 1996: xi). Anglo-American commentators frequently describe France as an inquisitorial system, because it is not adversarial. Yet, every French text on criminal procedure begins by describing the transition from the stark extremes of a purely inquisitorial, written and secret procedure, to the present 'mixed' system in which defence lawyers may challenge pre-trial decisions and the accused is tried in public. In studying criminal processes, it may, on occasions, be inappropriate to place, for example, French criminal justice concepts and activities into English criminal justice boxes. We have seen that we cannot group all those carrying out the prosecution function together without also considering their additional roles, contrasting values and different training. The comparativist needs to shed her preconceptions of legal categorization, but without losing the benefit of her own experience in maintaining a critical perspective.

Once in the field for some time, the researcher may become so familiar with her environment that she is unable to objectify it, taking for granted much of what she observes and fails to record it as meticulously as before.

This presents problems when trying to write up and analyse data some time later. There may also be confusion as she tries to convey aspects of the process studied, whilst at the same time confronted with her own inescapable bias and the distorting effect of her own cultural perspective. In my own research, some things which seemed obvious when reading French texts, or when observed in the *Palais de Justice*, lose something in the translation when presented at a conference in Birmingham.[24] How to describe the legal culture studied, to convey its nuances of meaning in a language which is understood by an audience to whom it is foreign, without distorting the original data, is difficult and not simply in terms of translation. Much of the context of the studied culture is implicit but absorbed and understood. This is not only the case in observational study. Literature read and analysed during the period abroad, in the full throes of foreign experience, may seem cold and more difficult to piece together once back at the university. Only when one comes to present findings to a 'home' audience do the gaps in explanation and background become apparent. The task of comparing seems never-ending, the related contextual areas of study endless – politics, history, economics, philosophy. The foreign observer has no cultural foothold and can take nothing as given. It may be that every French law student is familiar with the Revolution, the Napoleonic codes and the successive constitutions amending them and this may operate as an unconscious background to their understanding of French legal institutions. But the foreign student is insecure about relevance and sees the job of penetrating and describing another culture in a meaningful way as an unending task.

A Concluding Example

What I have sought to do here is to highlight some of the problems encountered in my own area of criminal justice research and reflect upon the role of the comparativist as ethnographer and the way in which this may inform the process of comparison. Among the shortfalls identified in earlier studies, the paucity of empirical work is perhaps the most difficult in terms of building equivalent pictures of jurisdictions and so one of the most fruitful areas of future research. One of the most recent examples of comparative research in England and Wales was that conducted under the auspices of the Royal Commission on Criminal Justice (1993) whose job was to critically assess many aspects of the criminal justice process. The Commission was established in the wake of a string of miscarriages of justice, and the abuse of police powers revealed in many of these cases brought about popular calls for a more inquisitorial styled system. In commissioning a research agenda, an ideal opportunity for the wider study of other jurisdictions was presented, but an agenda driven by a combination of efficiency and reform proved fatal. As in many other areas, its approach to comparative work lacked any theoretical grounding and reflection, providing a rather bad example of the use of comparative study.

I have suggested here that the comparativist should retain a broad outlook and not become too easily captivated by ethnocentric categories. A real attempt at understanding the structure and operation of a legal process in its own context is required and not simply a cursory glance to see 'if they do what we do, better'. The Royal Commission rejected out of hand the idea of any change in an explicitly inquisitorial direction,[25] without affording it any proper consideration. Researchers were specifically asked to examine other jurisdictions with a view to their reception into England and Wales (Leigh and Zedner, 1992: 67). This may be an eventual consideration, but to set down such narrow terms at the outset forecloses much of the research enterprise. There is a need to explore in depth the workings of other systems, the relationships between legal actors, institutional structures and daily practice and thus the strengths and the weaknesses of the process. Only then can we begin to learn about foreign systems in their own context, as well as about their possible relevance within our own. The failure of something in one jurisdiction does not preclude its adoption in a modified and improved form in another. Even if this is rejected, broad consideration across a number of countries may reveal better ways for the *procureur*, the *juge d'instruction* or the police to operate, suggesting ways in which the English system might be modified. Is it important that a judge supervise police investigation? Or should it simply be someone outside the police service? Should that be their only role, in order to avoid conflict later in the case? To what extent should their function be supported by that of other legal personnel? And why has the *juge d'instruction* been abandoned in some jurisdictions? For local or structural reasons? Issues such as these can be just as useful in the process of reform and are probably more realistic in application. In understanding better the functioning and context of French, Dutch or German criminal justice we can begin to reflect upon the structural weaknesses in our own malfunctioning process in England and Wales and to consider alternative approaches.

Many have criticized the absence of any theoretical framework in the UK Royal Commission's report – although others have identified the implicit theorizing behind many of its proposals.[26] In examining what other jurisdictions might have to offer it appeared to be searching for the perfect bolt-on system. Inevitably disappointed in this superficially constructed objective, it rejected all inquisitorial systems as 'no better than our own' and, with them, anything rooted in an inquisitorial tradition – structures, institutions, training, personnel. The Commission's approach characterized much of the bad practice identified above, being reform-driven, unable to go beyond ethnocentric functional equivalence and allowing rules and procedures (rather than an understanding of the wider context) to dominate its understanding. There was no process of reflection and re-understanding of one's own system in a new light. In short, very little of other legal 'cultures' emerged from the report. Despite this lost opportunity, from which other jurisdictions might have been better understood and myths exploded within the high profile of a Royal Commission Report, scholars continue to research and raise the quality of comparative work beyond 'pick-and-mix' reform.

Notes

1 Countries such as France, Germany, the Netherlands and pre-1988 Italy are often procedurally described as inquisitorial and historically categorized as civil law jurisdictions. These are broad groupings and may not be recognized by those claimed (by adversarially-based jurisdictions) to be within them.
2 Not a random example, language considerations being crucial.
3 Some descriptions, in their culturally biased selection, may not even accurately reflect this. See below.
4 For example, Cooper (1991) cites the 95 per cent conviction rate after jury trial in the *Cour d'Assises* as evidence of the high quality of the pre-trial investigation. He argues this would be preferable to our own 'criminal court system in its current overblown and expensive form'. Others may point to the *lack* of adversarial behaviour by trial counsel and the damage which a biased *juge d'instruction* may do in pre-judging and foreclosing the defence case.
5 Though note that the recent Law Society/Legal Aid Board accreditation scheme goes some way to improving the quality of legal advice. See Bridges and Choongh (1998).
6 See, for example, Legrand (1996: 236) who, in the same way that many of us would argue for the necessity of a contextual approach to the study of all areas of law, argues for consideration of the 'socio-historical or socio-cultural context' in comparative studies.
7 Presentational data 'concern those appearances that informants strive to maintain (or enhance) in the eyes of the fieldworker, outsiders and strangers in general, work colleagues, close and intimate associates, and to varying degrees, themselves' (Van Maanen, 1983: 42).
8 Earlier presentational data can then be reinterpreted in the context of observation, and may take on a new significance: if the fieldworker has been consciously or unconsciously misled by research subjects, that is of interest – what perspective was projected and why? It should also be remembered that people often lie about what matters most to them.
9 For example, there is a much stronger human rights discourse in debate surrounding French criminal procedure than is the case in the UK. The recent reform body, the Delmas-Marty Commission (1991), couched its discussion and proposals in the language of the European Convention on Human Rights.
10 See e.g. Pakter (1985), who compares the ways in which evidence is excluded in France, Germany, Italy and the USA. Set in the context of the courts' willingness to exclude evidence in practice, as well as potential alternative remedies, this provides the

reader with a feel for the very different approaches adopted in relation to evidence admissibility.
11 Even the more well known terms such as *juge d'instruction* are not easily translated, as anything including the word judge or magistrate is likely to mislead. *Procureurs* are *juges* in France, which is commonly translated as 'judge'. On more than one occasion, a *procureur* has commented to me, 'So you see, it is very different here in France. We are not old men in wigs like in England.'
12 See, further, Langbein and Weinreb (1978) for criticism of Goldstein and Marcus as being preoccupied with their own false model.
13 The use of tables and statistical comparisons can be especially hazardous; see Frase (1990). For example, figures comparing assaults or public order offences need to be interpreted in their local context as they may represent different values, activities and levels of seriousness (Zedner, 1995: 14).
14 'Cross-national research provides an especially useful method both for the further development of sociological theory, and for establishing the generality of findings and the validity of interpretations derived from studies of single nations' (Øyen, 1992: 3, referring to L. Kohn, 1989). 'Cross-national Research as an Analytical Strategy' in M.L Kohn (ed), *Cross-national Research in Sociology*, Newbury Park: Sage.
15 Participant observation is described by McCall and Simmons (1969: 1) as a blend of methods, as, 'some amount of genuinely social interaction in the field with the subjects of the study, some direct observation of relevant events, some systematic counting, some collection of documents and artifacts, and open-endedness in the directions the study takes'.
16 One reading of which is a desire to limit the power of the judiciary *vis-à-vis* the elected government, the sovereign will of the people. See, for example, Magendie and Gomez (1986). The independence of the *procureur* is the subject of current reform.
17 See, further, Magendie & Gomez (1986) who discuss to what extent the judiciary are independent or are in fact constrained by the executive, their apparent independence acting as a legitimator of state power.
18 The change in terminology in 1958, from *pouvoir judiciaire* to *autorité judiciaire*, is also of interest in relation to the separation (and status) of powers.
19 In France, for example, the notion of a university academic (and moreover an English one) conducting an observational study was generally greeted with surprise.
20 See Ferrari (1992: 68) for a discussion of the problems of translating concepts into legal language.
21 Van Maanen, who took part in training with police recruits he was studying, was accused by friends of 'growing a badge' (Van Maanen, 1981: 194). Flood describes his overempathy with the position of the barrister's clerk, accentuated when he actually became a clerk for a short time (Flood, 1981: 179).
22 See May (1993: 72) for an interesting discussion of the 'discourse of objectification, not only in relation to the subjects of research, but also of the researchers themselves'.
23 The researcher, however carefully disguised...is always the elephant in the room' (Foreword by Geoffrey Pearson to Hobbs and May, 1993: viii).
24 The ethnographer needs to be in two places at the same time. Geertz (1988) describes this as 'In itself, Being There is a postcard experience...It is Being Here, a scholar among scholars, that gets your sociology read, published, reviewed, cited, taught' (cited in Hobbs and May, 1993: 51).
25 There were, however, a number of proposals with a distinctly inquisitorial flavour. See Field (1994).

26 See, for example, many of the contributions in McConville and Bridges, *Criminal Justice in Crisis* (1994), Edward Elgar.

References

Berlins, M. and Dyer, C. (1986), *The Law Machine*, Harmondsworth: Penguin.
Bridges, L. and Choongh, S. (1998), *Improving Police Station Legal Advice: The impact of the accreditation scheme for police station legal advisers*, Research Study No. 31, London: The Law Society and Legal Aid Board.
Cooper, J. (1991), 'Criminal Investigations in France', *New Law Journal*, 381–2.
Damaska, M. (1975), 'Structures of Authority and Comparative Criminal Procedure', *Yale Law Journal*, **84**, 480–544.
Delmas-Marty, M. (President) Commission Justice Pénale et Droits de l'Homme (1991), *La mise en état des affaires pénales*, Paris: La Documentation Française.
Devlin, P. (1979), *The Judge*, Oxford: Oxford University Press.
Ferrari, V. (1992), 'Socio-legal Concepts and their Comparison' in E. Øyen (ed.), *Comparative Methodology*, London: Sage.
Flood, J. (1981), 'Researching Barristers' Clerks', in R. Luckham (ed.), *Law and Social Enquiry: Case Studies of Research*, Uppsala: Uppsala Offcenter Ab.
Frankenberg, G. (1985), 'Critical Comparisons: Re-thinking Comparative Law', *Harvard International Law Journal*, **26** (2), 411–55.
Field, S. (1994), 'Judicial Supervision and the Pre-Trial Process', *Journal of Law and Society*, **21** (1), 119–35.
Frase, R.S. (1990), 'Comparative Criminal Justice as a Guide to American Law Reform: How Do the French Do It, How Can We Find Out, and Why Should We Care?', *California Law Review*, **78**, 539–683.
Goldstein, A. and Marcus, M. (1977), 'The Myth of Judicial Supervision in Three "Inquisitorial" Systems: France, Italy and Germany', *Yale Law Journal*, **87**, 240–83.
Hobbs, D. and May, T. (eds) (1993), *Interpreting the Field: Accounts of Ethnography*, Oxford: Clarendon Press.
Kohn, M.L. (1989), 'Cross-national Research as an Analytical Strategy', in M.L. Kohn (ed.), *Cross-national Research in Sociology*, New Park, CA: Sage.
Langbein, J.H. and Weinreb, L.L. (1978), 'Continental Criminal Procedure: "Myth" and Reality', *Yale Law Journal*, **87** (8), 1549–69.
Legrand, P. (1995), 'Comparative Legal Studies and Commitment to Theory', *Modern Law Review*, **58** (2), 262–73.
Legrand, P. (1996), 'How to compare now', *Legal Studies*, **16** (2), 232–42.
Leigh, L.H. and Zedner, L. (1992), *A Report on the Administration of Criminal Justice in the Pre-Trial phase in France and Germany*, London: HMSO.
McCall, G. and Simmons, J. (eds) (1969), *Issues in Participant Observation: A Text and Reader*, Reading, MA: Addison-Wesley.
McConville, M. and Bridges, L. (1994), *Criminal Justice in Crisis*, Aldershot: Edward Elgar.

McConville, M. and Hodgson, J. (1993), *Custodial Legal Advice and the Right to Silence*, London: HMSO.
McConville, M., Hodgson, J., Bridges, L. and Pavlovic, A. (1994), *Standing Accused: The Organisation and Practices of Criminal Defence Lawyers in Britain*, Oxford: Clarendon Press.
Magendie, J.-C. and Gomez, J.-J. (1986), *Justices*, Paris: Atlas Economica.
Mansfield, M. and Wardle, T. (1993), *Presumed Guilty*, London: Heinemann.
May, T. (1993), 'Feelings Matter: Inverting the Hidden Equation', in D. Hobbs and T. May (eds), *Interpreting the Field*, Oxford: Clarendon Press.
Merle, R. and Vitu, A. (1979), *Traité de Droit Pénale*, Vol. 2 *Procédure Pénale*, (3rd edn), Paris: Cujas.
Mendelson, W. (1983), 'Self Incrimination in American and French Law', *Criminal Law Bulletin*, **19**, 34–50.
Øyen, E. (ed.) (1992), *Comparative Methodology: Theory and Practice in International Social Research*, London: Sage.
Pakter, W. (1985), 'Exclusionary Rules in France, Germany and Italy', *Hastings International Journal of Comparative Law Review*, **9** (1), 1–57.
Puchalska-Tych, B. and Salter, M. (1996), 'Comparing legal cultures of Eastern Europe: The Need for a Dialectical Analysis', *Legal Studies*, **16** (2), 157–84.
Rogowski, R. (ed.) (1996a), *Civil Law*, Aldershot: Dartmouth.
Rogowski, R. (1996b), 'The Art of Mirroring: Comparative Law and Social Theory', in G. Wilson and R. Rogowski (eds), *Challenges to European Legal Scholarship*, London: Blackstone Press.
Rose, D. (1996), *In the Name of the Law*, London: Cape.
Rose, R. (1991), 'Comparing Forms of Comparative Analysis', *Political Studies*, **XXXIX**, 446–62.
Sanday, P.R. (1983), 'The Ethnographic Paradigm(s)' in J. Van Maanen (ed.), *Qualitative Methodology*, Beverley Hills, CA: Sage.
Tomlinson, E.A. (1983), 'Nonadversarial Justice: The French Experience', *Maryland Law Review*, **40** (1), 131–95.
Van Maanen, J. (1981), 'Notes on the Production of Ethnographic Data in an American Police Agency', in P. Luckham (ed.), *Law and Social Enquiry: Case Studies of Research*, Uppsala: Uppsala Offcenter Ab.
Van Maanen, J. (1983), *Qualitative Methodology*, Beverley Hills, CA: Sage.
Zedner, L. (1995), 'Comparative Research in Criminal Justice', in L. Oaks, M. Maguire and M. Levi (eds), *Contemporary Issues in Criminology*, Cardiff: University of Wales Press, 8–25.

7 Prosecutor Culture in Japan and the USA

David T. Johnson

The intent of all my work...has been to display and analyze the different assumptions and intentions the Japanese bring to public life, compared to the Americans, and to uncover the likely consequences of these Japanese orientations. (C. Johnson, 1995: 11)

Culture is to an organization what personality is to an individual. (Wilson, 1989: 91)

Introduction

How different is Japan, the first major industrial society to emerge from outside the Western tradition? No question more engages students of Japan, and no question breeds more, or more rancorous, disagreement. For every scholar who insists that there is no need to invoke 'the peculiarities of Japanese culture' in order to understand the essence of Japan, another scholar can be heard contending for the converse.

The chief aim of this chapter is to construct an empirically adequate answer to the parallel question about prosecution in Japan: how different is it? I focus on two important aspects of prosecutor culture: prosecutors' preferences, or what prosecutors want, and prosecutor beliefs about the factors which should and do influence their discretion. I show that Japanese and American prosecutors have markedly different work objectives and that, in important respects, they also hold different beliefs about how to exercise their discretion to charge.

Most works on Japanese law and society either assume or argue that Japan possesses a unique legal culture which is extraordinary in its effects. John Haley, for example, posits 'the paradoxical distinctiveness of the

Japanese system' (Haley, 1991; Haley, 1993: 39–40). Similarly, the other best known English book on Japanese law and society is built on a contrast between 'two Western models' and 'a Japanese model' of law (Upham, 1989: 7). This stress on the distinctiveness of Japanese legal culture is equally evident in works on criminal justice. In his classic comparative study of police in the USA and Japan, David Bayley argues that 'what stands out between the two [countries] is culture', and he urges Americans concerned about crime control to reconsider culture's powerful influence on crime by attending more carefully to the Japanese case (Bayley, 1991: ix, 189). Other legal scholarship uses less of the 'culture-structure' language employed by social scientists such as Bayley, although the cultural thrust is much the same. Daniel Foote's article on 'The Benevolent Paternalism of Japanese Criminal Justice' (1992) stresses 'an underlying orientation toward specific prevention', 'concern for rehabilitation and reform of the offender', 'a high degree of trust in criminal justice officials', and 'a relatively broad societal consensus on certain core values' (ibid.: 321, 327, 363, 386). Foote contends that these distinctives of Japanese criminal justice, all 'legal-cultural' in so far as they refer to 'ideas, values, expectations, and attitudes about law and legal institutions' make Japanese criminal justice unusually successful at maintaining social order by preventing recidivism (ibid.: 363). Likewise, John Haley's account of 'policemen and prosecutors' in Japan asserts that the 'determinative elements in the decisions whether to report, to prosecute, or to sentence' Japanese offenders are cultural 'factors that appear to be missing elsewhere – at least in the West' (Haley, 1991: 129). For Haley, the two most important factors are 'the attitude of the offender in acknowledging guilt, expressing remorse, and compensating any victims' and 'the victim's response in expressing willingness to pardon'. Finally, John Braithwaite, author of one of the most celebrated theories of crime causation in recent years, notes that since the Second World War 'the only case of a country which has been clearly shown to have had a falling crime rate...is Japan' (Braithwaite, 1989: 49). Braithwaite's general thesis is that 'the key to crime control is cultural commitments to shaming in ways that are reintegrative', and his account of Japan's crime control successes is rooted in cultural distinctives.

Despite this penchant for stressing the peculiarities of Japanese culture, scholars have done little to document how different Japan's legal culture is or, for that matter, even *what* it is. Many works which cite secondary literature in support of their cultural claims (Braithwaite, 1989; Westermann and Burfeind, 1991) turn out, on inspection, to rest tenuously on other secondary sources (Clifford, 1976), on selected anecdotes (Wagatsuma and Rosett, 1986) or, not infrequently, on the writer's expertise and thus authority as an interpreter of Japanese law and society. If what distinguishes social science from journalism is the systematic analysis of large amounts of purposefully collected evidence (Ragin, 1994: 8), then much of the work on Japan's legal culture – and especially the part pertaining to criminal justice – seems more like journalism than social science. Moreover, it is notable that the most rigorous attempt to measure and compare legal cultures in Japan and the USA finds that, at least with respect to serious crime, the two countries share far more legal culture than the prevailing accounts suppose (Hamilton and Sanders, 1992: 157).

This chapter describes and interprets certain key aspects of the legal culture of Japanese prosecutors by systematically analysing evidence – primarily survey evidence – that I collected for this purpose. Although the meaning of the concept of legal culture is far from settled (Nelken, 1995: 437), I follow Lawrence Friedman and others in using the term to denote 'ideas, values, expectations, and attitudes toward law and legal institutions' (Friedman, 1975). By analogy, prosecutor culture refers to prosecutors' mental products – the ideas, values, expectations and attitudes they have about criminal law, behaviour, and justice. I say little about the 'external' or 'public' legal culture of the general Japanese population and instead focus chiefly on the 'internal' legal culture of prosecutors, for three reasons: because prosecutor attitudes and values are often invoked but little documented; because there is good theoretical reason to believe that the culture of legal professionals has a particularly significant effect on the workings of a criminal justice system (Friedman, 1975: 194; Rutherford, 1993); and because, as a practical matter, I cannot say something about everything.[1]

In describing and interpreting the 'working personality' of Japanese prosecutors, I make frequent comparisons to prosecutors in other nations, chiefly the United States. That is the country, in addition to Japan, which I know best, and it is also the country to which students of Japanese criminal justice most frequently compare. Researchers often note that 'those who know only one country know no country' since 'it is impossible to understand a country without seeing how it varies from others' (Lipset, 1996: 17). The same may be said of prosecutor culture – it 'cannot but be comparative', for only through comparisons can its specific properties be assessed or even recognized (Guarnieri, 1997). Unfortunately, even in Western countries 'remarkably little is known about the beliefs and sentiments that impact upon the work of criminal justice practitioners'. While it is surprising that this remains relatively uncharted territory 'given the profound social and political implications of the activities of personnel working at every stage of the criminal justice process' (Rutherford, 1993: xi), it is nevertheless a baseline fact which severely limits the kinds of comparisons I can make. Thus, although this chapter is comparative it is asymmetrically so. The journey through the data is much less a direct flight to a clearly discernible destination than it is a matter of 'tacking backwards and forwards' between Japan and my own country of origin (Nelken, 1995: 444) and of trying, along the way, to point out a few of the most noteworthy features of the landscapes of prosecutor culture.

The structure of this chapter is as follows. In the opening section I provide background information on who Japanese prosecutors are so that readers may better assess the survey responses I present in subsequent sections. Then, relying on the survey results, I focus on two key aspects of prosecutor culture. First, what do prosecutors want, both in becoming prosecutors and in performing their everyday jobs? And second, what do prosecutors believe about how they should, and do, exercise their discretion to charge? The final section poses several important, but still unanswered, questions about Japanese prosecutor culture.

Who are the Prosecutors? Some Background Information

In 1994–95, I surveyed 235 Japanese prosecutors and assistant prosecutors about a variety of work-related attitudes and behaviours. In all, the survey asked 153 questions, about personal background, work objectives, suspension of prosecution, or the exercise of charging discretion, and various other aspects of the prosecutor's job. Although the survey is long,[2] almost all the questions provided respondents with multiple responses to choose from, so that most respondents took between 30–60 minutes to complete this closed-question format. All completed the questionnaire outside my presence. I heeded the advice of professional survey designers to 'search for questions on the same topic that have been asked by other researchers' (Sudman and Bradburn, 1982: 14) and adopted many items from surveys of American prosecutors, adapting them, where appropriate, to fit the Japanese context.

The original draft of the questionnaire was almost 30 per cent longer than the version actually administered. However, 64 of the original questions were cut at the insistence of prosecutors, while an additional ten were substantially rewritten at their behest. Thus, in order to get the questionnaire into the field I was required to omit or change nearly one-third of the survey items I wanted to ask. The cut and altered items fit into several identifiable types: questions about other people, whether defence attorneys, judges, police or prosecutor bosses; items asking for evaluations of the procuracy's performance; and queries about prosecutor practice which have been previously criticized (such as prosecutors' alleged overreliance on confessions or refusal to admit mistakes).

The questionnaire was first administered in January 1994 to 40 prosecutors (*kenji*) and assistant prosecutors (*fukukenji*) in a large urban office in western Honshu. After that, I used a snowball sampling technique to generate an additional 195 responses from 24 other district prosecutors offices. In all, I received responses from exactly one-half of the 50 district offices, as well as from prosecutors working in the Ministry of Justice. Like the procuracy itself, the 235 respondents were spread unevenly throughout the archipelago: 12 in Hokkaido (5.1 per cent). 158 in Honshu (67.2 per cent), 19 in Shikoku (8.1 per cent), 33 in Kyushu (14 per cent), and five in the Ministry of Justice (2.1 per cent) (eight respondents did not provide their office location). Nearly one-half of the responses (n=113) came from three urban offices.

'A Man's World'

Prosecutor respondents were overwhelmingly male (93.5 per cent male, 6.5 per cent female), as is the procuracy on the whole. Indeed, a book authored by a prosecutor executive and published in September 1993 (just three months before I began the survey) states that only about 50 of Japan's approximately 1130 prosecutors (4.4 per cent) were then female (Sato, 1993: 33). Since that book was published, the percentage of female prosecutors has increased steadily. In fact, in 1995 the percentage of new prosecutors who were female exceeded the percentage of new private attorneys who were female, although the percentage of new female judges was nearly twice as high as either.[3] Even with the increase, however, women still comprise considerably less than 10 per cent of the total prosecutor force.

Hence, Japan's procuracy is very much 'a man's world' (*otoko no sekai*), as many prosecutors freely admit. Of the 15 female respondents in my survey, I interviewed six. All spoke impassively about the problems they encountered in an overwhelmingly male office. Moreover, although all described being given case or job assignments which would have invited charges of invidious discrimination had they occurred in the USA, only one was critical of this in the interview. The others stolidly stated that some male prosecutor bosses 'were just like that' – that is, inclined to treat women differently than men simply because they are women – and that 'there is no use complaining' (*shikata ga nai*).

In fact, women prosecutors are seldom assigned to positions in either of the two launching pads for prosecutor elites – the Special Investigation Division (SID) of the Tokyo District Office and the Criminal Affairs Bureau (CAB) of the Ministry of Justice. Only in the last five years have women been admitted to the ranks of the SID's 'elite troops', and then only on what several prosecutors describe as a 'token' basis – one at a time (out of an SID force of about 30). Similarly, while I was doing research in Tokyo the sole female prosecutor in the CAB told me that she was only the second woman ever to work there, in the most elite bureau in the entire Ministry. The CAB's first female prosecutor, she vaguely explained, had 'not worked out very well'. Female prosecutors are also treated differently outside the 'elite career courses'. Sato Michio, the former superintending prosecutor of the Sapporo High Prosecutors Office (and thus one of the 11 most elite prosecutors in the entire procuracy) and now a member of the upper house of the Diet, has written a story about a young female prosecutor in which he notes that many women prosecutors are assigned trial work instead of investigations. Sato observes that the managers and executives who make such assignments say that 'trial work suits women best because trials are the face of the procuracy' but contends that 'in reality they believe investigations are too difficult for women to perform' (Sato, 1993: 33). Sato's assessment is consistent with everything I observed in Japan. Since most Japanese trials are more akin to 'mere ceremonies' than to adversarial battles, it is difficult to avoid the conclusion that, even in the procuracy, women are status inferiors, much as women are in other large Japanese organizations (Pharr, 1990).

Age

The prosecutors I sampled spanned four decades in age, ranging from 24 to 63 (one respondent, long retired, was 84) with a mean age of almost 41 years. Five out of six respondents were below age 50, while 102 of the 235 were in their thirties. Rookie prosecutors tend to be about two years younger than new judges and two years older than new lawyers. In 1995, when a record number of 86 legal apprentices were appointed to the procuracy, the average age of the new prosecutors was 29.3 years, while the corresponding figures for new judges and new lawyers were, respectively, 27.44 years and 31.11 years (*Japan Times*, 5 April 1995).

Education

Compared to the diverse college and law school backgrounds of American prosecutors, prosecutors in Japan receive strikingly similar educations. All the prosecutors (*kenji*, n=149) in the survey had graduate degrees, as did about 56 per cent of assistant prosecutors (*fukukenji*, n=86). They come from a wide range of colleges (45 in all), but more than half (104 of 197) from only four universities: Chuo (46), Waseda (26), Tokyo (20) and Kyoto (12). Thus prosecutors are heavily concentrated in the schools which have long been regarded as the main feeders for the judiciary, the private bar and the procuracy, not to mention much of the rest of the elite bureaucracy and business worlds. The larger number of Chuo and Waseda graduates is partly a function of the large number of law graduates produced by these two colleges. By contrast, in 1984 about 64 per cent of all candidates who passed the Type-A Higher Civil Service Examination were graduates of Tokyo and Kyoto universities – 55 per cent from Tokyo alone (Koh, 1989: 97).

Prosecutors' educational homogeneity extends to major areas of study as well. In the survey 181 of the 197 college graduates – nearly 92 per cent – majored in law at college. No other major had more than five prosecutor graduates. Unlike the USA, where legal education is primarily post-baccalaureate, legal education in Japan is largely undergraduate, as it was for all the law graduates in the survey. One result is that, as a group, the bar passes who embark on the two-year legal apprenticeship which precedes their choice of legal profession have received comparatively narrow educations and hardly any of the practical legal training that many American law students acquire at law schools. Their educational focus is further narrowed by the difficulty of the Japanese bar examination – probably the most difficult credentialling test in the world (Abel and Lewis, 1988: 15). In 1987 the bar pass rate was 1.98 per cent (489/24 690), but by 1994 it had skyrocketed to 3.28 per cent (740/22 554). In order to pass this exam nearly half of these aspiring legal professionals take the bar (which is only offered once a year) six times or more (Oki *et al.*, 1995: 21). Most devote themselves to full-time study during these years, often attending special cram schools (*shiho shiken yobiko*) which charge from US$1000 to US$5000 a year for tuition. Among other purposes, the two-year legal apprenticeship for bar-passers aims to broaden candidates' 'knowledge of the world' after a long, cloistered period of narrowly legal study, and to impart some of the skills necessary for their subsequent legal careers.

Family Background

In most respects, prosecutors' fathers and mothers have decidedly different occupational backgrounds. Over three-quarters of all mothers worked primarily as housewives, and none was a legal professional. In contrast, prosecutors' fathers were about evenly distributed between four of the survey's five occupational categories: as public officials, company employees, self-employed, and 'other'. Only nine of the 235 prosecutor respondents (3.9 per cent) reported that their father is, or was, a legal professional – far lower than the 19 per cent reported in a survey of private practitioners in the former West Germany (Abel and Lewis, 1988: 37). It thus seems that, like many other entrance exams in Japan (Rohlen, 1983: 61, 82, 311–13), the Japanese bar exam is a relatively open, meritocratic screening procedure – at least when compared to the screening systems used in other industrialized democracies.

Job Assignments

The largest proportion of prosecutors (n=114) worked in small district offices or branches that employ a continuous or 'vertical' prosecution system in which the same prosecutor stays with a case from the pre-charge investigation through trial. About an equal number worked in larger district offices that have bureaus. They prosecute cases 'horizontally': an investigative prosecutor (n=45) transfers cases to a trial prosecutor (n=49) immediately after the case is charged. In descending order of frequency, the other prosecutor respondents worked in general affairs bureaus (n=15), the special investigation division in Tokyo (n=4), and the traffic (n=4) and public security (n=2) bureaus. Prosecutors in the larger district offices played a wide range of more specific roles, the great majority as front-line 'operators'. Only 14 prosecutor respondents came from the management or executive ranks. As a consequence, the survey results are biased toward the culture of front-line operators, not managers or executives. This, however, is an insignificant problem, for prosecutors are best studied 'bottom-up' rather than 'top-down' (Wilson, 1989: 11).

Working Hours

Finally, prosecutors report working an average of 50 hours a week. The range is wide, running from 29 hours per week at the low extreme to 100 hours per week at the high. The distribution of hours worked is bimodal: 52 respondents said that they worked 40 hours per week and the same number said they worked 50 (the survey question was open-ended). Thus, although a few prosecutors report that they are extraordinarily busy, most do not. This is further evidence that, as I have demonstrated elsewhere (Johnson, 1996: 80), Japan's procuracy does not suffer from 'institutional incapacity' – the press of heavy caseloads – as many have claimed (Haley, 1991: 121; Abe, 1968).[4]

What Do Japanese Prosecutors Want?

Prosecutor preferences are a core constituent of prosecutor culture. Unfortunately, what prosecutors want and why they want it are two of the great unanswered questions in the sociology of criminal justice. Indeed, since for the most part these questions go unasked altogether, our understanding of prosecutor culture is severely deficient.[5] Even the minority of scholars who concern themselves with 'what prosecutors want' do so not by trying to measure, describe, interpret or explain those preferences, but by postulating them at the outset as if they were as self-evident as the Euclidean geometry axiom that 'two points determine a line'.

The prevailing postulate about prosecutor preferences states that prosecutors – or at least the American prosecutors who have been the focus of most of the social science writing on this profession – want to 'maximize the expected number of convictions weighted by their respective sentences, subject to a constraint on the resources or budget available to the office' (Landes, 1971; Forst and Brosi, 1977). This claim – the most often-repeated assertion of prosecutor preferences found in the literature – stands on no confirmatory evidence. It rests instead on 'logical' inferences about what prosecutors must want in an adversarial system of criminal justice and, perhaps more importantly, on its consistency with other assumptions in the 'law and economics' and 'rational choice' traditions. Corollary formulations of prosecutor preferences teeter on equally weak empirical foundations: prosecutors want to maximize the overall number of convictions (Chambliss and Seidman, 1984) or, a little less strongly, want a high number of felony convictions (Neubauer, 1974); prosecutors are preoccupied with their record of punishment (Reiss, 1975) and are in the business of producing favourable statistics (Sutherland and Cressey, 1978); and, as an organization, a prosecution office's dominant goal is a high conviction record (Stanko, 1981).

While the prevailing view stresses that American prosecutors want to impose harsh punishments, other views posit different preferences, albeit in a similarly axiomatic style. Consider these three examples. Pressed by a heavy volume of cases, prosecutors want to process them efficiently – to 'keep the cases moving' (Blumberg, 1979; Utz, 1984). Or, prosecutors want 'not so much to win as not to lose' (Kaplan, 1965; Skolnick, 1967). Or, enmeshed as they are in networks of relationships with police, judges, defence attorneys and political elites, prosecutors want to accommodate each of their major 'clients' (Cole, 1970; Feeley and Lazerson, 1983). Former US Supreme Court Justice Robert Jackson's (1940) claim that 'the duty of the prosecutor is not to win a case but to see that justice is done' has often been invoked as a normative standard to which prosecutors should aspire, but it is rarely regarded as what prosecutors actually want as a matter of occupational fact. In only a handful of works are prosecutors portrayed as intent on doing justice, and even then the point is seldom stated or demonstrated explicitly (Cole, 1970; Carter, 1974; Littrell, 1979; Mather, 1979; Feeley, 1992; Tevlin, 1993).

What Japanese prosecutors want is also poorly documented. Indeed, the claims which have been made stand on even weaker empirical foundations than do counterpart claims about American prosecutor preferences. Above all, Japanese prosecutors are said to be greatly concerned with rehabilitating offenders and reintegrating them into their communities (Foote, 1992; Bayley,

1991; Haley, 1991; Braithwaite, 1989; Parker, 1984; Itoh, 1982; Aoyagi, 1986). Ironically, historical works provide better evidence about what Japanese prosecutors wanted in the past than contemporary works proffer about what they want now. The best histories regard the pre-war procuracy as a central agent of state control which utilized reintegrative strategies in order to help 'solve the crucial problem of maintaining the integration of Japanese society during the dual crises of political modernization and impending war' (Steinhoff, 1991: 6; Mitchell, 1976; Mitchell, 1992).

This section attempts to better establish what contemporary Japanese prosecutors want and, in the process, to interrogate the prevailing but unsubstantiated claims that what they want is distinctly rehabilitative and thus distinctively Japanese. In order to assess how different Japanese prosecutor preferences are, I compare them to what is known about American prosecutor preferences. I present the evidence in two installments – first, by briefly describing the variety of reasons for becoming a prosecutor in the first place and then, and in more detail, by documenting Japanese prosecutors' work objectives.

Reasons for Becoming a Prosecutor

To learn why Japanese prosecutors become prosecutors instead of judges or lawyers, I employed a number of complementary research methods. First, the survey included an open-ended question asking each respondent his or her 'motives for becoming a prosecutor'. Of the 235 respondents, 193 provided valid responses, ranging in length from a few terse words to several carefully crafted paragraphs. Second, in follow-up interviews with 30 of the respondents I probed for more detailed descriptions of their career choices. In addition, in one large city I spent hundreds of hours working and relaxing with the legal apprentices who were then in the process of choosing which of the three legal professions they would enter (private attorney, judge, or prosecutor). Similarly, in Tokyo I had many opportunities to interview prosecutors (most of whom had not filled out a questionnaire) about why they became prosecutors. Finally, I have searched several autobiographical 'retrospectives' for descriptive accounts of prosecutors' reasons for becoming *kenji* and have compared them to the accounts I gathered directly (Aoyagi, 1986; Bessho, 1983; Itoh, 1982, 1987; Kawai, 1979; Sato, 1993; Yasuhara, 1985).[6]

These methods reveal that Japanese prosecutors enter their profession for a variety of reasons. A comprehensive account is beyond the scope of this chapter, but a content analysis[7] of the 193 valid questionnaire responses suggests that prosecutors' stated motivations fit into five general (and overlapping) categories: the desire to do justice; the appeal of investigations; the perceived 'fit' between job content and personality; the influence of 'significant others'; and the attraction to authority.

The desire to do justice   By far the most frequently mentioned reason for becoming a prosecutor is the desire to do justice (n=84). Many prosecutors employed the same shorthand phrase about wanting 'to realize justice', while others elaborated at greater length their desire to protect the rights of victims and society by 'not letting the bad guys sleep'. Almost as common as the desire to secure justice for victims and 'society' is the desire to do the same for criminal suspects and offenders. As one respondent wrote:

... since prosecutors wield so much control in the criminal process, and at relatively early stages in the process, they are in a privileged position to protect suspects' rights. And isn't preventing abuses of rights in the first place at least as important as trying to identify abuses after the fact and seeking remedies for them [as defence attorneys do]?

Another interview respondent put it differently when he said that: 'of all the legal professions, only prosecutors are in a position to cry with victims and get mad at offenders. We can do both.'

The appeal of investigations   Another large subgroup (n=21) emphasized investigation work as their primary motive for becoming a prosecutor. For those in this category investigations are 'interesting' because they reveal the true character of people better than trials do, or because they 'teach' truths about the world one otherwise could not know. Most respondents discovered that investigation is an interesting aspect of the prosecutor's job during their legal apprenticeships. One respondent colourfully explained that he became a prosecutor because investigations make the job 'smell of humanity'. Other prosecutors span categories one and two by linking their desire to do justice to prosecutors' special capacity to discover the truth during the pre-indictment investigation: 'If you want to do justice, you have to know what happened. Investigations enable us to know.'

The perceived fit between job and personality   A third category of respondents (n=32) became prosecutors because being a prosecutor fits their individual character better than other jobs do. Most in this category framed their decision narrowly, as a choice between becoming a judge, a private attorney or a prosecutor, but in fact many prosecutors decide to become a prosecutor in stages. First, one resolves to take the formidable bar exam, often in order to acquire the security *and* autonomy which come with being a Japanese lawyer (Haley, 1991: 111). Only after passing the bar do many aspirants give serious thought to which of the legal professions is most suitable. For some, a judge's job is too passive – reading documents all day long [as judges do] without encountering any "raw humans" is too tedious – while the profits that private attorneys must pursue make that alternative the source of so much stress, insecurity and potential failure that it may be judged a 'disgusting occupation'. Thus, the perceived drawbacks of becoming a judge or lawyer push some people away from those legal professions. Simultaneously, opportunities to 'actively make cases' by conducting investigations and exercising discretion pull them into the procuracy.

The influence of significant others The motives of the fourth group are distinctly other-directed. These respondents were encouraged by people they liked, trusted or respected to pursue the prosecutor path (n=23). Many administrative assistants (*jimukan*) become assistant prosecutors (*fukukenji*) because their supervisors urged them to take the requisite exams. Likewise, one does not have to probe prosecutors (*kenji*) very deeply to learn that many were strongly influenced to become prosecutors by a teacher or supervising prosecutor during their days as legal apprentices. More broadly, other respondents say they were swayed by parents or relatives already in the procuracy or by college 'seniors' who had preceded them on the same course. In one account, a 37-year-old prosecutor who had been in the procuracy for seven years explained that, as the eldest son in his family, Japanese custom calls for him to take care of his parents in their old age – something he could not do as a prosecutor because of the frequent transfers. Fortunately (for this prosecutor liked his job), his parents did not oppose his desire to become a prosecutor because they could rely on a younger child for support when necessary. Thus, parental permission, together with the intense dislike his girlfriend (now wife) held toward private attorneys, pushed him into the prosecutor profession.

The attraction to authority Finally, some respondents (n=7) stressed their desire to wield the vast power inherent in the prosecutor role. These prosecutors said that they wanted to become the 'fulcrum' or 'pivot point' of the criminal justice system, as Japanese prosecutors are widely and accurately held to be. More specific descriptions stress the legal authority prosecutors have to 'suspend prosecution' even in cases where there is sufficient evidence to charge and convict. As one prosecutor put it, this authority is a

> ... flexible power which judges do not possess. It can be used, of course, to benefit suspects, but at the same time if it is applied unfairly one will inevitably be criticized. Thus, prosecutors must exercise this power with great care.

Clearly, these five categories are neither mutually exclusive nor do they exhaust the wide range of motives prosecutors have for entering the procuracy. Indeed, in interviews many prosecutors give multiple, overlapping reasons for having joined the profession. Nonetheless, even the most elaborated prosecutor stories generally get spun around these principal motivations. Above all, in choosing to become prosecutors Japanese men and women select a profession which they find 'meaningful' (*ikigai ga aru; yarigai ga aru*) because it confers both the obligation and the power to 'do the right thing' routinely. The vast majority are happy with their choice: 88 per cent of respondents say that they are glad they became a prosecutor and 73 per cent say that they will remain a prosecutor until they retire.[8]

Prosecutor Work Objectives

I turn next to what Japanese prosecutors aim to achieve *after* entering the procuracy. As above, the data on 'work objectives' come mainly from the survey (n=235) and from interviews conducted with survey respondents and other prosecutors.

Part II of the survey presented respondents with 17 prosecutor work objectives. For each objective, respondents were asked to circle one of four answers in order to 'indicate how important you believe it is to try to achieve the following objectives when disposing of cases'. The four responses were: (1) not an objective, (2) not a very important objective, (3) an important objective, and (4) a very important objective. I generated the 17 objectives in the survey from the socio-legal literature on prosecutors, from several months of field observations in Japan prior to constructing the questionnaire and from a small, informal pretest of this part of the survey.

The analysis which follows is based on the percentage of prosecutors who regarded each work objective as either 'important' or 'very important'. Table 7.1 ranks the 17 objectives accordingly, from most important to least important. Most strikingly the table shows that many work objectives are salient to Japanese prosecutors. Indeed, 13 of the 17 objectives were considered 'important' or 'very important' by two-thirds or more of all prosecutor respondents. This finding belies the assertions, common in the literature, that prosecutors pursue one, or one primary, objective, such as maximizing convictions, sentences or some other index of punishment (Landes, 1971; Forst and Brosi, 1977; Chambliss and Seidman, 1984; Stanko, 1981). As a matter of fact, Japanese prosecutors seem to want least precisely what pundits of the American procuracy presume they want most.[9]

I have grouped the 17 prosecutor objectives into four categories based on the aggregate percentage of prosecutors who found them important or very important: cardinal objectives (ranks 1 and 2), primary objectives (ranks 3

Table 7.1 Prosecutor Work Objectives

Rank	Objective	Percentage
1	Discovering the truth about a case	99.6%
2	Making 'proper' charge decisions	97.9%
3	Invoking remorse in offenders	92.7%
4	Rehabilitating and reintegrating offenders	91.5%
5	Protecting the public	91.1%
6	Treating like cases alike	90.7%
7	Respecting the rights of suspects	83.9%
8	Reducing the crime rate	83.8%
9	Giving offenders the punishment they deserve	82.5%
10	Maintaining good relations with the police	80.8%
11	Have public understand that office is responding properly to crime	77.4%
12	Repairing relations between offender and victim	67.6%
13	Disposing efficiently of as many cases as possible	65.5%
14	Maintaining and improving the reputation of the prosecutor's office	36.6%
15	Invoking public condemnation of the crime and criminal	28.6%
16	Maximizing the punishment imposed on criminals	21.9%
17	Prosecuting and convicting as many cases as possible	8.6%

to 6), secondary objectives (ranks 7 to 13), and tertiary objectives (ranks 14 to 17).[10]

Cardinal objectives The two cardinal objectives – 'discovering the truth about a case' (99.6 per cent) and 'making a proper charge decision' (97.9 per cent) – are important to virtually all Japanese prosecutors. Indeed, only one prosecutor regarded the former, and only five the latter, as 'not very important' objectives, and no one regarded either as 'not an objective'. 'Discovering the truth' is such an important work objective that it constitutes the 'core task' for front-line operators. Moreover, commitment to this objective sharply distinguishes Japanese prosecutors from their American counterparts who by and large consider 'discovering the truth' either an epistemological impossibility or else the responsibility of other actors or stages of the criminal process (Johnson, 1996). 'Discovering the truth' is linked symbiotically with the other cardinal objective, 'making proper charge decisions'. As interview respondents made clear, discovering the truth is necessary in order to make good charge decisions, while good charge decisions can only be made after constructing an adequate account of the 'truth' of any given case. In short, for Japanese prosecutors, 'justice is truth in action'.

Furthermore, and notwithstanding prominent claims to the contrary, Japanese prosecutors are *not* content to discover merely the 'rough truth' or to fix their account of the truth in imprecise language. Kawashima Takeyoshi (1979), the eminent sociologist of law, argues that a 'traditional, non-Western' way of thinking permeates legal decision-making and the practice of law in Japan. To Kawashima, Japanese words, meanings and reasoning are at once indefinite, unfixed, imprecise, indeterminate, vague and ambiguous. Anyone who has ever observed Japanese prosecutors prepare dossier during a criminal investigation must greet Kawashima's claims with devout disbelief, for almost without exception the prosecutor's dossier records the official version of the facts – the truth as the prosecutor discerns it – with painstaking precision. Even for a simple bicycle theft where the suspect fully confesses, prosecutors (and police) commonly produce written accounts of the crime that exceed 50 pages. For more complicated cases, the dossier, stacked one on top of another, look from a distance like an unbound Japanese version of the *Encyclopedia Britannica*. In short, Japanese prosecutors do not merely aim to uncover the truth of each case which they process, they also convey the facts they have discovered in a manner which is 'non-Western' primarily in that it is far more 'precise' than the versions of truth produced by their peers in other dossier-producing countries.[11]

Primary objectives Each of the four primary objectives is important to at least 90 per cent of all prosecutor respondents. The first two, 'invoking remorse in offenders' (92.7 per cent) and 'rehabilitating and reintegrating offenders' (91.5 per cent), stand in much the same logical relationship to one another as do the two cardinal objectives. That is, Japanese prosecutors frequently aim to invoke remorse in offenders because they believe that acknowledging moral and legal guilt is an essential step on the road to rehabilitation. Thus, to achieve the second primary objective one must first perform the first.

The strong Japanese commitment to the first two primary objectives serves to further distinguish the preferences of Japanese and American prosecutors. Students of Japanese criminal justice have long posited a strong prosecutor preference for rehabilitation, albeit with little empirical support for their claims (Foote, 1992; Haley, 1991). The results of this study strongly support such assertions. In contrast, American prosecutors seem largely unconcerned with rehabilitative and reintegrative aims, except in cases involving juveniles or first-time, non-serious offenders. The 'decline of the rehabilitative idea' so evident in the USA (Allen, 1981) and the UK (Rutherford, 1993: 25) finds no parallel in Japan. Rather, Japan's Confucian past continues to cast a long shadow over contemporary legal culture. The Confucian tradition assumes original virtue and the perfectibility of people rather than, as in the Judeo-Christian tradition, original sin and immutable character (Smith, 1983). In criminal justice (as in industrial relations) these different assumptions lead to different beliefs and behaviours – the latter to a set of prosecutor preferences and practices pessimistic, or at best agnostic, about the possibility of rehabilitating offenders, and the former to efforts to reform most of the offenders who enter the system (Foote, 1992). Crucially, the less adversarial nature of the criminal process in Japan, together with other critical contexts of criminal justice (light caseloads, enabling law, political quiescence and the absence of juries) enable prosecutors to consider objectives besides the punitive ends of retribution and general deterrence (Johnson, 1996: 75).

The following case clearly reveals the resolutely rehabilitative ethos of Japanese criminal justice. A 45-year-old defendant was on trial for violently raping a female acquaintance twice in the same day. To use John Irwin's (1985) evocative description, the defendant was Japanese 'rabble'. He was an outsider, neither well integrated into mainstream society nor the holder of conventional values and beliefs. He was also dirty, unkempt, uneducated and disreputable; most Japanese undoubtedly considered him irksome, offensive and threatening as well. Somehow I was unsurprised to learn that he had a long prior history of felony convictions, including two prison terms for rape. Years earlier the defendant had lost much of his right arm in a prison factory accident, but this did not keep him from gesturing with the stump as he spoke.

This defendant's trial was straightforward. Police and prosecutors had secured several mutually corroborating confessions from the defendant and had recorded them in the dossier which they submitted to the court. Since the defence did not oppose the prosecutor's motion to introduce these written documents as evidence, the court's verdict and sentence were based mainly on the dossier. The investigating authorities also submitted the victim's statement in written form, thus making it unnecessary for her to make what might have been an emotionally painful appearance in court.

Since there was no disagreement about what the defendant did, the trial focused on what he deserved as punishment. The prosecutor called no witnesses, choosing instead to simply, even perfunctorily, remind the three-judge court of the defendant's prior record and the seriousness of the present offences. The defence attorney, a state-appointed lawyer who appeared to be at least a few years on the far side of 70 (I later learned he was a retired judge), called only one witness – his client. The defence attorney first tried to get the defendant to show that he was genuinely sorry for what he had done. At this he succeeded. As if on cue, the defendant proclaimed his heartfelt sorrow for the pain he had caused the victim and announced his intention never to do such a thing again. However, the defence attorney's attempts to get his client to tell the court how, exactly, he would try to reform himself generated only incomprehensible mumbling and vague promises that the defendant would 'do his best'. At this point the defence attorney saw fit to expound on the rehabilitative effects of composing *haiku* poetry.[12]

'Have you ever written haiku poetry?' the lawyer asked.
'Never have,' replied the confessed rapist.
'You should,' retorted the lawyer. 'I write *haiku* often, and there's nothing like it for focusing the mind and purifying the spirit.'
'I see.'
'Have you ever heard of Basho?' queried the attorney. 'He's a famous *haiku* poet you know.'
'I've never heard of him.'
'Well, you should read him, and you should write your own *haiku* too. I think it would do you some good. Basho wrote this *haiku*. It's famous. "An old pond/A frog jumps in/Plop." Pretty good, huh? Haven't you ever heard this poem?'
'No I haven't,' replied the defendant.
'Well, I think you should begin studying *haiku* poetry. Something like this could really help you to reform your ways.'
'Yes,' responded the defendant, 'I'll try it. Thank you.'

On hearing the defence attorney recite Basho's famous frog poem (the most well known verse in *haiku* history), I struggled to smother a snicker, unsuccessfully. The defendant was clearly the kind of person James Q. Wilson had in mind when he declared that 'wicked people exist'. Like Wilson, I believed that all that could be done with this particular defendant was to set him apart from the innocent. He was, I was sure, completely beyond hope. To treat him otherwise would 'make sport of the innocent and encourage the calculators' (Wilson, 1983: 260). Could this defence attorney really be serious?
He was quite serious. Indeed, even the prosecutor agreed with him. After that trial session ended I cornered the prosecutor and the three legal apprentices who had observed the trial, reminded them of the defence attorney's exhortations and asked what they thought. Unlike me, all found the defence

attorney's remarks perfectly appropriate and all shared the belief that, with effort, the defendant could be restored to something approximately his original virtue.

'Why not?' the prosecutor responded to my incredulous inquiry. 'Maybe *haiku* poetry could help the defendant turn his life around.'

Another primary prosecutor objective, 'treating like cases alike' (90.7 per cent), is widely held to be a goal that American prosecutors cannot, and thus should not, even try to achieve. Lief Carter (1974), for example, argues that the American ideal of justice embodies two mutually incompatible ideals – individualization 'treating different cases differently' and uniformity ('treating likes alike', or what Carter calls 'order') – but that the bureaucratic model of management necessary to achieve uniformity does not fit the nature of the job of prosecution. Hence, Carter claims, prosecutors should seek to individualize case dispositions without worrying about uniformity, as they do in fact in the California office he studied. Similarly, prevailing accounts of Japanese criminal justice assert that Japanese prosecutors do 'not seek simply to process cases as quickly as possible according to highly uniform standards', but instead emphasize 'the importance of individualized determinations based on careful considerations of the individual's personal circumstances and other factors' (Foote, 1992: 341; Haley, 1991). In short, scholarship on both Japanese and American prosecutors concludes that neither does much, or even cares much, about treating like cases alike.

That orthodoxy, at least as it applies to Japanese prosecutors, is wrong. In fact, survey results demonstrate that 'treating like cases alike' is a key objective for Japanese prosecutors. Indeed, only two of 235 prosecutors said that it was 'not an objective'. In the rank order of work objectives this goal was deemed significantly more important than even 'repairing relations between offender and victim' – an aim often deemed one of the chief distinctives of Japan's procuracy (Haley, 1991). Furthermore, prosecutor respondents were not simply reciting *tatemae* (the officially accepted view) when they emphasized the importance of this goal; treating likes alike is clearly their *honne*, or real intention, too. Prosecutor responses to questions in part four of the questionnaire on *kessai* consultations with superiors (questions 33, 34, 35, 36, 37, 38, 72, 95) and office precedents and guidelines (questions 70, 71, 73, 78, 80) reveal that organizational structure and practice are dedicated to the ideal of 'treating likes alike', and ethnographic observations further reinforce that conclusion. In fact, this work objective is so primary to Japanese prosecutors that I consider it a principal hallmark of the Japanese way of justice (D. Johnson, 1996: 311).

Secondary objectives The seven secondary objectives, while significantly less important to Japanese prosecutors than either cardinal or primary objectives, were still deemed important by four or five of every six prosecutor respondents (65.5–83.9 per cent). As mentioned above, 'repairing relations between offender and victim' was important to slightly more than two-thirds (67.6 per cent) of all prosecutors, but its rank order of 12 indicates that Japanese prosecutors regard other aims as more salient. Moreover, 2.5 times as many respondents said this objective is 'important' rather than said it is 'very important' and, in follow-up interviews, many prosecutors declared that, even when they wanted to help mend relations between an offender and victim, unless both parties are similarly motivated there is little that even the most determined prosecutor can do.

The importance ascribed to the last secondary objective – 'disposing efficiently of as many cases as possible' (65.5%) – suggests that while prosecutors possess relatively light caseloads, they still consider efficiency a relatively important aim. Here too, interviews helped provide a more nuanced understanding of this value. Because the eight High Prosecutors Offices review the district offices in their respective jurisdictions at the end of the year, front-line operators feel pressure during the last weeks of each calendar year to dispose of cases that have been on the books for a long time (particularly 'at-home' cases in which the suspect has not been arrested). Several prosecutors reported that pressures to 'clear the books' for the new year were far greater in the past than at present, but even today managers in the various district offices and their executive bosses in the High and Supreme Offices continue to expend considerable energy trying to ensure that the office statistics for which each is responsible reflect well on their respective individual and team performances.[13]

Tertiary objectives The final category of prosecutor work goals I call tertiary objectives, although the weak aggregate commitment to these objectives means some may be better labelled 'non-objectives'. Only one of the four goals in this category was regarded by more than a third of prosecutors as either important or very important ('maintaining and improving the reputation of the prosecutor's office') and, even then, the level of support barely exceeded one-third (36.6 per cent). The level of commitment to this objective probably would have been higher if I had been able to sample prosecutor executives more broadly, for one key executive task is to preserve the procuracy's external legitimacy by guarding its organizational reputation. Nevertheless, concerns about the reputation of the office appear to influence routine prosecutor decisions only weakly – an unsurprising fact given that prosecutors' job security does not depend, either directly or indirectly, on electoral scrutiny.

The survey included the next tertiary objective, 'invoking public condemnation for the crime and criminal', because John Braithwaite's much publicized theory of 'reintegrative shaming' predicts that it must be an important Japanese criminal justice objective and because Braithwaite urges other researchers to test his theory with ethnographic and survey research (Braithwaite, 1989). The weak level of support (28.6 per cent), however, reveals that 'invoking the public's condemnation' is not an important prosecutor objective.

Braithwaite believes that 'the key to crime control' lies in cultural commitments to reintegrative shaming and that, of all the countries in the postwar era, Japan has most successfully controlled crime precisely because it has been committed so strongly to reintegrative shaming, both informal and formal. Thus, one key concept in Braithwaite's theory is 'shaming', which he defines as 'all social processes of expressing disapproval which have the intention or effect of invoking remorse in the person being shamed and/or condemnation by others who become aware of the shaming' (Braithwaite, 1989: 100). As shown above, since 'invoking remorse in offenders – the first method of shaming in Braithwaite's definition – *is* a primary prosecutor objective (92.7 per cent), my survey provides partial support for Braithwaite's claims about crime control in Japan. However, Braithwaite's second method of shaming appears much less important to Japanese prosecutors than the first – so unimportant, in fact, that it hardly merits mention as a prosecutor objective at all. Indeed, prosecutor commitment to this work objective was so weak that when I was trying to gain approval for this part of the survey (so that it could be administered), two of the prosecutors reviewing the item had difficulty understanding what it meant. When they finally comprehended what the question was designed to measure one asked quizzically, 'Why would we want to do that?'. It seems, then, that no matter how well other features of Braithwaite's theory fit Japan (more research is needed), 'invoking condemnation of the crime and criminal' is not something prosecutors do.

Ironically, the last two work objectives in Table 7.1 express the prevailing wisdom about what American prosecutors want (Landes, 1971). Whether American prosecutors aim at these goals or not (and my research suggests few do), Japanese prosecutors unequivocally do not. The first, 'maximizing the punishment imposed on criminals', was considered important by only 20.9 per cent of Japanese respondents and 'very important' by a trifling 0.9 per cent (for a total of 21.9 per cent). The second, 'prosecuting and convicting as many cases as possible', proved even less popular. Indeed, it is by far the least important of all 17 objectives (8.6 per cent). Clearly, one cannot draw an accurate picture of what Japanese prosecutors want by using the assumptions, speculations and stereotypes provided by accounts of American prosecutor preferences. Japanese prosecutors are not the bad guys, the princes of punishment, that their American counterparts are so often characterized and caricatured to be. In fact, as my own observations and interviews in American prosecutors' offices make clear, neither are prosecutors on this side of the Pacific (Gottfredson and Gottfredson, 1988: 113).

The aim of this section on objectives has been to paint a collective portrait of the preferences held by Japanese prosecutors. Although the picture resembles a rough sketch more than a high-quality close-up, it is an improvement over the acts of faith that too often substitute for data. Much more, of course, remains to be done in order to better understand prosecutor preferences in Japan and the USA. We still know little about this critical corner of criminal justice culture. Until we learn more, Freud's aphorism should speak reprovingly to students of prosecutors in both countries: 'ignorance is ignorance; no right to believe anything can be derived from it'.

The Suspension of Prosecution and the Exercise of Discretion

Attitudes and beliefs about how prosecutors should, and do, exercise discretion constitute the second core element of prosecutor culture. This section examines prosecutors' views on their authority to suspend prosecution, one of their most important discretionary powers.[14] It does so in three parts. First I recount a story which is famous among Japanese prosecutors and suggest what the story teaches about their perceptions of risk. Then I briefly summarize the suspension of prosecution doctrine so that the last part can examine prosecutors' beliefs about the exercise of discretion.

'Prosecutors Mature by being Deceived': A Homily about Risk

The most widely read essay ever written by a Japanese prosecutor is almost certainly Itoh Shigeki's (1982) 'A Prosecutor Gets Tricked' (*'Damasareru Kenji'*), a three-page discourse which introduces a book of essays by the same title and which was followed five years later by a similar book of essays entitled 'A Prosecutor Gets Tricked Again' (*'Mata Damasareru Kenji'*). The verb in the titles – *damasareru* – is what the Japanese call a 'suffering passive'. It covers a range of related meanings: to be tricked, cheated, deceived, suckered and made a fool of. All imply that the prosecutor has 'been had'.

In the 1982 essay, Itoh tells a story about a burglary case he handled in 1949 at the Tokyo district prosecutors' office on his very first day on the job. The suspect, a middle-aged man, had just confessed to the burglary when a woman carrying an infant on her back (papoose-style) rushed into Itoh's office to reproach the man for his crime.

'How could you do such a thing?' the woman bawled. 'Aren't you ashamed for the baby?'

From the way the suspect and woman interacted Itoh inferred, reasonably enough, that they were husband and wife and that the baby was their child – an impression which was reinforced when the man tearfully swore that he would not 'cause you guys any more trouble'. During training, Itoh had been instructed that this was the kind of case which calls for a suspended prosecution, so he obtained the approval of his superiors, warned the man not to slip up again, and released him without filing any criminal charges.

Two days later Itoh observed the same man entering the office of a veteran prosecutor – in handcuffs. The prosecutor informed Itoh that the man was the head of a gang of thieves who had committed over 200 burglaries in the area, and that immediately after Itoh had released him the police had re-arrested him for a related crime. Perplexed by this sequence of events, Itoh telephoned the police officer in charge who told him that the police had brought the thief to a different prosecutor for the second offence because 'a rookie just can't cut it in a case like this'. Itoh's frustration was further fuelled when he learned that the thief's 'wife' and 'child' were nothing of the kind. In fact, the woman was an acquaintance of the gangs and had been paid to put on a performance designed to deceive Itoh into suspending prosecution.

Itoh concludes the story with a maxim that is widely repeated in prosecutor circles: 'prosecutors mature by being suckered and suckered again'. To Itoh and, as we shall see, to the vast majority of Japanese prosecutors, the aim of suspending prosecution is to help reform offenders and reintegrate them into society. In so aiming, prosecutors are occasionally tricked by dramatic performances of the kind that bamboozled Itoh in his first day on the job. Even then, however, prosecutors believe some such tricksters return to society and, as Itoh puts it, 'reform perfectly'. More importantly, the opposite error – wrongly prosecuting a case which should not be prosecuted – is considered much the graver mistake, so much so that, even for a rookie *kenji*, it is 'absolutely unforgivable'.

Itoh's story and commentary teach two central truths about prosecutor culture in Japan. First, the tale exemplifies the strong commitment of the prosecutor organization and the individuals in it to learn from their mistakes so as not to repeat them. Prosecutors may 'mature by being deceived', but since maturity is not a quality the inexperienced naturally possess, mistakes are to be anticipated and, if at all possible, avoided. One sees evidence of the procuracy's organized hunt for mistakes almost wherever one looks: in the ubiquitous guidelines for charge and sentence decisions, in the two or three levels of *kessai* consultations required for all major discretionary decisions, in the yearly after-the-fact audits of case dispositions and, perhaps most strikingly, in the great lengths to which prosecutors go in order to avoid making, or being perceived to make, mistakes. Like elite bureaucrats in other Japanese ministries, prosecutors are judged chiefly on the basis of 'the demerit principle' (*shittenshugi*) (Miyamoto, 1994: 22). Since office peers and (especially) superiors translate mistakes into aspersions, criticism, undesirable job and case assignments, and other negative career repercussions, Japanese prosecutors are extraordinarily prudent (Tojo, 1968: 62, 219).

But to Japanese prosecutors all mistakes are not equally grave, and herein lies the second and (for present purposes) more important lesson to be learned from 'A Prosecutor Gets Tricked'. Stated broadly, prosecutors may take two types of risk when deciding whether or not to charge a case: they may choose not to charge an offender who then reoffends (a type I risk), and they may charge someone who is subsequently found not to deserve criminal punishment (a type II risk). More concretely, a prosecutor takes a type I risk when, as rookie Itoh did, he decides not to charge an offender who then goes on to commit additional and, arguably, avoidable harm. Conversely, a prosecutor takes a type II risk when he charges a suspect who does not deserve to be punished. The accused may deserve no criminal punishment either because there is reasonable doubt about whether he really committed an offence or because punishment will not achieve any legitimate jurisprudential purpose (such as rehabilitation or deterrence).

A second Itoh essay stands in counterpoint to the first. This one, which concludes Itoh's 1982 book and is probably the second most famous piece ever written by a Japanese prosecutor, is entitled 'Prosecutors do not Let the Wicked Sleep' ('*Warui yatsu o nemurasenai kensatsu*'). As the title suggests, this essay exhorts prosecutors to aggressively investigate and prosecute criminal behaviour. Thus, while the first story implores prosecutors to seek the reform of offenders through suspended prosecutions, even at the cost of being deceived, this story entreats them to 'cry together with the victim' and to deal harshly with criminal offenders. The policies advocated in the two stories, like the plural purposes of punishment more generally, often cannot be reconciled in particular cases. When that tension makes it impossible for Japanese prosecutors to pursue both aims simultaneously, they systematically favour the teachings of the first Itoh essay over the second – they prefer, in other words, to err on the side of less punishment rather than more.

Cultures are biased towards some risks and against others. Since no person or group can attend equally to all hazards, some sort of priority must be established among them. The culture of Japanese prosecutors is biased toward type I risks of the kind Itoh describes in the story – suspending prosecution in cases where there is clearly enough evidence to convict and punish an offender. In contrast, American prosecutor culture is more inclined to take type II risks, by pursuing conviction and punishment in serious cases even when there are doubts about the probability of gaining conviction. Why the difference?

Consider the USA first. American prosecutors also possess legal authority to 'suspend prosecution', but are extremely reluctant to use it because their political permeability leaves them vulnerable to public criticism (Johnson, 1996: 91). American chief prosecutors are elected, and the electorate on whom they depend demands increasingly harsh punishments. The ghosts of Willie Horton and Richard Allen Davis (among a host of others) constantly remind American prosecutors (not to mention police chiefs, parole boards and politicians) of what the public wants and of the price they will pay in public criticism and job insecurity if they disregard it.[15] In short, for American prosecutors the cost of a failed type I risk usually surpasses the cost of a failed type II risk. Moreover, since unpredictable juries make it difficult for American prosecutors reliably to predict whether a type II risk will fail, it is extremely difficult for them to systematically eliminate type II risks, as have Japanese prosecutors (Johnson, 1997a).

In contrast, Japanese prosecutors incur few personal or collective costs when a type I risk is taken and fails, for crime is far less a public problem in Japan than it is in the USA, and public criticism of prosecutors for not being sufficiently punitive is almost unheard of.[16] However, prosecutors in Japan *are* harshly criticized when a case that they have charged results in acquittal (that is, when a type II risk fails). Indeed, even acquittals or partial acquittals in minor theft and assault cases generate media headlines and public fury about the procuracy's 'sloppy investigations', 'reckless practices', and 'fascist intentions' (Hatano, 1994). This intense criticism of type II mistakes has helped create Japan's 'high-precision' criminal justice system, wherein few criminal indictments end in acquittal. Critics allege that Japanese prosecutors are 'cherry-picking airtight cases' (*Wall Street Journal*, 18 December 1995) and in choosing to charge only cases which are certain to end in conviction, prosecutors do their utmost to avoid type II mistakes. However, if Japanese prosecutors are 'cherry-picking' cases, it is largely because the Japanese people strongly prefer cherries to lemons. Significantly, in cases where the public is most willing to accept the risk of an acquittal – mainly corruption cases involving Diet politicians – the acquittal rate is an astounding 45 per cent (Nomura, 1994: 55). Thus, the preference of Japanese prosecutors for type I risks arises from Japan's general legal culture, just as American prosecutor culture rests on broader cultural foundations.[17]

The Suspension of Prosecution: An Overview

The authority to suspend prosecution is widely regarded as one of 'the most important characteristics' in Japanese criminal justice (Inagawa, 1994: 14). Indeed, judged by how much prosecutors write and talk about it and by how much they and criminal suspects are affected by it, suspension of prosecution may be the most noteworthy prosecutor practice of all.

Japanese writers commonly describe suspension of prosecution as a uniquely Japanese practice which resonates well with other distinctives of Japanese culture (Aoyagi, 1986: 194). This compound assertion is half-correct; the most important half is the second part, and it is true. To be sure, American prosecutors possess similar discretion to divert offenders from the criminal process even in cases where there is enough evidence to convict (Gottfredson and Gottfredson, 1988: 114). Prosecutors in many other countries – such as Denmark, France, the UK, Holland, Norway and South Korea – do this too (Tak, 1986: 33). Thus, in this regard, there is nothing uniquely Japanese about the power to suspend prosecution. However, the practice does fit well with other features of Japanese culture, especially the propensity for wrongdoers to confess (Wagatsuma and Rosett, 1986) and the disposition to believe that people are 'perfectible' through social engineering (Smith, 1983). Although the doctrine was not formalized by statute until 1922, prosecutions have been suspended in Japan since the 1880s (Foote, 1992: 347). In the early years, however, prosecutors used the practice primarily to mitigate prison overcrowding and thereby reduce demands on an already overburdened national budget. By the early 1900s the formal justification had shifted to stress reforming offenders and ensuring their reintegration into the community (Aoyagi, 1986: 194; Goodman, 1986: 18), and it continues to be justified in similarly rehabilitative terms today (Inagawa, 1994). Furthermore, when prosecutors are considering whether to suspend prosecution, one important factor is the likelihood of rehabilitation (Mitsui, 1974; Goodman, 1986: 36).

In recent years prosecutors have disposed of between 30 and 40 per cent of their caseloads by suspending prosecution. For a variety of reasons this figure has declined since the pre-war years when more than a half of all criminal cases were so disposed (Aoyagi, 1986: 195), but the still high percentage reflects how significant the practice remains to prosecutors and suspects alike. As such, any account of prosecutor culture must consider prosecutor beliefs and attitudes about it. Unfortunately, with the exception of Mitsui Makoto's unduly neglected research from the 1970s, no one has tried to measure the kinds of factor which influence prosecutors to suspend prosecution. Part 3 of my survey was designed to do just that. It is, in other words, one means of probing another important but neglected segment of Japanese prosecutor culture.

Part 3 of the survey had two sections, both straightforward. Section 1 asked prosecutors to indicate how strongly they agreed or disagreed with ten statements about suspension of prosecution. The answer scale ranged from (5) 'strongly agree' to (1) 'strongly disagree', with the midpoint meaning that respondents 'cannot say either way'. Section 2 asked prosecutors to indicate the importance of each of 18 factors in determining whether or not to suspend prosecution' when you are investigating a case and think that suspending prosecution is a possible disposition for the case'. The answer scale for section 2 had three categories: (1) 'not an important factor', (2) 'depending on the case, sometimes important and sometimes not'; and (3) 'an important factor'.

The original draft of part 3 of the survey included a detailed hypothetical similar to those used by W. Boyd Littrell (1979) in his study of New Jersey detectives and prosecutors. Use of the hypothetical would have enabled me to compare prosecutor responses on the same set of case facts. Unfortunately, my prosecutor handlers would not permit the questionnaire to be administered in a form which included the detailed case. They feared (they said) two deleterious consequences: that the published results would encourage the calculators to take as many bites from the apple of leniency as the survey evidence seems to allow (a deterrence concern), and that the results would be interpreted as an official statement of procuracy policy which might give defence attorneys a new resource for arguing that indictments were unfair. One wonders, of course, whether the prosecutors' opposition also stemmed from what would be an equally understandable desire to keep their practices insulated from external scrutiny and potential criticism. Whatever their real reasons, the data were generated by a question which leaves plenty of room for different prosecutors to imagine differently the circumstances shaping their suspension of prosecution decisions.

Responses to the general questions on suspension of prosecution show that Japanese prosecutors regard this decision as an important, difficult and rewarding part of their job. Of the 235 respondents, 230 (97.9 per cent) agreed or strongly agreed that 'the decision whether or not to suspend prosecution is one of the most important judgments a prosecutor makes'. Only one disagreed. Furthermore, almost three-quarters of all prosecutors believed that the suspension of prosecution decision is 'difficult' to make, while nearly three in five said that such judgments are 'one of the most rewarding, meaningful parts of my job'. Indeed, virtually all prosecutors who have written memoirs of their careers give primacy of place to decisions to suspend prosecution and the effects that such decisions had on themselves and offenders (Aoyagi, 1986; Bessho, 1983; Itoh, 1982, 1987; Kawai, 1979; Sato, 1993; Yasuhara, 1985).

The aim of the suspension of prosecution system is, as Itoh Shigeki (1987: 188) notes, 'to prevent offenders from reoffending by rehabilitating and reintegrating them into society without stigmatizing them' (literally, 'without stamping them with a branding iron'). For nearly 90 years this goal has also served as the official justification for the practice. The vast majority of individual prosecutors believe that suspended prosecution often realizes this aim in practice. In fact, more than four out of five prosecutors agreed or strongly agreed that 'in some cases suspending prosecution better helps to rehabilitate and reintegrate offenders than does prosecution'. Although scant, the available research evidence supports their view that suspending prosecution has the intended rehabilitative effects (Foote, 1992: 363).

At the same time, however, suspension of prosecution is occasionally applied for less laudable reasons as well. Setsuo Miyazawa (1992: xi) has argued persuasively that Japanese police detectives are under such intense pressure to solve cases efficiently that they often violate the rules of due process to do so. Miyazawa further suggests that since 'prosecutors also are under pressure for efficient case disposition' (1992: 220), they also take procedural short-cuts, chiefly by suspending prosecution in cases where there is insufficient evidence to convict. Of course, such short-cuts, when taken, violate the office policy that allows prosecutors to suspend charges *only* in cases where there is sufficient evidence to convict. Sometimes prosecutors do suspend charges in order to curry police favour (*kempu teki kiso yuyo*; Johnson, 1996: 158), but survey and interview results demonstrate that prosecutors seldom do so out of efficiency considerations. Prosecutor respondents were almost evenly divided about whether 'compared to prosecuting a case, suspending prosecution saves time and effort'. Nearly half said that they 'cannot tell either way' (45.5 per cent) – that is, it depends on the case – while the remaining half was about equally split between those who agreed (30.2 per cent) and those who disagreed (23.4 per cent). In an interview one prosecutor said that:

... suspending prosecution does save time when the choice [as to whether to suspend prosecution or not] is clear, but in many cases the choice is not clear. In those kinds of cases I have to acquire a great deal of information in order to make a good judgment and convince my superiors. That takes time.

In addition, only 6.1 per cent of prosecutors agreed with the more precise statement that 'I sometimes suspend prosecution in order to save my time and effort for other cases', whereas about four out of five said they do not. In interviews, many prosecutors reported that they cannot suspend prosecutions in order to conserve resources because they must justify their disposition decisions both in writing and, more importantly, in *kessai* consultations with as many as three office managers. Whether or not to suspend prosecution is a primary topic in such consultations, with almost four in five prosecutors saying that 'at *kessai* I frequently discuss whether or not to suspend prosecution'.[18]

Finally, my survey asked two questions about the conditions imposed on offenders whose prosecutions are suspended. Nearly four in five respondents said that before suspending prosecution they usually make the offender promise to do some things after the case is suspended, such as 'maintain good conduct' or 'make reparations' (*jidan*) to the victim. In many of the interrogations and interviews which I observed prosecutors exhorted suspects to reform their ways and exacted promises accordingly. However, since prosecutors rarely obtain information about an offender's behaviour following the suspension of prosecution decision, they are unable to monitor compliance with the pre-disposition promises (Tojo, 1968; Dando, 1970). Of course, since suspended prosecutions are recorded by the organization, if a once-forgiven offender reoffends, the prosecutor in charge of the second case often learns of the earlier disposition.

Prosecutor Beliefs about the Exercise of Discretion

Engraved in stone on the Department of Justice Building in Washington DC are the words 'Where law ends tyranny begins'. In truth, where law ends discretion begins, and how that discretion is exercised means either justice or injustice, reasonableness or caprice (Davis, 1969: 3).[19] The discretion to suspend prosecution is critical because it is the paradigm instance of prosecutor power and because how it is used strongly shapes the quality of Japanese criminal justice.

Unfortunately, scholarship on Japanese criminal justice reveals little about this crucial category of decision which is empirically corroborated. This section describes what Japanese prosecutors believe about the factors that do, and should, influence their suspension of prosecution decisions. Thus, the focus remains squarely on prosecutor culture – that is, beliefs and attitudes about prosecutor behaviour.

Prior Research

Previous works on criminal justice in Japan emphasize several distinctively 'Japanese' factors that influence suspension of prosecution decisions. John Haley, for example, states that Japanese police, judges, and prosecutors 'take a variety of factors into account in their decisions on how to treat a particular suspect or defendant'. Such factors include 'considerations common to most criminal justice systems' (such as prior record and gravity of offence) as well as 'additional factors that appear to be missing elsewhere – at least in the West'. On this view, two distinctively Japanese factors 'are determinative elements in the decision whether to...prosecute...the offender': first, 'the attitude of the offender in acknowledging guilt, expressing remorse, and compensating any victims' and, second, 'the victim's response in expressing willingness to pardon' (Haley, 1991: 129). Similarly, although Marcia Goodman's study of prosecutorial discretion in Japan discerns several 'common threads' in prosecutor decisions to suspend prosecution, it stresses above all an offender's remorse (*hansei*), without which 'it is most unlikely...that lenient treatment will be accorded' to the suspect (Goodman, 1986: 46). The best Japanese research reaches much the same conclusion. Using written records from prosecutor offices and trial courts, Mitsui Makoto has conducted a statistical analysis of suspension of prosecution decisions. Mitsui concludes that prosecutors emphasize 'special prevention' or rehabilitation factors for both property crimes and violent offences (Mitsui, 1974: 1693, 1736).

Survey Findings: The Primary Factors

As Table 7.2 makes clear, Japanese prosecutors believe that a wide range of factors influence their suspension of prosecution decisions. In fact, the most striking feature of this table is how few factors are considered unimportant. Of the 18 factors listed, only the last three (suspect's cooperativeness, suspect's marital status, and police opinion) were deemed unimportant by at least a quarter of the prosecutor respondents, whereas fully 12 of the 18 were considered important by 25 per cent or more.

Clearly, however, some factors are more important than others. The first seven factors in Table 7.2 are *primary factors*, for two related reasons. First, between 70 and 90 per cent of all respondents regarded these seven as important – a range far higher than the corresponding percentages for the other 11 factors. There is a clear break in level of importance between the seventh and eighth ranked factors ('prior record', at 70.1 per cent, is considered 'important' by 50 per cent more prosecutors than 'future effects of prosecution on suspect', at 46.8 per cent). In addition, almost no one regarded the primary factors as unimportant. In fact, for six of the seven primary factors, not even one prosecutor answered 'unimportant', while for the seventh ('whether suspect repents') only one prosecutor so answered.

Thus, analysis of the culture of prosecutorial discretion should attend closely to these primary factors. Previous accounts of Japanese criminal justice stress the distinctively Japanese considerations that influence prosecutor decisions (Foote, 1992; Goodman, 1986; Haley, 1992), yet the first

Table 7.2 Prosecutor Beliefs about Factors Influencing Suspension of Prosecution Decisions

Rank	Factor	Percentages*
1	Damage done by the offence	90.1, 9.9, 0.0
2	Likelihood of reoffending	90.1, 9.9, 0.0
3	Whether suspect repents	80.3, 19.3, 0.4
4	Suspect's motive	76.4, 23.6, 0.0
5	Whether suspect compensates victim	76.0, 24.0, 0.0
6	Victim's feelings about punishment	70.8, 29.2, 0.0
7	Prior record	70.1, 29.9, 0.0
8	Future effects of prosecution on suspect	46.8, 51.5, 1.7
9	Legally prescribed punishment	44.6, 49.4, 6.0
10	Suspect's prior relationship with victim	34.1, 64.7, 1.3
11	Suspect's age	32.2, 65.2, 2.6
12	Suspect's demeanour during interrogation	28.9, 55.2, 15.9
13	Suspect's family ties	24.0, 66.1, 9.9
14	Public opinion	20.2, 72.1, 7.7
15	Suspect's social status	19.3, 72.5, 8.2
16	Suspect's cooperativeness with police and prosecutors	9.9, 50.9, 39.2
17	Suspect's marital status	3.4, 69.1, 27.5
18	Police opinion	2.6, 43.8, 53.6

* The three figures in this column reflect the percentage of prosecutors (n=235) who regarded each factor as 'important', 'sometimes important and sometimes not' and 'not important'. For example the suspect's motive (rank 4) was considered important by 76.4 per cent of the respondents, sometimes important by 23.6 per cent and unimportant by no one.

two primary factors, three of the first four, and four of the first seven (ranks 1, 2, 4 and 7 in Table 7.2) are case characteristics considered important in most criminal justice systems worldwide – and certainly in the USA. These are, in other words, 'universal primary factors'. In fact, the best reviews (Gottfredson and Gottfredson, 1988: 132; Forst, 1983: 170) conclude that American prosecutor decisions are 'influenced primarily by...seriousness of the offence' and 'prior record' (and thus the probability of reoffence) – considerations which correspond closely to 'damage done by the offence' (rank 1 in table 2), and 'likelihood of reoffending' and 'prior record' (ranks 2 and 7).[20] Likewise, the other 'universal primary factor' – the suspect's motive – is a key index of the suspect's mental state at the time of the offence and is therefore an important indicator of culpability, in the USA no less than in Japan. In fact, a large experimental survey in the USA and Japan showed that, when judging responsibility and punishment for relatively nonserious wrongs, an offender's state of mind is a more influential factor to Americans than to Japanese, but that *when the offence is serious* people in the two countries make similar use of information about the offender's mental state (Hamilton and Sanders, 1992: 183). In sum, the survey responses suggest that most of the 'primary factors' influencing suspension of prosecution decisions in Japan – and the most important factors at that – are not uniquely Japanese but are, rather, relevant considerations in most discretionary prosecution systems (Abrams, 1971; Blankenburg et al., 1978, Downes, 1988; Fionda, 1995; Frase, 1990; Goldstein and Marcus, 1977; Grosman, 1969; Guarneri, 1997; McConville et al., 1991; Weigend, 1980; Weinreb, 1977).

The survey provides further evidence that, in exercising the discretion to charge, Japanese prosecutors emphasize many of the same considerations as their American counterparts. Almost 93 per cent of all Japanese respondents agreed or strongly agreed that 'the most important single consideration in determining the sentence to impose should be the nature and gravity of the offence', and almost 78 per cent said that 'most people charged with serious crimes should be punished whether or not the punishment benefits the criminal'. Both questions are translations from American surveys first used in research on criminal court communities in the USA (Nardulli et al., 1988: 687), and both are designed to measure the 'punitiveness' of respondents. These responses show that Japanese prosecutors strongly believe punishment is an appropriate response to criminal offenders – especially serious ones – a fact which previous works on Japanese criminal justice have not sufficiently underscored.

However, this strong belief in punishment co-exists with a similarly strong commitment to some of the Japanese norms stressed by previous scholarship. For example, Daniel Foote (1992: 341) claims that 'the Japanese system emphasizes the importance of individualized determinations based on careful consideration of the individual's personal circumstances'. Consistent with that claim, over 96 per cent of Japanese prosecutors are convinced that 'it is important to individualize treatment of each suspect' (note also that no prosecutor disagreed with this assertion). Prosecutors' strong beliefs in the three remaining primary factors (ranks 3, 5 and 6 in Table 7.2) also provide support for John Haley's (1991: 129) claim that norms of 'confession, repentance, and absolution' influence Japanese criminal justice officials. First, just over 80 per cent of respondents regarded the suspect's repentance, or lack of it, as an important factor. In addition, Haley and others have noted that Japanese offenders often make restitution (*jidan* or *higai bensho*) to victims in order to repair harms and demonstrate the sincerity of their remorse, and about 76 per cent of prosecutor respondents believe restitution is an important factor influencing suspension of prosecution decisions. Finally, 'the victim's feeling about punishment' are deemed important by 71 per cent of prosecutors. As for the items tapping the repentance and restitution factors, not even one prosecutor said the victim's feelings were unimportant.[21]

The question, then, is not whether the norms of repentance, confession and absolution are important to Japanese prosecutors, for clearly they are, but rather whether in the service of rehabilitation and reintegration Japanese prosecutors are more deeply influenced by such norms than their American counterparts. They are.

Repentance and Rehabilitation in the USA and Japan

That Japanese prosecutors remain committed to a rehabilitative ideal is less remarkable than the extent to which American prosecutors seem to have foresworn it. In the words of one California prosecutor (a 'politically correct' liberal democrat, active in the gay and lesbian rights movement, and living in what is widely considered one of the nation's most progressive cities), 'it is not the prosecutor's job to help suspects'. Of course, prior to trial most American prosecutors have little direct contact with suspects. The same prosecutor states that increased contact with suspects in interrogation or interviews might be 'fun' and probably would help her 'understand the streets better', but that she still does not want it:

> I don't want to be swayed by emotional arguments. Everyone looks pathetic and sympathetic behind bars [after arrest]. My job is to give offenders the punishment they deserve, and hearing their sad stories just gets in the way.

Another American prosecutor – this one a 20-year veteran and the boss of seven prosecutors in another California office – declares that:

> ... since the [California] legislature is out of the business of rehabilitation, we should be too. Our role is not to rehabilitate. The even hand of justice must not be swayed by concerns for the individual circumstances of particular cases.... To be professional, we must avoid all favoritism and inconsistency.

Ironically, this prosecutor invokes the fear of 'inconsistency' as a reason for forsaking rehabilitative concerns even though American prosecutors make far less 'ordered' decisions than the Japanese prosecutors who have not foresworn rehabilitation (Johnson, 1996: 325).

The second California prosecutor explained that disregard for the rehabilitation of offenders is also the official policy. Whenever a criminal suspect is 'booked' by the police but not charged by a prosecutor, the prosecutor must report the 'reject reasons' to the Department of Justice. There are 11 categories of reject reasons (or 'T reasons', as they are known in the office), each with between two and 12 subcategories. They are printed and distributed to all prosecutors in the office. The main reject categories are:

- T1 – Lack of corpus (insufficient evidence to prove crime occurred)
- T2 – Lack of sufficient evidence (witness not credible)
- T3 – Inadmissible search and seizure (questionable probable cause for arrest)
- T4 – Victim unavailable/declines to testify (victim requests no prosecution)
- T5 – Witness unavailable/declines to testify (witness privilege)
- T6 – Combined with other counts/cases (more/less severe charge filed)
- T7 – Interest of justice (nature of offence, relationship of the parties)
- T8 – Other (other due process or jurisdictional considerations)
- T9 – Prosecutor prefiling deferral (district/city attorney hearing)
- U2 – Referred to out-of-state jurisdiction (US Attorney General, military authority and the like)
- U3 – Deferred for revocation of parole/probation.

Most of the reject reasons concern questions of evidence (T1, T2, T3, T4, T5) or describe other prosecution alternatives to charging the count booked by the police (T6, T8, U2, U3), but the title of the T7 category – 'interest of justice' – would, at least at first glance, seem to suggest rehabilitation as one legitimate reason for not filing a criminal charge. It does not. Nowhere among T7's dozen subcategories does one find the notion that not instituting charges (the American analogy to 'suspended prosecution') may better promote rehabilitation and thereby serve the 'interest of justice'. The closest official policy comes to that idea is the 'made restitution' reason, about which more will be said shortly.

A third Californian prosecutor told me that, even if office policy allowed prosecutors to take into account an offender's repentance, it would make little difference to charge decisions anyway because offenders rarely repent or display remorse. American suspects and offenders, she explained, are more inclined to shout obscenities at prosecutors and judges or wear shorts, caps and 'fuck the police' t-shirts to court. 'Those people don't *want* to be rehabilitated', she exclaimed. Indeed, it only takes a half-hour of observation in American and Japanese courtrooms to notice the radical difference in defendant demeanour in these two countries. While Japanese defendants are unfailing polite, deferent and respectful, many American defendants display a 'defiant individualism that confronts authority and power with few indications of deference, fear, or remorse' (Sanchez-Jankowski, 1991: 26).[22] Through friends and relatives, the defiant attitude of American defendants even gets physically inscribed in graffiti on the backs of courtroom chairs. My own quick count in one California courtroom revealed that the preferred graffito is in the 'fuck prosecutor (or judge) so-and-so' genre.[23]

Minnesota prosecutors seem to share these attitudes about the irrelevance of remorse and repentance. One, formerly a deputy sheriff, said that in dealing with juveniles remorse and willingness to get treatment are, and should be, important factors, but that he has 'a whole different attitude with adults', which he summarized as 'Tough shit! You should have been remorseful before committing the crime'. When I pointed out that, actually, one could only be remorseful about a *past* wrongdoing, the prosecutor elaborated: 'I am hard-core with adults – tough but fair. I am into fairness, not excuses. You couldn't be that remorseful if you did it.' In another interview, one of his colleagues seemed to agree. 'In intentional crimes', this former public defender declared,

> no contrition is possible. In this job you have to be cynical of human nature because everyone acts out of self-interest. Many suspects believe that manufacturing remorse will get them something. I rarely see real contrition.

Thus, American prosecutors resist allowing evidence of an offender's remorse to influence charge decisions and plea bargains. Conversely, however, American prosecutors do use an offender's 'bad attitude' to justify extra severe treatment. Prosecutors in one California office have a name for such considerations – 'asshole enhancements'. In a case involving a young man arrested for possession of one rock of crack cocaine, the prosecutor raised her original plea bargain offer and bail requests because the offender cursed at his public defender, was unruly and uncooperative during his preliminary hearing and generally behaved 'like a jerk' throughout the investigation period. In short, and in the main, suspect's attitudes influence American prosecutors negatively but not positively.

A suspect's defiant, non-compliant, or unreasonable attitude also influences Japanese prosecutors to be more punitive, at least in certain cases. Japanese prosecutors have their own version of the American 'asshole enhancement', albeit less colourfully captured as a 'denial tariff' (*hininryo*). When a suspect insists that he is innocent even in the face of substantial evidence to the contrary, Japanese prosecutors sometimes charge cases they otherwise would not or, more commonly, recommend a more severe sentence at trial.

A Japanese prosecutor imposed the first type of 'denial tariff' on a middle-aged British foreigner arrested for selling hashish. Since I translated during interrogations, I knew this case and the prosecutor well. In the early stages of the investigation the prosecutor wanted to suspend prosecution because the amount of hashish was small, the suspect had no prior record and prosecution would have badly disrupted the Japanese family into which the suspect had married. In order to have prosecution suspended, the suspect only had to acknowledge he had done wrong and promise not to possess, use or sell illegal drugs again. However, the suspect elected not to confess, despite the prosecutor's repeated instructions that doing so would be in his own best interests. Over the subsequent three days of interrogation I observed the prosecutor's attitude evolve from the original desire to forgive the suspect in order to encourage reform into the conviction that charging the suspect and seeking real time (that is, a non-suspended prison sentence) were necessary in order to 'teach him a lesson'. John Haley (1982) has described an analogous case in which two suspects, also foreigners, refused to confess even though it seemed clear they would have benefited by doing so, but the 'denial tariff' is imposed on Japanese suspects and offenders as well. In fact, almost four in five prosecutor respondents acknowledge the existence of a denial tariff by agreeing or strongly agreeing that 'in a case which will result in conviction, if a suspect denies the facts and does not express remorse, this influences the sentence we recommend'.

Scholars have argued that there is one other noteworthy difference in how American and Japanese prosecutors make charge decisions. Victims, it is said, are routinely neglected in the American criminal process while Japanese prosecutors consistently pay them careful attention (Haley, 1991: 129). This view is half-correct. Japanese prosecutors do take into account the victim's feelings about punishment, at least in most cases (but see also Morita, 1994). As described above, prosecutors believe that the victim's feelings about punishment and whether or not the victim has been compensated are two of the primary factors influencing their suspension of prosecution decisions.

However, since the first part of the claim – that American prosecutors disregard victims' attitudes – is exaggerated, there is less cross-national difference in this respect than others have supposed. Of course, many scholars argue that victims play too minor a role in the American criminal process (Fletcher, 1995), but there is actually little systematic evidence to support such a position. On the contrary, in a classic study of the disposition of nearly 2000 felony arrests in New York City, the Vera Institute of Justice concluded that:

...prior relationships were often mentioned by prosecutors...as their reasons for offering reduced charges and light sentences in return for a plea of guilty. Even more commonly, prior relationships led to dismissals.

The Vera study goes on to explain that, in these 'prior relationship cases', prosecutors most often cited the victim's non-cooperation as the main reason for dismissal, and reconciliation between the victim and offender as the main reason for non-cooperation (Vera Institute of Justice, 1981: 19). In his foreword to the Vera report, Malcolm Feeley argues that, just as American police have long tried to resolve criminal conflicts through negotiation, compromise, and temporary separation rather than through formal arrest, so prosecutors and courts also apply informal considerations. Furthermore, although the Vera study looked at only a single city nearly 25 years ago, Feeley warns that 'it would be a shame to dismiss these findings as being out of date, or as revealing no general insights into the criminal process' (ibid.: xi). Indeed, Hans Zeisel's (1982) re-analysis of the Vera data reaches similar conclusions about the importance of victims' feelings, as have other major studies of prosecutor discretion in the USA (Kerstetter, 1990; Stanko, 1981; LaFave, 1970; Miller, 1969; Newman, 1966).[24] Moreover, in the years since the Vera study the victims' rights movement has, if anything, only strengthened victims' influence in the American criminal process. In short, and contrary to the much repeated claim that Japanese prosecutors (and other criminal justice officials) are uniquely attentive to victims' attitudes and desires, the best available American research reveals that, at least in this regard, the two countries share considerable common ground.[25] Reports from Germany (Blankenburg et al., 1978) and France (Frase, 1990) show that many European prosecutors also take victims' views seriously.[26]

Conclusion

As measured by what prosecutors say in surveys and interviews, there are some striking similarities in the factors which seem to shape American and Japanese charge decisions. Several of the 'primary factors' are the same in both countries – especially the seriousness of the offence and the likelihood of reoffending. Likewise, the urges to be 'extra severe' towards offenders who are unrepentant and to consider the victim's attitude and relationship to the offender are characteristics shared by prosecutors in both countries.

However, one significant difference sharply distinguishes American and Japanese charge decisions: American prosecutors are deeply distrustful – even cynical – of virtually all offender displays of remorse, while Japanese prosecutors try hard to elicit real remorse and believe that genuine repentance can lead to reform. Of course, the Japanese propensity should not be overstated, since Japanese prosecutors do scrutinize confessions for sincerity. Indeed, as seen in Itoh Shigeki's homily, many Japanese prosecutors have learned the hard way that offenders put on insincere 'performances' (*engi*) in order to obtain more lenient treatment. Yet Japanese prosecutors also believe that one of their chief duties is to discern which offenders are genuinely repentant and which are not. They are empowered to do so by a number of enabling contexts: the long pre-charge investigation period; the many legal levers for acquiring information; the less adversarial nature of Japanese criminal justice; and the propensity of offenders to acknowledge wrongdoing (Miyazawa, 1992; Bayley, 1991). Thus, there is a close fit between the cultural imperatives which animate Japanese prosecutors and the structural realities which make their attainment possible.

The other feature of prosecutor culture considered in this chapter – work objectives – also differs markedly between the USA and Japan. Discovering the truth, invoking remorse, rehabilitating offenders and treating like cases alike appear to be more primary aims for Japanese prosecutors than for Americans. Conversely, American (and British) prosecutors are more inclined to stress the objectives of efficiency and 'just deserts' (Rutherford, 1993).

I have not addressed other interesting questions about prosecutor culture – questions which deserve far more attention than they so far received. Where, for example, does prosecutor culture come from, and how does one explain the emergence of such strongly held norms as the need to 'discover the truth', the importance of an offender's attitude, or the imperative to treat like cases alike? How does the 'internal culture' of prosecutors relate to the broader 'external cultures' of Japan's society and polity? Are there identifiable subcultures within Japan's procuracy? What are the strengths and weaknesses of Japan's prosecutor culture (Wilson, 1989: 93)? Concerning the culture of Japanese criminal justice more generally, are Japanese trials as compelling a cultural form as American trials, acting out great moral, social and political dramas? Or is Japanese culture so little beset by conflicting social values – freedom versus order, group allegiance versus individual autonomy, equality of opportunity versus equality of outcome – that trials are a less revealing symbolic venue than they are in the USA?

In closing, I raise one final question about the causal efficacy of Japan's prosecutor culture. Do prosecutors' stated commitments to 'discover the truth', 'invoke remorse', and 'treat like cases alike' actually influence prosecutor behaviour? The sociologist Paul Lazarsfeld once advised that 'if you want to know why people do something, ask them!'. The research on which this chapter is based has followed that suggestion, as do many studies of prosecutors and criminal justice practitioners (Fionda, 1995: 4; Rutherford,

1993: 2). However, some research on the relationship between the attitudes of American prosecutors and their actual decisions reaches a decidedly non-Lazarsfeldian conclusion: that the impact of attitudes on behaviour is 'marginal at best, nil for the most part'. This conclusion led the trio who conducted the study to move beyond 'the tip of the proverbial iceberg' (that is, beliefs and attitudes) to explore the iceberg's base – that is, its 'structures and contours' (Nardulli et al., 1988: 360).

Elsewhere I explore the iceberg's base – the 'structure and contours' of Japan's procuracy – and the processes and outcomes of Japanese prosecution (Johnson, 1996). In the end, prosecutor culture *does* shape how cases are processed and suspects are treated. At times, the difference culture makes seems small in comparison to the influence of structural constraints, and often the cultural distinctives seem to arise from the structures that create and maintain them. However, the assumptions, attitudes and beliefs of Japanese prosecutors do significantly shape the Japanese way of justice. The desire to elicit remorse, for example, motivates prosecutors to pursue not merely a confession but, rather, *the right kind of confession*. Once it is obtained, it may mean the difference between a suspended prosecution and a trial. Similarly, the prosecutor imperative to treat like cases alike means, among other things, that front-line charge decisions must be reviewed and approved by two or more prosecutor superiors (*kessai*) in order to ensure that Japanese justice not only aspires to but actually achieves a tolerable level of consistency. Even when it is impossible to demonstrate the presumed causal efficacy of prosecutor culture, it is clear that prosecutors' beliefs, attitudes, and assumptions justify and support particular procedural arrangements (Damaska, 1986: 14). The *kessai* system of consultation and review, for instance, rests on a foundation of cultural presumptions: that hierarchy works; that organization matters; and that decisions should, where possible, be made collectively. In short, prosecutor culture matters in Japanese criminal justice, as both cause and justification. Culture is created and culture counts. The two statements are not incompatible (Bayley, 1994).

Notes

1 In a recent review of the concept of legal culture, James Gibson and Gregory Caldeira (1996) distinguish three 'dimensions of legal values': *legal consciousness* refers to 'specific attitudes toward legal issues and institutions', *legal cultural values* are the 'more general values relevant to the legal systems but not necessarily closely connected to it'; and *general cultural values* represent such things as 'a preference for individualism over collectivism, trust in people' and so on. This chapter (and the survey on which it is based) focuses primarily on what Gibson and Caldeira call 'legal consciousness'.

2   The survey is too long to present and interpret all of the results in a single chapter. I plan to explore additional survey findings in future work.
3   In April 1995 the Ministry of Justice announced that 86 people were appointed as new prosecutors that year – the largest number ever. (The previous high was recorded in 1952, when 81 prosecutors were appointed). Of the 86 new prosecutors, 16 (18.6 per cent) were women – also the largest number ever. These increases have been attributed to Japan's protracted economic recession which made the security of a prosecutor position more appealing to many new legal professionals, to bar examination reforms which expanded the number of bar passers from 500 to 700, and to the increase in the percentage of female bar passers.

In 1995, 633 people graduated from the Legal Research and Training Institute of the Supreme Court after passing the bar exam and completing a two-year apprenticeship (a slightly large number, 712, had passed the bar two years earlier). Thus, 13.5 per cent (86/633) of the new graduates became prosecutors. By comparison, in the same year 99 people were appointed to the judiciary (15.6 per cent), of whom 34 (34.3 per cent) were women. Of the other 453 graduates (71.6 per cent of the total) who became private attorneys, an estimated 78 (17.2 per cent) were women (*Japan Times*, 5 April 1995; *Yomiuri Shimbun*, 6 March 1995; *Tokyo Shimbun*, 6 April 1995).

The percentage of female Japanese bar-passers has increased steadily over the last four decades. In the 1950s, women constituted 3 per cent of all bar-passers. The figure rose to 5 per cent between 1965 and 1975, and to about 10 per cent in the mid-1980s (Abel and Lewis, 1988: 36). From 1987 to 1991, the percentage ranged from 12–15 per cent and, in each of the three years from 1992 through 1994, 20 per cent of all Japanese bar-passers were female (Oki *et al.*, 1995: 22). In comparison, 'women represented a third of all French *stagiaires* in 1960 and a quarter of all *avocats* in Paris and its suburbs', while in Italy in 1966 women constituted about 4 per cent of all lawyers (Abel and Lewis, 1988: 36).
4   It is interesting to compare the background characteristics of Japanese prosecutors with 'the most outstanding characteristics of Japan's administrative elite' more generally (Koh, 1989: 252). Prosecutors and other high-level Japanese bureaucrats share many characteristics. They: are predominantly law graduates; chosen from among the educated elite; wield great power; and work as generalists in organizations which stress seniority and consensual decision-making. Prosecutors and elite bureaucrats also tend to retire early and get re-employed. Koh concludes that 'Japan shares many attributes of its bureaucracy with the three advanced industrial countries of Western Europe [Britain, France, and West Germany]', but not with the USA. In several key respects, prosecutor culture in Japan appears to most closely resemble prosecutor culture in France (Frase, 1990; Guarnieri, 1997; Carbonneau, 1995).
5   Indeed, Michael and Don Gottfredson (1988: vi, 117) argue that 'a profound lack of clarity of definition and of adequate measurement of objectives abounds' in studies of the criminal justice system, although their own work on 'the decision to charge' is one of few to attempt to explain what purposes animate prosecutor activities.
6   For the classic account of why 'newcomers' enter and how they adapt to American criminal court communities, see Heumann (1977).
7   The basic premise of content analysis is that the many words of a text can be classified into fewer content categories. One important use of the method is to generate indicators which 'point to the state of beliefs, values, ideologies, or other culture systems' (Weber, 1985: 9).
8   In the late 1980s more Japanese prosecutors seemed discontent with their jobs. In an article entitled 'The Prosecutor Crisis' one Japanese magazine reported that about 50

prosecutors were quitting the procuracy each year, mainly because of dissatisfaction with the office's personnel and transfer decisions and its rigidly bureaucratic character (*Sunday Minichi*, 26 April 1987). Similarly, in 1989 the Tokyo Bar Federation (*Hoso Shikaku ni kan suru Shiken Seido no Kenkyu*) reported the results of a survey administered to 144 former prosecutors who quit the procuracy and joined the private bar between 1967 and 1987. The 56 respondents answered 11 questions about their perceptions of the procuracy and their reasons for leaving it. Many expressed discontent over transfers, personnel decisions and the procuracy bureaucracy.

9   In his study of a large prosecution office in California (36 prosecutors), Lief Carter (1974: 179, 195) asked prosecutors to rate the importance of nine work goals and to evaluate how well the office accomplished each. Unfortunately, Carter did not provide a summary of the survey results. In a footnote, however, he did say that the most important three objectives for his California prosecutors were: (1) maintaining a high level of professional high performance; (2) separating the innocent from the guilty; and (3) striking a fair balance between the conflicting interests and desires of victims, police, judges, defence counsel, the public and so on. I borrowed from Carter's survey in order to construct my questionnaire, although many objectives which are centrally important to Japanese prosecutors – such as 'clarifying the truth' – are not found in his study.

10 The original version of the questionnaire also asked prosecutors to evaluate how well they achieved the various work objectives. However, prosecutors cut that section before allowing me to administer the survey. One prosecutor said that they wanted me to avoid the public criticism which would result if word got out that prosecutors believe some objectives are not accomplished.

11 The process used to uncover and construct the truth also intrudes far more deeply on the suspect's autonomy (Miyazawa, 1992).

12 A *haiku* is a three-line poem consisting of seventeen syllables (5-7-5). Most *haiku* employ special 'season words' that prompt associations to nature. Basho Matsuo, the most famous *haiku* master, helped popularize *haiku* in the Tokugawa period (1600–1868).

13 Japanese prosecutors operate under pressure to produce favourable office statistics, but police operate under much more (Miyazawa, 1992). One prosecutor told me the following story about the extraordinary lengths to which police will go in order to produce good statistics for self and office. The story gives new meaning to the subtitle of Setsuo Miyazawa's book on Japanese detectives – *A Study on Making Crime*.

Japanese police stations compete against one another twice a year to see which can seize the most guns, drugs, or organized crime members (*boryokudan*). These competitions (called *gekkan*) go a long way towards determining which police get promoted, both at the lower, front-line levels and at the managerial levels. In Tokyo, a former member of a *boryokudan* (call him B) found himself in front of my prosecutor informant being grilled about how and where he had acquired the gun for which he was arrested. After several hours of intense interrogation and confused, contradictory statements, B finally told the prosecutor that the police had ordered him to bring a gun into the police station by the end of the month (also the end of the *gekkan* competition period), had threatened him with arrest for an unrelated assault if he did not comply, and had promised him summary prosecution (and thus a light fine) if he cooperated. B told the police he did not have a gun to bring in, but the police were adamant. Indeed, B told the prosecutor the police angrily retorted that the gun B had brought to the police five years earlier did not even shoot, and they warned him that he had better not repeat the same mistake again.

Prosecutor Culture in Japan and the USA   197

B consulted with his fiance and employer about what to do. The latter urged B not to cooperate with the police. However, the police pressure persisted, and a day before the *gekkan* period ended B bought a model gun (*kaizo*) from a friend, borrowed a drill, and attempted to modify the model so it could actually shoot bullets. His fiance and employer joined him in the project and, after modifying the gun, held a small going-away party for B, drinking and toasting until the early hours of the last day of the *gekkan*. B's compatriots urged him to take care of his health during what they expected to be an uneventful ten-day detention, and promised to help B pay for the fine the police had promised he would receive. Early on the morning of the last day of the month, B turned the gun and himself into the police.

After the prosecutor confirmed B's story in interviews with B's employer and fiance, he had another prosecutor interview the relevant policeman. The police officer admitted pressurizing B to bring in a gun, but said he had not ordered B to *make* one. In the end, B's prosecution was suspended, so neither he nor his comrades in arms had to pay a fine. The responsible police officer (a detective in the organized crime branch) was pressurized to resign. He was neither arrested nor prosecuted, although legally (according to my informant) he could have been (for *kyoyozai*, or being an accomplice). The prosecutor further noted that cases this extreme of *gekkan*-induced misconduct are rare, but that less serious abuses abound. Most commonly, police compel a *boryokudan* member to bring in a gun or drugs by threatening to arrest him or his wife or boss on other charges.

14 Japanese prosecutors can divert offenders from the criminal process by not bringing charges even when there is sufficient evidence to convict at trial, whatever the severity of the offence (Code of Criminal Procedure, Article 248). This practice is known as 'suspension of prosecution' (*kiso yuyo*). In many countries (including Austria, Finland, Germany, Ireland, Italy, Poland, Spain, Sri Lanka, Sweden and Turkey) prosecutors do not have comparable discretion to withhold charges (Tak, 1986: 33). For an excellent comparative account of prosecutorial discretion in sentencing, see Fionda (1995).

15 Willie Horton is the black murderer who escaped from a prison furlough in Massachusetts and committed more violent crimes. In the 1988 presidential campaign, Republicans used his story to attack Massachusetts Democratic governor and presidential candidate Michael Dukakis as 'soft on crime' (Anderson, 1995).

Richard Allen Davis confessed to kidnapping and murdering 12-year-old Polly Klaas when he was on parole in California in 1993. Following Klaas's murder and the revelation that Davis had a long criminal record, 'three strikes and you're out' legislation gained widespread support in California and throughout the nation (Winchell, 1995).

16 The most significant exceptions occur when the public believes prosecutors have not pursued elite corruption aggressively enough, as in the Sagawa Kyubin scandals of 1992-93 (Mukaidani, 1993).

17 The methodological lesson is that to accurately understand prosecutors in any country one must resist the temptation to separate prosecutor culture from the institutions in which it works. Such arbitrary separations only generate insoluble questions (Douglas, 1986).

18 Marcia Goodman (1986: 48) and Daniel Foote (1986) disagree about how often prosecution is suspended in cases where there is insufficient evidence to convict. I believe that such cases are more common than Goodman supposed (Johnson, 1996: 158).

19 The dictionary defines 'discretion' as 'the freedom to act according to one's judgement'. This definition is close to what I mean by the term, but since it presumes that

discretion is exercised individually, not collectively, I modify it. The nature and extent of collective discretionary decision-making in Japan's procuracy distinguishes it from prosecution systems in many other countries. Hence, prosecutors have 'discretion' whenever the effective limits on their power leave them free to make a choice among possible courses of action or inaction (Davis, 1969: 4).

20 These reviews and other studies of decision-making by American prosecutors (Frase, 1980; Greenwood *et al.*, 1976) stress that in addition to the factors mentioned in the text, 'the quality of evidence' strongly influences prosecutor charge decisions. I did not include this factor in my survey because prosecutors in Japan must have sufficient evidence to convict in order to dispose of a case by suspending prosecution (Itoh, 1987: 186). In other words, they may consider suspending prosecution only in cases which have no evidence problems. Actual practice, however, is another matter (Johnson, 1996: 158).

21 Responses to related questions in the survey show that Japanese prosecutors regard the victim's attitude as a slightly stronger influence on the charging decision than the suspect's attitude, although whether or not restitution has been made appears more important than both.

22 In his 'theory of gang behavior and persistence', Martin Sanchez-Jankowski (1991: 23) states that American gang members 'have, to varying degrees, developed...a *defiant individualist* character', composed of seven attributes: competitiveness, mistrust or wariness, self-reliance, social isolation, a survival instinct, a Social Darwinist world view and a defiant air. Viewed in comparison with Japan, it is not just gang members who present a defiantly individualist demeanour. Many American non-gang suspects and offenders do so as well.

23 David Heilbroner (1990: 14) tells a story which vividly illustrates the propensity of many American offenders to deny wrongdoing and defy authority, even when literally 'caught in the act'. In Manhattan, where Heilbroner worked as an assistant district attorney for three years, kids often 'slip a folded piece of paper into the [subway] token slot so the token won't go into the token box. After a passenger loses a token and walks away, the kids come back, suck it out of the slot, and sell it for a buck on the street.' One token booth clerk became so frustrated over this 'stuff 'n' suck' technique that she smeared Krazy Glue all over the token slot. The next person to try a 'stuff 'n' suck' found himself instantly bonded to the turnstile by his lips and teeth. The first police officer on the scene called Emergency Medical Services, which injected a saline solution between the turnstile metal and the perpetrator's lips. The saline dissolved the glue and the token-sucker was arrested on the scene. His first words to the arresting officer? 'Listen, man, I wasn't sucking tokens.'

24 For example, in his assessment of pretrial diversion programmes in American criminal courts in the 1970s, Malcolm Feeley (1983: 107) concludes that 'contrary to myth, [American] prosecutors are often willing to drop charges when the interests of justice are compelling'.

25 The victim's willingness to pardon has been deemed a factor important in Japan, but is missing elsewhere. According to one scholar, Richard Frase's (1980) study shows that the response of the victim is not taken into account by American prosecutors (Haley, 1991: 121). However, since many of the federal crimes Frase studied (such as 'fraud against the government' and 'counterfeiting and forgery') did not have identifiable victims, it is unremarkable that prosecutors did not take victims' attitudes into account (personal communication with Richard Frase, 15 August 1995).

26 Whether prosecutors *ought* to concern themselves with the attitude and well-being of victims is, of course, a separate and contested issue. Some scholars strongly advocate

victim–offender reconciliation programs. Others disagree, arguing that such programs can hurt victims (by denying them the vindication of a public finding of the offender's guilt) and offenders (by relying on arbitrary criteria, eliminating procedural protections, and allowing a private party to exploit the leverage of public authority for private gain that may not lie in the wider social interest).

References

Abe, Haruo (1968), 'Shinkensatsukanron', *Chuo Koron*, May, 162–75.
Abel, Richard and Lewis, P. (1988), *Lawyers in Society*, Berkeley, CA: University of California Press.
Abrams, Norman (1971), 'Internal Policy: Guiding the Exercise of Prosecutorial Discretion', *UCLA Law Review*, **19**, 1–58.
Allen, Francis A. (1981), *The Decline of the Rehabilitative Ideal: Penal Policy and Social Purpose*, New Haven, CT: Yale University Press.
Anderson, David C. (1995), *Crime and the Politics of Hysteria: How the Willie Horton Story Changed American Justice*, New York: Times Books.
Aoyagi, Fumio (1986), *Nihonjin no Hanzai Ishiki*, Tokyo: Chuo Koronsha.
Bayley, David H. (1991), *Forces of Order: Policing Modern Japan*, Berkeley, CA: University of California Press.
Bayley, David H. (1994), 'Review Essay Rejoinder', *Law & Society Review*, **28**, 963–64.
Bessho, Otaro (1983), *Oni Kenji Oboegaki*, Tokyo: Yomiuri Shimbunsha.
Blankenburg, Von Erhard, Sessar, Klaus and Steffen, Wiebke (1978), *Die Staatsanwaltschaft im Prozes Strafrechtlicher Sozialkontrolle*, Berlin: Duncker & Humboldt.
Blumberg, Abraham (1979), *Criminal Justice: Issues and Ironies*, New York/London: New Viewpoints Press.
Braithwaite, John (1989), *Crime, Shame and Reintegration*, Cambridge: Cambridge University Press.
Carbonneau, Tom (1995), 'Truth on Trial', *World & I*, 314.
Carter, Lief H. (1974), *The Limits of Order*, Lexington, MA: Lexington Books.
Chambliss, William J. and Seidman, Robert B. (1984), 'The Use of Guilty Pleas in the Legal Process', in William J. Chambliss (ed.), *Criminal Law in Action*, New York: John Wiley & Sons.
Clifford, William (1976), *Crime Control in Japan*, Lexington, MA: Lexington Books.
Cole, George F. (1970), 'The Decision to Prosecute', *Law & Society Review*, **4**, 331.
Damaska, Mirjan R. (1986), *The Faces of Justice and State Authority: A Comparative Approach to the Legal Process*. New Haven, CT: Yale University Press.
Dando, Shigemitsu (1970), 'System of Discretionary Prosecution in Japan', *American Journal of Comparative Law*, **18**, 518.
Davis, Kenneth C. (1969), *Discretionary Justice: A Preliminary Inquiry*, Urbana and Chicago: University of Illinois Press.

Douglas, Mary (1986), *How Institutions Think*, Syracuse: Syracuse University Press.
Downes, David (1988), *Contrasts in Tolerance: Post-war Penal Policy in the Netherlands and England and Wales*, Oxford: Clarendon Press.
Eisenstein, James, Flemming, Roy B. and Nardulli, Peter (1988), *The Contours of Justice: Communities and Their Courts*, Boston, MA: Little, Brown and Company.
Feeley. Malcolm M. (1983), *Court Reform on Trial: Why Simple Solutions Fail*, New York: Basic Books.
Feeley, Malcolm M. (1992), *The Process is the Punishment*, New York: Russell Sage Foundation.
Feeley, Malcolm M. and Lazerson, Mark H. (1983), 'Police–Prosecutor Relationships: An Interorganizational Perspective', in Keith O. Boyum and Lynn Mather (eds), *Empirical Theories About Courts*, New York: Longman Press.
Fionda, Julia (1995), *Public Prosecutors and Discretion: A Comparative Study*, Oxford: Oxford University Press.
Fletcher, George P. (1995), *With Justice for Some: Victims' Rights in Criminal Trials*, Reading, MA: Addison-Wesley Publishing Co.
Foote, Daniel H. (1986), 'Prosecutorial Discretion: A Response', *Pacific Basin Law Journal*, 5, 96.
Foote, Daniel H. (1992), 'The Benevolent Paternalism of Japanese Criminal Justice', *California Law Review*, 80, 317–90.
Forst, Brian (1983), 'Prosecuting and Sentencing', in James Q. Wilson (ed.), *Crime and Public Policy*, San Francisco: Institute for Contemporary Studies.
Forst, Brian and Brosi, Kathleen B. (1977), 'A Theoretical and Empirical Analysis of the Prosecutor', *Journal of Legal Studies*, 6, 177.
Frase, Richard S. (1990), 'Comparative Criminal Justice as a Guide to American Law Reform: How Do the French Do It, How Can We Find Out, and Why Should We Care?', *California Law Review*, 78, 539–683.
Friedman, Lawrence (1975), *The Legal System: A Social Science Perspective*, New York: Russell Sage Foundation.
Gibson, James L. and Caldeira, Gregory A. (1996), 'The Legal Culture of Europe', *Law & Society Review*, 30, 55.
Goldstein, Abraham S. and Marcus, Martin (1977), 'The Myth of Judicial Supervision in Three "Inquisitorial" Systems: France, Italy, and Germany', *Yale Law Journal*, 87, 240.
Goodman, Marcia E. (1986), 'The Exercise and Control of Prosecutorial Discretion in Japan', *Pacific Basin Law Journal*, 5, 16.
Gottfredson, Michael R. and Gottfredson, Don M. (1988), *Decision-making in Criminal Justice: Toward the Rational Exercise of Discretion*, New York: Plenum Press.
Greenwood, Peter W. *et al*. (1976), *Prosecution of Adult Felony Defendants: A Policy Perspective*, Lexington, MA: Lexington Books.
Grosman, Brian A. (1969), *The Prosecutor: An Inquiry into the Exercise of Discretion*, Toronto: University of Toronto Press.

Guarnieri, Carlo (1997), 'Prosecution in Two Civil Law Countries: France and Italy', in David Nelken (ed.), *Comparing Legal Cultures*, Aldershot: Dartmouth.
Haley, John O. (1982), 'Sheathing the Sword of Justice in Japan: An Essay on Law without Sanctions', *Journal of Japanese Studies*, **8**, 265.
Haley, John O. (1991), *Authority without Power: Law and the Japanese Paradox*, New York: Oxford University Press.
Haley, John O. (1993), 'A Response to Johnson', *Law & Society Review*, **27**, 639.
Hamilton, V. Lee and Sanders, Joseph (1992), *Everyday Justice: Responsibility and the Individual in Japan and the United States*, New Haven, CT: Yale University Press.
Hatano, Akira (1994), *Tsuno o Tamete Ushi o Korosu Koto Nakare: Kensatsu Kenryoku wa Kokumin no Teki ka*, Tokyo: Kobunsha.
Heilbroner, David (1990), *Rough Justice: Days and Nights of a Young D.A.*, New York: Dell.
Heumann, Milton (1977), *Plea Bargaining: The Experiences of Prosecutors, Judges, and Defense Attorneys*, Chicago: University of Chicago Press.
Inagawa, Tatsuya (1994), 'The Criminal Justice System in Japan: Investigation and Prosecution', Tokyo: UNAFEI.
Irwin, John (1985), *The Jail: Managing the Underclass in American Society*, Berkeley, CA: University of California Press.
Itoh Shigeki (1987), *Mata Damasareru Kenji*, Tokyo: Tachibana Shobo.
Itoh Shigeki (1982), *Damasareru Kenji*, Tokyo: Tachibana Shobo.
Jackson, Robert H. (1940), 'The Federal Prosecutor', *Journal of the American Judicature Society*, **24**, 18–20.
Johnson, Chalmers (1995), *Japan: Who Governs? The Rise of the Developmental State*, New York: W.W. Norton & Company.
Johnson, David T. (1996), 'The Japanese Way of Justice: Prosecuting Crime in Japan', University of California at Berkeley Boalt Hall School of Law Program in Jurisprudence and Social Policy, Ph.D dissertation.
Johnson, David T. (1997a), 'Japan's Dazzling Acquittal Rates and the Procuracy's Pursuit of Perfection', Harvard University Program on US–Japan Relations, Center for International Affairs and the Edwin O. Reischauer Institute of Japanese Studies, USJP Occasional Paper.
Johnson, David T. (1997b), 'Why the Wicked Sleep: The Prosecution of Political Corruption in Postwar Japan', Japan Policy Research Institute, Working Paper No. 34, June.
Kaplan, John (1965), 'The Prosecutorial Discretion – A Comment', *Northwestern University Law Review*, **60**, 174.
Kawai, Nobutaro (1979), *Kensatsu Tokuhon*, Tokyo: Shoji Homu Kenkyukai.
Kawashima, Takeyoshi (1979), 'Japanese Way of Legal Thinking', *International Journal of Law Libraries*, **7**, 127.
Kerstetter, Wayne A. (1990), 'Gateway to Justice: Police and Prosecutorial Response to Sexual Assaults Against Women', *The Journal of Criminal Law and Criminology*, **81**, 267.
Koh, B.C. (1989), *Japan's Administrative Elite*, Berkeley, CA: University of California Press.

Lafave, Wayne R. (1970), 'The Prosecutor's Discretion in the United States', *The American Journal of Comparative Law*, **18**, 532.
Landes, William M. (1971), 'An Economic Analysis of the Courts', *The Journal of Law and Economics*, 61.
Lipset, Seymour M. (1996), *American Exceptionalism: A Double-edged Sword*, New York: W.W. Norton & Company.
Littrell, W. Boyd (1979), *Bureaucratic Justice: Police, Prosecutors, and Plea Bargaining*, Beverly Hills, CA: Sage Publications.
McConville, Mike, Sanders, Andrew and Leng, Roger (1991), *The Case for the Prosecution*, London: Routledge.
Mather, Lynn M. (1979), *Plea Bargaining or Trial? The Process of Criminal Case Disposition*, Lexington, MA: Lexington Books.
Miller, Frank W. (1969), *Prosecution: The Decision to Charge a Suspect with a Crime*, Boston, MA: Little, Brown and Company.
Mitchell, Richard H. (1976), *Thought Control in Prewar Japan*, Ithaca, NY: Cornell University Press.
Mitchell, Richard H. (1992), *Janus-Faced Justice: Political Criminals in Imperial Japan*, Honolulu: University of Hawaii Press.
Mitsui Makoto (1974), 'Kensatsukan no Koso Yuyo Saiyro: Sono Rekishiteki oyobi Jisshoteki Kenkyu', *Hogaku Kyokai Zasshi*, **91**.
Miyamoto, Masao (1994), *Straitjacket Society: An Insider's Irreverent View of Bureaucratic Japan*, Tokyo: Kodansha International.
Miyazawa, Setsuo (1992), *Policing in Japan: A Study on Making Crime*, Albany, NY: SUNY Press.
Morita, Hisashi (1994), *Fukiso no Giwaku: Chonan no Kotsu Jikoshi Kara*, Tokyo: Nihon Toshokankokai.
Mukaidani, Susumu (1993), *Chiken Tokusobu*, Tokyo: Kodansha.
Nardulli, Peter F., Eisenstein, James and Flemming, Roy B. (1988), *The Tenor of Justice: Criminal Courts and the Guilty Plea Process*, Urbana and Chicago: University of Illinois Press.
Nelken, David (1995), 'Disclosing/Invoking Legal Culture', *Social and Legal Studies*, 435.
Neubauer, David W. (1974), 'After the Arrest: The Charging Decision in Prairie City', *Law & Society Review*, **8**, 495.
Newman, Donald J. (1966), *Conviction: The Determination of Guilt or Innocence Without Trial*, Boston, MA: Little, Brown and Company.
Nomura, Jiro (1994), *Nihon no Kensatsukan*, Tokyo: Waseda Keiei Shuppan.
Oki, Kazuhiro *et al.* (1995), *Saibankan ni Narenai Riyu*, Tokyo: Aokishoten.
Parker, L. Craig jr (1984), *The Japanese Police System Today: An American Perspective*, Tokyo: Kodansha.
Pharr, Susan (1990), *Losing Face: Status Politics in Japan*, Berkeley, CA: University of California Press.
Ragin, Charles C. (1994), *Constructing Social Research*, Thousand Oaks: Pine Forge Press.
Reiss, Albert J. jr (1975), 'Public Prosecutors and Criminal Prosecution in the United States of America', *Juridical Review*, **20**, 1.

Rohlen, Thomas P. (1983), *Japan's High Schools*, Berkeley, CA: University of California Press.
Rutherford, Andrew (1993), *Criminal Justice and the Pursuit of Decency*, Oxford: Oxford University Press.
Sanchez-Jankowski, Martin (1991), *Islands in the Street: Gangs and American Urban Society*, Berkeley, CA: University of California Press.
Sato Michio (1993), *Kenji Chosho no Yohaku*, Tokyo: Asahi Shimbunsha.
Skolnick, Jerome H. (1967), 'Social Control in the Adversary System', *Conflict Resolution*, 11, 52.
Smith, Robert J. (1983), *Japanese Society: Tradition, Self and the Social Order*, Cambridge: Cambridge University Press.
Stanko, Elizabeth Ann (1981), 'The Impact of Victim Assessment on Prosecutors' Screening Decisions: The Case of the New York County District Attorney's Office', *Law & Society Review*, 16, 225.
Steinhoff, Patricia G. (1991), *Tenko: Ideology and Societal Integration in Prewar Japan*, New York: Garland Publishing Inc.
Sudman, Seymour and Norman M. Bradburn (1982), *Asking Questions: A Practical Guide to Questionnaire Design*, San Francisco: Jersey-Bass Publishers.
Sutherland, Edwin H. and Cressey, Donald R. (1978), *Criminology*, Philadelphia: J.B. Lippincott Co.
Tak, Peter J. (1986), 'The Legal Scope of Non-Prosecution in Europe', Helsinki: Helsinki Institute for Crime Prevention and Control.
Tevlin, Aidan (1993), 'Motives for Prosecution', *Journal of Criminal Law*, 288.
Tojo, Shinichiro (1968), 'The Prosecutor's Discretion and its Control in Japan and the United States', Master of Law Thesis, Boalt Hall School of Law, University of California at Berkeley.
Upham, Frank K. (1989), *Law and Social Change in Postwar Japan*, Cambridge: Harvard University Press.
Vera Institute of Justice (1981), *Felony Arrests*, New York: Longman.
Wagatsuma, Hiroshi, and Arthur Rosett (1986), 'The Implications of Apology: Law and Culture in Japan and the United States', *Law & Society Review*, 20, 461.
Weber, Robert Philip (1985), *Basic Content Analysis*, Beverly Hills, CA: Sage.
Weigend, Thomas (1980), 'Continental Cures for American Ailments: European Criminal Procedure as a Model for Law Reform', in Norval Morris and Michael Tonry (eds), *Crime and Justice: An Annual Review of Research*, Chicago: University of Chicago Press.
Weinreb, Lloyd L. (1977), *Denial of Justice: Criminal Process in the United States*, New York: Free Press.
Westermann, Ted D., and James W. Burfeind (1991), *Crime and Justice in Two Societies: Japan and the United States*, Pacific Grove: Brooks/Cole.
Wilson, James Q. (1983), *Thinking About Crime*, New York: Basic Books.
Wilson, James Q. (1989), *Bureaucracy: What Government Agencies Do and Why They Do It*, New York: Basic Books.
Winchell, Hilary (1995), 'Unanticipated Consequences: The Economic and Social Impact of "Three Strikes" Legislation on California', *California Legal Studies Journal*.

Yasuhara, Yoshio (1985), *Kensatsu no Mado Kara*, Tokyo: Kobundo Shuppansha.
Zeisel, Hans (1982), *The Limits of Law Enforcement*, Chicago and London: The University of Chicago Press.

8 Contrasts in Victim–Offender Mediation and Appeals to Community in France and England[1]

Adam Crawford

Introduction

The 1990s saw the proliferation of experiments and developments in mediation and reparation in, and around, formal court processes across Europe. Most recently in the UK, the new Labour government has committed itself to the expansion of reparation through victim–offender mediation, particularly with regard to young offenders, via proposals in the Crime and Disorder Act 1998. Meanwhile, the French government has promised to extend the role of mediation and reparation in both criminal and civil justice, with particular regard to minor offences, juvenile crime and family disputes (Guigou, 1997). Taken together, these developments represent what one commentator has called 'a practice in search of a theory' (Matthews, 1988: 2), rather than a series of well formulated and coherently implemented policies. In this chapter I will consider and contrast the comparative developments and practices of victim–offender mediation and reparation, and the nature of their appeals, in both France and England and Wales.[2] The aim of the chapter is to identify some of the conceptual tools for comparative criminological and socio-legal research through the examination of what, at face value, may seem like similar developments in practice.[3] In so doing, I will seek to excavate the cultural embeddedness of particular strategies of crime control. By locating the growth of victim–offender mediation and reparation within a wider cultural framework, I will begin to identify the manner in which given strategies are shaped by, and reflect, their meaning, appeal and place within different judicial and wider social cultures.

Victim–offender mediation and reparation constitutes a particularly fertile field for the study of the interconnectedness of culture and crime control given its seemingly successful transference across differentiated social contexts. However, this proliferation highlights numerous questions concerning the nature and impact of its transferability, immersion and institutionalization into different legal cultures. The extent of the reception of mediation across different legal cultures has led some commentators to discount the very relevance of such differences in explaining developments in different countries. For some, this appears to imply a 'convergence' of criminal justice practice or the emergence of a common criminal justice policy (Jung, 1993). What is clear is that the apparent proliferation of a singular model of dispute resolution across very different criminal justice systems, linguistic boundaries and cultural traditions, initially, does seem to call into question the extent of the interconnectedness of culture and strategies of crime control, whilst providing an environment in which such considerations are exposed for all their potency. For, as Nelken warns, 'many claims about...crime control which purport to be universal in fact take their sense and limits of applicability from such cultural connections' (Nelken, 1994: 221). He correctly stresses the importance of research agendas that shift between crime and culture, so that culture can inform us about crime rates and forms of crime control, whilst the latter can help us make sense of differences in culture (ibid.: 229). At the same time, we need to be wary of the dangers of slipping into cultural relativism (Beirne, 1983) and overexaggerating either the differences between cultures or their separateness from global trends (Nelken, 1995).

In addition, victim–offender mediation carries significant symbolic weight beyond its relatively small numerical importance in terms of case referrals. The practice of mediation brings into sharp relief issues and debates with much wider ramifications which inform and transcend whole criminal justice systems. This is particularly evident for three reasons: first, its conceptual location which is simultaneously both 'inside' and yet 'outside' criminal justice systems – this dual position of being in two places at the same time is alluded to by Zedner in her assessment of mediation and reparation schemes as constituting a 'conceptual cuckoo' in the criminal justice nest (Zedner, 1994: 234); second, its organizational location or bureaucratic positioning, which connects with, is influenced by, and seeks to influence, a wide variety of criminal justice agencies; and, third, the diverse interests with often conflicting motivations from which mediation and reparation draws support, or that proponents claim for it. In relation to this last point, forms of mediation have met with enthusiasm from different quarters, across the political spectrum and within professional and community groups.

The divergent nature of the interests and groups promoting 'alternatives to criminal litigation' has resulted in mediation meaning different things to different people. On one level this has allowed the 'movement' to gain support from diverse sources and to fit into the prevailing political rhetoric at a given moment. However, it also means that specific initiatives can be pulled in different, and often competing, directions as they try to meet the multiple aims and objectives and satisfy the divergent demands of the different constituencies. In attempting (or claiming) to do too much, the danger is that mediation and reparation initiatives can end up falling short on a number of fronts. Consequently, many of the salient debates and contradictions concerning the nature and shape of criminal justice come together around the development and practice of victim–offender mediation.

Finally, at a discursive level victim–offender mediation directly connects crime and culture by way of two relatively autonomous appeals around which a host of normative and moral, as well as administrative and managerial, concerns coalesce. The first is a *critique* (implicit or explicit) *of existing formal criminal proceedings and the institutions available for the processing of disputes*. Informalism is, after all, merely a movement away from traditional criminal proceedings. Thus, the perceived failings of formal proceedings define the characteristics of the 'informal'. The nature of the critique differs somewhat across substantive areas of criminal law, depending on the nature of the relationship between the parties in dispute and, more importantly for our purposes, across judicial cultural contexts. This is what we might call the 'negative attraction' of mediation. In order to understand this attraction we need to comprehend that which is being rejected in the movement away from the formal process. In different ways these concerns have found expression in critiques in relation to: *economy* (that is, they cost too much), *efficiency* (that is, they operate too slowly), *effectiveness* (that is, they fail to achieve their objectives of reducing crime and fear) and *legitimacy* (that is, they inadequately meet the interests and needs of the parties – often leaving them dissatisfied with, and alienated from, the process – and fail to pacify public concerns regarding expectations of justice).

The second element embodied in appeals to mediation is *a quest to revive some notion of 'community'* in which informal social institutions act to regulate conflict by means of social control processes. Crime is an emotionally compelling symbol of lost community. The doubling of recorded crimes in the UK between 1979 and 1990 and the similar, though less dramatically steep, rise in the rate of crime in France over the same period, are seen as symbolic of the erosion of traditional communities and the social cohesion that they are said to sustain.[4] The perceived decline of a 'sense of belonging' and the fracturing of actual communal institutions, such as trade unions, political parties and the extended family in the late twentieth century, are associated – in the minds of some – with a crisis of social regulation. These two appeals are not inversely related, but frequently coalesce and fuse. In order to understand the relative recourse to mediation and reparation and the cultural position that they are accorded, we need to be aware of the diverse institutions (both formal and informal) available for the processing of disputes. While the plurality of types of dispute suggests that different conflicts may be better handled in different ways and at different procedural levels, there remains the question as to whether there is anything intrinsic about given cases which places them into one forum of justice or another. This is evident, for example, in the potential overlap between victim–offender and neighbourhood mediation, as well as between criminal litigation and so-called 'alternatives'. Therefore, we need to be sensitive to the extent to which the processing of a dispute and many of the taken-for-granted assumptions and practices which accompany it actually transform it, so that, as a consequence, it becomes reconfigured as something which is rendered 'suitable' by extracting that which the process chooses to treat as the salient features of a dispute for its own purpose (Nelken, 1985). Hence, whether or not a dispute is processed through mediation as well as its subsequent form and outcome, are products of complex social and cultural processes. The concern here is with legal culture as a 'juridico-political' phenomenon constructed and reformed at the interface between legal and political discourses, institutional practices and the ways in which professional and lay actors make sense of normative and administrative arrangements through shared codes of understanding, myths, habits and traditions. The study of legal culture requires the 'unravelling of the cognitive structure that characterises that culture' through a 'focus on assumptions, attitudes, aspirations and antipathies' (Legrand, 1996a: 60–1). In this context, legal culture constitutes the collective *mentalité* and *sensibilité* – or what Legrand refers to as the 'collective mental programme' (ibid.: 60) – through which institutional and behavioural maps are interpreted and redrawn. The focus, therefore, is on the ideas and practices of those who work within the available institutions, as well as on public attitudes, political and legal consciousness and social behaviour (see Geertz, 1983; Blankenburg, 1996; Zedner, 1995).

It is my contention that both appeals to 'community' and critiques of existing legal processes have different cultural meanings which influence the resultant policies, practices and their attraction. In this chapter I will consider, solely, the former *appeal to community* in order to begin to illustrate the implications of such an insight and simultaneously outline the scope and shape of my own research agenda. Before doing so, it is necessary briefly to address one of the central problematics in comparative research – that of translation. Translation occurs at both linguistic and cultural levels. In relation to the former, Legrand (1996a) correctly chastises much comparative legal research for ignoring issues of translation and the 'foreignness of languages' (Benjamin, cited in ibid.: 235). However, following Sacco, he argues that 'the comparativist must learn *not* to translate' (ibid.: 234, emphasis on original). Language needs to be related to a much wider horizon of interpretation. This is particularly pertinent in this context for, as Garapon notes, the term 'community' does not translate easily into French. He suggests that it is not best understood as *communauté*, 'the meaning of which is too spiritual' (Garapon, 1995: 499). However, this does not render comparative research in this field unproductive. On the contrary, we merely need to look deeper. Its sense is embodied in various analogous terms such as *collectivité, solidarité, proximité* and *ethnicité*. Moreover, there is a growing debate in France about the appropriateness of '*communauté*' as a term for group identity precisely because of its association with an Anglo-American social experience. Hence, French *communauté*, unlike the rural idylls which English 'communities' conjure up, is directly connected with a more recent process of social disintegration. One French commentator has recently noted:

> It seems to me that the notion of *communauté* should be treated with due care, as the *communautés* in question are not at all the surviving remains of historic and embedded communal bonds, but communal inventions and creations tied to a process of massive marginalization. It is for this reason that the term *néo-communauté* or *ethnicité* seem to be more acceptable in depicting their imprecision. (Dubet, 1995: 145–6, my translation)

Despite the direct connection between appeals to community and mediation, in the English context, this is not to be found in France where any such connection is more likely to be denied within dominant political discourse. For to recognize the existence of distinct 'communities' is interpreted as undermining the efficacy of the republican model to which French political discourse clings (Wieviorka, 1997). Instead, mediation in France is located within debates about the need for, and appropriateness of, a *justice de proximité* which has come to assume a central place within French political discourse (Haenel and Arthuis, 1994; Vignoble, 1995; Wyvekens, 1997). This expression references three interconnected strands (Wyvekens, 1996). The first is a 'territorial proximity' which is captured in decentralizing programmes of recent French governments. It concerns attempts to decentralize judicial institutions such that there is a greater geographic proximity between the law and the people. This is an essential mission of the burgeoning *Maisons de Justice et du Droit* in France through which much victim–offender mediation is delivered (Wyvekens, 1995). A second element concerns a 'temporal proximity' which seeks a faster and more timely form of justice.

The final element is a 'human proximity' which seeks to give the parties greater agency and voice within the criminal justice process, as its subjects and not its objects (Vidal-Naquet 1994). All three of these elements have their grounding in critiques of current French criminal justice – that it is too remote, over centralized, too slow, too formal and does not allow the parties sufficient agency and voice – as well as in appeals to some notion of 'community' whether or not specified.

Hence, whilst language and terminology have a specific cultural place, they are neither static nor impermeable but, rather, subject to challenge and change. The essential lesson for comparative criminology is to recognize the need simultaneously to be aware of the deeper cultural sense of words and their ability to be transformed and take on external referents. Thus, as I hope to show, the transference of modes of victim–offender mediation from different cultural and linguistic contexts has been accompanied by an infiltration of associated language and terminology born of different contexts and out of which such models took their initial form and *raison d'être*. It is not surprising, therefore, that the recent rebirth of mediation in advanced industrialized societies, which first took root in the USA, should be accompanied by terminology which does not translate easily into, or may be alien to, French language and culture. Nonetheless, this does not deny its significance nor its effects.

In relation to the cultural level of translation, Nelken appropriately notes that:

> ...the attempt to grasp the meaning of a concept in another culture always parts from and returns to ideas derived from one's own culture. An account of another culture is never a 'view from nowhere' but is the particular product of this process of shifting between meanings in the culture under consideration and those of the observer. Difference or even uniqueness is always relative. (Nelken, 1994: 226)

Again, the point here is to recognize the importance of standpoints in the comparative process. In a concept as rich as appeals to 'community', cultural and linguistic translations are both constraining and limiting in their specificity but nevertheless opens up new avenues of explanation.

Appeals to 'Community' in Mediation

It has become an academic *cliché*, in both France and England, to protest that there are few concepts in social science as nebulous as 'community' (Houchon, 1984: 204–5, Bell and Newby, 1971). Nevertheless, it is a concept indisputably rich in symbolic power and one with enduring significance and appeal. It is also a notion infused with cultural reference (Lacey and Zedner, 1995). As a defining concept, 'community' connects crime control – mediation in particular – with culture, both in terms of direct appeals to a 'sense of community' and in the sense that community is essentially a cultural formation. In relation to the latter, cultures are a fundamental function and product of 'community', its expression of identity and belonging. Hence, it is one of those 'key concepts whose nuances are thought to provide insights into the secrets of legal culture' (Nelken, 1995: 442). Three principal appeals to community in victim–offender mediation in France and England can be identified, and these are discussed below.

'Community' as Empowerment through Communication

The involvement of the parties in the process of disputing through mediation is seen by proponents to be an essential element of community membership (Wright, 1991: 76–7). Disputes and crimes arise where 'normal' community controls have broken down. Consequently, the response to crime is an activity which is conducted both on behalf of the community and one which reflects a community's moral sensibilities. Conflict processing is, therefore, a highly *communal* act. It represents not only a 'potential for activity, for participation' but also allows the parties 'opportunities for norm-clarification' (Christie, 1977: 7–8). Hence, resolving a conflict between parties is understood as instrumental to the construction of shared values and commitment among the local community of residents. Consequently, mediation is believed to empower the parties and the wider community through a heightened form of communication. It is an aspect of a wider ideology of 'social transformation' (Harrington and Merry, 1988). On the one hand, mediation is seen to be 'an age-old practice, natural to any functioning community' (Sandwell Mediation Scheme, 1993: 3); on the other hand, it is something that, as a society, we appear to have forgotten about – either because community has broken down or because the courts and other professionals have appropriated the role from communities – hence, the need for schemes to restore people's capacity for mediation.

Often 'strengthening the bonds of community' is believed to occur, either by solving interpersonal conflicts and thus alleviating tension or, more often, through 'mediation as education'. Here, mediation is seen as a tool through which people can learn to communicate their feelings and enable them to have the ability to solve their own problems in the future. To this end, a significant number of neighbourhood mediation schemes actively 'teach' or 'facilitate' mediation skills in schools and other local institutions. Victim–offender mediation schemes, by contrast, are more likely to emphasize their impact on the community by stressing the influence of mediation on offending behaviour. Indeed, some victim–offender schemes also identify their potential impact on 'community safety' more generally, by addressing victims' fears and anxieties.

However, social transformation and community empowerment through mediation are difficult to assess. Clearly, the parties may be given a greater sense of control, but the extent to which this has an enduring impact is less evident. The somewhat pessimistic conclusion reached by Yngvesson, in relation to the San Francisco Community Boards, was that community empowerment may be possible only for a privileged 'internal community' of volunteers, rather than the external 'community of neighbours' (Yngvesson, 1993: 381). Certainly, the aim of community empowerment through communication for the internal community of volunteers and scheme workers may be a more easily obtainable goal and one which is accorded greater significance than the empowerment of the wider community of residents. It is a significant challenge for mediation to explicate and demonstrate how enhancing participation in the process of conflict processing has the potential to change communities.

'Community' as Obligations to Others

The restorative priorities of mediation identify the importance of ongoing and future relations – the mainstay of 'community'. Mediation seeks to give prominence to mutual responsibility, shared values and interconnectedness. This finds expression through different normatively informed notions of justice, which emphasize the reparation and restoration of communal bonds in response to crime and harm, rather than retribution through punishment (Zehr, 1990; Wright, 1991). Thus, an importance is accorded to interpersonal accountability through interparty dialogue. This carries with it a role, and concern, for the wider community. Therefore, 'encouraging the parties to acknowledge their own responsibility' is an important prerequisite for individual empowerment through mediation and a recognition of a connection to a wider community. This sense of obligation or responsibility resonates with appeals to community in mediation, which are consequentialist by way of their future orientation.

Moreover, these appeals to community embody a tension between 'voluntarism' – in the sense of the individual autonomy and agency of the parties – and the form of communication which individuals need to accept as the premise for mediation – that is, mutual responsibility, a concern for the future and the importance of how their actions impact on others. The ambiguity lies in the fact that this requires a shift from one dialogic frame to another and yet must be voluntarily embraced and freely chosen. However, in reality, this transformation of the 'self' may not be forthcoming and may require encouragement by mediators. Consequently, victims and offenders may feel a suasive community pressure to enter into the mediation process, as their actions have potential consequences for others. Further, this consequentialism implicitly, and sometimes explicitly, is referenced and reinforced within mediation practice. More often, this suasive potential is likely to affect the victims of crime who may, and often do, feel that through their meeting with the offender(s) they may be able to 'help' them confront their offending behaviour, thus resulting in fewer victims in the future. Similarly, offenders may feel the need, or may need to be 'encouraged', to 'help the victim get over what has happened to them' by explaining their actions and answering the question which the victim may have about the offence. However, given the complex interrelationship between forms of mediation and the court process, it is questionable whether they can ever be truly voluntary. The considerable incentives, 'subtle coercive pressures' and inducements to participate run counter to the notion of voluntariness. Yet the therapeutic and socially constructive aspects of mediation as negotiation or ceremonies of 'reintegrative shaming' are unlikely to be fully realized if some, or all, of the parties to the conflict are coerced into the process.

Mediators and the 'Moral Community'

One of the central claims of many mediation schemes is that conflicts should be handled by the disputants' social peers. In local victim–offender mediation the mediator often aspires to represent a given community, even if only symbolically – to be *from* and *of* the community. Many schemes deliberately seek to recruit 'ordinary lay volunteers'. The rationale for using community volunteers as mediators often lies in the expectation that such people will be 'like' the disputants and share their values and social practices, even if only figuratively. Here, community is conceptualized in one of two ways. The first concept is as a geographic or social field which is structured by homogenous values and shared interests. Mediators are supposed to represent the whole community and embody its values. They are cast, symbolically, in the role of representatives of the 'moral community'. However, outside of highly specialized professional groups and small-scale rural villages, it is difficult to find examples of this type of community in the contemporary world. Such a conception of community assumes organic wholeness of a given fixed collectively and neglects intra-community conflict and diversity of value systems.

A second, and more radical, approach to 'community' is to be found where schemes recognize social, cultural or ethic differences and seek to accommodate them through 'incorporation' within the body of mediators.

Thus, specific interests, often identified in terms of ethnicity, are recognized for their differences and included into the social identities represented within the 'moral community' of mediators. This approach, familiar in some English schemes, is epitomized by the *Boutiques de Droit* in Lyon, which have:

> ...chosen mediators from among residents, taking into account selection criteria favouring the most representative of the social and ethnic categories living in the neighbourhood. Among the selection criteria is the candidate's mode of insertion in the neighbourhood (e.g. the fact of belonging to a community group) or involvement with community life. (Bonafé-Schmitt, 1992a: 187)

However, this recognition of multicultural heterogeneity raises a number of normative, as well as practical, dilemmas. For example, which cultural identities are sufficiently appropriate or worthy to be acknowledged and accommodated within the process of 'representation'? How inclusive can such a 'moral community' be before it loses any sausive capacity it may have? And, consequently, how many different interests can be accommodated within the mediation process without fragmenting the unity of mediators (and thus the notion and possibility of a 'moral community') or destroying the process itself?

Second, there is a tension here between 'voluntarism' – in the sense of volunteers as people – and community representation. The correspondence between actual volunteers and the types of social identities that mediation schemes seek to incorporate in the name of 'representativeness' may be limited. Mediation schemes confront the dilemma that many 'ordinary volunteers' are not necessarily representative of such social identities. This reality has required some mediation schemes to look to other ways of attracting mediators from the diverse groups which are traditionally underrepresented among volunteers, such as paying them a nominal fee (as in the Leeds scheme). The problem is that by paying mediators, schemes may begin to erode the very attraction of mediators as disputants' social peers – their symbolic 'lay' connectedness. As a result, mediators may begin to look and behave more like 'quasi-professionals' than ordinary lay people.

Third, there is a troublesome contradiction in the conception of 'community' in the mediator role. The more attached to the 'community' mediators are, the less likely they are to hold the required detached stance which constitutes a central value in establishing mediator neutrality and legitimacy. The more mediators represent interests or value systems the greater the danger that the central triadic relationship (between the parties to the dispute and the third party mediator) will break down or will be perceived to have broken down, into a 'two versus one' situation (Crawford, 1996). As Harrington and Merry have commented in relation to the American experience: 'Precisely because of their participation and membership in the community, it is difficult for them to assume the required detachment' (Harrington and Merry, 1988: 730). However, as they go on to suggest, ironically, it is the interest in providing neutral and detached mediators that increases the pressures to develop a core of professional mediators whose claims to expertise as specialists in mediation, eventually set them apart from that 'community'. Over time many schemes come to rely on a group of core mediators who increasingly are seen as semi-professionals by virtue of their work turnover, their training and experience, the fact that they are paid workers (as for example, in the Leeds scheme), or their value and importance to the scheme.

Finally, there is a further contradiction here between the analysis of the problem – that there is a loss of sociability on which conflict is constructively negotiated in some neighbourhoods – and the solution – settlement by mediators well integrated into the local community so that their actions are rendered legitimate. If there are already existing figures within the local community who are sufficiently legitimate in their own authority then it would seem that local sociability has not altogether broken down and mediation could take place outside of formal schemes attached to criminal justice systems. Or, if there are no sufficiently legitimate agents within the community, it is questionable whether any scheme will be sufficient to manufacture such legitimacy. The concern is that the legitimacy of mediation schemes derives not from their moral attachment to 'community' but from the (coercive) authority that stems from their attachment to the formal criminal justice system.

Comparative Conceptions of Community

What these different appeals to community in mediation suggest is the need for analytic tools with which to make sense of the different place and meaning of community in divergent cultural contexts. The literature provides little by way of assistance. In debates surrounding victim–offender mediation – as well as other forms of mediatory processes like family group conferences (Alder and Wundersitz, 1994; Morris et al., 1993; Hudson et al., 1996) and 'sentencing circles' (LaPrairie, 1995) – the nearest we come to this is Braithwaite and colleagues' generalized schema in which 'communitarian' and 'individualistic' societies, cultures or groups are said to stand at contrasting ends of a continuum (Braithwaite, 1989; Braithwaite and Daly, 1994). Communitarian societies are defined by Braithwaite as being those in which,

... individuals are deeply enmeshed in interdependencies which have the special qualities of mutual help and trust... A communitarian culture rejects any pejorative connotation of dependency as threatening individual autonomy. (Braithwaite, 1989: 100).

By contrast, individualistic societies or groups, are marked by social fragmentation, a lack of personal obligation to others and a cultural celebration of individual autonomy and self-interest (ibid.: 168). The understanding of 'community' is relative; it goes beyond locality and embraces a multiplicity of groups and networks to which, it is believed, we all belong. It does not rely on a fixed assumption of where a 'community' will be found. Rather, it develops on the notion of 'communities of care' – the networks of obligation and respect between the individual and everyone who cares about him or her the most – which are not bounded by geography (Braithwaite and Daly, 1994: 195). This marks a significant development in the understanding of contemporary communities. These 'communities of care', it is argued, are more relevant to contemporary modern living in urban societies. They encompass an expanded notion of 'community' which, in part, is a subjective one, in that the ascription to community membership or social identity is personal and not necessarily one which carries any fixed or external attributes of membership. In other words, 'communities of care' do not carry connotations of coerced or constrained membership. This is one of its appeals, and, yet, it is also its weakness, for, as 'community' is subjectively ascribed, there is little by way of external criteria through which the nature of community can be assessed. Community here begins to look more like bilateral relations of trust than 'semi-autonomous social fields' which have rule-making capacities and the means to induce compliance, but which are simultaneously set in a larger social matrix which can, and often does, affect and invade it (Moore, 1973: 720).

Whilst Braithwaite and colleagues' contribution represents an important development it is but a partial understanding of the nuances of cultural formations. In this schema we find little to assist us in *measuring* intra-community relations, either in terms of the nature of interdependency or the suasive capacity of given communities. Furthermore, it fails sufficiently to address the nature of inter-community relations, which also will be constitutive of intra-community relations. In order to locate the transferable potential of mediation and to make sense of its operationalization and value within given social and cultural contexts, we need to develop alternative analytical tools with which to locate the construction and meaning of appeals to community in comparative settings.

At the level of *intra*-community relations we need to consider the nature and meaning of 'voluntarism' therein, both in terms of the cultural tradition of volunteers and the place accorded to individual volition or 'agency'. This raises subquestions about a community's homogeneity, its members' commitment, its regulation of members' behaviour, and the nature of its boundaries – internality and exclusion. *Inter*-community relations, by contrast, can be understood at two conceptual levels. First, at a horizontal level, we need to ask what is the nature of the relations between one 'community' and another. Communities have potentially divergent values and conflicting interests and are frequently in competition for scarce economic resources and political power. Thus, the relationship between given communities and the market, both as a source of resources and as a lever for community self-realization, is of considerable importance. Second, at a vertical level, we need to ask what is the nature of the interrelationship between different hierarchical formations – between communities and the wider community of communities, the nation-state. The former issue highlights the importance of power differentials between interest groups and communities, thus raising dimensions of political and economic inequality. The latter question concerns how specific communities, with their own moral codes, fit within an overarching set of state institutions. From an economic perspective this questions the extent of state interventionism on behalf of communities. From a political perspective it problematizes the nature of the state's regulation (and 'policing') of given communities in the name of the collective national (or even international) cultural identity. It interrogates the extent to which the state adheres to or claims 'universalism' or 'diversity' as an *ideal typical* approach to communities' cultural and moral differences. 'Diversity', on the one hand, celebrates cultural and communal difference and seeks to accommodate 'multiculturalism' by exerting a looser suasive control or normative assertion over the constituent communities. Nevertheless, it raises the question whether we should forego the notion of a supra-community, with its own identity, which seeks to cohere the pastiche of subcultural, ethnic and racial groups. A multiculturalism lacking any sense of the commonalities or shared interests of the constituent ingredients of the 'melting pot' can give rise to a variety of 'differentialist' discourses which vie with each other for economic resources and political power or patronage. 'Universalism', on the other hand, appeals to an homogenous collective value system to which the constituent communities are deemed to adhere. It holds out the expectation of one people, one culture and a single nation without internal differences along lines of communal affiliation. However, in doing so, it is in danger of asserting a cultural superiority and thus alienating those who do not easily fit within the dominant 'moral community'.

The tension between 'diversity' and 'universalism' is neither one of mutually exclusive categories nor of an inverse relationship where more of one necessarily results in less of the other.[5] However, for our purposes, it raises the question as to what extent given societies seek to articulate cultural and communal differences within a set of social or universal values. It highlights important aspects of inter-community relations, particularly within and between the state and civil society. It also alerts us to an important slippage, which persists within much of the communitarian literature, between a sociological and ideological understanding of 'community' – between what 'community' *is* and what it *ought* to be – the empirical authenticity of 'community' as distinct from its normative appeal (Frazer and Lacey, 1993: 154). The rhetorical claims to 'diversity' or 'universalism' should not be read as reflecting empirical reality. Rather, it is often the nature and extent of the dissonance between the two which is more indicative of the nature of social order within a society. It is with these additional conceptual tools that we now can begin to excavate the place and understanding of 'community' within the structures, claims and practices of mediation and reparation in both France and England. In sum we need to develop a culturally specific understanding of 'community' which locates it at the intersection of the 'state', 'market' and 'civil society', with particular regard to traditions of voluntarism.

Comparative Contexts

In the remainder of this chapter I will begin to sketch out how such a culturally sensitive understanding of 'community' helps highlight differences in the operationalization of mediation in France and England. In dominant French political discourse 'community' is conceived of as homogenous, inclusive and grounded in notions of citizenship. 'We are all French' is the often heard rallying cry of French political discourse. At a certain theoretical level 'community' is an anachronism, as it contradicts the constitutional principle that France is one and indivisible (Gaspard, 1995: 96). Nevertheless, diversity is taken to exist. As a 'nation of immigrants', France has always relied on integration and assimilation (Weber, 1995: x). As André Frossard has noted: 'The French people were born of a Christian mother and an unknown father... I say unknown father because France is a nation of immigrants and always has been' (quoted in Marnham, 1993: 8). Consequently, it is the assumed role of social institutions to 'include' and 'integrate' those peripheral and diverse elements outside of mainstream culture into the existing normative frameworks. Where social exclusion or a lack of social integration exists, the failure and consequential responsibility lies largely with the relevant social institutions (the state), not merely the individuals or groups in civil society. The meaning of community in political life in France, therefore, is fundamentally linked with the role of the state, with *étatisme*. French political scientists see the state as the embodiment of the general will. In law it is accorded special powers and status (Bell, 1995: 72).[6] The relations between individuals and the notion of a collective identity lie within the nation-state and are associated with a 'republican contract' which sees integration not as a coercive infringement on group or individual autonomy but as the basis of mutuality. The state holds a prominent place in constructing the meaning and practices of 'community' in France. As a political ideal the state – at different levels and in different spheres of activity – is identified as a 'moral unifier' – a role which requires it to be strong and prominent in order for it to stand above and transcend particular interests (Prosser, 1995: 510).

This conception of 'community' permeates the Bonnemaison Committee Report (1983), *Face à la Délinquance, Prévention, Répression, Solidarité*, and subsequent crime prevention policy discourse in France. A key element in the report was its emphasis on two central terms which remain embedded in the essential dominant discourse. The first is the concept of *solidarité*, a notion by which the French are conceived as a homogenous, rather than heterogeneous, people. Accordingly, all French citizens are assumed to belong to the same unified nation in which they work towards the fulfilment of nationally consensual goals, despite cultural or ethnic differences. Community implies citizenship which is the embodiment of 'universalism'. This may be idealized rhetoric (often recognized as such) but it, nevertheless, does have real discursive, strategic and institutional effects. It is, in part, the 'rhetorical cement holding together the various disparate elements' (King, 1991: 91).

The second concept is that of *intégration* by which those groups and individuals perceived to be at the margins of the bonds of social *solidarité* are deemed to require (re)incorporation. Social isolation and exclusion of certain groups were seen by the Bonnemaison report as the central problem affecting French society. The enduring hold exerted by this dominant discourse over French political life was reaffirmed in the recent French presidential elections, in which all the candidates (apart from Jean Marie Le Pen and his National Front party) declared the centrality of *intégration* and the struggle against social exclusion. Consequently, failure to integrate marginalized groups – particularly sensitive in relation to immigrant populations – is perceived as a failure of the local and national state. In France the concept of 'community' is an integrating force (Bonnemaison, 1987; King, 1987). There is a clear gulf between, on the one hand, the rhetoric or ideology of citizenship, nationhood, *solidarité* and social inclusion which permeates French politics and life, and, on the other hand, the lived reality or institutional practices which constitute, and are constituted by, that idealized vision. This dissonance between the imaginary and the real is an important element which frames French culture generally and French legal culture specifically (Garapon, 1995, but see Bell 1995: 75).

In England 'community' has become a policy buzzword, the dominant definition of which has its own distinct inflexions. Social identities outside of the national frame are accorded considerable significance. As in France, the notion of community appeals to, and references, homogeneity and shared interests. However, in England, unlike France, the understanding of community invokes a celebration of diversity and difference. This is not unproblematic since, in reality, this amounts to a celebration of 'voluntarism'. Hence, 'community' is often a shorthand term for 'collective voluntarism' as a source of resources on which responsibility for the provision of collective goods can (and should) be bestowed. As a consequence, the articulation and practice of community involvement often embody a localism and particularism, an important part of which is the power to exclude. Membership involves significant social processes of inclusion and exclusion. Diversity embodies important power relations, of 'belonging', around which boundaries are formed. Membership of community in England comes closer to the concept of the 'voluntaristic consumer' who is formally free to enter and consume but whose entry, in reality, is restrained by the requirement that he or she shares certain prerequisites. For some, this is less oppressive because it does not coerce compliance and conformity because there exists a greater recognition of diversity and multiculturalism. However, those who fail – who are unable or unwilling to meet the dominant normative standards – are left behind. The exclusive nature of the construction of community can, and often does, undermine the extent of tolerance between communities.

Unlike in France, appeals to community in England connect with, and are nourished by, an anti-statism. Community is seen as an alternative to the public provision of services. In political discourse the state is seen as 'a vaguely threatening monolith' (Prosser, 1995: 510). It is argued – most vehemently (but not solely) by neoliberal commentators – that the state has morally damaging effects on people, producing passivity and a 'culture of dependency' by misleadingly cultivating a view that it is the role of the state to provide for individuals and communities (Murray, 1990). It is the antithesis of 'collective voluntarism'. The practical implication of this anti-statism is that in England, unlike France, community is often a byword for parochialism (Crawford, 1997). A considerable gulf exists between 'the communal' and 'the social'. While this allows for innovation and a bottom-up generation of practices, it also allows for narrowmindedness and the differential local use of discretion. This is rendered particularly problematic in England by the absence of tiers of government between the nation-state and community which seek to mediate and integrate localized communities within a wider 'community of communities' – that is, a public civic polity. France, with a centralized state tradition, has begun to develop a much more fragmented system of urban government – three layers of subnational government (with 36 000 communes as well as 96 departments and 22 regions). England, by contrast, has fewer units of local government (some 400). The centralizing dominance of the French state has always been mediated by safeguards (which do not exist in England), such as the overlapping roles of politicians and administrators at national, regional, departmental and local level (the *cumul de mandats*). It is argued that this system integrates the different levels of the state and places greater emphasis on negotiation. In contrast with France, England has no specifically regional administration and since 1986 has had no metropolitan level government. Indeed, the movement throughout the 1980s, in England, was away from regional, or city-wide policies. Meanwhile France strengthened regional institutions (de Montricher, 1995): the neighbourhood focus of early French decentralization was abandoned, and the wider urban area became the basis of policy in order to promote greater solidarity across fragmented urban areas. Most significantly, the *Contrat de Villes* scheme – an attempt to create links between the state and local authority or inter-communal groupings within a framework of a contract negotiated between the two sides – was developed to integrate all existing initiatives. It was out of the subsequent *politique de la ville* (urban policy) that the *Maisons de Justice et du Droit* – offering victim–offender mediation under the direction and control of the *parquet* (prosecutor's office) – emerged.[7] The first *Maison de Justice* was set up in 1990 in the Val d'Oise by the prosecutor of the Pontoise Tribunal and, by the beginning of 1997, these had increased to 49 with a further ten planned for that year and another ten for the year after. In addition, victim–offender mediation also takes place through dedicated associations or delegated mediators.

The role and powers of local authorities in England have been dramatically changed and limited since the early 1980s. Since 1979 there have been almost 50 separate parliamentary Acts affecting local authorities many of which have restricted their autonomy. The power of local authorities has been further undermined through the establishment of numerous centrally controlled agencies and quangos whose work parallels that of elected local authorities and, one might argue, deliberately circumvents them. Consequently, local authorities have played no significant part in funding local victim–offender mediation initiatives, although some housing (and environmental) departments have been willing to support neighbourhood mediation schemes to deal with neighbour disputes on public sector housing estates (although sometimes at the cost of local autonomy). In fact, it is the probation service which has provided the principal funding route for victim–offender mediation in England, raising questions as to their independence of the criminal justice process.

In France decentralization has taken place within a context in which the nation-state still has a forceful role which is confirmed and reinforced. As DATAR (*Délégation à l'Aménagement du Territoire et à l'Action Régionale*) stated in a recent report:

> two different patterns of development can be considered for this country. The first is a model in which people and territories evolve separately, acquire dissimilar characters, and reject a national community of interests. In this situation, national uniformity would collapse over the diversity of the systems in crucial sectors like education, social affairs, and taxes. The second pattern restores coherence in a renewed 'republican contract'. The goal is to bring back equity and to establish solidarity among the various territories'. (DATAR, 1994)

The path of recent French politics has been concerned with attempting to reassert, at every critical turn, republican integration and 'universalism', despite the reality of considerable social *différence*. The existence of powerful social identities and group interests outside of, and sometimes in conflict with, that expressed by the universal notion of French citizenship is something that French law and politics refuse to acknowledge. Witness, for example, the public neurosis engendered by the furore, a few years ago, surrounding the wearing of the veil by Muslim girls in French schools. Here, the national French principle of *laïcité* (secularism) collided head-on with a desire to affirm cultural difference on the part of a segment of the population. The wearing of religious affiliation, such as a headscarf, was not incompatible with the secular nature of French schools (properly referred to as *écoles de la citoyenneté*) but, as the Conseil d'État ruled in its advisory opinion of 1989:

> ... this freedom cannot permit pupils to bear signs of religious affiliation which, by their nature, by the circumstances in which they are worn, individually or collectively, or by their ostentatious or campaigning character constitute an act of pressure, provocation, proselytism or propaganda. (cited in Bell, 1990: 124)[8]

More recently, the absence of a public discourse acknowledging the existence and importance of social identities other than the abstracted citizen caused a political storm when graphically depicted by the semi-factual film *La Haine* ('The Hate') which portrayed the decaying relations between the police and marginalized youths on a peripheral estate in a *banlieu* of Paris. It also posed fundamental questions about the reality and viability of accepted strategies of *integration*.

Hence, it would be disingenuous to suggest, as some commentators have done (King, 1991), that the integrative 'universal' French concept of community is culturally unproblematic or preferable. It has resulted in a damaging silence surrounding different cultural and ethnic identities in France, their place and their claims for recognition (Wieviorka, 1997). The universalist approach adopted by the French state and political élite is simultaneously culturally stifling, on account of its totalizing and, what for some are perceived as, coercive effects. Whilst a larger gulf exists in England between the communal and the social, in France the social can be overbearing in its universality.

In many senses, the growth of victim–offender mediation in France both reflects, and is the product of, a much wider crisis in relations between the state and civil society, as it is in England albeit for different reasons. Garapon (1995) refers to this crisis as the 'shock of globalisation. This crisis is particularly evident as regards the role of the law. French penal law has increasingly colonized areas of social life (Garapon and Salas, 1996) with its own universalistic discourse which is increasingly at odds with contemporary cultural pluralism at the local level and a 'foreign' global culture, at the international level. The traditionally self-assured appearance of the French state, law in particular, is being weakened both from above and below. By and large, this challenge has been met by an uncertainty and ambivalence (Robert, 1997).

French legal culture places a traditional emphasis on authoritative formal rules which carry a symbolic and ritualised importance. The law, Garapon (1997) suggests, is infused with a Catholic tradition which idealizes the 'sacredness' of legal texts. Hence, in this analogy, the *Code Pénale* is invested with a quasi-biblical significance. This notion of the law as 'sacred ideal' hinders its flexibility and applicability in practice, producing a significant dissonance between the ideal and the reality. Here, mediation would appear to offer French legal culture a degree of flexibility, which in part explains its appeal. However, it also makes mediation a very 'unFrench' judicial response. First, mediation is a form of 'empirical justice' – or 'khadi justice' in Max Weber's (1966) terminology – whereby outcomes are arrived at on the basis of criteria internal to individual cases, rather than in accordance to preordained (external) normative rules. As such, mediation is the antithesis of a traditional French legal mentality that, as an ideal, starts from the universal normative rule into which cases are deemed to fit. First, mediation – in theory at last – is partly driven and necessitates the application of discretion within a judicial framework. Second, it offers less space for symbolism in its informal settings, tending to dispense with the sacred iconography of formal legal processes. Finally, mediation, as I have argued, appeals to a diversity of community norms and values, which simultaneously threatens universal normative categories to which French culture clings.

The practice of mediation in France expresses these contradictions in legal culture. Mediation tries to provide space for different normative systems and yet imposes the pervasive logic of the prosecutor's office. Moreover, as we have seen, it embodies a paradox of French justice which simultaneously seeks to construct an associative order outside of the state – in order to delimit the boundaries of state intervention – whilst at the same time responsibilizing the citizen in a paternalistic manner through state institutions. As Garapon suggests, 'French positivism responsibilizes the citizen-as-legislator but infantilizes the citizen-as-actor' (Garapon, 1997: 175, my translation). This is particularly evident in the practice of mediation, in many parts of France, where mediation occurs immediately after, or as part of, what is referred to as *rappel à la loi*. This distinctly French practice does not translate easily into English – the closest functional equivalent in English practice is the formal caution, but this comparison underplays the responsibilizing and paternalistic nature of the process. It involves the parties, both victim and offender, as the passive recipient of a 'lecture' – often punctuated with reference to, or extracts from, the *Code Pénale* – on the law and their social responsibilities to it. In this sense, mediation in France has come to assume a role which follows in a long tradition of strategies of social integration (Wieviorka, 1997). Victim–offender mediation, whilst aspiring to respond to a plurality of normative and cultural value systems, is transformed into the carrier of an idealized, central normative order. As such, it occupies a somewhat anomalous position within French legal culture – one which simultaneously expresses that culture, together with its ambiguities.

Conclusion

This different cultural place and meaning of mediation in France can help explain why victim–offender mediation has been accorded a different, more favourable and yet, in many ways, more problematic reception in France than in England. In a considerably shorter period of time mediation in France has secured a prominent place on the legal agenda. Nevertheless, it embodies and expresses many of the contradictions evident within wider French legal and political culture. It also explains why mediation is intimately tied to the needs of the courts and the prosecutor's office (Bonafé-Schmitt, 1992b; Wyvekens, 1996), as a result of which it is largely restricted to minor juvenile cases – *la petite délinquance des mineurs* – which are perceived to block the criminal justice system.

In this chapter I hope to have begun to demonstrate that, in order to understand the manner in which similar judicial and normative strategies are constructed in different social and legal contexts, we need to be sensitive to nuanced differences in those culture. We need to develop ways of understanding *contrasts* and *differences* without slipping into cultural relativism. It has been suggested that a cultural excavation of key discursive concepts, such as 'community' in the appeal of victim–offender mediation, can open up new ways of understanding the interconnectedness between crime control and culture. However, such an analysis also poses implicit and difficult questions about what counts a culture and also about the purpose of comparative research (Nelken, 1996). It also reminds us that culture is temporally bounded: it is continually undergoing a process of change and adaptation. Thus, as Nelken suggests, we need 'to treat culture as a process of becoming and a point of departure as much as a functioning whole' (Nelken, 1995: 444). I have sought to use culture as a means of explaining variations in the recent histories, institutional location and practices of victim–offender mediation and reparation in both England and France. In so doing, I have hoped to show that, despite trends towards Europeanization, the way in which societies handle disputes is culturally constructed and that the meaning of disputes and their resolution varies greatly from one cultural framework to another (Harrington and Merry, 1988: 731). The specific nature and practice of victim–offender mediation in France and England thus depend on, and are informed by, the social location of both the critique of existing formal disputing procedures as well as appeals to 'community'.

Notes

1 Earlier versions of this chapter were presented to the Australian and New Zealand Society of Criminology Conference, Victoria University of Wellington, New Zealand, 30 January–1 February 1996; an international seminar on 'Mediation' at the IISL Oñati, Spain, 6–7 June 1996; and the American Law and Society Conference at the University of Strathclyde, 10–13 July 1996. The ideas expressed in this chapter have benefited from helpful comments and criticisms by John Braithwaite, John Bell, Antoine Garapon, Jean-Pierre Bonafé-Schmitt, Johannes Feest, Susan Flint, Martin Wright, Anne Wyvekens, Jacques Faget and the various participants of the above mentioned seminars, for which I am grateful.
2 Throughout this chapter reference will be made to 'England' as shorthand for 'England and Wales'.
3 This chapter outlines a comparative research agenda, which is the subject of an empirical investigation supported by ESRC grant R000221717, see Crawford (2000a; 2000b).
4 More recent data suggests a very similar rise in crime between the two countries. Between 1985 and 1995 recorded violent crime in England and Wales rose by 60% and in France the rate rose by 71%. Of 13 OCED countries for which information is

available only New Zealand experienced a greater increase of 80% (Alun Michael in a parliamentary answer to Stephen Twigg MP, on 9 June 1997).

5 The argument here is not meant to imply that the rallying cry of 'unity in diversity' is an unattainable ideal, but rather to highlight that this 'balance' constitutes one of the most fundamental and yet problematic political dilemmas confronted by modern states.

6 By contrast, in England there is no clear legal conception of the state, even though this situation is changing under pressures of European law (see Bell, 195: 73).

7 In 1995 the Vignoble Report identified some 32 generic *Maisons de Justice* structures in France, most offering some form of mediation. The funding for setting up the *Maisons de Justice*, like those in Tourcoing, Lyon and Pontoise (the oldest of the schemes, established in 1990) was split between the *délégation interministérielle à la ville*, the Ministry of Justice and the *collectivités locales*.

8 As Bell (1995: 75) notes, this view was later confirmed in the same language by decisions from its judicial section. While two cases declared a total ban on having headcovering in schools to be too wide (CE 2 November 1992, *Kherouaa and others*, AJDA 1992, 833 and CE 14 March 1994, *Mlles Nesinur et Zehranur Yilmaz*, Rfda 1994, 630), in a later case (CE 10 March 1995, *Aoukili*, ADJA 1995, 332) the suspension of two girls for refusing to remove their headscarves during physical education lessons was upheld.

References

Alder, C. and Wundersitz, J. (eds) (1994), *Family Conferencing and Juvenile Justice*, Canberra: Australian Institute of Criminology.

Beirne, P. (1983), 'Cultural Relativism and Comparative Criminology', *Contemporary Crises*, 7, 371–91.

Bell, C. and Newby, H. (1971), *Community Studies: An Introduction to the Sociology of Local Communities*, London: George Allen and Unwin.

Bell, J. (1990), 'Religious Observance in Secular Schools: A French Solution', *Education and the Law*, 2, 121–28.

Bell, J. (1995), 'English Law and French Law – Not So Different?', *Current Legal Problems*, 48, 63–101.

Blankenburg, E. (1996), 'Indicators for Studying Legal Culture', in D. Nelken (ed.), *Comparing Legal Cultures*, Aldershot: Dartmouth.

Bonafé-Schmitt, J.-P. (1992a), 'Penal and Community Mediation: The Case of France', in H. Messmer and H.-U. Otto (eds), *Restorative Justice on Trial*, Dordrecht: Kluwer.

Bonafé-Schmitt, J.-P. (1992b), *La Médiation: Une Justice Douce*, Paris: Syros Alternatives.

Bonnemaison, G. (ed.) (1983), *Face à la Délinquance, Prévention, Répression, Solidarité*, Paris: Documentation Française.

Bonnemaison, G. (1987), *La Securité en Libertés*, Paris: Syros.

Braithwaite, J. (1989), *Crime, Shame and Reintegration*, Cambridge: Cambridge University Press.

Braithwaite, J. and Daly, K. (1994), 'Masculinities, Violence and Communitarian Control' in T. Newburn and E.A. Stanko (eds), *Just Boys Doing Business? Men, Masculinities and Crime*, London: Routledge.

Christie, N. (1977), 'Conflicts as Property', *British Journal of Criminology*, **17**, 1–15.
Crawford, A. (1996), 'Alternatives to Prosecution: Alternatives to, or Exits from, Criminal Justice?' in R. Young and D. Wall (eds), *Access to Criminal Justice: Legal Aid, Lawyers and the Defence of Liberty*, London: Butterworths.
Crawford, A. (1997), *The Local Governance of Crime: Appeals to Community and Partnerships*, Oxford: Clarendon Press.
Crawford, A. (2000a), 'Justice de Proximité - The Growth of "Houses of Justice" and Victim/Offender Mediation in France: A Very UnFrench Legal Response?', *Social & Legal Studies*, **9** (1), 29–53.
Crawford, A. (2000b), 'Why British Criminologists Lose their Critical Faculties upon Crossing the Channel', *Social Work in Europe*, **7**, 1–9.
DATAR (1994), *Débat National pour l'Aménagement du Territoire*, Paris: La Documentation Française.
de Montricher, N. (1995), 'Decentralization in France', *Governance*, **8**, 405–18.
Dubet, F. (1995), 'La Délinquance Juvénile et les Figures de la Ville', in C. Fijnaut, J. Goethals, T. Peters and L. Walgrave (eds), *Changes in Society, Crime and Criminal Justice in Europe: Vol. I Crime and Insecurity in the City*, The Hague: Kluwer.
Frazer, E. and Lacey, N. (1993), *The Politics of Community*, Hemel Hempstead: Harvester Wheatsheaf.
Garapon, A. (1995), 'French Legal Culture and the Shock of Globalization', *Social & Legal Studies*, **4**, 493–506.
Garapon, A. (1997), *Bien Juger: Essai sur le Rituel Judiciaire*, Paris: Edition Odile Jacob.
Garapon, A. and Salas, D. (1996), *La République Pénalisée*, Baume-les-Dames: Hachette.
Gaspard, F. (1995), *A Small City in France*, London: Harvard University Press.
Geertz, C. (1983), 'Local Knowledge, Fact and Law in Comparative Perspective', in C. Geertz (ed.), *Local Knowledge: Further Essays in Interpretive Anthropology*, New York: Basic Books.
Guigou, E. (1997), 'Discours de Mme Guigou au Colloque de Villepinte sur la Sécurité', Paris: Ministère de la Justice, 24 October.
Haenel, H. and Arthuis, J. (1994), *Proposition pour une Justice de Proximité*, Paris: Document Ministère de la Justice.
Harrington, C. and Merry, S. (1988), 'The Ideology of Community Mediation', *Law and Society Review*, **22**, 709–35.
Houchon, G. (1984), 'A la Recherche du Temps Perdu', *Déviance et Société*, **8**, 199–206.
Hudson, J., Morris, A., Maxwell, G. and Galway, B. (eds) (1996), *Family Group Conferences: Perspectives on Policy and Practice*, Annandale, NSW: Federation Press.
Jung, H. (1993), 'Criminal Justice – A European Perspective', *Criminal Law Review*, 237–45.
Lacey, N. and Zedner, L. (1995), 'Discourses of Community in Criminal Justice', *Journal of Law and Society*, **23**, 301–25.

LaPrairie, C. (1995), 'Altering Course: New Directions in Criminal Justice', *Australian and New Zealand Journal of Criminology*, 28, 78–99.
Legrand, P. (1996a), 'European Legal Systems are not Converging', *International and Comparative Law Quarterly*, 45, 52–81.
Legrand, P. (1996b), 'How to Compare Now', *Legal Studies*, 16 (2), 232–42.
King, M. (1987), 'Crime Prevention in France', *Home Office Research Bulletin* (24), London: Home Office.
King, M. (1991), 'The Political Construction of Crime Prevention: A Contrast between the French and British Experiences', in K. Stenson and D. Cowell (eds), *The Politics of Crime Control*, London: Sage.
Marnham, P. (1993), *Crime and the Académie Française*, Harmondsworth: Penguin.
Matthews, R. (ed.) (1988), *Informal Justice?*, London: Sage.
Morris, A., Maxwell, G. and Robertson, J.P. (1993), 'Giving Victims a Voice: A New Zealand Experiment', *Howard Journal*, 32 (4), 304–21.
Moore, S.F. (1973), 'Law and Social Change: The Semi-Autonomous Social Field as an Appropriate Subject of Study', *Law and Society Review*, 7, 719–46.
Murray, C. (1990), *The Emerging British Underclass*, London: Institute for Economic Affairs.
Nelken, D. (1985), 'Community Involvement in Crime Control', *Current Legal Problems*, 38, 239–67.
Nelken, D. (1994), 'The Future of Comparative Criminology', in D. Nelken (ed.), *The Futures in Criminology*, London: Sage.
Nelken, D. (1995), 'Disclosing/Invoking Legal Culture: An Introduction', *Social & Legal Studies*, 4, 435–52.
Nelken, D. (ed.) (1996), *Comparing Legal Cultures*, Aldershot: Dartmouth.
Prosser, T. (1995), 'The State, Constitutions and Implementing Economic Policy: Privatization and Regulation in the UK, France and the USA', *Social & Legal Studies*, 4, 507–16.
Robert P. (1997), *Le Monopole Pénale de l'Etat*, paper presented to the IHEJ seminar 'Violence et Sécurité', 26 May.
Sandwell Mediation Scheme (1993), *Annual Report*, Sandwell.
Vidal-Naquet, P.A. (1994), *L'Action Judiciare dans la Ville. L'Exemple de l'Antenne de Justice de Gennevilliers*, Lyon: CERPE.
Vignoble, G. (1994), *Les Maisons de Justice et du Droit*, présenté au Garde des Sceaux, Paris: Document Ministère de la Justice.
Weber, E. (1995), 'Foreword', in F. Gaspard, *A Small City in France*, London: Harvard University Press.
Weber, M. (1966), *On Law and Economy in Society*, in M. Rheinstein (ed.), Cambridge, MA: Harvard University Press.
Wieviorka, M. (1997), *Commenter la France*, Marseille: Éditions de l' Aube.
Wright, M. (1991), *Justice for Victims and Offenders*, Milton Keynes: Open University Press.
Wyvekens, A. (1995), *Analyse de l'Activité des Maisons de Justice et du Droit du Tribunal de Grande Instance de Lyon*, Montpellier: ERPC.

Wyvekens, A. (1996), 'Justice de Proximité et Proximité de la Justice: Les Maisons de Justice et du Droit', *Droit et Société*, **33**, 363–88.

Wyvekens, A. (1997), *L'Insertion Locale de la Justice Pénale*, Paris: L'Harmattan.

Yngvesson, B. (1993), 'Local People, Local Problems, and Neighbourhood Justice: The Discourse of "Community" in San Francisco Community Boards', in S.E. Merry and N. Milner (eds), *The Possibility of Popular Justice*, Michigan: The University of Michigan Press.

Zedner, L. (1994), 'Reparation and Retribution: Are They Reconcilable?', *Modern Law Review*, **57**, 228–50.

Zedner, L. (1995), 'In Pursuit of the Vernacular: Comparing Law and Order Discourse in Britain and Germany', *Social & Legal Studies*, **4**, 517–34.

Zehr, H. (1990), *Changing Lenses: A New Focus For Criminal Justice*, London: Metanoia.

PART IV
LIVING THERE

9 Telling Difference: Of Crime and Criminal Justice in Italy

David Nelken

... the comparative study of law cannot be a matter of reducing concrete differences to abstract commonalties ... law is local knowledge not placeless principle. (Geertz, 1983: 215, 218)

Introduction

In this chapter I shall be taking further earlier discussions of the challenges to be faced in studying crime and criminal justice comparatively (see, for example, Nelken, 1994b; Nelken and Levi, 1996; Nelken, 1997a; Beirne and Nelken, 1997). In particular I shall return to the classical problem of 'starting points' in comparative research and the way this affects the task of discovering similarities and differences amongst systems of criminal justice. These questions arise as part of my current interest in the peculiarities of the viewpoint of the foreign expatriate observer, whom I shall be calling an 'observing participant'. But although the illustrations used will be based mainly on what I have learned during my experience of living and working in Italy over the past ten years, the methodological issues discussed should be of wider relevance.

As is suggested by my choice of opening quotation, in seeking to communicate the experience of 'being there' in the study of other cultures I, like many others, have found inspiration in the work of Clifford Geertz. The activities known as criminal justice are certainly ones which are particularly rich in symbolic themes, and there are many local cultural differences which need to be interpreted carefully. At the same time, however, for those studying European systems of criminal justice some caution is needed in taking Geertz as a model, despite this being recommended in some of the best recent British work on comparative criminal justice (for example, Zedner, 1995a). There are, after all, important differences between the cultures he

233

studies (Morocco, Bali or South East Asia) and carrying out research in contemporary France, Germany or Italy – countries whose cultures are much more similar to, and interconnected with, the cultures of origin of those studying them and which are increasingly being tied together by European and global exchanges of all kinds. Even Geertz's famous formulation of the aim of comparison (though less his actual practice) can present us with a misleading dichotomy. By emphasizing the importance of 'local knowledge' he rightly warns us to look for what is specific and not only what is universal. But what we find when looking at criminal justice in contemporary Europe is a law which can no more be described as 'local knowledge' than as 'placeless principle'. Rather, criminal justice needs to be approached as a system of actions and ideas which claims also to be 'placeless knowledge' (deriving from science, technology and other forms of expertise, including even 'legal science') as well as representing 'local principle'. Moreover there are a variety of forces and influences at work which, in one way or another, *are* actually having the effect of 'reducing concrete differences to abstract commonalties' (Geertz, 1983, *op. cit.*).

On Not Starting from Here

The puzzle to be discussed in this chapter is easier to pose than to resolve. What can and should the comparative researcher do about the way in which previous experience and expectations condition his or her understanding of the culture under observation? On the one hand, the ability to look at a culture with new eyes is supposed to be the great strength of the ethnographer. On the other hand, what if the observer's questions have more relevance to the country of origin than that under observation? Can we be sure that knowledge about criminal justice in England is helpful in understanding crime and criminal justice in Italy? Could it not even be a handicap? These questions are often left begging because of the implicit collusion between the writer and the audience which privileges what the audience wants to know as if it is what it *should* want to know. What therefore tends to be highlighted are those aspects of the society under investigation which seems especially relevant in confirming or disconfirming previous expectations. One result of this is that it can often be instructive to read comparative work, whatever its purported aims, not for what it says about the country or culture being observed but for what it reveals about the cultural viewpoint of the observer and his or her home audience (as if we were looking through the other end of the telescope). It is easy for us to see that what an Italian scholar finds strange and problematic about law in the USA is likely to tell us at least as much about Italian assumptions about the role and rule of law as it is does about how things are organized in the USA (Ferrarese, 1997). We are less quick to appreciate that the same is true in reverse.

The comparative study of criminal justice therefore makes it particularly necessary (as well as offering particular opportunities) to develop what I have called a 'reflexive criminology' (Nelken, 1994a). Whatever may be the case elsewhere, it is impossible to engage in comparative research without paying close attention to the definition and reach of the concepts of crime, of criminal justice and of social control which the observer and the observed employ; the changing local and global social contexts which shape what is being studied; the persuasive expressions used in the discourse of criminal justice officials, politicians and criminologists themselves; the sources of the standpoints being adopted; and the practical purposes and possible implications of the research (Nelken, 1994a).

For an 'observing participant', learning about another country's or culture's system of criminal justice involves paying close attention to the unfolding relationship between the observer and what is observed. Not only will this reveal how much the starting point of any comparison shapes what is found noteworthy in the foreign culture but also how this starting point is reformulated over time. Because there can be no 'view from nowhere' – no neutral or innocent point of reference – many attempts at comparison are deeply, and sometimes fatally, conditioned by taken-for-granted assumptions about the cultures explicitly, or implicitly, being compared. Even as accomplished a criminologist as Marshall Clinard has been criticized for failing to examine the extent to which his own experience as an American (rather than someone used to living in Europe) influenced what he found remarkable about the alleged lack of crime in Switzerland (Clinard, 1978; Balvig, 1988).

Much of the voluminous American research on the specificity of Japanese criminal and civil justice can be criticized for attempting to explain as singularly Japanese matters which could better be attributed to the Continental European models which shaped, and still shape, legal institutions in Japan. In my own case, too, beginning from English preconceptions and writing for an audience which shares them, I face the ever-present danger of describing features of criminal justice as peculiarly Italian which should better be characterized as part of larger differences between common law and civil law legal systems. In particular, much of Italian criminal procedure – the discipline which is in some respects the nearest equivalent in Italy to the academic study of criminal justice – is heavily influenced by *German* legal culture![1]

A particularly vivid encounter which throws light on the importance of starting points, as well as on the 'specificities' of Italian culture, occurred during a visit I made to Copenhagen some time ago. My teenage daughter had been keen to see Christiana, the counter-cultural enclave where soft drugs are bought and sold openly. In the main street where this was carried on we met a young man from Palermo weighing out hashish for sale. He looked a bit glum and, in the course of conversation with him, he voiced his complaint that the Danes in particular and Northern Europeans in general were, in his view, terrible conformists as compared to Italians. 'How can you say that?' complained my daughter (dressed in British teenager grunge), 'It is we who are the individualists! Just look at the way you Italians all dress with the same conformist "elegance".'

'No, no', he replied, 'clothes are not the point here, it is you Northerners who are all alike, for it is you who have the state in your hearts!'

There are a number of ways of trying to make sense of the strange-sounding claim that Northern Europeans have 'the state in their hearts'. In the first place it may reflect something of how residents of Christiana see themselves in relation to other members of straight society in Denmark – almost the party line for those who choose to live in some respects on the margins of the law. It may also have something to do with the extent to which many Danes in general do seem to be particularly proud of being law-abiding and patriotic (and not only as compared to many Italians). But, above all, it is important to see how this judgement tells us something both about the observer's own preconceptions and about those he is observing. It is only someone brought up in Italy (or possibly some other southern European countries) who would be likely to talk about the state as such as an object of love and hate. In particular this accusation (which is more likely, I think, to leave Northern Europeans puzzled rather than offended) expresses all the contradictory feelings of someone brought up in the South of Italy and in Sicily in particular. These are parts of Italy which have, on the one hand, regularly experienced external and internal colonization and, on the other hand, can, with reason, lament continued neglect and abandonment by an absentee state. To have such a state in our hearts would indeed be worthy of reproach. But most Northern Europeans, and especially those used to Anglo-American political discourse in which the term 'the state' hardly appears, do not think of their relationship with government in these terms. Still less would they accept that it is this background sentiment – which they are unaware of having – which permits their individualistic expressions of non-conformity. What the substance of this accusation brings out so well is the possibility that 'we' have indeed internalized the state as such a deep level of our hearts and minds that we simply can no longer recognize this (as Foucault would well have agreed). But the way in which it is formulated also reminds us just how much our observations of others also express our own concerns.

The force of this point is so strong that it can be tempting to deal with it by saying that the goal of a comparative project should be to learn more about our own society rather than to seek to characterize another. Going abroad is then justified in terms of the opportunity it provides to understand our own country or culture better in the light of 'the other' (see, for example, Balvig, 1988). But this solution is flawed. Even to succeed in the aim of learning more about our *own* country or culture we need to be clear about whether we have in fact made sense of the foreign culture being observed. Otherwise we can end up simply constructing 'the other' as a projection of our own culture. Inevitably we will have to make some claims about how things work *elsewhere* – and, in any case, we will certainly be perceived as doing so. Thus the problem remains: if comparison is so conditioned by our starting point, what sort of claims can be made and with what sort of licence?

We must, it seems, accept that our embeddedness in our own culture of origin makes it difficult not only to put forward appropriate 'solutions' for others but also even to understand their problems. But this should not lead to a relativism which would make it impossible ever to engage in understanding anything outside ourselves (Leavitt, 1997). We all have to start from somewhere, but we do not have to end there. This said, many of the most important gains of comparative work do come from interrogating the very sense of making comparisons. Whether a 'problem' exists, and what sort of problem we need to explain, is inextricably bound up with starting points. And some questions do make little or no sense when transferred across cultures because the linguistic and cultural categories simply do not match.[2]

Yet even questions couched in terms which *are* salient in both (or more) cultures being compared may look different depending on which cultures one starts from. Someone coming from Mexico might find Italian criminal justice relatively efficient, whereas someone from Denmark is unlikely to do so. If the Italian system of criminal justice has relatively more built-in leniency than the Anglo-American system[3] (as Italians refer to it), is the problem which needs to be explained the harshness of the one or the indulgence of the other? (Compare Nelken, 1994b with Melossi, 1994.) Does the distinction between 'white-collar crime' and 'organized crime', the basically legitimate businessman and the Mafia-like figure, correspond to an ontological reality? Or does it reflect a Protestant conception of the ethics of wealth production which presupposes the inherent respectability of money-making (Ruggiero, 1997). The more we range into wider aspects of society and culture the more prior expectations matter. British observers are likely to be struck by the strength of family ties in Italy; many recent Muslim immigrants, on the other hand, consider that there is not enough emphasis on family values and that there is insufficient respect for mothers (Ginsborg, 1998: 133)! All these perspectives may have something to teach us about

Italy or about ourselves (and different cultural expectations provide no argument for relativism).

But does this mean that all we can do is add together such diverse views as if we were blind men describing an elephant? Is there really no way of describing or explaining Italian criminal justice 'in itself'? In one sense, it may indeed be impossible to explain Italy 'in itself' (what the insider takes for granted the outsider may make problematic, but only from some other point of view). But there are two sources of information and ideas which can, and should, be used as at least a partial corrective to the parochialism of any given starting point. In the first place we can interview members of the culture under observation and sample their discourses. The corrective provided by the insider point of view can be salutary. Once, having waited four years for official confirmation in Italy that Cambridge was a university I let fly the remark that this was Kafkaesque. To this a colleague replied sharply: 'It's Kafka to you!'. In some sense this was normal for her.

On the other hand, insider observers must also 'start from somewhere', are subject to their own biases and follow their own agendas and methodologies. And greater familiarity with the relevant features of general or legal culture (life in Italy, the tradition of civil law, Catholicism, or whatever) will also tend to obscure, for these informants, what for outside observers could be some of the most interesting features of the culture to which they belong! For this reason we must also refer (although not necessarily defer) to the wider scientific literature. Faced with perplexing practices in Italian criminal justice it is of great help to consult what has already been written about crime and criminal justice there, or else in other civil law countries. It can be of even greater value to consult the wider literatures of comparative law, anthropology, political science or history. After immersion in these literatures our starting point is less likely to reflect our own experiences or expectations and, instead, can be based on what both insiders and outsiders have contributed to the relevant social scientific and other literatures. The country or culture under observation can thus be related to a series of other cases which go beyond the experience of any one observer. We can search for overarching themes such as trust versus distrust, order versus disorder, tolerance versus punitiveness, or exclusion versus inclusion, which allow aspects of criminal justice in both the country under observation and in the country of origin to be embraced in a larger comparative framework.

However, if we would be mistaken simply to adopt the insiders' perspective neither can we rely slavishly on the scientific literature to do the job of comparison for us. To decide what the literature really means and how far it relates, or is relevant, to what we are trying to understand is far from easy without direct experience of the culture in question. It is a quite different matter to merely read about 'clientilism' as opposed to actually encountering this intricate combination of instrumental friendship and sponsored cooptation, and then consult the literature to learn more about the varieties of this form of social and political ordering. Many other matters which have to do with contrasts between personal and impersonal forms of coordination can only really be grasped through direct experience rather than linguistic description. The nature of this 'experience', however, is always and necessarily marked by expectations based on previous socialization. But, more than this, the scientific literature itself is also inevitably constructed by scholars with specific viewpoints and standpoints. One of the important practical findings of comparative research is therefore the discovery that the scientific literature is often less universalistic than it purports to be. Much Anglo-American scientific criminological literature, for example, is a carrier of entrenched culturally specific assumptions about the nature of crime and role of criminal justice, all of which can easily obstruct sensitive cross-cultural research.

The 'observing participant' who lives and works in a new country or culture has the responsibility – and opportunity – of going beyond the existing literature by drawing on and relating scientific texts to his or her life experiences. He or she will have valuable opportunities to learn through engagement, rather than only through observation. This sort of observer is likely to have a greater range and depth of experiences than a visitor who stays for a shorter period. He or she can more easily become a sort of 'insider/outsider', experiencing some of the advantages of each role. He or she will have more chance of transcending the early stages of 'culture shock' which so often tells us much more about traumas arising from the observer's previous expectations than it does about cultural struggles in the country under observation. The gradual mastery of social rules and cultural expectations achieved by the observing participant can itself serve as a guarantee that he or she has increased his or her understanding of how things actually work.

But the insider/outsider has no absolutely privileged perspective in that he or she also occupies a role in the society and therefore is subject to its specific constraints. Even being able to draw on direct experience, as well as consult the scientific literature, does not obviate the need to relate his or her opinions and observations to those of the native members of the culture with whom he or she interacts. He or she may find him or herself serving as a translator, commentator or counterpoint in respect to their views. Not always able or wishing to be consistent, the observing participant will sometimes use the conformity of his or her findings with the views of the natives as evidence for the soundness of an observation and, at other times, emphasize the freshness of the outsider's perspective. As is the case for other comparative researchers, special importance will be attached to explicit (or implicit) conversations with scholars or legal actors in the society under investigation – all the more so if they are themselves insider/outsiders looking at their own culture in the light of others (Balvig, 1988; Downes, 1988, 1990; Franke, 1990; Killias, 1989). Yet, most importantly, like any other stranger, the 'insider/outsider' also moves between past socialization in a specific culture and present, willing or unwilling, resocialization into a new way of doing things. A crucial part of his or her discovery of 'the other' still necessarily passes through self-discovery.

Differences and Absences

Some of the implications of the argument so far are relatively uncontroversial. The disciplined investigation of cultural variability is all about the search for similarities and differences. It requires avoiding the assumption of similarity at all costs whilst also taking care not to be deceived by what may turn out to be only apparent difference. Getting beyond first impressions of curiosity, pleasure or shock at uncovering differences means being open to the similarities hidden by apparent and persisting differences in the midst of alleged similarities. But other matters are less clear-cut. In the light of what we have said so far about the role played by our expectations in recognizing differences, what do these differences actually represent? And how can we be sure whether we have correctly identified them? As Sztompka puts it, 'when is the same really the same, when is the same really different' (Sztompka, 1990).

If we set out to find examples of similarities we can certainly find parallels in Italy to many of the developments and concerns which are at the centre of research on criminal justice in the UK and other English-speaking countries. In both settings there is considerable discussion of the exponential increase in crime since the Second World War and the more recent apparent growth in the fear of crime. The same type of socially and economically marginal people fill up the prisons, usually for offences involving theft or drug dealing. Likewise, the evolution of crime prevention follows much the same pattern in Italy as in most of the rest of Europe including the UK. Local government initiatives try to take some of the responsibilities previously monopolized by the state. Along with increasing resort to technology – such as investment in closed circuit television – there is a massive growth in private policing in securing the safety of banks, and the 'public–private' spaces of shopping malls, although not as yet as part of housing developments for the rich. In Italy, too, we can discover experiments in mediation between offenders and victims, especially in cases involving juveniles. (Early results in Turin confirm the general finding that such schemes are more favoured by offenders than victims.)

Italy takes part in international victim surveys and is, finally, also organizing annual national victim surveys to internally monitor its crime problem. Following a period in which medical and psychological approaches dominated, sociological criminology is again becoming important, and research projects and criminological texts take great account of English-language theories and initiatives in the field of crime and delinquency (Barbagli, 1995, 1998). Slogans such as 'zero tolerance' are used by political campaigners of different persuasions, both by the mayor of Milan responding to social alarm over increased street crime, and by women's groups taking forward their struggle against assault and harassment in the home and at work. All over the world, Italy included, public opinion about crime is increasingly shaped by the 'virtual' knowledge produced by the media and this, in turn, shapes police action as it seeks to defend its legitimacy and resources.

Given other differences in history, political and social structure and culture, the existence of such common trends can itself be noteworthy. And seeking explanations of such similarities can take us far beyond the strict realm of criminal justice. We may be facing convergence, as a result of similar responses to the problems and exigencies which face modern industrial societies or as the inevitable effects of globalization. Or we could be dealing with deliberate borrowing and imitation irrespective of whether institutions or practices are really 'functional necessities' for the importing country.

As this suggests, however, we must be as much on the look-out for differences as for similarities if we are not to commit the error well categorized as 'confusing the familiar with the necessary' (Langbein and Weinreb, 1978). Whereas ostensibly different institutions and practices in the society under observation *may* be performing similar 'functions' to those in the society from which the researcher comes, 'functional equivalents' do not always exist. As I wrote soon after moving to Italy:

> ... living in another country has given me a jaundiced view of the sort of comparative research which sets out to show that all societies face basically similar problems even if they may solve them in somewhat different ways. What is more striking is the power of culture to produce relatively circular definitions of what is worth fighting for and against and the way institutions and practices express genuinely different histories and distinct priorities. (Nelken, 1992: 2).

If only because 'seeing is believing', observing participation is one of the best ways of experiencing this point. In the first few years of my stay in Bologna a deviant band of local police officers was discovered to have been engaged in a systematic campaign of robbing and murdering up to 20 people. But even when, after eight years, these crimes were demonstrated to have been the work of the police and not of professional criminals, there was – from a British point of view – amazingly little public debate about what these events revealed about the role of the police or the need of new methods of recruitment or control to avoid a recurrence. Those on the political Left had difficulty in categorizing these crimes as representing a 'political' cause rather than as an isolated phenomenon, in contrast to their attitude towards the role played by the police in dealing with strikers and students during the 1970s; in any case, the local left-wing administration would have been reluctant to upset its delicate balance with the national state. Equally, the Right would not normally make political capital out of police misbehaviour. By contrast, the attention devoted to discussing the role of the judges, especially after their investigations into political corruption, is massive and unending and is out of all proportion to that dedicated to the police. Presumably because of the threat criminal court judges represent to them, politicians see judges as 'out of control' because *they* cannot control them!

The cognitive unfamiliarity of a different conceptual order itself often serves as a clue to the way in which problems, dilemmas or solutions are constructed by other systems of 'criminal justice'. Differences in language pose issues which go well beyond the technical problems of translation and link up with differences in the 'place' occupied by concepts of criminal law and justice, ideas about institutions and their role in society, which all point to, and reflect, important contrasts calling for further investigation. Examples of this, for someone coming from an 'Anglo-American' background, include: the diverse connotations of the term 'community' (in its central sense in Italy it conjures up religious communities rather than local groups of civil society); the lack, in the Italian language, of the separate terms 'politics' and 'policy' (social policy becomes *le politiche sociale*); or, conversely, the absence of an easy translation of what in English is termed 'enforcement' which, in Italian, would need to be separated into considerations which have to do either with 'bringing the law into force' or with 'making the law respected'. More fundamentally, there is not even any obvious equivalent in Italian for the term 'criminal justice', conceived as a series of empirically mapped stages of everyday decision-making by police prosecutors or judges. There is a great paucity of empirical research into such everyday decisions, and little, if any, analysis of the interrelationship between such decisions.

Such variations in ways of thinking, talking and researching criminal justice reflect and reproduce – albeit in complex ways – differences in institutional and social practices. In Italy two of the three police forces are militarized and there seems to be no call for this to be changed. Sometimes even the army itself (drawing on those serving their compulsory military service) is itself involved in crime control. The role of the news media in reacting to announcements of forthcoming prosecution are crucial in shaping the social effectiveness of the criminal law (given the delays in actually coming to trial). Yet, on the other hand, the main newspapers make little or no use of investigative journalism in their reporting on crime and political corruption, so that the reports of prosecutors and judges undergoing investigations and trial are almost always the major source of *empirical* information about crime – especially organized crime. These same authoritative sources quite regularly find themselves accused of crimes ranging from revealing reserved information to acting in collusion with the Mafia. The role of the Catholic Church in shaping public opinion and behaviour is another of the many issues which escapes easy comparison. At the time of the *Tangentopoli* corruption trials it seemed that some priests were advising politicians (and others caught up in these investigations) that, once they had shared their confessions with them, they need not also confess to the authorities. But priests are also in the front line in trying to prevent the recruitment of youths to the ranks of organized crime, and some – like judges and policemen – have lost their lives in such battles.

Such similarities and differences come to life for an observer – more than for a native – when they are exemplified by what Nicola Lacey and Lucia Zedner (1998) have recently called 'significant absences'. The problem, of course, is then deciding why and to whom these absences are significant. We could add that the same role is played by the discovery of 'surprising presences'. After investigation an observer may conclude that much of what seems different is only a result of his or her unfamiliarity with the new culture; with time he or she may also succeed in finding unexpected equivalents in his or her own country. But, in so far as he or she remains convinced that there are real differences, it will often be the correlative *absence* or *presence* of comparable phenomena in his or her country of origin that itself then becomes problematic – often for the first time. Understanding the causes, consequences and meaning of 'significant' differences thus requires interpretation and explanation of *absence* and *presence* in each of the cultures concerned. For example, to understand the role played by laymen in criminal justice in the UK, as opposed to Italy, it would be necessary to investigate both the reasons why laymen are favoured in the UK and what state officials and state law symbolize in Italy.

But working out the significance of absence and presence can be even more complicated than this. Not all presences or absences are equal: some are constitutive of self-identity, others more contingent. Absence is often as important as presence – it can even be a form of presence. *Absence has a shape* and can function as cause and consequence both in the realm of social structure and that of meaning. Many Italians bemoan the lack of a well functioning state; and, although they mainly lambast their politicians, they also sometimes blame themselves (the expression 'we don't have the sense of the state' is heard frequently). However, the state of which they feel the absence is quite definitely the French or German concept of the state, with its collective project taken forward by the organs and officials of the nation, rather than the 'foreign' English or American liberal conception of government as the servant of civil society. In the European tradition 'the legal system is the way the state makes ethical the system of needs of civil society' (Melossi, 1990: 100–102). From this Continental perspective it was Anglo-American ideas of the state – one in which popular sovereignty replaced the role of the ideal representative of social and political stability and in which private interests have an inherent legitimacy – which seemed, and can still seem, alien (Ferrarese, 1997).

When it comes to identifying distinctiveness on the basis of 'presence' and 'absence', differences in legal and political discourses may have only an uncertain relationship to differences in social practices. Both practice and discourse therefore need to be studied independently, as well as in relation to each other. In one country debate may centre on public order policing while, in practice, police surveillance goes on unnoticed; another culture may be concerned about the risks of private surveillance and take for granted the role of public police patrols (Zedner, 1995b: 526–27).

The relationship between discourse and practice may often be complex and even paradoxical. The Italian national state is *in theory* a collective impersonal project (Dyson, 1980; Costa, 1986) but, *in practice*, its survival with any sort of credibility often comes down to the calibre and integrity (or the lack of these qualities) of a very limited number of individual politicians, judges or policemen – some of whom even risk martyrdom in its name. There is incessant public debate regarding the danger of the personal intruding into the realm of the impersonal – so much so that some observers see this as partly explaining why Italy is attributed such a relatively high degree of corruption (Eve, 1993, 1996). Yet, at the same time, some of the current Italian political parties are simply named after their leaders. In the UK there is much less use of the notion of 'the state' as compared to simply talking in a relatively personalized way about the government of the day. But there seems to be no contradiction at all between this tal of individ politicians and strong identification with the nation-state (which is surely not reducible to, the institution of the monarchy). And the and continuity of the British state are not in question.

Much the same applies to the notion of 'communit discourse in Germany, France and Italy makes much ss re role of 'community involvement' in criminal justice England or the USA (Lacey and Zedner, 1995 A' countries have this in common, each also has special reasons to avoid such terminology. In Germany, for example, the reasons suggested include the inconsistency of the appeal to community with the claims of the *Rechstaat*, the well entrenched respect for professionalism, as well as the competition this might pose to the well organized and well funded system of local government. Talk of community or of any other type of 'informal justice' may also be deliberately avoided because it is reminiscent of the way in which informers were encouraged to use the Nazi totalitarian legal system as a way of settling old scores. However, this does not, in fact, mean that 'the community' is not expected to be active in monitoring and censoring behaviour. Indeed, it may be that these habits are already so strong that they are simply taken for granted. As Lacey and Zedner put it:

> ... the assertion that community is 'absent' in Germany should be understood, therefore, to refer to the fact that the term barely figures in the vocabulary of German criminal justice politics. It is not a claim about the nature or lack of particular social arrangements. Indeed, paradoxically, it may be that it is the very stability of social relations in Germany, or more particularly the strength of community as an institutional entity, which deprives this term of rhetorical appeal. (Lacey and Zedner, 1998: 8)

In Italy, likewise, talk of community involvement in crime control is also slow to make headway, perhaps because of a tradition of state responsibility for public order, as well as a background of Church and state conflict over who represented the community. Nevertheless, the appeal to 'solidarity', drawing on either Catholic or communist roots, can be all-important in the way Italian civil society is mobilized and held together, especially, but not only, in regions such as Emilia Romagna or Tuscany.

Finally, however, it is worth remembering that 'absence' and 'presence' are contingent and changeable qualities. The observer who includes in his or her report of other systems of criminal justice the different way in which local discourses conceptualize such issues may thereby contribute to redrawing them.[4] Studies of criminal justice in the UK have been rightly criticized for obscuring the role of the state by concentrating only on the lower level echelons of criminal justice (McBarnet, 1981). In Italy, by contrast, it is impossible to forget that one is dealing with the state, but it is still hard to find attention given to the importance of variability and unexpected outcomes in organizational practices. But, in Italy, as elsewhere in Europe, ideas of what counts as crime, and how it should be dealt with, do presently seem to be converging on Anglo-American ideas about such matters (Van Swaanigen, 1999). The spread of international crime surveys can be seen as part of a steady process through which the conception of social control is changing from one linked to the state to one relating it to civil society (Melossi, 1990: 101-20). Whether writing as a comparative researcher or, even more, when serving as a member of the Secure Cities Crime Committee created by the Emilia Romagna regional government, I too am part of these developments (in however small a way).

Drawing the Contrasts

It is with these points in mind that I shall now seek to highlight some of the continuing differences in *crime, criminal justice* and *discourse about crime* in Italy which underlie, accompany or retard European or global trends. My assumption will be that many of the Anglo-American ideas about crime which I was socialized into taking for granted are also those which are currently striving for hegemonic influence. Thus the aim will be not so much to deny my starting point as to use it to highlight what it is about Italy which renders these expectations problematic and which helps us to reflect about their source and meaning.

The Meaning of Crime Rates

In comparative indexes of crime or incarceration rates, Italy's 'natural' place seems to lie somewhere in the middle of the range of other European countries. Yet it should come as no real surprise that we can easily show that such statistics need considerable interpretation before they can be used. It is no exaggeration to say that one needs to know the culture well in order to decide whether and what significance to give to such statistics. At the most obvious level there is the problem of reliability. At one meeting of the Emilia Romagna Secure Cities Crime Committee a senior official of the government statistical service commented that, with the exception of a very few crimes such as murder or kidnapping, he would not place much trust in the statistics because of the haphazard way in which they were compiled. At a later meeting we were told that the police admitted that some of the local figures for fraud they had reported to the Ministry were in error by a factor of ten to one. But technical problems do not end there. Even within different regions of Italy, let alone between countries, it is difficult to tell how far differences in the tendency to report crimes to the police biases alleged crime rates. What sense should be made of the fact that it is where women are most emancipated, in the North (and not the South) of Italy, that there is the highest level of reporting sexual assaults?

Whatever else they are measuring, statistics which appear to refer to similar phenomena are primarily registering the activities of criminal justice agencies. Such agencies in Italy often operate in ways which are, in many respects, quite different from common law countries and – at least as far as delay is concerned – can also be distinguished from those in other Continental systems. It is impossible to know what would be the 'real' rates of convicted crimes and incarceration if there were not such enormous backlogs in the processing of crimes and the holding of trials. Rates in Italy have to be understood against the background of the various stages of judgement, the possibilities for formal objections, the existence of periodic amnesties, paying a penalty to avoid a conviction ('condoni'), and so on. Were it not for the fact that many cases end up being time-barred (through cases running over the maximum time allowed for prosecution, 'prescription') the rates of crime and incarceration would certainly be much higher. But then which is the real rate – that for which the system is formally geared up or that which it actually produces? Pre-trial detention provides a particularly tricky example of the difficulties of fair comparison. Those in prison awaiting trial are counted for the purpose of incarceration rates, but their behaviour does not count as a criminal conviction until their cases have passed through all the stages of the trial system (which usually means two stages of trial on the merits and then one appeal on the law). Should those held in prison waiting to go to appeal after conviction at the first trial stage or, at least, those waiting to appeal after conviction at the second stage be held comparable to those in other countries serving sentence after conviction? Or should they be equated (as is common) to those in common law countries being held on pre-trial? Form and substance can diverge, especially as there is more than a suspicion that some judges do make use of imprisonment before final conviction as a resource of punishment.

Just because these rates play such an important role in international comparisons they are also sometimes subject to deliberate manipulation. It has been suggested to me by an insider that Italy embarked on a large prison building programme in the 1980s after it discovered that it had a relatively low rate of imprisonment (on the other hand, Finland is alleged to have done its best to reduce its incarceration rate to correspond more to the mean). But even when dealing with similar rates it can be instructive to see the different route that each system takes to get there. In Italy, as elsewhere, immigrants are more likely than others to be suspected of involvement in crime and more often stopped and questioned (although this does not apply to those stopped whilst driving cars). But the technical reasons why they fill the prisons out of all proportion to their number in the society, especially while awaiting trial, also has much to do with their failure to possess the formal identification requirements which all native Italians can provide. There is also some evidence that they are often advised to use the Italian equivalent of plea bargaining or shortened trials rather than take their chances by drawing out the criminal process to the utmost. And this, too, has the effect of increasing their representation amongst those in prison.

Since the problems which official statistics pose for disentangling crime from criminal justice are notorious, it is logical to turn to victimization surveys as a better basis for comparison. Since 1992 Italy has collaborated in the International Victim Surveys which have indeed generated valuable and essential information about many aspects of the crime phenomenon. However, even here, we should be aware of how much can remain implicit and taken for granted in apparently common sense notions of crime. As compared to other European countries Italy turned out to have roughly similar rates of victimization and concerns about crime. One of the few differences seemed to be the relatively lenient public attitudes to punishment in Italy. (By contrast it is the UK which stands out from most European countries in its level of public approval of sending burglars to prison.)

But what were the crimes being compared in this victim survey? The 1992 survey limited itself to the following offences. Under the heading of household crimes it covered theft of cars and from cars, vandalism to cars, theft of bicycles, burglary with entry, attempted burglaries and break-ins to outbuildings. For what it called personal crimes it asked about robbery, theft of personal property, pickpocketing, non-contact theft, sexual incidents, sexual assaults, offensive behaviour, assaults, threatened assaults with force and threats without force (Van Dijk and Mayhew, 1993). Why did it examine these crimes in particular? Can we be sure that they are equally central to the meaning of crime in different cultures? Is there any way we can decide this? The way in which national criminal statistics are arranged may be at least as important a guide.[5] The Italian criminal statistics, for example, are organized in terms of the following categories: crimes against the person; crimes against the family, public morality and good customs; crimes against property; crimes against the economy and public trust; crimes against the state and other social institutions and the public order.[6] Daily decision-making in first-level criminal courts in Italy certainly does also involve the crimes picked out in the victimization surveys, but it also routinely includes allegations of criminal negligence in causing accidents at work, criminal medical recklessness, and pollution cases, not to mention a large number of cases involving bouncing cheques, outraging public officials and a host of minor administrative contraventions.

Another source of valuable information is the type of work and specialization of criminal defence lawyers (Di Federico et al., 1994). A recent survey of a large and representative sample of lawyers, according to the main type of crimes, divided respondents into the following categories: those who do all types of work (21 per cent); those who gave various general responses (34 per cent); organized crime (2 per cent); violence against person and rape (10 per cent); drugs alone (4 per cent); crimes against public administration (4 per cent); business, commercial and financial crimes (7 per cent); tax and tax evasion (7 per cent); building offences (3 per cent); manslaughter and accidents (6 per cent); fraud and pollution (2 per cent). As might be expected, more of the work of the lawyers in the North than those in the South involves business crime although some lawyers in the large Southern cities have similar numbers of such clients.

There are obvious reasons why victim surveys privilege an 'ordinary crime' definition of their object. It would certainly be more complicated to study, for example, white-collar, organized crime or state crime with survey methods. Victims of these crimes are often diffuse, sometimes unaware of their victimization, may collaborate in the crime or be afraid to report it. The focus of such surveys might also perhaps be defended as reflecting what people are most worried about. But this easily becomes part of a self-fulfilling prophecy. Fear of crime is often only an indication or substitute for much wider concerns. Moreover, if what matters is what most disturbs people why stick to the legal definition of crime – why not extend such surveys to include those incivilities or disturbances to expectations that are not even crimes? (And why, then, avoid asking about racism and intolerance?) Whatever the justifications advanced, the impression remains that such surveys help to spread exactly those ideas of crime, of victimization and of the appropriate role of criminal justice agencies which fit well with liberal–individualistic Anglo-American culture but which are presented as if they were 'cultural universals'.

This process can be witnessed vividly in present-day Italy. The term used to characterize ordinary crimes, such as burglary and robbery, is *microcriminalità* – the use of this diminutive clearly intending to indicate the lack of public importance of such criminality. However, unease has developed about using this term, and there have been proposals to talk instead of 'diffuse crimes'. There is also mounting evidence that the Italian police are sometimes overstating the severity of ordinary crimes (so that what were once thefts become robberies), and recent legislative proposals to sharply increase penalties for burglary or robbery show the consequences which such cultural homogenization can produce.

The question of cultural variability becomes all the more relevant when the results of victim surveys are employed, as they so often are, in service of the positivistic goal of finding the causal factors which underlie different rates of crime as indexed by reported levels of victimization. Van Dijk (in Van Dijk and Mayhew, 1993) deduces from the findings of the international victim surveys that higher levels of violence are a product of 'beer drinking cultures' as compared to 'wine drinking cultures'. But it is clearly unsatisfactory to describe culture in such reductive terms. It is far from obvious whether it is the type of drink which makes the difference or the social context in which it is consumed which matters – that is, where drinking takes place, with who, whether it is surrounded by a taboo, whether it is competitive, how it relates to the expectations on young males, the cultures of masculinity and so on. Again, we would need to get to know the culture first in order to make full sense even of the findings of victim surveys.

Controlling the Controllers

The steadily growing political pressure to recognize the seriousness of 'micro-criminality' in Italy means that the *criminal justice* apparatus is likely to be asked to respond more effectively to popular demands for the effective control of crime. Such pressures, which are all too familiar to those used to Anglo-American systems, are in many respects novel in what is still very much a 'top-down' type of Continental legal order. But the influence of Anglo-American models has already led to other important changes in the way crimes are dealt with. In the late 1980s, for example, the Italian political class took steps to bring their country's criminal justice procedures more in line with those of the common law world by introducing its well known reform of the Code of Criminal Procedure.[7] This explicitly set out to move the criminal process away from the inquisitorial model and imported large parts of the accusatorial model. This included a quite new emphasis on oral testimony and on the trial as a contest between prosecution and defence. It also introduced indigenous versions of shortened trials and plea-bargained sentences. (The latter involves automatic reductions of sentence for avoidance of trial, together with the eventual cancellation of the criminal record, but does not require an admission of guilt.)

But criminal justice systems do not change overnight and so we should not be surprised if these reforms have had limited effects so far. Plea bargains, as well as the other routes to avoiding trial, are probably used, in no more than a quarter to a third of cases.[8] Most offenders continue to gamble on the benefits of delay, hoping that this will affect the recall or motivation of witnesses and victims. Prosecutor overload and other factors (cases can take up to ten years to end if they are at all complicated) always offer the possibility that they will never have to face the charges or the sentence. Although there are no other accusatorial systems with so many stages of trial there is still little support for the idea of abolishing the guarantee represented by the second stage of trial on the facts.

There is also some resistance from older members of the judiciary, whether from habit or vested interest, to the more demanding standards of proof required by the new Code. Moreover there are deep-seated cultural factors at stake here: given the connection between law and state in civil law cultures it will take a long time before defence lawyers are really seen as much as 'servants of the court' as 'the state' prosecutor who has hitherto uniquely represented the state's interest in ascertaining the truth. There are constant difficulties in reconciling the ethos of the new Code with the different requirements of dealing successfully with the challenge of organized criminals. And, in practice, the measures taken to strengthen the hand of the defence seemed to make little difference to the power of the prosecutors in the 'Mani Pulite' corruption investigations (Nelken, 1996b, 1997a, 1998).

Many other continuing differences in criminal justice can best be explained in terms of self-validating cultural presuppositions. The fact that two out of three police forces in Italy are militarized is still widely seen as a guarantee of their trustworthiness, by keeping them from being too easily corrupted by their social environment rather than, as would be the case in the UK, as an index of their lack of accountability to the populations they are supposed to serve. Someone from an Anglo-American background finds it surprising that an important method of legitimating criminal justice agencies is by mean of a constitutionally entrenched rule which purports to deny the prosecution any use of discretion. But although this attempt to eliminate discretion can easily be attacked as merely a 'myth' (Di Federico, 1991), it is one which does have many practical consequences – both bad and good (Nelken, 1997a).

Single prosecutors have little chance of openly exercising discretion to handle their massive caseloads, especially where the heads of offices take a bureaucratic attitude to maximizing throughput, treating all cases alike and avoiding cases 'falling into prescription'. One judge I interviewed was threatened with disciplinary proceedings by the head of her office if she carried out her plan to give priority to preparing solid indictments in cases involving accidents at work and pollution rather than to the thousands of, as she saw it, more petty crimes and contraventions. On the other hand, the absence of any exception to prosecution even for reasons of 'the public interest' strengthened the hands of prosecuting judges in their fight against high-level political corruption (Nelken, 1997a, 1998). So much so that, in the Italian context, the debate over the need to recognize and structure prosecution discretion is heavily (excessively?) conditioned by the fear that this would lead judges and prosecutors to fall under the control of the (potentially corrupt) executive.

These same fears, which date back to the mutual distrust amongst the post-war political elites holding to very different ideologies who drafted the constitution, also explain other apparent anomalies such as the rules about promotion. Judges receive automatic promotion in terms of pay and status from first court level to Supreme Court status merely on the basis of seniority – simply by growing older – even if they do not move court. This 'makes sense' in the Italian context because of fears that promotion on merit might otherwise lead to political interference. But it is a 'sense' which is not easily captured by seeking for 'functional equivalents' in 'Anglo-American' systems where political influence comes in at the stage of appointing judges rather than afterwards. The emphasis on 'guarantees' for defendants, has, at least up until now, united politicians of the Right and Left more effectively than populist calls for crime control. This helps explain many salient features of Italian criminal justice *in action*, such as the interminable built-in delays in the criminal process, the enormous expenditure of time and resources needed to bring to conviction a tiny proportion of the cases which are prosecuted, or the way in which higher criminal courts are forced to give priority to hearing claims against orders for preventive detention rather than hearing new cases. It can be instructive to realize how much difference it can make if those shaping criminal justice processes cannot be certain that they will never need to take advantage of the protections available to the defence (as if they were trying to work out the safest system in a situation similar to the veil of ignorance hypothesized by John Rawls in his *Theory of Justice*).

Patterns of Discourse

As we have already had cause to notice, whatever the evident, and increasing, similarities in discourses about crime there are also important and persistent differences. The picture is complicated by the need to distinguish, for some purposes, academic, official and technical discussions from political, popular and public discourses. All these discourses can be more or less differentiated within a society and some can have more similarities across societies than they have in common with other types of discourses in the same society. What is most striking, for someone coming from an Anglo-American background, is the relative lack in Italy of populist exploitation of the crime problem. But in a wider panorama it may be that the common law countries should be treated as the exceptions, even if it is now *their* discourse and practices which are nonetheless coming to be treated as the norm.[9]

Until recently at least, crimes such a burglary, wounding or mugging – the very stuff of 'moral panics' in the UK and the USA – stimulated relatively little media coverage or political debate in Italy. Even on the local news, bank raids or art robberies are given routine, rather than overdramatised, coverage with – what to an outsider – often seems like grudging admiration of particularly daring exploits. The explanation does not seem to be – as in some other societies – that ordinary crime is played down because of the desire to present 'a good face'[10] but rather that such crime pales into relative insignificance beside the greater threats such as international or homegrown terrorism (now unexpectedly re-emerging), political corruption (never far from the news) or organized crime (in its different varieties). There is an incredible variety of sensational crime-related activity to choose from. An 'ordinary' day can bring news of the arrests for drug trading of a gang of 'Albanians',[11] charges and countercharges connected to the progress of the long-running national anti-corruption investigations or more locally-based cases of corruption, continuing enquiries about a lawyer murdered in mysterious circumstances, the arrest of the son of a Mafia boss or the discovery of a Mafia arsenal. More infrequently, newsworthy crimes can include animal liberationists threatening to poison Nestlé products or the national court of auditors describing charges being brought for cases of misappropriation of public funds going back as far as the 1970s.[12] The news value of most crime events seems to depend on their capacity to trigger concern about wider problems of political confrontation, political untrustworthiness, fears about immigration or whatever. A simple burglary does not have this potential.

The emphasis in news stories on some offences rather than others, in Italy as elsewhere, is no measure of their actual distribution or the way in which this changes over time. Nor does it correspond to the harm caused. Why is so much attention in Italy devoted to the threat posed by usury while there is no similar attention to this problem in England and Wales? Certainly this may in part reflect differences in social structure: the centrality of small business in the Italian economy; the reluctance of many Italian banks to provide loans to all but the most secure of customers (and the way in which the major bank credit card companies in the UK deflect stigma for their overdue payment charges); and, not least, the different levels of organized crime. But it almost certainly also links back to a long Catholic cultural tradition of concern over the 'just price' and an instinctive rejection, at the ideological level at least, of the exploitative tendencies of capitalism. Newspapers in both countries personalize the news. But there are deep-seated contrasts in their ways of linking personal and political morality. In the UK it used to be very unusual to devote space to corruption – although it helped a lot if it could be linked to some angle of sexual deviance. In Italy sexual peccadilloes are rarely discussed unless they can be linked to corruption![13]

The use of the term *micro-criminalità* to indicate ordinary crime may well have underestimated the importance of these crimes for the general public in the past, as much as it does for the present. In any case, 'street crime' is now, finally, gaining in political and public salience, because of its association with the perceived 'threat' of criminal immigrants – a clearly identifiable target group of 'suitable enemies'. This may successfully overcome the difficulty previously encountered in mobilizing populist outrage against criminals. Shamefully, even the most otherwise insignificant breaches of law can now become newsworthy merely by being tinged with the theme of immigrants, known euphemistically as *extra-comunitari* (technically this term means those coming from outside the European Union but in practice it is reserved for those coming from poor countries).

Over the past 150 years the crime problem in Italy has been mainly linked to internal political, ideological and geographical divisions, especially the 'problem of the South' (Davis, 1988), rather than to society mobilizing itself against its 'dangerous classes', as it is in the UK. For the post-Second World War period the absence of a conventional 'law and order' discourse has been explained as the result of strong ideological divisions whereby all social issues were thought to be resolvable by taking the correct political stand (Pavarini, 1997). Politically speaking, each side had better 'suitable enemies' than petty criminals. Although there were recurrent concerns about crime, especially as a sign of falling morality during the post-war economic boom, it is thus only recently that discourse about 'ordinary crime' has begun to take on something like its central position in Anglo-American discourse. This was seen, for example, in the social and political reaction to eight murders by predatory criminals in Milan in as many days in early January 1999. It can also be detected in newspaper campaigns in other cities.[14] If such a change in popular consciousness takes hold (which is not yet certain) it will have significance well beyond criminology. Truly, we would be witnessing 'the end of ideology', even in Italy.

However, if some differences are attenuating, others seem destined to remain. In particular, the daily public reporting and discussion of organized crime and political corruption has no close equivalents in the UK. Conversely, there is still no parallel in Italy to the profound concern over juvenile crime found in many English-speaking countries. The term 'delinquency' is reserved for adult rather than juvenile criminality – young people are almost always seen as in need of care rather than punishment, the principal and important exceptions being those youths enrolled by organized criminals, or the way in which young immigrants and gypsies are dealt with. As an extreme example, two youths were accused some years ago of killing their parents in order to come into their inheritance sooner rather than later, and a leading national newspaper sent a journalist to sound out the reactions of their neighbours in the Northern Italian suburb where they lived. He reported back that they were described as 'good boys who were good workers'. It is an empirical question (and one I hope to pursue further) whether there is actually a lower rate of youth criminality or merely a different 'reaction' to young people in trouble – and both of these issues will vary between regions in Italy. In my region of Italy, for example, three recent cases of teenagers reported for murder are all being dealt with by means of re-education projects which are aimed at diverting their cases before, and in substitution of, criminal trial (and not only punishment). It is certainly of some relevance that a large proportion of Italian youngsters live at home with their parents – and are therefore in some sense subject to control – until they are into their thirties.

Some of the differences in discourse about crime which strike the observer from common law countries mainly reflect what Italian institutions have in common with those in other civil law countries, despite important differences in the actual level of faith in the state or other relevant matters. In Germany, too, the theme of victimization by street crime has hitherto been given relatively little emphasis because of the central focus on crime as, above all, a challenge to, and offence against, the state (Zedner, 1996: 11–12). Likewise, the popularity of 'the little judge', fighting for the collectivity, in his or her battle against the powerful, as in the recent anti-corruption investigations in Italy, has close parallels in France. For some commentators, criminal court judges can even come to represent the real 'state' as compared to corrupted politicians. The heated public debate after the shock of the *Tangentopoli* investigations concerning the alleged dangers of Italy being governed by criminal court judges, rather than by properly elected politicians, is kept alive by members of the political opposition largely for their own instrumental reasons. But it is difficult to imagine such a controversy ever arising in the UK.

However, even where we seem to be dealing with debates which have much in common, it is important to look beyond superficial similarities. A good example is provided by the classic issue of the conflict between those advancing the goal of 'crime control' and those giving more importance to the goal of 'due process'. Discussion of such a contrast, even if not exactly in these terms, can certainly be found also in Italy, both in political and academic circles.[15] But, as compared to common law countries such as the UK and USA, however, *at the level of public discourse* there tends to be less support for 'crime control' in Italy (as in many other civil law countries). This can already be seen in the terms used to describe the two sides, which are biased in favour of the supporters of 'due process'. Those who stress the protection of defendants' rights describe themselves, positively, as *garantisti*, and the prestige of this position is such that, in order to attack it, their opponents are often obliged to call them *falsi garantisti* or, at least, to denounce the excesses of what Italians call *hyper-garantismo*. Those who emphasize 'crime control', on the other hand, are unlikely to adopt this as their slogan. In fact they lack an easy rallying cry, especially as their (many) opponents may describe them as *giustizialisti* (or sometimes *Giacobini*, referring to the Revolutionary period in France) – terms which carry overtones of a desire to rush people to punishment without any consideration for legal protections.

The constituency for *garantismo*, or 'due process' in the broadest of senses, is thus much wider than that of academic lawyers and left-leaning civil libertarians. As compared to common law countries, politicians in Italy are more likely to seek votes by stressing their support for *garantismo* rather than for effective crime control, and not only because they (and some of their supporters) themselves fear being caught up in the criminal process. We should recall the fact all the previous parties of government were swept from office as a result of the *Tangentopoli* investigations based on the ordinary criminal law in the early 1990s. Currently, Silvio Berlusconi, the leader of the main opposition party, and a previous prime minister, is still involved in a series of criminal court processes (as is true of some of his collaborators), but successfully heads up the party which obtained by far the largest number of votes in the 1999 elections for the European parliament. There are internal divisions within all the parties over strategy and principle, but the majority of politicians, both on the Right and Left, are cautious about campaigning on the platform of crime control. Indeed, it was a member of the ex-fascist party (now the National Alliance) who in 1998 gave his name to a law designed to enable even some of those who receive definitive sentences at the end of all stages of the court process to benefit from an alternative to actually imprisonment.

The contest between the goals of 'crime control' and 'due process' is particularly complicated in Italy because of the way in which the criminal justice system needs to deal simultaneously with both the processing of normal crime and the special problems posed by organized crime. In some respects, a double-track system does exist – for example, regarding the use of the *pentiti* ex-Mafia informers. But a large amount of newspaper space is dedicated to periodic criticisms of the reliability of many *pentiti* and how using their testimony can involve abandoning the normal standard of protection for defendants. Certainly there is pride in the fact that the challenge of Red Brigade terrorism was faced by the ordinary courts without resort to special tribunals. Applying the normal trial procedures to Mafia cases, however, adds to the already difficult task of obtaining convictions – and the Mafia have more resources and local support than did the Red Brigade.

Sometimes there may be improper motives for exaggerating formal guarantees in Mafia trials. During the 1980s controversy surrounded the decisions of Judge Carnevale, head of a penal section of the Supreme Court (*Corte di Cassazione*). Carnevale (known as the 'killer of sentences'), together with his colleagues, quashed numerous complex Mafia trials at the last hurdle before definitive sentence, after years of preparation and previous sentences, on what seemed the slightest formalities, such as a previous court's failure to inform all the various lawyers of the many defendants of the dates of hearings in the correct manner. Subsequently, in the 1990s, Carnevale found himself on trial for alleged collaboration with the Mafia though he was eventually acquitted.

But, even apart from such extreme cases, the issue of whether exceptions to normal protections for the accused should be made in Mafia trials, and the dangers of so doing, remains a much debated issue. The move in the 1980s to a much more accusatorial type of trial has made this dilemma more acute. For much of 1997 and 1998 parliament and the Constitutional Court were embroiled in a struggle over the application of Article 513b of the Criminal Procedure Code which requires witnesses to reconfirm in open court any evidence previously given to police or prosecutors privately for their testimony to have legal force. In Mafia trials this requirement exposes witnesses and their relatives to the real threat of coercive violence aimed at forcing them to retract their evidence throughout the long periods of waiting for trial and appeal. In this debate (which, as so often in Italy, also turned into a jurisdictional turf war) the Constitutional Court favoured allowing the previous evidence to stand, so parliament is redrafting the law to confirm its more *garantisti* intentions. On other occasions, however, it is the courts which insist on the fullest respect for defendant's rights even in Mafia trials. In 1999, for example, the Supreme Court again ordered a complete retrial of a Mafia case after many years of investigation, trial and appeals, arguing that, since in the course of proceedings one of the judges had been substituted, it was necessary – in the light of the requirements of orality of the New Code of Criminal Procedure – that all the evidence of witnesses be reheard.

Even leaving politics aside, interview data suggest that criminal court judges and prosecutors both prefer to see themselves as primarily responsible for the correct and even-handed interpretation of the law rather than as ranged alongside the police in a 'war against crime' (Berti *et al.*, 1998). The important exceptions here are anti-Mafia judges, and those involved in pursuing political corruption or white-collar crimes: the *Tangentopoli* judges, for example, were clearly called on, or elected, to play the role of enforcers of the criminal law. But it is especially those judges and prosecutors who take on powerful interests who are regularly attacked, on *garantismo* grounds, for failing to respect defendant's rights – and some of these judges may, indeed, sometimes give precedence to 'crime control' considerations given the power and danger of those they are dealing with. Although they received widespread support at the time, whether the *Tangentopoli* judges were right to act as a political 'supplement' by using criminal law to unblock a corrupt and paralysed political system is now the subject of considerable debate.

At the level of ordinary crime, irrespective of their theoretical dedication to *garantismo*, judges and prosecutors have considerable power to make or break defendants. One of the major current concerns, for example, has to do with the way in which advising defendants that an investigation is underway has been turned from a protection for the accused into a license for newspapers to announce to the world that an investigation is underway. Because police powers are exercised under the nominal direction of prosecutors and magistrates too little attention has been given to the actual determinants of many of their gatekeeping and street-level decisions (an absolute priority for future empirical research). Defence lawyers regularly go on strike to protest what they see as behaviour which limits their capacity to protect defendants' rights, and their representative associations are much weaker than in common law countries.

The power of culture is well displayed in the solutions proposed for the problems of criminal justice. In the UK and the USA the continual emphasis on the need for *more* efficiency and managerialism takes place against a background which, in comparative terms, is already far down that road. In Italy, on the other hand, there is remarkably little debate (except within closed professional circles) about practical problems or the more effective use of resources – and this is in itself both cause and consequence of the lack of empirical research into these matters. Although terms like 'mediation', 'compromise' or 'pragmatism' are rarely given a positive meaning in Italian discourse and are often thought to suggest a dangerous absence of principle, they can be all-important in actually resolving or avoiding conflict on the ground. Within and between different criminal justice agencies the very insistence on strict independence and autonomy often has the (perverse?) effect of making informal and unregulated collaboration even more essential if anything is to be achieved (Guarnieri, 1997).

There are also, as would be expected, many significant differences in the way academic discussion of criminal law and criminal justice actually proceeds. Italy shares with much Continental philosophical and legal thinking a much more idealistic and normative approach to discussing crime problems. In parallel with the difference between civil and common law itself, there is less tendency to start from actual situations. The role of discourse is taken very seriously, getting the theory right is seen to have a 'saving effect'. Maximizing the ideals which a theory can satisfy is paramount, and intellectual coherence is all-important. These matters are well illustrated in the work of Luigi Ferrajoli, a former magistrate and a leading left-wing philosopher of law, who in 1988 published a 1000-page masterpiece called *Law and Reason* which set out to rethink the requirements of the ideal of *garantismo* in Italy (Ferrajoli, 1988). His analysis is mainly philosophical and, even though it sets out to consider these ideals in the light of what is known about the inadequacies and failures of the actual existing normative protections, the main criticisms are at the level of principle (thus he condemns the New Code of Criminal Procedure for the pressure it can place on defendants not to use their rights). The very high procedural standards that he advocates are deliberately not linked to piecemeal modification of existing practices but rather presuppose the success of his campaign for a 'minimum penal law' which depends on a massive effort at depenalization (although there is no real political will for this, or likelihood of political agreement about what or how much should be depenalized). At no point does Ferrajoli discuss the conflict between 'crime control' and 'due process' as two competing and entrenched visions of criminal justice and nor does he refer to this literature. What is striking is how he seeks to reconcile such dilemmas in a way that is theoretically coherent rather than treating them as requiring the need for difficult or tragic choices between competing goals or values.[16]

Conclusion

I have argued in this chapter that the criterion of salience which we use to identify matters of difference owes as much to the structures of our expectations as to the structure of what is observed. But this being (unavoidably) so has a number of implications for our efforts to portray and explain the workings of other cultures. It is hard to resist the temptation to describe 'the other culture' in terms of its differences from ours, since this is what makes it interesting. But do we really have enough reasons to think that these differences could, even potentially, have any basis of connection other than the process of (angled) observation which generated them? What if these differences go together only *for us* – both in the sense of striking our former expectations and offering us necessary working pictures which act as our guide to finding our way in unfamiliar territory? If this is the case we must beware of trying to summarize another culture in terms of its 'differences'. What about those similarities which we have neglected because they were 'unproblematic' from our particular comparative viewpoint? Perhaps the similarities are also, or even mainly, responsible for what we wish to explain? What is certain is that they form an essential part of the pattern of the social structure and culture under observation just as much, if not more, than any observed differences. (How far we can build explanations of culture by putting similarities and differences together is, however, another story.)

The lesson, for now, is more limited. It is precisely because the starting point of the observer – and of his or her audience – so conditions those themes which are found salient that we must always bear in mind the source of our perspective. But having said this, the contrasts it reveals can have significance – depending on the purposes of comparison – both for the host society and the society of origin. Exploring these contrasts can, as I have tried to show, help us trace plausible relationships between crime, criminal justice and discourse about crime in different cultures which can go beyond the simple reporting of 'culture shock'. Such an enterprise can also be relevant (though never determinative) for assessing the effects of likely or proposed social or legal changes. For example, the enormous number, range and potential reach of penal laws and administrative offences in Italy should make us cautious about what would really be the effects of introducing 'zero tolerance' as advocated by the Mayor of Milan in January 1999 after flying to New York for an on-the-spot inspection.

More fundamentally, we can also be led to ask how far the achievement of greater 'efficiency' at any one stage – for example, by speeding up trials – could really improve the operation of Italian criminal justice overall. If this recently proclaimed goal were ever to succeed where would all the convicted prisoners be placed? It is implausible and misleading to identify a homeostatic mechanism behind the apparent disorganization of criminal justice in Italy, but it is probable that 'modernization' on only one front will often add to, rather than resolve, underlying problems. More important, however, is the way in which we become aware that criticizing attempts to achieve the goal of greater 'efficiency' in Italian criminal justice *only from an efficiency point of view* is itself to participate in cultural impoverishment. As René Van Swaaningen has recently reminded us, there may be much which more pragmatic cultures such as the UK or the USA could gain from thinking about criminal justice in deliberately counterfactual ways such as that put forward by Luigi Ferrajoli (Van Swaaningen, 1999). But to learn how to do that requires living, and not only observing, a culture.

Notes

1. On the meanings of 'legal culture' see Nelken (1995, 1997b). There is also the opposite risk of describing, as typically Italian, aspects of legal and social life which are characteristic of only one region or part of the country, such as the region of Emilia Romagna or the town of Bologna with which I am most familiar.
2. I once received a questionnaire sent from a French university asking me to comment on the significance in the British legal system of the equivalent difference between the terms 'law' and 'right' in the French system.
3. The currency of this hybrid term is itself interesting for how it shows the degree to which 'cultural objects' are created by the observer's starting point.
4. As can also be the case within a culture. Thus Ditton *et al.* (1998: 10) make the strong claim that 'there was no fear of crime in Britain until it was discovered in 1982'.
5. As a more extreme example Balvig (1988) stresses the importance given to traffic accidents and traffic control in Switzerland as part of its downplaying of crime statistics.

6   For detailed analysis of the figures of criminality before and after the 1989 reform of the Code of Penal Procedure see Rosario (1997).
7   It is interesting to note that Giuliano Vassali, the then Socialist Minister of Justice who sponsored the introduction of the New Code of Criminal Procedure, wrote a long introduction to the Italian translation of Herbert Packer's *Limits of the Criminal Sanction* (which includes his famous distinction between 'due process' and 'crime control').
8   This estimate is based on consulting national statistics and local in-house court reports. But reliable information based on systematic empirical research on this or other matters regarding the operation of criminal justice is not readily available.
9   'In Germany the mass of "traditional crimes" (public order offences, property crimes, sexual and violent assaults) which so preoccupy in Britain receive little attention from the public, politicians, or significantly from agents of the criminal justice system itself' (Zedner, 1996: 3).
10 Balvig (1988) offers this as one of the main reasons why, in Switzerland in the 1980s, newspapers – even scandal sheets – did not treat crime as newsworthy.
11 The identification of offenders as 'Albanians' is often far from reliable.
12 For example, early in 1999, 109 people in the South of Italy, including numerous professionals involved in estimating damage and supervision work, were charged with 850 billion lire damages for misusing the funds made available for rebuilding after the 1972 and 1973 earthquakes.
13 The *Tangentopoli* investigations, as well as other recent political scandals, were in fact helped on their way by evidence provided by ex-wives or lovers.
14 The local newspaper in Bologna, *Il Resto di Carlino*, ran a campaign throughout the late 1990s under the slogan 'we must retake the city' which was aimed at the alleged degradation of public spaces brought about by the presence of illegal immigrants, vagabonds, drug dealers and so forth. As a further sign of the times a centre-right 'civil list' candidate was surprisingly elected mayor of Bologna in 1999, which had been the showpiece of effective left-wing administration for the past 50 years. The new councillor in charge of public security matters ('imposed' on the new mayor by the right-wing *National Alliance* party which had supported the mayor's campaign) was a former senior policeman (*vice-questore*) who had been involved in considerable controversy only the previous year. The accusation was that, while participating in a local radio phone-in programme, he set up his own policemen, posing as ordinary citizens, to phone in complaints about the illegal behaviour of immigrants. In the same election, Massimo Pavarini, a leading international criminologist and founder of the Region's Secure Cities initiative, was not re-elected.
15 Cf. Zedner (1996: 11) 'German criminal justice culture, like English, is characterised by a series of tensions. It is drawn in one direction by repression, quite another by welfare... these values and principles are rarely compatible with one another... the demands made daily on criminal justice officials, limits on resources, and pressure to produce quantifiable results are all likely to privilege some goals over others. What is remarkable about German criminal justice culture is that these tensions have not created the atmosphere of penological crisis by which England is currently riven.' A question raised by this account is how far the observer can speak about the existence of 'tensions' independent of the extent to which they enter into the discourses of the culture under observation.
16 Alternatively, such dilemmas are treated as part of the judge's inalienable sentencing discretion, rather than seen as a problem for the legal philosopher. I raised these issues in a contribution to a book about Ferrajoli's work (Nelken, 1993) to which Ferrajoli responded in the same volume. But the exchange mainly reinforced the (cultural?) differences in our approaches.

References

Balvig, F. (1988), *The Snow White Image: The Hidden Reality of Crime in Switzerland*, Oslo: Scandinavian Studies in Criminology, Norwegian University Press.
Barbagli, M. (1995), *L'Occasione e L'Uomo Ladro*, Bologna: Il Mulino.
Barbagli, M. (1998), *Immigrazione e Criminalità in Italia*, Bologna: Il Mulino.
Beirne, P. and Nelken, D. (eds) (1997), *Issues in Comparative Criminology*, Aldershot: Dartmouth.
Berti, C., Mestitz, A., Palmonari, A. and Sapignoli, M. (1998), *Avvocati, Magistrati e Processo Penale. Analisi Socio-Psicologica di una fase di Transizione*, Rome: Carocci.
Clinard, M.B. (1978), *Cities with Little Crime*, Cambridge: Cambridge University Press.
Costa, P. (1986), *Lo Stato Immaginario*, Milan: Giuffré.
Davis, J.A. (1988), *Conflict and Order: Law and Order in Nineteenth-Century Italy*, London: Macmillan.
Di Federico, G. (1991), 'Obbligatorietà dell' Azione Penale, Coordinamento delle Attività del Pubblico Ministero e Loro Rispondenza alle Aspettative della Comunità', *La Giustizia Penale*, 96, 148–71.
Di Federico, G., Gori, G.D., Marino, A. and Negrini, A. (1994), *Gli Avvocati Penalisti in Italia*, Bologna: Quaderni del Centro Studi e Ricerche sull'Ordinamento Giudiziario Universita di Bologna n.1 Anno IV, March.
Ditton, J., Farrall, S., Bannister, J. and Gilchrist, E. (1998), 'Fear of Crime', *Criminal Justice Matters*, (31), Spring, 10.
Downes, D. (1988), *Contrasts in Tolerance*, Oxford: Oxford University Press.
Downes, D. (1990), 'Response to H. Franke', *British Journal of Criminology*, 30, 94–6.
Dyson, K. (1980), *The State Tradition in Western Europe*, Oxford: Martin Robertson.
Eve, M. (1993), 'Paradigmi Nazionali: Percezioni del 'Particularismo' in Italia e in Inghilterra', *Rassegna Italiana di Sociologia*, XXXIV, 3.
Eve, M. (1996), 'Comparing Italy: The Case of Corruption', in D. Forgacs and R. Lumley (eds), *Italian Cultural Studies*, Oxford: Oxford University Press, 34–51.
Ferrajoli, L. (1988), *Diritto e Ragione*, Rome: Laterza.
Ferrarese, M.R. (1997), 'An Entrepreneurial Conception of the Law? The American Model Through Italian Eyes', in D. Nelken (ed.), *Comparing Legal Cultures*, Aldershot: Dartmouth: 157–81.
Franke, H. (1990), 'Dutch Tolerance: Facts and Fallacies', *British Journal of Criminology*, 30, 81–93.
Geertz, C. (1983), *Local Knowledge*, London: Fontana.
Ginsborg, P. (1998), *L'Italia del Tempo Presente*, Turin: Einaudi.
Guarnieri, C. (1997), 'Prosecution in Two Civil Law Countries: France and Italy', in D. Nelken (ed.), *Comparing Legal Cultures*, Aldershot: Dartmouth, 183–94.
Killias, M. (1989), 'Book Review (of Balvig)', *British Journal of Criminology*, 29, 300–5.
Lacey, N. and Zedner, L. (1995), 'Discourses of Community in Criminal Justice', *Journal of Law and Society*, 22, 301–20.

Lacey, N. and Zedner, L. (1998), 'Community in German Criminal Justice: A Significant Absence?', *Social and Legal Studies*, 7, 7–25.
Langbein, J.H. and Weinreb, L.L. (1978), 'Continental Criminal Procedure: "Myth" and Reality', *Yale Law Journal*, 87 (8), 1549–69.
Leavitt, G. (1997), 'Relativism and Cross Cultural Criminology', in P. Beirne and D. Nelken (eds), *Issues in Comparative Criminology*, Aldershot: Dartmouth, 25–50.
McBarnet, D. (1981), *Conviction*, London: Macmillan.
Melossi, D. (1990), *The State of Social Control*, Oxford: Polity Press.
Melossi, D. (1994), 'The Economy of Illegalities: Normal Crimes, Elites and Social Control in Comparative Analysis', in D. Nelken (ed.), *The Futures of Criminology*, London: Sage, 202–19.
Nelken, D. (1992), 'Law and Disorder in Italy', *Socio-legal Newsletter* Winter, 3–5.
Nelken, D. (1993), 'Le Giustificazioni della Pena e i Diritti del'Imputato', in L. Gianformaggio (ed.), *Le Ragioni del Garantismo*, Turin: Giappichelli, 275–307.
Nelken, D. (1994a), 'Reflexive Criminology?', in D. Nelken (ed.), *The Futures of Criminology*, London: Sage: 7–42.
Nelken, D. (1994b), 'Whom Can You Trust? The Future of Comparative Criminology', in D. Nelken (ed.), *The Futures of Criminology*, London: Sage, 220–44.
Nelken, D. (1995), 'Understanding/Invoking Legal Culture', in D. Nelken (ed.), *Legal Culture, Diversity and Globalization*, special issue of *Social and Legal Studies*, 4, 435–52.
Nelken, D. (1996), 'Judicial Politics and Corruption in Italy', in M. Levi and D. Nelken (eds), *The Corruption of Politics and the Politics of Corruption*, Oxford: Blackwell, 95–113.
Nelken, D. (1997a), 'Studying Criminal Justice Comparatively', in M. Maguire, R. Morgan and R. Reiner (eds), *The Oxford Handbook of Criminology*, (2nd edn), Oxford: Oxford University Press, 559–76.
Nelken, D. (ed.) (1997b), *Comparing Legal Cultures*, Aldershot: Dartmouth.
Nelken, D. (1998), 'Il Significato di Tangentopoli: la risposte Giudiziaria alla Corruzione e i suoi Limiti', in Luciano Violante (ed.), *Storia d'Italia 14: Legge, Diritto e Giustizia*, Turin: Einaudi: 597–627.
Nelken, D. and Levi, M. (1996), 'Introduction', in M. Levi and D. Nelken (eds), *The Corruption of Politics and the Politics of Corruption*, Oxford: Blackwell, 1–18.
Pavarini, M. (1997), 'Controlling Social Panic. Questions and Answers about Security in Italy at the end of the Millennium', in R. Bergali and C. Sumner (eds), *Social Control and Political Order*, London: Sage, 75–96.
Rosario, M. (1997), *Il Controllo della Criminalità*, Florence: La Nouva Italia.
Ruggiero, V. (1997), *White Collar and Corporate Crime: Offers which Cannot be Refused*, Aldershot: Dartmouth.
Sztompka, P. (1990), 'Conceptual Frameworks in Comparative Inquiry: Divergent or Convergent', in M. Allbrow and E. King (eds), *Globalization, Knowledge and Society*, London: Sage.
Van Dijk, J.J.M. and Mayhew, P. (1993), 'Criminal Victimisation in the Industrial-

ised World: Key Findings of the 1989 and 1992 International Crime Surveys', in *Understanding Crime: Experience of Crime and Crime Control*, Rome UN no. 49, reprinted in P. Beirne and D. Nelken (eds) (1997), *Issues in Comparative Criminology*, Aldershot: Dartmouth, 203–70.

Van Swaaningen, R. (1999), 'Reclaiming Critical Criminology: Social Justice and the European Tradition', *Theoretical Criminology*, 3, 1, 5–29.

Zedner, L. (1995a), 'Comparative Research in Criminal Justice', in L. Oaks, M. Maguire and M. Levi (eds), *Contemporary Issues in Criminology*, Cardiff: University of Wales Press, 8–25.

Zedner, L. (1995b), 'In Pursuit of the Vernacular; Comparing Law and Order Discourse in Britain and Germany', *Social and Legal Studies*, **4**, special issue on *Legal Culture, Diversity and Globalization*, (ed.) D. Nelken, 517–34.

Zedner, L. (1996), 'German Criminal Justice Culture', paper presented at the first *Oñati Workshop on Changing Legal Cultures*, 13–14 July.

10 Through *Other* Eyes: On the Limitations and Value of Western Criminology for Teaching and Practice in Trinidad and Tobago

Maureen Cain

Introduction

For eight years, from 1987 to 1995, I worked at the University of the West Indies' campus in Trinidad and Tobago, and for the last five of these I taught criminology to undergraduates, as well as to research students. This discussion arises largely, but not entirely, from that experience: from the embarrassment of teaching about youth cultures in a society which is not rigidly age stratified; of teaching community policing and democratic accountability while lacking a language to describe a post-colonial service lacking a sense of direction, having lost its *raison d'être*; of talking ethnic minorities where historically – and, arguably, today as well – it is the culture and identity of the black former *majority* which is under threat.[1] The examples are as numerous as the topics in a year-long course. Out of shame, therefore, and because the students would so obligingly learn that the answers lay in Western books, rather than in their so often contrary experience, I made it my project to develop a criminology for, and to some extent with, them (for a first adventure in this, see Cain, 1996a).

The 'with', above, is arrogant, as such claims must always be. My relative wealth and my own ethnicity, being Caucasian and English, made sure of that. However, in one area, that of penal reform, I did work with and for the people, making the most of my prestigious position (in that education-conscious society) as Professor of Sociology, while being held in spiritual and political place by local friends in the Catholic Church, in the women's movement, and in the Alternatives to Custody Group. For my small efforts I was rewarded with much love. Today I miss being called 'family' and 'sister' and *'tante'* by strangers met in the road.

However, I can no longer work for or with Caribbean people within their own society. What I can, and must, do is try to limit the harm that we, the well intentioned academics of the West, do daily by peddling our intellectual wares as universal and so deepening the silence and the vanishment of those self-defined non-Westerners to the west of 'here' who are not Eastern either – the people who call us Western and, by default, seem to define themselves as being from nowhere or, at best from somewhere else. I mean, of course, the Trinidadians. What they achieve, in this alternative geography, is a challenge to the Eurocentric way of ordering even physical reality. Just such a challenge to Anglo-European conceptual ordering is the aim of the emergent Caribbean criminology.

In this chapter I will address the two questions of youth and age and of policing, first, in each case, descriptively and then to consider the harm that can result from the importation of false understandings. In the final section I consider the benefits for Western theorizing of moving beyond that form of criminological accidentalism which presumes the applicability of 'our' theories to all 'normal' societies. Such an approach can find confirming instances, it can identify non-Western 'curiosities', but it cannot grow or develop or make itself relevant to the majority of the world's peoples – those we identify as being of the south and of the east.

In conclusion I shall reiterate the familiar argument that Western (criminological) theory may be irrelevant or even harmful when exported, unless used critically and selectively. I shall also argue the less familiar point that a better theory can be constructed for 'home' use, too, if universalist presumptions can be eliminated.

Age and Crime

The maleness of offenders, always strikingly in evidence, has only recently been conceived as a problem (Allen, 1989; Cain, 1990; Newburn and Stanko, 1994). Conversely, and just as perversely, the youth of offenders has been 'known' by the sociology of crime since its inception. It is on the list of 'known' relationships with criminality that John Braithwaite presents as the starting point for his arguments about integration and shaming. He cites:

Hirschi and Gottfriedson (1983) [who] conclude that this age structure of offending [ie peak ages 15–25] has been essentially invariate across cultures and historical periods and for different types of crime. (Braithwaite, 1989: 45–6)

Thrasher, Cohen, Cloward and Ohlin, Brake; Miller, Matza, Morris, Mays, – the two preoccupations have been with young males spending time together in public places (gangs, youth cultures) and with learning to be a criminal (subculture theory, social background of delinquents). Learning is presumed to be something that we (and they) do more of when we (they) are young. Thereafter people become set in their ways and, for this reason, prevention and re-education are also believed to be more effective with young rather than mature people. And there is, indeed, convincing evidence, from self-report studies as well as official data, that the 'offending years' in both the USA and UK are from 13 to 25 (see, for example, Wolfgang *et al.*, 1972; West, 1982).

Today there are strong reasons to challenge this preoccupation with the youthful criminal, both nationally and internationally. Within nations we know that white-collar crime is more damaging to the fabric of society, whether assessed monetarily or symbolically, than most youth crime (see, for example, Snider, 1992). We also know that white-collar crime is rarely committed by teenagers and that opportunities and the relevant skills may increase with age. Yet young people remain the objects of our fears (Mawby and Walklate, 1994) and of our remedial intentions.

Under pressure from the women's movement it has been established that female victimization most frequently occurs in the home and other private places (Dobash and Dobash, 1979). The perpetrators in most cases may be presumed to be more or less the same age as their adult victims. Assaults on children in the domestic sphere are now considered to be more widespread than had previously been believed: again, the perpetrators are not predominantly in the 13–25 age groups.

So, even on a Western and national level there are grounds for challenging the theory of *uniquely* dangerous youth. The baton is picked up by older men with less public practices of incivility.

The international challenge to the implicitly universal claims of the classical theories can be carried by the nations of the southern West Indies. Data are available from Guyana, Trinidad and Tobago, and Barbados which suggest that the relationship between age (as measured in Western chronology) and offending may vary from context to context, so problematizing all theories which depend on notions of identity-seeking adolescents or 'growing out' of crime.

The first hint that the age profile of Caribbean offenders might be different appeared in the early 1980s (Jones, 1981: chs 2 and 3). Jones pointed out that those aged between ten and under 16 were not dominant in the offender statistics in Guyana once a rate per 10 000 in the age group was calculated: for this age group in Guyana, the figure was 71.3, the 16 and under 20 and 20 and under 30 groups had higher, and almost identical, rates (89.6 and 89.7), and therefore the rate of conviction dropped markedly. In England and Wales, by contrast, the highest rate of conviction was in the 16 and under 20 age group, with the 10 and under 16 year group coming second, and the 20 and under 30 group having a rate less than half that of the 16 under 20 group (ibid.: 39, table 3.9). But Jones' main focus was on ethnic variations in offending and sentences, so the age data, which appear in purportedly descriptive chapters called 'The Research' and 'The Crime Picture', have had no impact on academic thinking.

Three more recent studies suggest and demonstrate, respectively, that the age profile of offenders in some Caribbean nations is sufficiently different from that in the USA and UK as to call into question not just the central place given to theories of criminality based on a high reported rate of juvenile and youthful involvement, but also the validity of those theories (Sampson, 1994; Cain, 1996a; Brathwaite, 1996). A Cabinet Appointed Committee was set up in 1992 'To Examine the Juvenile Delinquency and Youth Crime Situation in Trinidad and Tobago' in order 'to determine strategies for the mitigation of the problem of escalating criminal activity among that sector of the population' (Sampson, 1994: i). However, in spite of its terms of reference, the committee noted 'an uneven decline [in reported juvenile offending] throughout the last decade', although the possibility of increases in unreported drug use and offending in schools was acknowledged.

Cain's most detailed analysis of the work of the juvenile court in Trinidad and Tobago (Cain, 1996a) supports the committee's finding about the decline in reported juvenile offending. 57.5 per cent of offences for which juvenile court proceedings were held related to status offenders; 5.6 per cent involved 'minor crimes', and just over one-third (36.9 per cent) involved serious offences (ibid.: 101). The national crime data reveal that 'offences committed by juveniles are not a major contributor to the overall crime rate' (ibid.: 100) with juvenile matters accounting for only 5 per cent of all prosecutions instituted and only '1.9% of those cases in which the offender was caught and a prosecution instituted' for an activity in the serious crime category (ibid.).

Brathwaite's (1996) sample was drawn from police files of those sentenced in 1993 in Barbados and does not include such very young children as those who, for one reason or another, appeared in the juvenile court described by Cain. His youngest age category is 14–19 years. However, his findings point in the same direction, in that the 14- to 19-year-olds in

Barbados accounted for only 9.4 per cent of those sentenced. Indeed, the modal age group for offenders sentenced in 1993 was 31–40 years (33.1 per cent). Those over 25 – the age at which in the UK offenders typically 'grow out of crime' – constituted *70 per cent* of all those sentenced. Even allowing for the fact that periods on remand are longer in the West Indies than in the UK, we have here conclusive evidence that the crime problem in Barbados, as in Trinidad and Tobago, is a problem of adult offending rather than of childish behaviour.

In itself, it does not matter in the least that the age profile of offenders in Trinidad and Tobago and Barbados differs from that in the USA and UK. The problem lies not in the facts of the situation but in the evidence that the situation is seen and understood through the lens of Western theory. During the eight years I lived in the region no one ever spoke to me about the special needs of adult or mature offenders, nor did anyone pay any special attention to the age of the inmates when the regime for a new maximum security prison in Trinidad was under consideration, yet inevitably, given this age profile for offending, both remandees and convicted offenders in Barbados and Trinidad and Tobago are older. The social work profession – and I accept my share of responsibility for this – was age-blind, insofar as the later age of offending was never put on the agenda for public discussion nor, it must be admitted, did I or my colleagues raise the issue in our teaching. Rather, as I shall argue later, the approach to the problem was on occasion age-distorted, presuming the pattern found in Western texts, in spite of available, if under publicized, evidence to the contrary. And while the Commissioner of Prisons and the prison welfare department staff plainly knew whom they were housing, they too were age-blind, failing to see mature men (in particular) as having specific needs.

As in the social work profession and the prisons, so too in academe. The grand theories of sociology were early found wanting in societies where ethnic differences carry a greater salience and the life-chance consequences of ethnicity are perceived to be greater than those of class. Weber and Marx were seen to offer inadequate or incomplete interpretations of the lived reality (L. Braithwaite, 1953; Smith, 1965; Beckford, 1972). But, notwithstanding Pryce's (1976) call for a Caribbean criminology (Pryce, 1976), the agenda for academic teaching is in the grip of the Western canon – the New Criminology, plus drugs and violence. These additions, carried largely by the Jamaican and Guyanese works of Stone (1988), Danns and Parsad (1989), Headley (1996) and Harriott (1996), have not yet driven a reappraisal of the classical theories, although the data, which could provide the basis for such a challenge, reveal cradle to grave alternative life-styles, state complicity in street crime, the dependence of legitimate lifestyles on the liquidity provided by illegitimate ones, as well as the persistent problem of familial violence (which has not adequately been integrated into Western criminological theorizing either). Sumner's (1994) theory of the politics of censure could provide a starting point, although that, too, might well need transformation in the context.

Serious crime even as conventionally defined is not age-specific in the Caribbean, and the research presented here reveals that those forms of offending which perhaps epitomize criminalty in the region – drug dealing and related activities – may depend organizationally on the continued participation of mature people. In the case of the less spectacular, individual, unorganized, and possibly most widespread offences, which would epitomize the region if people elsewhere knew about them – that is to say domestic violence and praedial larceny – perpetrators may be of any age, whether 'beating' their partner (Danns and Parsad, 1989) or simply stealing fruit and vegetables to resell and 'make a little change'. This last is not boyish 'scrumping' but a way of making a living. My hunch is that property is *thought* differently in a land where the ancestors of the governing classes were themselves once constituted as owned.

The argument, then, is that Western theories, because they are based on Western experiences, have embedded in them presumptions about the youthfulness of most offenders. Such presumptions shape perceptions (the misperception of a juvenile crime wave in Trinidad in the early 1990s) and policies, which are directed to the youth and the young employed. Western presumptions may also be responsible for slowing down the moment when the theoretical and policy implications of the new data can be identified, and intellectual and political debate honed in the light of relevant local knowledge enable the region to respond in an appropriate way to its own characteristic crime problem.

Policing

The problems of post-colonial police forces are well known, if not as yet well documented. Apart from the classic accounts of the chequered transition to independence collected in Anderson and Killingray (1992a), and their own summary of the difficulties in their Introduction (1992b) there now exist readily accessible accounts of the contemporary aftermath of empire in Nigeria (Ahire, 1991; Alemika and Tannibi, 1993; Odekunle, 1979), India (Bayley, 1969; Gupta, 1974) and South Africa (Scharf, 1989; Brogden and Shearing, 1993; Cawthra, 1993). In Northern Ireland the debate continues. What is the appropriate way forward for a centralized paramilitary police force which was quite clearly established to serve the needs of the metropole and, in the case of the West Indian territories, the local planter class? Whatever their differences – over the abolition of slavery, over excise duties and so on – the metropole itself, metropolitan outpost governments in the colonies, and the local planting and trading classes were agreed about the need for a steady supply of disciplined labour and no challenges to either their way of being (their culture) or their trade. A bare chronology may illustrate this for Trinidad and Tobago, since more detailed accounts appear elsewhere (Ottley, 1964; Trotman 1986; Cain 1994; 1996).

In 1835 – after Emancipation but during the phoney freedom of the apprenticeship years – a full-time police force was established under a chief of police. They were required, *inter alia*, to apprehend 'all idle and disorderly persons lying in any highway, yard, or street between sunset and sunrise' as well as 'persons ... playing at bat and ball in the streets' (Ottley, 1964; 23). At full Emancipation in 1838 the police were organized in the rural areas as well, and their powers under the vagrancy laws considerably expanded (Cain, 1994: 51). From 1846 on the police also had to enforce labour contracts. Breaches of the Master and Servants Ordinance of 1846 were punishable by fines or imprisonment, and committals of mainly East Indian plantation workers remained high throughout the 1840s and 1850s (Trotman, 1986: ch. 6). Recruitment even to the lower ranks of the police remained barred to Trinidadians, and constables were important from Barbados and other islands. After the bar on local recruitment was lifted in 1864 the force was reorganized in 1869 as a paramilitary organization. Local recruits needed a tighter control over their loyalty. The military capabilities of the police were strengthened in 1889 after the regiment left the island, and at the end of a turbulent decade of street rioting and what might almost be described as cultural warfare (Brereton, 1979: ch. 8; Ottley, 1969; Trotman, 1986: ch. 8). 'Raids' on non-European cultural gatherings continued to take place into the 1940s when the future first black commissioner, Eustace Bernard, participated in dispersing 'a large crowd singing, dancing, and beating drums' in the village of San Juan (Bernard, 1991).

After Independence in 1962 the name was changed from the police force to the police service, but the paramilitary organization persists. Until very recently, a style of policing which combined passivity with sporadic raids also persisted, the latter now being justified by searches for drugs rather than by the 'need' to police culture. This 'passive policing' involved staffing police posts to which members of the public, such as myself, would repair as best they could when they had such matters as an armed robbery to report. The passivity was enhanced by the lack of serviceable vehicles: a British team invited to review the Trinidad and Tobago Police Service reported in 1991 that some 40 per cent of vehicles were off the road and unserviceable and that the police driving school had no functioning vehicle at all (O'Dowd, 1991: 18). Lack of clear and strict procedures for routine maintenance and the issuing of spare parts epitomized, in my view, a dilatoriness that pervaded the police administration. With Independence, the purpose of control on behalf of a foreign power became irrelevant. Subsequently, official neglect and underresourcing led to low morale and undercommitment at all levels, leading in turn to malfunctioning management structures and, among the junior officers, a crude choice between a self-serving restriction of the job to going through the motions or do-it-yourself community work (running police youth clubs and so on) by those officers who managed to hold on to some kind of service ideal. However, throughout the 1990s, under international pressure to control drugs and commercial pressure to keep the tourist areas safe, there have been changes. Foot patrols in the capital, Port of Spain, were strengthened; a form of community policing was introduced in two housing estates on the main link road to the capital, the 'east–west corridor'; a neighbourhood watch scheme was initiated; an influx of foreign money has enabled more mobile patrols to be carried out (although vehicles available to CID officers and those wishing to attend scenes of crime are still scarce); a special and reputedly elite unit to deal with drug related crime has been established; and in 1998 Commissioner Mohammed (now retired) visited the resort island of Tobago to negotiate further advances on the already successful enhanced patrols in the high-density tourist areas (interviews with hoteliers, August 1998). While the Community Relations Branch continues to specialize in work with juveniles, a senior officer committed to community policing has been posted to the Police Training School (interview with the head of the Community Relations Branch, 17 August 1998). Finally, a *Community Policing Plan* was published by the Office of the Commissioner in 1996 (Trinidad and Tobago Police Service, 1996).

What may inhibit these well intended measures is the tendency to tackle each problem by creating a new specialized section to deal with it. O'Dowd (1991: 13) remarked on the complexity and resulting confused accountability of the organizational structure, as well as an acute lack of trust between departments which compounds the lack of organizational systems of communication (ibid: 4, ch. 5). This may have been exacerbated by the proliferation of yet more specialized roles, each with its own mini-hierarchy and, also, some claim to organizational autonomy. Moreover, we have known since the beginning of sociological police studies some 30-odd years ago that specialist roles with a community orientation may be seen as 'soft options' or 'perks', and, in any case, not 'real police work'. In the West they do not impact on the practice or value system of the main structure, from which they are organizationally separated, as well as marginalized in terms of core police values. This may not be the case for centrally organized police: in theory it should be easier to change core values and modes of practice in a top-down way. On the other hand, if, over the years, organizational centralism has been converted by departmental proliferation and confused accountability into *de facto* sectional autonomy the hoped for changes are unlikely to occur. Key players here will not be specialist units but senior line managers at divisional level, supported, of course, from the Commissioner's Office. This was acknowledged in the 1996 *Plan* (Trinidad and Tobago Police Service, 1996: 23). I cannot say whether, or to what extent, this change of practice at divisional level has occurred.

The above is a version of the Trinidad and Tobago story. Each island has its own. In Jamaica the problem was not, as in Trinidad, one of loss of direction and purpose after Independence but rather the seizure of the police by rival political forces (Harriott, 1997: 1–6). In St Lucia Independence came a decade later than elsewhere in the region and British influence has been stronger. Between 1991 and 1993 the Service had a British national as commissioner (Royal St Lucia Police, 1993). While recommending 'self-help' in the form of neighbourhood watch schemes and crime prevention panels (ibid.: para. 31), the retiring Commissioner also noted 'police failure to kick start crime prevention initiatives (ibid.: para 13). Since that time, such initiatives have emerged, largely tourism led (see below). Those initiated, or at least staffed, by the police include beach patrols, community policing (which means getting out of the vehicles and patrolling) and intensive mobile patrolling of the high-density tourist zone. There is an enthusiastic Community Relations Branch which, once again, deals primarily with juveniles.

In Bermuda the situation is different again (Pratt and Simmons, 1990) because the tradition of foreign and paramilitary policing was not as deeply entrenched as in Jamaica and Trinidad. A new police force was (of course) established in 1840 after Emancipation but 'this new Police Force was distinctly non-military in character' (ibid.: 13) and remained so for 50 years. When the West Indian Regiment withdrew, the Secretary of State for the Colonies indicated here, as elsewhere, that a strengthening of the police would be 'quite suitable as a replacement for the troops' (ibid.: 32). Because there was local opposition to a non-Bahamian force, this strengthening was accomplished in 1892 by the recruitment of 42 men from Barbados who were organized into a *separate* police force alongside the local one. However, a single commandant for both forces was appointed in 1894, and the two forces were combined in 1909. Such a history could produce a culture amenable to community policing initiatives, but there are no research data on the topic. A Community Relations Branch which includes a crime prevention remit was established in 1987 (ibid.: 115).

This patchy and incomplete description of 'some police forces I know a little bit about' demonstrates both the past and the present variability of policing in the Anglophone Caribbean. It is intended to sound the cautionary note that there is not one 'there', any more than there is one 'West'. For this reason alone there cannot be one prescription about what to do next. Nor should it be overlooked that, even within small island states, different styles of policing may suit different interests: a style of policing and allocation of resources which suits the tourist industry may not be best suited to the control of drug trafficking. Maintaining peaceful residential communities and non-violent homes may require other strategies again. And this play of interests is complicated in the islands by an ambivalence about both tourism and drug trafficking: both bring in money, at a lifestyle price.

Insofar as there is an academic debate about policing in the Caribbean it has been between Anthony Harriott and myself. I have argued that, in Trinidad and Tobago, a movement to an effective community policing style, where officers are treated as professionals able to act alone while being accountable, cannot be established until a first stage of old-style technical professionalism has rebuilt morale, skill levels, managerial systems and control (Cain, 1996b). Moreover, in a society where communities are not politicized and have no developed conception of how they want policing to be, community control and accountability to the community are not possible. The situation is different from that in South Africa and Northern Ireland where the police have long been an object of political struggle. So in 1996 I advocated re-gaining central control of policing coupled with the instigation of debates and consultations about policing priorities and styles. I argued at the time that full-scale community policing should remain the longer-term objective to be approached by these means.

Harriott (1997) argues that, in Jamaica, the liberal model of technical and efficient professionalism has already been tried and found ineffective, as has indeed been the case in the UK and the USA also. In this situation greater responsiveness to the community is the first priority. This may be possible, because in Jamaica the police are already in stage 1, and also because control of the police has been a political issue there. This has not been as part of a freedom struggle but as part of a battle between rival political parties each representing a middle-class grouping eager to establish and maintain a position of patronage, in the absence of a clear constituency in class or ethnic terms (Campbell, 1976). This may have raised control of the police to a sufficiently high place on the political agenda that communities can now debate whom policing should be for and how it should be organized to deliver the service required.

What is notable, however, about both my work and Harriott's – not to mention police and official thinking on the matter – is that we are allowing debates and blueprints from other parts of the world to overdetermine the argument. Neither the UK nor South Africa is likely to provide a direction appropriate for the Caribbean, because, as we have seen, not all colonized places have the same policing histories and the experiences of the metropole are different again. In the final part of this chapter, therefore, I want to explore some models of community self-policing that have emerged in Trinidad and Tobago and St Lucia. The data are, at this stage, incomplete and suggestive rather than definitive. Nonetheless I am convinced that, methodologically, this is the correct way to proceed: to identify and then emulate those policing practices which, over the years, the citizens of the nations in question have developed for themselves, to deal specifically with local problems. As will be seen, the adoption of this method identifies hitherto unrecognized sites from which policing in terms of community choices and needs might indeed be developed. The immediate next step should be to make these widely known so that those in the situation can better formulate a conception of 'best practice' in relation to their own locally defined needs.

Policing by Communities in Trinidad and Tobago and St Lucia

Ironically, the first of the local alternatives to be considered in this section are in fact a colonial invention – namely, the five municipal police forces of Trinidad and Tobago and St Lucia.[2] Second, I consider self-policing in residential neighbourhoods and, finally, some self-help strategies adopted by small businesses.

Municipal Police Forces in Cities and Boroughs

The rules governing municipal authorities and their police forces are different in Trinidad and Tobago from St Lucia and, to complicate matters further, in Trinidad and Tobago a long-planned municipal reorganization is currently underway. Taking the simplest case first, therefore, in St Lucia, the Castries Constabulary employs ten constables and a head constable and the Act authorizing their employment empowers them to enforce the bylaws. However, their general police powers derive from the fact that each officer is also sworn in by the commissioner of police as a special constable. Neither the mayor nor the head constable indicated any problem of dual loyalty or confused accountability and, because I did not, at that stage of my work, anticipate such difficulties, I did not explore the matter further. Problems that were mentioned were:

- shortage of staff
- inadequate office facilities

- lack of recognition, compared to the national police, and
- lack of career development possibilities, leading to a high turnover of personnel.

In Trinidad and Tobago at the time of interview (December 1997) there were four municipal police forces. These, by Act No. 21 of 1990, replaced two city and two borough forces, when all cities and boroughs received the status of municipal corporations. The same Act, when amended by Act No. 8 of 1992, created nine regional corporations and one new borough (municipal corporation), giving a current total of 14 local authorities. Staff of the ten newer authorities are appointed by the Public Service Commission, in consultation with the Ministry of Local Government. Their funds come from central government via the Ministry of Local Government. Staff of the four older municipal corporations, including police officers, are appointed by the Statutory Authorities Service Commission and receive a direct grant to supplement the monies raised in local taxes and dues. Nonetheless, the Ministry with which they have to deal on, for example, development matters, is the Ministry of Local Government. As one official said, 'in the final analysis, the question of accountability is dual'.

Making matters still more complex was the fact that, while the nine regional corporations and the new municipal corporation were established by the 1990 and the 1992 Acts, that part of the 1990 Act which authorized them to set up municipal police corps had not been 'called' by the end of 1997, although implementation was anticipated during 1998, starting with the new municipal corporation and extending the implementation to the nine regional corporations in the course of the year. Pre-implementation, that is to say at the time of my interviews – these ten local authorities hired security staff who, when appropriately qualified, were then sworn in as Estate Constables by the commissioner of police under the Supplemental Police Ordinance Chapter 15:02 of 1906. This gave them full police powers in the area of the local authority and throughout the police division in which the authority was situated. However, while the commissioner of police could call upon the services of these officers in emergency situations, they were employed as public servants, and their accountability was to the employing authority and, ultimately, to the Ministry of Local Government.

Under the new regime currently being implemented, the officers will be employed not as estate constables but as municipal police. Their powers will come with their badge of office, and no delegation of powers by the commissioner of police will be necessary. Furthermore, these powers will be extended throughout the nation – that is, they will be identical with the powers of the national police. While training will continue to be provided by the national police, municipal police do not, and will not, have to pass the examination set centrally by the police commissioner as a criterion of eligibility for all estate constables. There is therefore a risk of more widespread powers being given to less qualified officers.

Compounding this undeniably complex situation is the relationship with the national police (the Trinidad and Tobago Police Service or TTPS). Municipal police have regular police powers plus special powers in relation to the bylaws. At the level of senior management, the commissioner of police can give instructions for municipal police to carry out police duties in the municipality for which they are engaged. One recently appointed officer in charge of a municipal force had gone so far as to consult the solicitor-general about the meaning of this clause. Perhaps as a result of this conversation, he argued that this clause, like the similar clause governing the work of estate constables, is intended to ensure the release and coordination of personnel in emergency situations. This interpretation makes sense, since the powers of the municipal police are not delegated, but it also makes for confusion at the middle management level and among the ranks.

In spite of this, only one area was found where there had been a long history of conflict between the TTPS and the municipal police. This had arisen from the perceived lower status of municipal police – 'they think we are supplemental police and we are not' – as well, sometimes, as over who may do criminal arrest work, the bread and butter of the police's self-image (to mix a few metaphors). But in this force, as elsewhere in Trinidad, those structure-generated problems were resolved on a daily basis by interpersonal negotiation, by a policy of employing ex-TTPS officers to head up municipal police forces, and by the fact that, in those areas where jurisdictions do in fact overlap, two practicalities were in play: the TTPS were quite often glad of assistance, and the municipal forces both recognized their limitations where specialist skills were required and, given their small staff, would quite usually hand over property crimes, as well as more serious matters, to the TTPS for prosecution.

On the ground, the work of municipal forces in both islands proved to be similar. They are responsible for guard duties at the council offices, where their own ammunition, as well as council monies, may be stored. They are responsible for maintaining order in council institutions such as abbatoirs and meat, fish, and vegetable markets and for overseeing the collection of market dues; for providing an escort to council officers seeking to enforce public health, building, or housing regulations; for providing escorts for the transport of council cash, both to the bank and on paydays; for maintaining order in the parks, streets, and public places within the boundaries of the municipality; for controlling traffic flows (although, in some muncipalities national police, or traffic wardens employed by them, do this); for dealing with the enquiries and concerns of citizens who visit the police station to discuss a problem; and for dealing with any 'general' police work that may crop up. Two of the larger towns reported that their proximity to the centre meant that reports of street crime were frequently made at the municipal, rather than the state, police station. One mentioned shoplifting as such a crime that frequently came their way for this reason, and another indicated that they might be told of people using drugs just nearby. If crimes are actually reported to them they usually deal with the investigations if they have the staff available.

Most importantly for the purposes of this chapter, community policing was also explicitly mentioned. Official policy in Trinidad and Tobago in late 1997 was to move towards community policing. As indicated in the preceding section, the TTPS had published a policy document in this regard and was reshaping its police training to enhance the emphasis on community. The Ministry of Local Government shared this view. Although the relevant Acts do not indicate that community policing should be a responsibility of the municipal police, the Ministry sees this as an appropriate role for them, consistent with a more general Ministry policy of encouraging participation at local level. Sadly, but not irrevocably, the various officials within the Ministry who discussed the matter with me had a limited view of community policing as a specialized form of work: work with juveniles, drug abuse programmes, scholarship programmes, youth clubs and so on. As with the TTPS, by implication crime and public order work are excluded. But at Ministry level in 1997, community policing strategies were not yet fixed, although a number of initiatives had already been undertaken in the largest municipalities. One had deployed 10 per cent of its staff to the welfare and community section. This force was creating community drop-in centres which, while retaining a focus on juveniles, provided skills-based social activities for adults and informal counselling and support.[3] Basic welfare, such as the provision of clothes and food was also undertaken. One of the officers in this section was a qualified social worker, and all the others were trained as counsellors. Most importantly, community policing in this force is presented as a flagship enterprise, although their more visible work, in terms both of media coverage and their own records, is on the city streets.[4] Another senior officer, while sending his officers on various training courses to equip them to work with violent families and to undertake counselling, also had a broader conception of what community policing might be. Of his client community he said, 'Here they see faces that are familiar to them over time, so that they may very often, they may very well feel more comfortable coming here': by which he meant, I believe, that the small things, the petty larcenies which are so difficult to clear up as well as the family quarrels, may none-the-less be taken seriously. Because most of the officers move to live in the municipality and remain there (since transfers are not possible) they become accustomed to 'this close interaction with the people'. This was seen as a distinct policing advantage, not something to be feared. Senior officers in the municipalities are aware of the tensions inherent in community policing. They live with the push and pull of local versus national politics, often played out in relation to vendors. All had sympathy for people who might otherwise be unemployed 'making an honest dollar', yet on health as well as legal grounds, not to mention pressure from political authorities, street traders had to be moved, or perhaps one should say moved with even-handed discretion, for vending might be tolerated at particular times and in particular places. Municipal police chiefs believed that policing was often used as a short-term solution for political and administrative problems, such as unemployment, homelessness, vagrancy and mental illness. Communities have lively and diverse interest groups, and policing accommodations have to be reached among them if public peace is to be maintained and underprivileged groups simultaneously offered protection.

In Trinidad and Tobago, and possibly also in St Lucia, because the institutions are currently in a state of flux, because the officers are looking for more status and job satisfaction than can be obtained by patrolling the markets and enforcing the bylaws, because senior and junior officers appear to agree about this, and because the political will is there, both old and new municipal police forces provide a site for the development of forms of community policing, involving not only traditional police–community work with juveniles but also community-based core police work, dealing with crime and public order as dictated by local circumstances while calling upon specialist colleagues as the need arises. Moreover, since they are all (so unusually for police officers) mindful of problems of family violence, a model of community policing might be developed which not only meets the aspirations and addresses the needs of the peoples of Trinidad and Tobago and St Lucia, but also provides an exemplar for 'the West'.

DIY Security in Residential Neighbourhoods

In one way or another, 11 neighbourhood 'policing' or security systems were identified. I came across four of them in the course of my participatory research with mobile patrols. These contacts resulted in one formal interview and three conversations while on patrol. Two other schemes were discussed in interviews with respondents who had been selected in samples designed to address other aspects of this multifaceted research; six interviews based on a snowball sample were held specifically to discuss neighbourhood security, two of which involved people associated with the same scheme. Put another way, I had seven interviews and three shorter conversations about residents' schemes, and two interviews about an umbrella organization for neighbourhood watch. Sadly, I ran out of research time while the snowball sample was still rolling. The data are sufficient, however, to demonstrate a wide range of ways that people have developed to police and secure the areas where they live.

Six of the 11 neighbourhoods were described to me as having 'neighbourhood watch' (NW). Three of these neighbourhood watch arrangements had been added to the functions of pre-exising, or separately existing, residents' associations, and three had been established in Trinidad in response to a combined police/Chamber of Commerce/Ministry of Community Development initiative in 1994. The four schemes that I encountered while on patrol involved the hiring of private security firms either by formal residents' associations or by groups of residents organized for the purpose. Lastly, one neighbourhood was secured by an informally organized group of young men who tended, in any event, to be up and about late at night.

The police/Chamber of Commerce scheme was got off the ground by the efforts of an enthusiastic and skilled police constable working in conjunction with a group conceived as a superordinate advisory committee (the umbrella group). The committee was large and consisted of people with high-level security experience, local businesspeople, professionals including teachers and clergy, and other residents of standing. The person first approached by the police officer was a member of a major service club which had independently been moving towards a neighbourhood watch initiative, so networks and know-how were pooled. This umbrella group worked with the police to spread NW values (no patrols, no vigilantism, cooperative area defence) to the burgeoning number of areas establishing schemes at this time. However, after a spectacular launch by the prime minister at the end of 1994 the umbrella group never met again. Three respondents felt that internal police politics (with varying degrees of legitimacy) were the reason, and certainly the constable whom all had identified as the mover and shaker was posted elsewhere. Another view was that the committee informally disbanded itself once police support diminished.

Be that as it may, many of the NW schemes had survived the intervening three years and set free from their defining focus on security, had in every case become more like the residents' associations. This is their strength.

The seven residents' groups which I interviewed ranged in size from 50 to 500 members, and their security problems varied too. The largest area had experienced burglaries (a generic term for housebreaking in Trinidad) and hold-ups, as well as a great deal of larceny from yards, porches, and galleries. Another area had trouble when 'an element' – that is, young people from outside the area – moved in on their park. Car theft was 'regular', as was petty larceny from yards. The smaller areas in Trinidad mentioned praedial larceny and thefts from yards, allegedly by 'guys off the hills' or coming up the 'drains' (streams in deep trenches carved during the wet season). In St Lucia one group had a problem with strangers because 'all the times things are happening and no action is being taken' about stealing, bag-slashing, and generally 'creating a problem ... around the area', while the other group reported no problems at all, but took preventive action when a new trunk road was built nearby.

All seven groups said that the various problems had been more or less eliminated since they took security into their own hands – even in the one area where a kidnap had since taken place. The day-to-day routine incivility of theft from people's gardens and trees had stopped. How was this reported success achieved? Three of the groups reported installing, or improving, lighting; three used neighbourhood watch signs or stickers which they designed for themselves; two had fenced the drains; one had closed its private road system and hired private security; one had supplied alarm bells for the aged; and one had effected a group arrest. Some created directories, or exchanged telephone numbers, or just put people in touch with those nearby. One retained an elaborately tiered reporting structure which had been encouraged by the police, but in another case I was told that the tiered system could not be relied upon to function, as the 'block captains' and others in the reporting chain were often out at work and those at the summit, being joiners and civically minded, were often out in the evenings too. In other words, security activity was relatively low-key. 'We watch out for each other', said one man, while others indicated that, since the group had started, people had got to know each other better. Which brings us to the crux of the matter – Most of the activities of most of the groups were social. The first objective in one constitution was:

> to provide closer interaction among residents of the Trace area by:
>
> a promoting a sense of community spirit;
> b promoting functions to encourage resident involvement.

Safety came further down the list. Other groups might vary the order and the wording, but there were always sociability clauses.

Only one group – the one with informal security provided by 'the boys' – reported no social activities. Another group had broadened the definition of security to include fire watch, environment watch, and price watch, in addition to crime watch: 'If you want to keep people interested and coming to meetings you can't just talk about security', explained one of the committee members. How right she was. The other five groups organized between one and three parties a year at Carnival, and possibly also Divali, Christmas, or for an anniversary (4 of 5); cared for or created parks, sports facilities, and other amenities (4 of 5); held informal socials in conjunction with meetings in people's homes (1 of 5); and organized public services such as roads, postal delivery, garbage collection and water supply (3 of 5). Activities included a junior football team, a sports day, painting, repairs to property, and general 'beautification'. These people made friends, got to know everyone by sight and by reputation, enjoyed themselves together, and in so doing created a world in which they could and would 'watch out for each other'. The secret of their success in reducing their victimization, which they all claimed, was their collective effort in enhancing their quality of life. Crime watching was not central to this process, Although the NW scheme had in some (but not most) cases precipitated the formation of the residents' groups, sociability was the reason for the crime-watching success.

Did the police, then, do the residents a favour by pulling their man out? That would be too strong, and unfair, for it seems that crime-watching was rarely the only activity of the groups, even in the early days when the officer was active. They valued the advice of the police and the umbrella group, but they never depended on it. What is clear is that British-style co-optation of these groups by the police, the attempt to use them as a source of criminal intelligence, was never really on anybody's agenda, including that of the police.

It is true, though, that elaborate ministerial structures, still on file, never set the heavy hand of planned bureaucracy on real-life events, thanks to whatever went wrong at the end of the first year. As a result, the groups were nudged in the direction of looking after themselves, they were given advice, but never taken over. They therefore developed as sites of fun and good fellowship which took on security as part of a broad definition of quality of life in a world in which safety bumps in the roads or an absence of garbage were equally important.

There is, of course a grey side and a dark side. The grey side is that I was talking to activists: while the tales of the Carnival fetes and cook-ups sounded plausible, I cannot say what has 'really' happened to the crime rate. I personally believe them when they say things have improved: and in any event, they felt better, and the pot holes in the road *are* mended, and the water does flow through the pipes.

The dark side is that two interviewees reported active hostility from the police, or from what both emphasized were 'segments' of the police. They 'came in here with guns' ... 'they've done that a few times – at least twice', said one respondent, while the other refused to be quoted. One thought that the police saw crime-watching and controlling the roads as a kind of turf war initiated by the citizens. Be that as it may, the notion of troublesome 'segments' while the 'regular' police cause no problem and the new community police are actively helpful at least supports my earlier analysis, building on O'Dowd's (1991) view of the TTPS as an organization which has broken down into quasi-autonomous subunits, and which is, as a result, dangerously unpredictable in its organizational responses. In this dark scenario it is all the more encouraging to have identified the safety of bright and neighbourly lights.

Policing, Security, Self-help, and Small Businesses

Serendipity is the stuff of knowledge. While engaged in a subproject on tourism and security in the Caribbean (Cain, forthcoming) I chanced upon a purpose-built locally owned 13-room hotel whose owner had found a unique way of solving (as he hoped) his alarming security problems. When he and his wife opened they employed a 'security watchman' at nights, but 'every time it rained, right, the chap wouldn't show up'. On these nights Mr O (the owner) 'had to man the fort as it were ... and also I would drop the staff home, my wife would hold on here until I came back ... and I would stay up the night and ... leave here at 5, 6 o'clock in the morning'. After several near-miss accidents through tiredness, they employed a different security man

> ... but he had a problem, falling asleep when he was supposed to be awake, or not turning up ... on the days when it was crucial. In fact we found that we couldn't go anywhere, to a function, ... any meeting on evenings ....

Theyn they had an attempted burglary on a guest room while 'the chap ... was apparently fast asleep', that guard was sacked, and two new men were employed. However,

> ... we still have the same problem. Up to this day I have to get out of bed and look out for these chaps and you know occasionally wake them and tell them they're not performing ... so I'm actually paying money and not getting value.

Mr O thought of hiring a firm, but that proved too expensive for a property the size of his hotel, but then, through his business contacts, Mr O hit on what he hoped would be a cooperative solution. A neighbouring firm, not connected with the tourism industry, had its own in-house security department. In order to maintain a three-shift system on a single site they have had to employ spare security capacity, to pay for surplus worker-hours. The suggestion is that they meet some of their costs by contracting security to Mr O on a non-profit basis. If he can buy in some of their excess hours in this way both parties could benefit. The beauty of the scheme, for Mr O, apart from its affordability, is that the large firm will supervise the security staff, so that Mr O will at last be sure of both a social life and a good night's sleep. Still at the planning stage when I left, this is a self-help scheme between indigenous businesses.

This example is important precisely because it was the smaller and middle-sized hotels, with fewer than 50 rooms, which reported the most problems with security staff (compared with the large hotels and smaller guest houses).

Another example is the Hotel Vendors' Association of St Lucia. The Ministry of Tourism, the Hotel and Tourism Association, the Tourist Board and the police all see persistent vending as a problem, and it is reported as 'harassment' by the tourists. Hoteliers also report this, but the vendors themselves have developed a solution to the problem, albeit an incomplete one.

The vendors' president told me on the phone, 'Stand by the bridge and I'll drive around until I see you'. (My whiteness and business clothes made me recognizable to people I had never met.) Later my respondent told me, 'The story is a very long one.' 'I've got time,' I said. 'I've got another tape …'

> When I started [vending at this hotel] in 1981 after the hurricane we used to be selling on the beach and in those days there was not a good relationship between management and the vendors. The relationship was very poor. So what we would do, there was a time, I think the last Friday in August, where the vendors would come together. Some people go to church and then they come back. They eat and drink and they would call it a vendors' feast and they would not probably bother to sell that day ….

The biblical cadences rolled, but I must cut my friend's story short. At his suggestion, the group decided to invite the management. This became an annual event. The vendors would have a cook-up, the hotel would supply the drinks, the management would come down to the beach and 'We would talk about our problems and they in turn would tell us what they don't like … And there was a very good relationship in those days.'

Another year a new Minister of Tourism came and in succeeding years as well. 'And he asked me to … make a national vendors' feast, get all the vendors from all the hotels.' About 70–75 per cent turned up and, from that meeting on the beach, the decision was made to start an association. This body now organizes and represents the vendors at seven of the largest hotels and will also organize those at the new vending sites being developed by the Parks and Beaches Commission (a quasi-autonomous body reporting to the Ministry of Tourism). Only licensed vendors may join the Hotel Vendors' Association; and the licensing system helps the Association by reducing the freelance competition.

> What we try to encourage members of the association is to abide by the constitution of the association, where the people on the beach does not have anything to

abide with. They do what they want and act how they want, so it created a problem because sometimes the feedback we are getting from some of the guests ... it doesn't make things look better for us ....

The constitution prohibits a vendor from creating 'problems' where he or she is working: 'Such things like obscene language, violent behaviour, well, drugs is completely out of it. You are caught with drugs on the premises ... you are no longer a vendor.'

On these terms the hotels build premises for the vendors and sometimes also arrange special market days.

Over the years members of the Hotel Vendors' Association have become a privileged group. It is a group which is hard to break into, as the hotels built market space only for the vendors already trading on 'their' beach and, without a vacant stall, a new member cannot be signed up. So although an effective self-policing method was devised, from the tourists' and hoteliers' point of view the vending 'problem' has re-emerged in the form of freelance beach vendors unable to join the association. The new beach facilities mentioned above will solve that at least temporarily, and the association will police and control the new members.

However, as well as the carrot there is the stick. To complement these self-policing efforts the Parks and Beaches Commission is establishing a squad of 20 beach wardens (in the first instance) to address the issue of harassment in particular, but also petty thefts, robbery and other beach crime. The wardens will not be special constables, will not have police powers, but will have a good communications network and a uniform. Their task will be prevention and, above all, they will have the task of preventing unlicensed vending. The vendors and the visitors will be pleased: the poor of St Lucia may find life a little harder.

The Hotel Vendors' Association model is replicated among boat owners and taxi drivers in St Lucia. Again, the functions are those of any professional association – to reduce competition and to maintain standards. Boat owners serve a largely tourist clientele, while the taxis serve both tourists and locals. In these cases, as with the vendors, the occupational association acts as a buffer between governmental and employers' powers and the unlicensed, uncontrolled entrepreneur. In these two areas – in St Lucia at least – this system of semi-co-opted self-policing offers an accommodation, creating a controlled space for some local small-scale entrepreneurs in exchange for restricting supply and policing the suppliers. Having observed, on another island, a local version of vending boom or bust – periods of unchecked vending interspersed with smashing up of stalls by the police – the St Lucian accommodation seems a fair compromise but, then again, I did not talk to any of those excluded.

Conclusion

These examples, of the age distribution of criminality, of policing problems and security solutions invented by local people, yield some expected and some more surprising results. For Westerners, the most important of these is contained in the discussion of age and criminality. Here there is clear empirical evidence that the claim to universality of Western theories is false. In some cases there may be global patterns – Ramoutar's (1996) work indicates that this may be the case for the gender–criminality relationship – but, from now on, the applicability of Western formulations must be a matter to be investigated and never a matter to be presumed.

The lesson here for people of the southern West Indies is that they must gather the confidence to read their own evidence, to trust their own data and to build an understanding and a theory upon that basis. That, at least, is the most obvious message. But there is a more complex and apparently contradictory one too, which is to trust your instincts – and their instincts tell them that they have a youth crime problem. I cannot resolve this contradiction: I know that the data are right and I suspect that the people are right too. They know their own place. So the more complex message is that in so far as they have a youth crime problem it is not one that is manifest in the conventional (colonial) ways of collecting evidence. This returns us to the same place: it does not seem to be a problem that can be addressed by conventional (colonial) theories. Whatever the problem may be that people sense but cannot put their theoretical finger on, it needs careful exploration using very open methods. That way, new concepts can be developed, together with data collection methods that will give them representation.

For the West the lesson is not just the moral one, of avoiding intellectual arrogance and theoretical imperialism. There is a way here, too, of improving our own understanding and formulations. Some theories – for example, about the pre-given problems of adolescence, purportedly the time of rapid physical development, puberty, unfamiliar emotional experiences and emergence into social adulthood – need to be picked apart at the least. Youth, in Caribbean culture, lasts much longer, certainly for males. 'I is ah young man,' said a crime victim encountered by chance in a St Lucian police station. He was over 30. So age is not a cross-cultural constant, and social age need not be tied to what is going on with the body. Nor, of course, are the emotions associated with 'growing up' cross-cultural, nor is gender constructed the same way in every place: but these are other stories, for a longer day.

Beyond this cultural and conceptual unpacking, however, there is reconstructive work that must also be undertaken. I have hinted – no more is possible – that the different forms of criminality are related to age *as it is constructed in the context* (hereafter just called age). This is obvious in the case of white-collar crime and domestic violence: however, the mists of pre-theory, in the Caribbean context, suggest that 'normal' crimes are intimately and integrally age-related as well. 'Pilferage', as my respondents called petty theft, and praedial larceny are not childish offences. Stealing of growing crops for resale is a way of making a living. Ask any farmer, ask anyone with a tree in their yard, grown men steal fruit to support themselves and their families of residence. It is done routinely to meet adult needs. Petty larceny is similar: it is not a child or a youth who steals a hose from the yard, or porch furniture inadvertently left unlocked. These things too are stolen for re-sale.

Cash is required by men of 25 plus in Trinidad and Tobago because unemployment remains high (down to 13.2 per cent for males in 1996) and there is no social security or unemployment pay for those without dependents – mainly males. Cash – although not very much – is also necessary to support a cocaine habit. I would argue that pilferage and praedial larceny were well developed forms of 'normal' crime before drug transhipment began to erode the social fabric. They were available forms, and people with added needs used them.

With the advent of wide-scale cocaine usage the new phenomenon to emerge is street crime and violence against strangers. Harriot (1996) has demonstrated the growth of stranger violence in Jamaica in recent years and, in Trinidad and Tobago, crimes against the person have continued to be high (although they peaked in 1993) despite unsteady falls in the overall crime rate since 1988 (*Annual Statistical Digest 1996*, Tables 47 and 48). These offences are related to the social organization of drug trafficking, dominated by adult males, and the social distribution of drug use in which more young people may be involved. I suggest that, just as fear of crime is related to a known but not documented (except in Jamaica) increase in stranger violence, so this sense that something is wrong with the youth – whatever the evidence says – may be related to a known increase in vulnerability because of association with traders or exposure to abuse.

For the West, then, the clear message is that each society is responsible for the crime patterns which it creates through its modes of social organization. As the nations of the West Indies are responsible for a society which creates angry adult males without means or life chances,[5] so also, in the same way, is the UK responsible for the pressures and opportunities it creates for its criminal boy children and male youth. This means that there is a policy lesson, as well as a theoretical lesson, in all this: treat your society's particular problem as one that your society has *created*. It is not a universal problem. It is not given by human nature. It is a problem shaped and created by the particular social order. And if the social structure is criminogenic, then change it.

So much for age. What do we learn from the policing examples? Here, the lessons for the West are simple: policing is a phenomenon structured in organizations which have been shaped by particular histories. Both discursive (cultural) relations and extra-discursive relations have a powerful past, as well as a powerful present context. Each organization is unique, therefore, in its opportunities for change. There can be no blueprints, although technical advice and an expansion of the pool of available ideas, if offered with due acknowledgement of the limitations of context, should always be welcome.

For the Trinidadians and others who are struggling to improve the service which they offer to their people, this analysis offers many further suggestions. Let me list them.

- The state police need to regain control of a segmented organization. Improved physical resources (police stations and vehicles) must have helped with the morale problem, but what is still needed is a vision. The new community policing thrust is meant to supply this, but here it seems the experience of the west is relevant. If community policing is designed as another segment, another specialism, then there will be no impact on the overall level of protection and service offered to the citizens. It is still my view that *centralization with a service message* will have to precede community-led policing in Trinidad and Tobago. The service message, of itself, will require greater transparency. Taxpayers, as well as the Minister of Internal Affairs, are entitled to know how the police budget is spent, and also about police activities in more detail than the present crime statistics offer. A National Consultation about the data to be included in a published annual report would be an ideal way to involve and empower the community within the context of strengthening managerial control.

Meanwhile, in Trinidad and Tobago, existing and much praised (O'Dowd, 1991: ch. 3) efforts in community policing (albeit largely restricted to the Community Relations Unit) should continue. There are few effective models here, so all local experiments add to the pool of possible models. For that to happen a lively record of the practice must be kept. The St Lucian Community Relations Branch, too, is worthy of best-practice study for its pioneering work with juveniles and abuse prevention programmes.

As to those other models – municipal police, residents' associations/crime watching, self-policing and self-protection by small businesses seeking alliances and accommodation where they can – what a wealth of possibilities. So how can cross-cultural information help?

Taking the municipal police first, here a variant of community-led policing seems a real possibility for the reasons already indicated: there is, in many respects, an ideal configuration of will and opportunity. These advantages, and the factors which might prevent the realization of this vision, can best be explored by comparing the situation in Trinidad and Tobago and St Lucia with the borough police in South Africa, whom Brogden and Shearing (1993) saw as a possible lead institution in the development of community-led policing in the post-apartheid era.

One huge advantage in the West Indian situation is that, although there have been some problems of status, and in one municipality some territorial disputes, in neither island is there a deeply embedded animosity between the municipal and state police. Furthermore, while in Trinidad the populace has been disappointed in, or cynical about, the poor performance of its police force, since Independence policing *per se* has not been a political issue: incompetence may have been deplored or accepted with a resigned shrug; the happy rats who allegedly ate a large batch of confiscated cocaine may have passed into delighted folklore; but there has been no sustained and active hostility between police and people in the post-Independence years. The citizens of the municipalities are open to trusting their police if their police can earn their respect. In this regard, the police of these islands have a head start over their South African counterparts.

On the other hand, because there has been no political struggle involving the police there are no innovative political ideas. People want a service, but this is a passive desire. Only in the area of family violence is there a demand for agenda-setting rights. I have heard no demands for transparency or accountability. The labour movement, strong in industrial Trinidad, has not considered the matter. The women's movement has restricted its demands to issues of female victimization. People have not yet considered what alternative they want from the current reorganizations, either on the local or the national levels. This, of course, is why regaining control must accompany a necessary shift to a service, rather than a power, model. And it is also why the immediate first model of a police service which is imbued in its structure and its practice with community values must be located in the municipalities.

So the new municipal police face a dilemma. They have the opportunity and the organizational space, but no serious demands coming in from the community which could shape their organization. Moreover, the new municipal police will be employees of the central state: only the four 'old' boroughs remain civil employees (ambivalently).

Teasing out the problem helps. The Western model will not do. The new South African model may come closer, but the conditions are not right. Instead, if the local government authorities and the central state, through the

Ministry of Local Government, want a more thorough-going community policing – not as a specialization but as a way of doing the job – then they must encourage, and even initiate, discussion not least to find out in what ways local communities want their local police to be answerable, as well as responsive, to them. Consultations have a long and effective political pedigree in Trinidad. Now is the time to hold one.

Residents' associations, my next example, provide evidence of an inadvertent stimulation by means of an imported idea – that of neighbourhood watch. However, these neighbourhood schemes work, whereas those in the UK demonstrably do not (Bennet, 1990). In the UK residents are disinterested, the local crime rates are not affected, and the increase in crime talk has been known to drive the fear of crime up! In St Lucia and in Trinidad[6] the effects were entirely positive. Enhanced sociability reduced fear and was believed to have reduced crime, as well as providing improved neighbourhood facilities and a lot of enjoyment. The lesson is that you can't solve neighbourhood crime problems by focusing on neighbourhood crime. Rather the medium – the sociability, the organization – is the message. And it is a message to which, reportedly, both helpful police officers and prudent potential offenders respond.

Here, then, are success stories to celebrate. And the policy message is encourage, stimulate, give support, respond when required but, beyond that for goodness sake leave the people alone to do what they want to do with their time and their energies and their resources, and to think of their own security remedies – whether this means turning an open 'park' into tennis courts, supplying alarm bells to the aged, cutting down the bush, fencing a drain or supplying the police with transport.

As for the two St Lucian businessmen, I cite these as examples of individual and collective inventiveness and of political wisdom. Both aimed for a possible improvement rather than an abstract ideal. I hope they flourish. They represent the future for St Lucians in St Lucia. On such a matter at least, the West, including myself, should maintain a respectful, if not a guilty, silence.

Acknowledgement

I am grateful to the Leverhulme Trust which supported this project under Research Grant RFG/96. This made possible two field trips to the Caribbean, one of six weeks duration and one of four months.

Notes

1 The 1991 census revealed approximately equal numbers of people of East Indian and people of African descent.
2 One new municipal police force has been created since the research. The nine regional authorities were also scheduled to have municipal police forces (rather than estate constables as hitherto). These arrangements were not in place at the time of the research.
3 Sadly, I missed my chance to spend time in one of these centres owing to an overcrowded diary in the last two weeks of my field trip.
4 Almost all the recorded work for this force involved the offence of 'obstruction', with 'pitching a stall' coming a poor second. For example of 17 recorded incidents in April 1997, 14 involved obstruction, two pitching a stall, and one breaking and entering.
5 Of course, the beneficiaries of global capitalism are also responsible for poverty in the region, but internal distribution of resources must, at least in part, be seen as a local responsibility (see also Miller, 1991).
6 I did not undertake this part of the research in Tobago.

References

Ahire, P. (1991), *Imperial Policing: The Emergence and Role of the Police in Colonial Nigeria 1860–1960*, Milton Keynes: The Open University Press.
Alemika, E. and Tannibi, E. (1993), 'Colonialism, state and policing Nigeria', *Crime, Law and Social Change*, 20, 187–219.
Allen, J. (1989), 'Men, Crime, and Criminology: Recasting the Questions', *International Journal of the Sociology of Law*, 17 (1), 19–39.
Anderson, D. and Killingray, D. (eds) (1992a), *Policing and De-Colonisation: Nationalism, Politics, and the Police 1917–1965*, Manchester: Manchester University Press.
Anderson, D. and Killingray, D. (1992b), 'An Orderly Retreat: Policing the End of Empire', in D. Anderson and D. Killingray (eds), *Policing and De-Colonisation: Nationalism, Politics and the Police 1917–1965*, Manchester: Manchester University Press, 1–21.
Bayley, D. (1969), *The Police and Political Development in India*, Princeton, NJ: Princeton University Press.
Beckford, G. (1972), *Persistent Poverty: Under Development in Plantation Economies of the Third World*, New York: Oxford University Press.
Bennet, T. (1990), *Evaluating Neighbourhood Watch*, Aldershot: Gower.
Bernard, E. (1991), *Against the Odds*, Port of Spain: Imprint Caribbean.
Brathwaite, F. (1996), 'Some Aspects of Sentencing in the Criminal Justice System of Barbados', in M. Cain (ed.), *For a Caribbean Criminology*, special issue of *Caribbean Quarterly*, 42 (2–3), 113–30.
Braithwaite, J. (1989), *Crime, Shame, and Reintegration*, Cambridge: Cambridge University Press.
Braithwaite, L. (1953), *Social Stratification in Trinidad*, special issue of *Social and Economic Studies*, 2 (2–3), 5–175.

Brereton, B. (1979), *Race Relations in Colonial Trinidad 1870–1900*, Cambridge: Cambridge University Press.
Brogden, M. and Shearing, C. (1993), *Policing for a New South Africa*, London: Routledge.
Cain, M. (1990), 'Towards Transgression: New Directions in Feminist Criminology', *International Journal of the Sociology of Law*, **18** (1), 1–18.
Cain, M. (1994), 'Crime and the Police in Trinidad and Tobago: The Colonial Legacy', in R. Deosaran, R. Reddock and N. Mustapha (eds), *Contemporary Issues in Social Sciences: A Caribbean Perspective*, St Augustine, Trinidad: Ansa McAl Psychological Research Centre, 44–58.
Cain, M. (1996a), 'Developing a Juvenile Justice Policy: Anomalies of Theory and Practice in Trinidad and Tobago', in M. Cain (ed.), *For a Caribbean Criminology*, special issue of *Caribbean Quarterly*, **42** (2–3), 99–112.
Cain, M. (1996b), 'Policing There and Here: Reflections on an International Comparison', *International Journal of the Sociology of Law*, **24** (4), 390–425.
Cain, M. (1998), 'Tourism and Security in Trinidad and Tobago and St Lucia', paper presented at the First International Conference on Criminology and Criminal Justice in the Caribbean, 14–16 October, in Bridgetown, Barbados.
Campbell, H. (1976), 'Crime and Violence in Jamaican Polities', *Caribbean Issues*, 22–34.
Cawthra, F. (1993), *Policing South Africa*, London: Zed Books.
Danns, G. and Parsad, B. (1989), *Domestic Violence and Marital Relationships in the Caribbean*, Georgetown: Women's Studies Unit, University of Guyana.
Dobash, R. and Dobash, R. (1979), *Violence Against Wives: A Case Against the Patriarchy*, New York: The Free Press.
Gupta, A. (1974), *Crime and Police in India*, Agra: Sahitya Bhawan.
Harriott, A. (1996), 'The Changing Social Organisation of Crime and Criminals in Jamaica', in M. Cain (ed.), *For a Caribbean Criminology*, special issue of *Caribbean Quarterly*, **42** (2–3), 61–81.
Harriott, A. (1997), 'Reforming the Jamaica Constabulary Force: From Political to Professional Policing', *Caribbean Quarterly*, **43** (3), 1–12.
Headley, B. (1996), *The Jamaican Crime Scene: a Perspective*, Washington DC: Harvard University Press.
Jones, H. (1981), *Crime, Race, and Culture*, New York: Wiley.
Mawby, R. and Walklate, S. (1994), *Critical Victimology*, London, Sage.
Miller, E. (1991), *Men at Risk*, Kingston: Jamaica Publishing House.
Newburn, T. and Stanko, E. (1994), 'Introduction: Men, Masculinities and Crime', in T. Newburn and E. Stanko (eds) *Just Boys Doing Business?*, London: Routledge, pp. 1–9.
Odekunle, F. (1979), 'The Nigerian Police Force: A Preliminary Assessment of Functional Performance', *International Journal of the Sociology of Law*, **7** (1), 61–83.
O'Dowd, D.S. (1991), *Review of the Trinidad and Tobago Police Service*, Report to the Government of Trinidad and Tobago, Port of Spain, unpublished.
Ottley, C.R. (1964), *An Historical Account of the Trinidad and Tobago Police Force from the Earliest Times*, Port of Spain: private publication.

Pratt, C. and Simmons, M. (1990), *A History of the Royal Bahamas Police Force*, Nassau: Royal Bahamas Police Force.
Pryce, K. (1976), 'Towards a Caribbean Criminology', *Caribbean Issues*, 11 (2), 3–20.
Ramoutar, K. (1996), 'Is Female Criminality Changing in Barbados? An Investigation Using Self-report and Official Data', in M. Cain (ed.), *For a Caribbean Criminology*, special issue of *Caribbean Quarterly*, 42 (2–3), 43–60.
Royal St Lucia Police (1993), *Review of the Force as at 1st July 1992*, Castries: Ministry for Home Affairs.
Sampson, J. (1994), *Report of the Cabinet Appointed Committee to Examine the Juvenile Delinquency and Youth Crime Situation in Trinidad and Tobago*, Port of Spain: Ministry of Social Development.
Scharf, W. (1989), 'Community Policing in South Africa' in *Policing and the Law*, special issue of *Acta Juridica*, Cape Town: Juta, 206–33.
Smith, M.G. (1965/74), *The Plural Society in the British West Indies*, Berkeley, CA: University of California Press.
Snider, L. (1992), *Bad Business: Corporate Crime in Canada*, Scarborough, Ontario: Nelson.
Stone, C. (1988), 'Crime and Violence', in P. Phillips and J. Wedderburn (eds), *Crime and Violence*, Department of Government Occasional Publication 2, Mona, Jamaica: UWI.
Sumner, C. (1994), *The Sociology of Deviance: An Obituary*, Buckingham: Open University Press.
Trinidad and Tobago Police Service (1996), *Community Policing Plan, 1996–1999* Port of Spain: Office of the Commissioner of Police.
Trotman, D. (1986), *Crime in Trinidad*, Knoxville: University of Tennessee Press.
West, D. (1982), *Delinquency: Its Roots and Careers*, London: Heinemann.
Wolfgang, M., Figlio, R. and Sellin, T. (1972), *Delinquency in a Birth Cohort*, Chicago: University of Chicago Press.

Index

Abe, Haruo 164
Abel, Richard 163
absences 42, 243–6
action research 41
administrative harassment 91
adversarial tradition 142–3
  see also common law countries
  coordinate structures of authority 140
  Italy 8, 250
  Japan 67
  language 79
  presentence detention 124
  proactive and covert policing 85–6
  prosecutors 165
  sentencing 124–5
  UK 98, 106–7
adversariality principle 79
age 13, 43–4, 266–70, 286–7
Alemika, E. 270
Allen, Francis A. 172
Anderson, D. 270
Anglo-American culture 3–4
  due process 8
  globalization 44, 246
  Italy 41–2, 250
  public concern over crime 252–4
  state 244
  victim surveys 249
anomie theory 13
Aoyagi, Fumio 166, 181, 182
appeal 53, 58, 62–3, 68
Armstrong, G. 87–8
arrest 50, 54, 59, 64

Arthuis, J. 209
authoritarian populism 89, 94
authority, structures of 140

Balvig, F. 26, 240
Barbagli, M. 241
Bayley, David H. 158, 165, 193, 194
'being there' 23, 24–7, 233
Beirne, P. 206
Bell, C. 210
Bell, J. 219, 220, 222
Bennet, T. 290
Berger, Peter 118
Berlins, M. 142
Bermuda 273
Bernard, E. 271
Bernat de Celis, Jacqueline 118
Berti, C. 257
Bertrand, Marie-Andrée 11, 13–14, 15, 33–4, 117–32
Bessho, Otaro 182
Blair, Tony 89
Blankenburg, E. 5, 6, 81, 90
Blumberg, Abraham 165
Bonafé-Schmitt, J.-P. 214, 224
Bonnemaison Committee Report (1983) 219
borrowing 11–12, 241
Bradburn, Norman M. 160
Brathwaite, F. 268–9
Braithwaite, John 158, 175–6, 215–16, 266–7
Brants, Chrisje 11–12, 14, 15, 31–3, 77–108

Brereton, B. 271
Brewer, J. 93
Brogden, M. 289
Brosi, Kathleen B. 165, 169
Burfeind, James W. 158
Busch, H. 90

Cain, Maureen 13, 41, 42–4, 265–90
Campbell, H. 274
Canada
  detention rates 126, 130, 131, 132
  women's prisons 33–4, 121, 122–3, 124, 126–7, 128, 129
Cape, E. 100
Carter, Lief 165, 174
Casanovas, Pompeu 66
Chambliss, William J. 165, 169
Christie, Nils 118, 130, 211
civil law countries
  see also inquisitorial tradition
  culture 3–4
  defence lawyers 250–1
  defendant protection 28–31, 64
  due process 8, 255–9
  as invention 150
  Japan 67
  police supervision 35
  public concern over crime 255
clientilism 238–9
Clifford, William 158
Clinard, Marshall 25–6, 235
cognitive structures 37
Cohen, Stanley 118
Cole, George F. 165
Colviz, M. 103
common law countries
  see also adversarial tradition
  due process 8, 255–6
  public concern over crime 252–3, 255
communitarian societies 215–16
communities of care 216
community
  crime as symbolic of erosion in 207–8
  culture 211

definitions 210–11, 215–16
England and Wales 40, 220–2, 244–5
France 40, 218–20, 221, 222–4
Germany 244–5
inter-community relations 217–18
intra-community relations 216–17
Italy 242, 244–5
mediation 211–15
neighbourhood watch schemes 44, 280–3, 290
obligations to others 212–13
policing 44, 272–3, 274, 278–9, 288–9
self-policing 279–85
and state 217, 218–19, 220, 221, 222
universalism 219, 222–4
USA 244–5
victim-offender mediation and reparation 207–25
voluntarism 216–17
comparative interpretation 78–80
comparative law 5–10
compensation *see* reparation
confessions 89, 143, 191, 194
constitutionalism 93
constructivism 118
Cooper, J. 148
coordinate structures of authority 140
correctionalisation (France) 144
corruption, Italy 251–2, 253, 254
Costa, P. 244
Cotterrell, R. 5, 80, 82
covert and proactive policing 31–3, 77–108
Crawford, Adam 12, 16, 26, 37, 39–40, 41, 205–25
Cressey, Donald R. 165
crime
  Italy 246, 248–50, 252–5
  management of 32–3, 90
  public concern 38, 252–4, 255
crime control
  culture 39, 40
  and due process 30–1, 255–9
  Italy 42, 255–9
crime rates 42, 43, 246–50

culture 13–15
  see also legal culture; political culture
  change and adaptation 225
  community 211
  crime control 39, 40
  definitions 80–2
  elements of 82
  experts and insiders 7–9
  Italy 235–8
  punishment 81
  of researchers 15–17, 140, 143–4, 234–8, 239
  translation 208–10
  universal 12
  victim-offender mediation and reparation 205–10, 225

Daly, K. 215–16
Damaska, Mirjan R. 14, 98, 140, 194
Dando, Shigemitsu 184
Danns, G. 270
DATAR (*Délégation à l'Aménagement du Territoire et à l'Action Régionale*) 222
Davis, J.A. 254
Davis, Kenneth C. 184
defence
  covert and proactive policing 86, 101
  UK 106–7
defence lawyers
  England and Wales 143–4
  France 143–4
  Germany 55, 56–7, 65, 66
  Italy 248–9, 251, 258
  Japan 60, 61, 65, 67, 68
  Netherlands 104–5
  Spain 51, 65, 68
  UK 98, 101, 141, 143–4
defendant
  demeanour in court 190
  protection of 28–31, 49–68, 179–80
Delmas-Marty, M. 79
Delphy, Christine 118
Denmark
  conformity 235–6

detention rates 126, 131–2
  women's prisons 121, 124, 127, 129–30, 132
detention rates 126, 130–2, 247
Devlin, P. 142
Di Federico, G. 248, 251
differences 15, 42, 240–6
diversion 32, 79–80
diversity
  England and Wales 220
  France 218
  state and community 217–18
Dobash, R. 267
Dorn, N. 78
Downes, D. 26, 90, 240
drug offences
  Netherlands 91, 99
  UK 88
  West Indies 43, 287
Dubet, F. 209
due process
  and crime control 30–1, 255–9
  Italy 8, 42, 255–9
  police autonomy 97
Dunningham, C. 78
Dyer, C. 142
Dyson, K. 244

ECHR see European Convention on Human Rights
Engel, D. 18
England and Wales
  centralization 221
  community 40, 220–2, 244–5
  covert and proactive policing 31–3, 77–108
  defence 143–4
  detention rate 126, 131, 132
  diversion 32, 79–80
  ECHR 100
  legal culture 93–4
  plea bargaining 80
  police autonomy 97
  police supervision 142, 151–2
  political culture 93–4
  prosecution service 100, 143

Royal Commission on Criminal
    Justice (1993) 151–3
rule of law 93
sentencing 143
state 220–1
victim-offender mediation 39–40,
    205–25
women's prisons 124, 125, 126–7,
    128, 129
environmental crime 91
ethnocentrism 27, 143–4
ethnographic research 35–7, 41, 139–53
European Convention on Human Rights
    (ECHR) 97, 100, 103, 104–5
Eve, M. 27, 244
Ewing, K. 106
exclusive society 3
expatriate researchers 41–4
experts *see* insiders

Feeley, Malcolm, M. 5, 11, 165, 192
Feest, Johannes 6, 11, 14, 18, 28–31,
    49–68
Feldman, E. 7
Ferrajoli, Luigi 258
Ferrarese, M.R. 235, 244
Field, Stewart 11–12, 14, 15, 31–3, 77–108
Fijnant, C. 87
Finland
    detention rate 126
    women's prisons 121, 124, 125, 127,
        128, 132
Fionda, Julia 194
Fletcher, George P. 191
Foote, Daniel H. 68, 158, 165, 171,
    172, 174, 181, 183, 185, 187
foreigners and immigrants
    Germany 58–9
    Italy 247–8, 253–4
    Japan 63, 191
    Spain 53
formalist accounts 141
Forst, Brian 165, 169, 186
Foucauldian approach 4
Foucault, Michel 118

France
    Code de Procédure Pénale 141, 223,
        224
    commission rogatoires 143
    community 40, 209, 218–20
    confessions 143
    correctionalisation 144
    decentralization 221, 222
    defence lawyer 143–4
    diversity 218
    inquisitorial tradition 140, 150
    insiders 7
    intégration 219
    investigation 145
    judges 146–7
    juge d'instruction 141, 142, 143,
        146–7, 148
    justice de proximité 209–10
    legal culture 223–4
    magistrats 147, 148
    police judiciaire 143
    police supervision 142, 143, 147–8
    procureur (prosecutor) 141, 142,
        143, 145, 146–8
    rappel à la loi 224
    research 142–3
    sentencing 143
    solidarité 219
    state 219, 221, 222
    victim-offender mediation 39–40,
        205–25
Franke, H. 240
Frankenberg, G. 150
Frase, R.S. 143
Frazer, E. 218
Friedman, Lawrence 5, 26, 38, 81, 98,
    159
Frossard, André 218
functional equivalents 5, 36
functionalism 143–4
Funk, A. 90

Garapon, A. 7, 209, 220, 223, 224
Garland, David 3–4, 81–2, 89–90
Gaspard, F. 218
Gearty, G. 106

Geertz, Clifford 27, 233–4
gender
  detention rates 131–2
  women's prisons 34
Germany
  arrest 64
  community 244–5
  defendant protection 28–30, 49, 54–9, 64–8
  detention rate 126, 131, 132
  legal culture 66–7
  Rechstaat 245
  women's prisons 121, 123, 124, 126–7, 128–9, 130
Gibb, F. 101
Ginsborg, P. 237
globalization 234, 245
  Italy 241
  policing 77, 86–7
  shock of 223
  West Indies 44
Glynn, J. 107
Goffman, Erving 118
Goldstein, A. 142–3, 144, 149
Goodman, Marcia 181, 185
Gottfredson, Don M. 177, 181, 186
Gottfredson, Michael R. 13, 177, 181, 186
Greer, S. 78
Guarnieri, Carlo 159, 258
Guigou, E. 205
Guillaumin, Colette 118

Haenel, H. 209
Haley, John 157–8, 164, 166, 167, 171, 174, 184–5, 187, 191
Hall, Stuart 93, 94
Hamilton, V. Lee 159, 187
Harding, Sandra 118
Harrington, C. 211, 214–15
Harriott, Anthony 274, 287
Hatano, Akira 180
Hay, D. 93
Heiland, H.G. 12
hierarchical structures of authority 98, 140

Hirano, Ryuichi 67
Hirschi, T. 13
Hobbs, D. 87–8
Hodgson, Jacqueline 11, 35–7, 41, 139–53
Hoogenboom, B. 85
Horowitz, R. 25
Houchon, G. 210
Howard, Michael 89
Hulsman, Louk 79, 118

immediacy principle 79
immigrants *see* foreigners and immigrants
Inagawa, Tatsuya 181
incarceration rate *see* detention rate
individualistic societies 93, 215–16
informalism 109
inquisitorial tradition 142–3
  see also civil law countries
  defendant protection 64
  France 140, 150
  hierarchical structures of authority 140
  Italy 8, 250
  Japan 67
  juge d'instruction 142
  language 79
  Netherlands 79
  presentence detention 124
  proactive and covert policing 85–6
  sentencing 124–5
  UK research into 151–3
insider/outsider 9, 17, 25, 41–4, 239–40
  see also participant observers
insiders
  culture of 7–9
  international collaboration 27–34, 49–108
  interviews of 17–18, 35, 142, 238
  Italy 24–5
  political affiliation 6–7
  reports 4
  shared meanings 31–2
institutions 82, 140
intellectual formations 82

international collaboration 27–34, 49–108
International Victim Surveys 248–50
interpretivism 4
interrogations 55, 65, 68
interviews
  by observing participants 25
  of insiders 17–18, 35, 142, 238
  limits on 122
  presentational data 35, 142
  reliability 39
interviews with experts 17–18
investigating magistrate 64, 104
investigation
  France 141, 142, 143, 145
  Japan 167
Inzake Opsporing 78
Irwin, John 172
Italy 41–2, 233–60
  adversarial tradition 8, 250
  community 244–5
  crime rates 246–50
  crimes 248–50, 252–5
  culture 235–8
  defence lawyers 248–9
  due process (*garantismo*) 8, 42, 255–9
  immigrants 253–4
  incarceration rates 247
  inquisitorial tradition 8, 250
  insiders 7
  judges 242, 243, 247, 251–2, 255, 257–8
  language 242
  media 243
  New Code of Criminal Procedure 8, 24–5, 250–1, 257, 258–9
  organized crime 237, 243, 254
  police 240–1, 251
  pre-trial detention 247
  prosecutors 243, 251, 257–8
  punishment 247
  state 236, 244, 245–6
  Tangentopoli investigations 6, 26, 255, 256, 257, 261
  victims 240, 248–50

youth crime 11
Itoh Shigeki 166, 177–9, 182, 183, 193

Jackson, Robert 165
Jamaica 273, 274, 287
Japan
  arrest 64
  confession 194
  defendant protection 28–30, 49, 59–63, 64–8, 179–80
  defender demeanour in court 190
  insiders 7, 157–94
  investigations 167
  judges 67, 168
  lawyers 168
  legal culture 66–7, 157–8
  prosecutors 11, 15–16, 28–9, 37–9, 157–94
  'reintegrative shaming' 176
  remorse in offenders 18, 29, 38–9, 158, 171, 176, 185, 187–92, 193
  victims 158, 175, 185, 187–8, 191–2
  women 39, 161–2
John, T. 78
Johnson, David T. 11, 15–16, 18, 37–9, 157–94, 170
Jones, H. 267–8
Jörg, N. 85, 98
judges
  covert and proactive policing 86
  France 146–7
  Germany 66
  Italy 242, 243, 247, 251–2, 255, 257–8
  Japan 67, 168
  Netherlands 95
  Spain 66–7
  UK 105–7
juge d'instruction (France) 141, 142, 146–7, 148, 152
Jung, H. 206
justice de proximité (France) 209–10
Juteau, Danielle 118
juvenile delinquency *see* youth crime

Kaplan, John 165

Kawai, Nobutaro 182
Kawashima, Takeyoshi 171
Killias, M. 240
Killingray, D. 270
King, M. 26, 219, 223
Klerks, P. 91
Koh, B.C. 163

Lacey, Nicola 211, 218, 243, 244–5
Landes, William M. 165, 169, 176
Langbein, J.H. 98, 142–3, 149, 241
language 242
  definition of legal concepts 78–9
  participant observers 148
  translation 208–9
  victim-offender mediation 208–10
Laurin, Nicole 118
lawyers
  see also defence lawyers
  Germany 67
  Japan 168
Lazarsfeld, Paul 193
Lazerson, Mark H. 165
le principe contradictoire 79
Leavitt, G. 237
Lebenswelt 118
legal anthropology 35–6, 139–40
legal culture 16–17, 66–7
  cognitive structures 37
  community 211
  covert and proactive policing 77–108
  definitions 81–2, 159
  dispute resolution 208
  elements of 82
  France 223–4
  Germany 66–7
  Japan 38–9, 66–7, 157–60
  participant observers 143–4, 150–1
  police accountability 96–8
  and political culture 33, 80–4, 93–6
  prosecutors 38–9
  protecting the innocent 67–8
  'restaging' 143–4
  Spain 66–7
  victim-offender mediation and reparation 40, 206–8, 223–4

legality principle 28, 55, 65
Legrand, P. 4, 139, 143, 144, 150, 208, 209
Leigh, L.H. 142, 152
Lester, A. 106
Lewis, P. 163
liberty, residual concept of 94, 96
life-world theory 118, 132
Lipset, Seymour M. 159
Littrell, W. Boyd 165, 182
'local knowledge' 233–4
Lofland, John 118
Luckmann, Thomas 118
Lustgarten, L. 97

McBarnet, D. 30–1, 245
McConville, M. 141, 146
MacKinnon, Catherine A. 118
McLennan, G. 93
magistrats (France) 147, 148
Maguire, M. 78
Mansfield, M. 142
Marcus, M. 142–3, 144, 149
Marx, G. 87
Massachusetts, detention rate 126
Mather, Lynn M. 165
Mathiesen, Thomas 118
Matthews, R. 205
Mawby, R. 267
Mayhew, P. 248
media
  Italy 241, 243, 252–5
  Netherlands 90
  UK 88, 90, 94, 97, 102
mediation 211–15
Melossi, D. 244, 246
Mendelson, W. 143
Merle, R. 142
Merry, S. 211, 214–15
Merryman, J.H. 83
Minnesota 34, 124, 125–6, 128
miscarriage of justice 28–31, 49–68, 179–80
Mitchell, Richard H. 166
Mitsui Makoto 181, 185
Miyamoto, Masao 179

Miyazawa, Setsuo 49–50, 183, 193
Moore, S.F. 216
multiculturalism 217
Murayama, Masayuki 6, 11, 14, 18, 28–31, 49–68
Murray, C. 220

Nardulli, Peter F. 187, 194
'nature of law' 141
neighbourhood mediation schemes 211
neighbourhood watch schemes 44, 280–3, 290
Nelken, David 3–44, 49–50, 233–60
  community 211
  culture 224
  legal culture 159
  translation 210
  victim-offender mediation 206, 208
Netherlands
  covert and proactive policing 31–3, 77–108
  diversion 32, 79–80
  ECHR 97
  inquisitorial system 79
  legal culture 94–6
  police accountability 96–8
  police autonomy 97–8
  political culture 80, 94–6
  politics of accommodation (pillarization) 80, 90, 92, 95–6
  prosecuting magistrate 97–8
  prosecutor 103–4
  Rechtstaat concept 96, 100
Neubauer, David W. 165
Newby, H. 210
Nomura, Jiro 180
Norris, C. 78
Norway
  detention rate 126, 131
  women's prisons 121, 123, 124, 125, 127, 128, 132

objectivism 117–18
observing participants *see* participant observers
O'Dowd, D.S. 271, 283, 288

offenders
  age 266–70, 286–7
  France 224
  rehabilitation 38–9, 171–4
  remorse 18, 29, 38–9, 158, 171, 176, 185, 187–92, 193
opportunity principle 30, 60, 65, 67
orality principle 79
organic intellectuals 7
organized crime 256–7
  Italy 237, 243, 254
  Netherlands 32–3, 91–2
  UK 88
Ottley, C.R. 271

Parker, L. Craig jr 166
parole systems 124–5
Parsad, B. 270
participant observers 18, 23, 24–7, 35–7, 41–4, 139–53, 233
  analysis 149–51
  culture of origin 27, 150–1, 234–8, 239
  differences 240–6
  effect on researcher 123, 149
  'going native' 26–7, 149
  immersion 147–9
  interviews by 25, 238
  language 148
  reflection 149–51
  use of literature 238–9
Pavarini, M. 254
Pennsylvania, detention rate 126
Pharr, Susan 162
'pillarization' (Netherlands) *see* politics of accomodation
'placeless knowledge' 234
plea bargaining 80, 143, 144, 247–8, 250
police
  accountability 96–8, 100–1, 106
  autonomy 97–8, 100
  confessions, Japan 68
  England and Wales 142, 151–2
  France 142, 143, 147–8
  Germany 56, 57

Italy 240–1, 251
Japan 61, 65
post-colonial forces 270–5
Spain 50–1, 53
supervision of 11–12, 35, 142, 143, 147–8, 151–2
Trinidad and Tobago 282–3, 288–90
UK 106
police judiciaire 143
policing
  community 272–3, 274, 278–85, 288–9
  covert and proactive 31–3, 77–108
  England and Wales 31–3
  Germany 54
  international cooperation 77
  Netherlands 31–3
  West Indies 43–4, 270–85
political culture 16–17
  covert and proactive policing 77–8, 93–6, 102
  and legal culture 33, 80–4, 93–6
  Netherlands 80
  UK 102
politics of accommodation (Netherlands) 33, 80, 90, 92, 95–6
positivism 4, 37, 117–18, 139, 141, 145
Poupart, Jean 118
Pratt, C. 273
pre-trial detention
  Germany 54, 55, 64–5
  Italy 247
  Japan 29, 59–60, 61–2, 64–5, 68
  Spain 64–5
  women's prisons 124–5
presences 42, 243–6
presentational data 35, 142
prisons
  detention rates 126, 130–2, 247
  education facilities 127, 132
  family visiting 127–8
  health facilities 127
  mother-and-child units 128–9
  women 33–4, 117–32
proactive policing *see* covert and proactive policing

procedural traditions 77–8, 80–4, 101, 107
prosecuting magistrate (Netherlands) 97–8
prosecution
  disclosure to defence 101, 106–7
  France 145, 147–8
  Germany 55–6
  Japan 60–1, 67, 168, 177–92
  Netherlands 95
  Spain 51
  suspension of 168, 177–92
  UK 101, 106–7
  USA 180, 181, 189
prosecutors
  covert and proactive policing 86, 103–4
  England and Wales 143
  France 141, 142, 143, 146–8
  Germany 55–6, 57, 58, 65, 66, 67
  goals of 37–9
  interrogation of suspects 65
  investigations, Japan 167
  Italy 243, 251, 257–8
  Japan 11, 15–16, 28–9, 37–9, 157–94
    background 160–4
    defendant protection 59–61, 65, 67
    preferences and objectives 164–77
    rehabilitation of offenders 171–4, 178, 181, 183–4, 185, 188–92
    suspension of prosecution 168
  Netherlands 99, 103–4
  Spain 65
  USA 15–16, 37, 38
    education 163
    objectives 174, 176–7
    preferences 165
    rehabilitation of offenders 171–2, 188–92
    suspension of prosecution 181
Prosser, T. 219, 220
Pryce, K. 269
public demonstrations 50–3, 54, 55–6, 59

Puchalska-Tych, B. 140, 141
punishment
  culture 81
  Italy 247
  Japan 176–7, 187
  UK 90
  victims feelings about 191–2
pyramidal organization 98

qualitivism 117–18
quantitavism 117–18

Ragin, Charles C. 159
Ramoutar, K. 286
rappel à la loi (France) 224
Rechtstaat 96, 100, 105
'reflexive criminology' 235
reform
  aim of research 11, 35, 36, 142–3, 148, 151–3
  aims of 24–5
  rehabilitation of offenders 38–9
    Japan 171–4, 178, 181, 183–4, 185
    USA 171–2, 188–92
  'reintegrative shaming' 38, 176, 213
Reiss, Albert J. jr 165
remorse
  Japan 18, 29, 38–9, 158, 171, 176, 185, 187–93
  USA 38, 39
reparation for victims 39–40, 158, 185, 187–8, 205–6
research
  aims 10–12
  at foreign sites 35–40
  comparative interpretation 78–80
  ethnocentric design 143–4
  field research in foreign culture 9–10, 35–40, 117–204
  international collaboration 27–34
  reform-driven 11, 35, 36, 142–3, 148, 151–3
  use by insiders 12
researchers
  see also participant observers
  change over time 123

culture of origin 15–17, 41–2, 140, 143–4, 234–8
expatriate 233
field research in foreign culture 9–10, 117–204
subjectivity 150
residents' associations 290
Riehle, E. 92
Robert, P. 223
Rogowski, R. 140, 150
Rohlen, Thomas P. 163
Rose, D. 101, 142
Rose, R. 143
Rosett, Arthur 158, 181
Ruggiero, V. 237
Rutherford, Andrew 159, 172, 194

St Lucia 273, 275–85, 288–9, 290
Salas, D. 223
Salter, M. 140, 141
Sampson, J. 268
Sanchez-Jankowski, Martin 190
Sanday, P.R. 149
Sanders, Joseph 159, 187
Sandwell Mediation Scheme 211
Sato Michio 162, 182
Schatzman, Leonard 118
Schutz, Alfred 118, 122
scientific literature 15, 238–9
Scotland
  detention rate 126
  due process 30–1
  women's prisons 124, 127, 128
Seidman, Robert B. 165, 169
sentencing
  adversarial tradition 124–5
  England and Wales 143
  France 143
  Germany 57–8, 65
  inquisitorial tradition 124–5
  Japan 62, 65
  Spain 52, 65
sex equality, women's prisons 125–6, 132, 133
Shearing, C. 289
'shock of globalisation' 223

short-term research abroad 17
significant absences 243
Simmons, M. 273
Skolnick, Jerome H. 165
Smith, Robert J. 172, 181
Snider, L. 267
social constructivism 118
South, N. 78
Spain
  arrest 64
  defendant protection 28–30, 49, 50–3, 64–8
  legal culture 66–7
Spencer, J. 100
Spronken, T. 100
squatters 50–3, 54
Stagg, Colin 102
Stanko, Elizabeth Ann 165, 169
state
  Anglo-American culture 3–4, 244
  and community 217, 218–19, 221, 222
  England and Wales 40, 220–1
  European culture 3–4, 236
  France 40, 218–19, 221, 222
  Italy 236, 244, 245–6
  Netherlands 94–5, 98
  UK 244
Steinhoff, Patricia G. 166
stigmatization, USA 39
Strauss, Anselm L. 118, 122
structure of feeling 82, 96, 103
Styles, J. 93
subjectivism 117–18, 122
Sudman, Seymour 160
Sumner, C. 270
surveys 17, 37–9, 160–1, 166, 169
Sutherland, Edwin H. 165
Swart, B. 97
Sztompka, P. 240

Tak, Peter J. 181
Tannibi, E. 270
Taylor, Laurie 118
Tevlin, Aidan 165
Thompson, E.P. 87, 93–4, 103

Toharia, José Juan 66
Tojo, Shinichiro 179, 184
Tomlinson, E.A. 148
tradition 82–3
translation 208–10
Travis, A. 103
trial
  Germany 56–8, 64, 65, 66
  Japan 61–2, 64, 65, 67, 68
  Spain 52, 64, 65
  UK 100–1
Trinidad and Tobago 265–90
Trotman, D. 271
truth, prosecutors, Japan 167, 170–1

UK, defence 98, 101, 106–7, 141
United Kingdom
  see also England and Wales; Scotland
  adversarial tradition 98
  age and crime 287
  covert and proactive policing 87–90, 92–3
  Criminal Procedure and Investigations Act 1996 101
  culture of constitutionalism 93
  custodial legal advice 141
  disclosure to defence 106–7
  ECHR 97, 103
  Judicial Commissioners 105–6
  police accountability 96–8, 100–1, 106
  Police and Criminal Evidence Act (1984) 89, 141
  political culture 102
  prosecution 101
  state 244
United States of America
  acquittals, mistaken 38, 180
  community 244–5
  confessions 143
  defender demeanour in court 190
  detention rates 126, 130–1, 132
  offender's ages 267
  plea bargaining 143
  police powers 143

prosecutors 15–16, 37, 38, 158–9
  education 163
  objectives 174, 176–7
  preferences 165
  rehabilitation of offenders 171–2, 188–92
  suspension of prosecution 180, 186–7, 189
  remorse in offenders 38, 39, 189–90, 193
  stigmatization 39
  suspension of prosecution 180, 181, 189
  victims 191–2, 212, 214–15
  women's prisons 33–4, 121, 122–3
universalism
  community, France 219, 222–4
  state and community 217–18
Upham, Frank K. 158
usury, Italy 253

Van de Wyngaert, C. 86
Van Dijk, J.J.M. 248, 249
Van Maanen, J. 146
Van Swaaningen, Ren, 6, 245, 260
verstehen approach 118, 132
victim surveys 42, 248–50
victim-offender mediation 39–40, 175, 240
victims
  feelings about punishment 185, 188, 191–2
  France 224
  Japan 185, 188, 191–2
  reparation 158, 185, 205–6
Vidal-Naquet, P.A. 210
Vignoble, G. 209

Vitu, A. 142
voluntarism 212–13, 214, 216–17, 220

Wadham, J. 103
Wagatsuma, Hiroshi 158, 181
Walklate, S. 267
Wardle, T. 142
Watson 5
Weber, M. 218
Weinreb, L.L. 142–3, 149, 241
West Indies 13, 41, 43–4, 266–90
Westermann, Ted D. 158
white-collar crime 11, 91, 237, 267, 286–7
Wieviorka, M. 209, 223, 224
Williams, Raymond 81–2
Wilson, James Q. 164, 173, 193
women
  Japan 39, 161–2
  prisons 11, 13–14, 15, 33–4, 117–32
Wright, M. 211, 212
Wyvekens, A. 209

Yasuhara, Yoshio 182
Yngvesson, B. 212
Young, H. 103
Young, Jock 3, 97
youth crime
  Italy 11, 254–5
  Trinidad and Tobago 266–70, 286
  UK 287

Zedner, Lucia 78, 90, 139, 142, 152, 206, 211, 243, 244, 255
Zehr, H. 212
Zeisel, Hans 192
zero tolerance 241, 260